THE DIVIDING PATHS

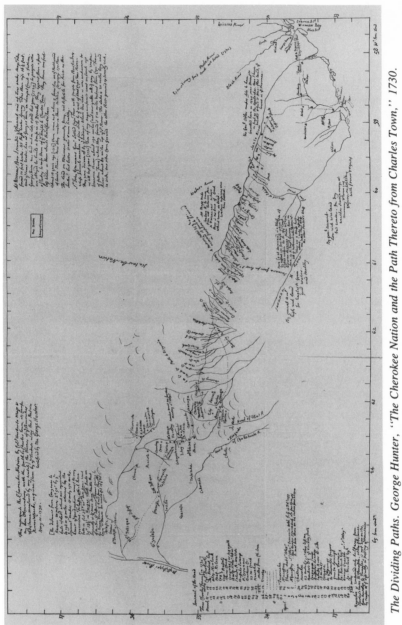

The Dividing Paths. George Hunter, "The Cherokee Nation and the Path Thereto from Charles Town," 1730. Courtesy, South Carolina Historical Society.

THE
DIVIDING
PATHS

Cherokees and South Carolinians
Through the Era
of Revolution

TOM HATLEY

New York   Oxford
OXFORD UNIVERSITY PRESS
1993

Oxford University Press

Oxford   New York   Toronto
Delhi-Bombay-Calcutta   Madras   Karachi
Kuala Lumpur   Singapore   Hong Kong   Tokyo
Nairobi   Dar es Salaam   Cape Town
Melbourne   Auckland   Madrid

and associated companies in
Berlin   Ibadan

Copyright © 1993 by Tom Hatley

Published by Oxford University Press, Inc.,
200 Madison Avenue, New York, New York 10016

Oxford is a registered trademark of Oxford University Press

Library of Congress Cataloging-in-Publication Data
Hatley, M. Thomas, 1951–
The dividing paths : Cherokees and South Carolinians
through the era of revolution /
Tom Hatley.
p.   cm.   Includes bibliographical references and index.
ISBN 0-19-506989-7
1. Cherokee Indians—History.
2. South Carolina—History—Colonial period, ca. 1600–1775.
3. South Carolina—History—Revolution, 1775–1783.
I. Title.
E99.C5H28.   1992   975.004'975   dc20   92-7605

975. 7
MH

2 4 6 8 9 7 5 3 1

Printed in the United States of America
on acid-free paper

For Jane
and
for Lizzie, Parker, and Rebecca

Preface

I was lucky to be led to this book, not by a dream in the way that Alexander Cuming was led to the Cherokees in 1730, but by valued teachers, friends, and guides: teacher Myrtle Kiker convinced me to look for history in the neighborhood; Lehman Kapp, Rowell Bosse, and Charles Moore of Brevard took me down the Horsepasture trail and showed me the stones of Cowee; Peter Wood hired me to investigate William Bartram's 1775 trip to the Cherokees for a video I still hope will materialize, and then he kept me on as a student and friend; he also supervised and prodded the best out of the dissertation that was the basis of this book.

There are many others who, sometimes knowingly and sometimes not, encouraged me or helped out along the way (in no order): Tom Mainwaring, Greg and Linda Waselkov, Tim O. Brown, Elisha P. Douglass, Peter Walker, Jack Hughes, Jerry Novesky, John Nelson, Tom Daggy, Barry Gaspar, Emily Russell, Jerry and Alice Cotten, Roger Manley, Keith Stewart, John TePaske, Sarah Hill, Allen Tullos, Dot Sapp, Howard Lamar, Bob Peet, John Richards, Jerry Hirsch, Russ Peithman, Cathy Davies, Ed Fersch and Kathy Berg, Mrs. B.W. Roberts, Ben Roberts, Roger Kennedy, Wes Taukchiray, Linda Willingham, John Kappelman, Karen Wolny, Robert Mitchell, and Theda Perdue.

The Cherokees and Carolinians have inspired writers and historians throughout their encounter, and I have benefited from this three-century stream of telling and insight. Equally important are the libraries and research institutions which answered my questions and pulled out boxes of material: the North Carolina and Southern Historical Collections of UNC-CH; the Western Carolina University Library; the South Caroliniana Library and Archives; the State Archives of Virginia, North Carolina, and Tennessee; the American Philosophical Society, the Cherokee Museum and Archives; the New York Public Library; the National Archives, the Library of Congress; the libraries of Duke and Vanderbilt Universities, and of the University of North Carolina at Chapel Hill; and the public libraries of Nashville, Tennessee, and Margaretville, New York.

"A critical boost was given to my research on the book by receipt of an Appalachian Studies Fellowship from Berea College.

I am most indebted to my family. My parents long ago gave me the freedom to be interested, and I would like to thank them for that; there is no way to pay them back. Lizzie, Parker, and Rebecca Hatley, and my wife, writer Jane Bosman, inspired me and kept my feet on the ground in the present while I was writing about the past.

Roxbury, N.Y.   T. H.
September 1992

Contents

Contents

Part IV Revolutions

Introduction

Outside the North Carolina town of Franklin, Highway 28 West follows the Little Tennessee River until the roadway is forced to higher contour in close hills. Today this is not disputed country, except for the quiet rustling of legal papers transferring ownership from local families to absentee buyers. But once, fifteen years before the Revolution, this land was a battlefield. During the last campaign of the Cherokee War, in 1761, victorious South Carolina forces marching against the tribe interrupted their march to bury their dead left uninterred in the haste of retreat on the same hillside the year before. Stone cairns built by the native Cherokee tribespeople to honor their warriors killed in battle stood beside the river trail that preceded the road.[1] While the Cherokees still held most of this land on the eve of the Revolution, a Presbyterian minister paused in 1776 at the evacuated Cherokee town of Cowee on the Little Tennessee and preached a sermon of victory against the tribe from the top of the mound.[2] Though Cherokees returned to live here after the Revolution, within a few decades the rich farmland passed from Cherokee to American hands, and the victors collected the cairn stones, mortaring them securely into the chimneys of their new houses.

The Cowee valley chimney stones are enduring, but mute, materials of history. Pottery washes out of cornfield furrows, and the charcoal from the extinguished fires of Cherokee town mounds, kicked out by burrowing woodchucks and pine voles, stains the soil with black splotches after a rain. Local traditions concerning this contested time among the descendants of the victors are hazy or non-existent. And even the story today supplied by the state on a historical marker standing in an overgrazed pasture simply notes the victory of the tribespeople there in 1760, without noting their subsequent losses. After the forced removal of the majority of the Cherokees in 1838, their history became confined within the remaining Cherokees themselves or banished to the Indian Territory. Strange folklore persisted. "One fact reported to me seems to prove that their nourishment is even better than our own," French traveler Louis-

Philippe reported in the early nineteenth century: "during the last war the bodies of Indians killed in battle were still fresh when the Americans' were already rotting."[3]

Today the place names—Cowee, Tugaloo, Elijay, Burning Town, Iotla—scattered across the hills of western North and South Carolina and Georgia seem to have strayed off another map, out of another past. But there is little in these seemingly out-of-place crossroad-names and the scatter of Cherokee rural communities to suggest the reality of decades of intense encounter between this Appalachian people, the Cherokees, and white and black colonists in South Carolina and Virginia. Nor is there anything to suggest the depth of time—perhaps ten thousand years—contained in the arbitrarily labeled pre-history of the Cherokees and their native neighbors before any contact with Euroamerican colonizers. In a sense, the sermon of victory preached to the American troops at Cowee during the first year of the Revolution betrays a willful forgetting, as if history were beginning with conquest in 1776. Even today, when the earliest years are remembered—whether on roadside signs or in textbooks—recollection is both fragmentary and selective. What has been lost is the most perishable part of history—the momentous transactions between two very different peoples, living as neighbors for more than one hundred years before 1785, the year of the first Cherokee treaty with the new American state.

So this book attempts to fill in a gap. It concerns itself with the important years from 1670, when the first permanent English settlement of South Carolina was made, through the first treaty with the new United States in 1785, a time when the traffic across the middle ground between the two cultures was thickest. The Cherokee lands lay at the center of their own pre-colonial world, and the mountain people came early into sporadic contact with many colonists—Spanish, French, African, and finally English. But their relationship with the latecomers in South Carolina was the closest and most consequential.

In a sense this is a comparative history, and fittingly so, for comparisons, over the shoulder and face-to-face, were themselves a vital reality, lived out as two societies regarded each other across the Piedmont and foothills of South Carolina for a century. Our story begins with the Cherokees in their homeland, and the Cherokee experience has a kind of priority throughout, in part because it has been told less frequently.[4] In following a historical path between the mountains and the coast, we pass along a natural transect of colonial period life. There are obstacles—dark spots in the records or willful deposits of prejudiced recollection; the dust kicked up by generations of travel—common to all historical journeys. The cultural distance actually traversed between Cherokee and colonial countries, the three-hundred-years from today, amplifies these problems. In an attempt to overcome these problems, wherever possible the same terms of analysis have been applied to the discussions of both Cherokee and colonial culture. For instance, though relationships between men and women are an underlying theme, the emphasis is not on defining at length the contrasting kinship lines or routines of inheritance. Instead, the male and female cultures—distinctive patterns of authority, myth, and economy—of Cherokee and white society are explored. There are few regions of North America where the contrast between colonist and native was as sharp or as sustained. Colonial patriarchy and Cherokee matriarchy were not perfect or unmixed, but these societies were set apart by widely divergent gender roles—a fact that was of great significance for both sides. Wherever possible the story is taken beyond the formalities of kinship to the personal accounts, reactions, and encounters of men and women in both societies.

Another factor in the slow process of alienation between the two societies—and one that is structurally related to differences in gender—has often been concealed by the flash of more dramatic historical events. The places of power and dependency were remarkably different within the two societies, and this contrast was reflected across the board—from family to diplomacy. The term dependency is usually understood in a purely economic sense as something that happened to native Americans, an economic or social impoverishment forced on them as their colonial or American adversaries gained the upper hand. Whatever the validity of economic theories used to explain this process and its disturbing outcome, this kind of dependency is not central to this study. Instead, issues of dependence and power are employed in another sense, as elements of numerous human relationships such as those between parents and children, commanders and troops, masters and slaves, warriors and farmers, husbands and wives.[5] People live their lives with a consciousness of these relationships, of proper and improper conduct. In the colonial southeast, from Virginia to Texas, colonist and tribesperson alike cast an eye toward their neighbors, black, white, and red, as much to criticize as to reassure themselves of the rightness of their own way. And at the foundation of the story of Cherokee and colonial relationships is a story which can be told with reference to the most intimate, as well as the most conspicuous, aspects of power and powerlessness.

Thus the strong are given attention, but not without the witness of the weak. Read together, the documents of both power and powerlessness are essential to understanding the tensions within Cherokee and colonial Carolina society, and also the destructive disassociation between the two cultures. Without this mirroring, the dehumanization and violence which were to characterize the events of the second half of the eighteenth century cannot be understood.

It was roughly 250 miles overland from Charleston, or Charlestown as it was written until the Revolution, to Keowee, the first of the Cherokee Lower Towns and a trade depot. Along its course the path traversed the coastal plain sands, the black ground crusted with a washed-out white sand-layer, entered the yam-orange and red clay of the raised Piedmont, and ended where it met the brown Appalachian loams of the Cherokee valleys. The distance was measured not only in miles, in twelve or fifteen days of travel, but in the mental units of imagination: expectation and fear. There was from the beginning a sense of minority at Oyster Point, as the precursor settlement of Charlestown was called. Charlestown had been settled as a Caribbean outpost of Barbados, as the population, white and black, spilled over its island and funneled into the harbor at the Ashley and Cooper rivers. For the colony's first four or five decades white Carolinians counted an Amerindian majority within territory imagined as South Carolina, setting it apart from other colonies. The most optimistic of the first generation *claimed* this majority as their own: "everybody knows well wee have the greatest quantity of Indians Subject to this Government of any in all America, and almost as many as all other English Governments put together."[6] By 1708 the population of enslaved Africans had overtopped the white residents of Carolina,[7] creating a double minority for the Anglo-Americans. The Cherokees were aware of at first, perhaps, but not as attentive to the transformation of the coast as its new occupants were to their distant presence. However, the coast-hugging Carolinians, half-oriented to the Caribbean, half-looking west, and the valley-fitted Cherokees were headed for intersection.

From the earliest days, intersections of commerce and diplomacy moved across both a metaphorical and literal path between the two peoples. The path between Charlestown and the Lower Towns was an actual trail and an image of village rhetoric. Carolina historian John Drayton borrowed the image in 1802: "The path over the mountain has been crooked or straight, bloody or clean according to the Indian talks, as war or peace have had greater influence."[8] After the 1730s the main path between Charlestown and the Cherokee villages was called the Dividing Paths, after a fork in the trail near the fall line, where one fork proceeded into the Cherokee town of Keowee while the other passed west toward the Creek settlements of the upper Flint and Chattahoochee. George Hunter's survey of 1730, which pinpointed the division and labeled the trail, made the Dividing Paths a cartographic fixture of colonial maps.[9] (Frontispiece)

Considered in retrospect, this place-name in map legends suggests the course and consequences of the accidental neighborhood of the Cherokees and South Carolinians. The course of contact between the two societies, even though separated by deep intercultural differences, was relatively open at the beginning of the eighteenth century. As the century progressed, and even as trade and communication skill crossed along the path, the branch of the trail leading toward increasing openness was shunned by Cherokees and colonists alike. And under the stress of an increasingly strained relationship, both sides came to or were forced into major decisions about the direction of life within their own societies. Choices were made about which path to take. From the present perspective, the unchosen alternatives—toward racial and cultural openness, toward a loosening rather than a tightening of routines of dependency, toward economic diversity—may seem perhaps implausible, even remote outcomes, yet their possibility once existed and therefore merit re-exploration. This book follows the divergent routes of Cherokee and Carolina societies as they moved from their first meeting into and across the difficult terrain of the eighteenth century.

. . . to manifest the Power of that Mighty Being, who to display His over-ruling Power, and as a proper lesson to Britons, rose up in mount *Perazim*, the place of breaches, the *Cherekee* mountains, the mountain of the Wild men that inhabit the Wilderness.

Alexander Cuming
Memoir

PART I

Appalachian Prologue

1

The Enchantment and the Leech: Cherokee Memory

L ATE in the seventeenth century, when the people who had only recently begun to call themselves Cherokee came into first contact with the Carolina colonists, these mountain-dwellers were already recovering from an earlier, troubled time. The dreams told by the Cherokee priests to their white visitors remembered a long period of shortage and depopulation. Especially vivid is the story of "enchantment" surviving in the record of an English trader named Alexander Longe who lived among the Cherokees from 1714 to 1724. At a town called Agustoghe, Longe was told, a "beloved man," or village elder, had through fasting discovered a hidden village disguised as a "turn pool," or whirlpool, in a river. The enchanted town was a place where "all things comes naturally without any trouble. The people never dies there nor never grows old . . . the light never fails. In the midst of winter there is green corn . . . and [the town] speaks Cherokee as we do." The elder added that he could lead the people to this village of refuge from the present only if they would undertake a fast. After the prescribed time the fast was suddenly broken by a mysterious entrance: in a darkened townhouse, with everyone present, "a troop of women [came] with all sorts of victuals as green corn, pumpkin, water and muskmelons and turkey, deer, bear and buffalo meat."[1] The people of Agustoghe disappeared into this better place in the whirlpool. For proof of what he was telling his disbelieving listener, the priest went on to point to the abandoned village site of Agustoghe nearby, "if you will to there you will see the pillars of the temple and the posts of the houses standing this very day."[2]

The time of the enchantment of Agustoghe, as told by the priest, was quite specific: "about ten years before the English were amongst them." In spite of this temporal specificity, the priest's story could have stood (as do many Cherokee myths) as a parable of sadness beginning prior even to the settlement of the English coastal enclave in 1670 and lasting for many generations. At one level, it shares the meaning of other traditions regarding the omnipresence of death and the sometimes destructive intrusion of a second, mythical reality into everyday life. Something as routine as the ford across the Valley River near the center of the Cherokee settlements, where a monstrous "great leech with red and white stripes along its body" captured the unwary, could thus become a supernatural crossing, a reminder of mortality.[3] Mythical stories such as these alluded to events within the collective life of the tribe as well as in the lives of hapless individuals. The reality of death was, of course, always with the tribe. And the harsh oscillations of population growth and contraction that seem to have characterized the ancestral Cherokee population patterns over millennia, were also made more manageable by the imaginary monsters.

The legend also was specific to the early colonial period, to the time of famine, warfare, and disease that prefaced the meeting of the Cherokee and English. For nearly two centuries before the conjurer related his tale, during the early colonial years between 1500 and the founding of Charlestown, the Cherokees had been first in arm's length contact with Euroamericans, via trade with middlemen tribes, and then in direct confrontation. In this period, the reality of extreme depopulation from new diseases and warfare must have made the lurking Great Leech seem very real. The exact location of the enchanted village never mattered; there had been many villages lost during the century and a half of early colonial contact, even before the English ventured away from the coast and into the towns of their neighbors, and reminders of their vanishing were everywhere.[4]

The Ghosts at Oakmulgee Old-Fields

The Cherokee language makes no "clear distinction" between the colors blue and green. Although this seems a puzzling imprecision, blue-green was true to the look of the landscapes around the Cherokee villages. In the Appalachian valleys where the Cherokees lived, the yellowish chlorophyll green of the forest is subdued in the summer, diffused into something darker by a bluish transpirational haze. In addition to this blue-green, the Cherokee language recognized three other colors—red, white, and black—as having significance beyond their place in the spectrum. The four were color-symbols, filters for viewing the world, lenses of good or bad fortune. Blue-green—the color of their own land—was traditionally the saddest of these hues and was associated with defeat and trouble.[5]

During the years from 1500 to 1715, this bluish mountain landscape was full of pain for the tribespeople. The landscape around their villages and those of their tribal neighbors bore witness to a damaged fabric of settlement. A green scar tissue of young forests and underwood newly invading old-fields symbolized something more to the Cherokees—a remembered sadness of dislocation and depopulation, largely brought about by the incursion of European diseases, pathogens which decimated tribal peoples even before the new coastal arrivals ever saw the interior.

The first, and most problematical, destabilization in the area bounding the Appalachians appears in archaeological horizons dating from the fourteenth and fifteenth centuries. West of the Cherokee core, the neocropoli of graves boxed with limestone slabs, covering many acres along the bluffs of the Cumberland River, point toward a period of settlement abandonment in the interior basins during the 1500s. Similarly, to the north along the mid-course of the Ohio, another population, the Fort Ancient people, lost cohesion and splintered into smaller less-organized groups during the same time.[6]

The second major episode followed closely on the heels of these earlier, but widespread occurrences. By the first decades of the 1500s, Spanish contacts along the Gulf and Florida coast introduced European diseases to native peoples, which in turn may have spread north to the Appalachians along long-distance trade paths.[7] By 1526, when Lucas Vasquez de Allyon established the doomed Chicora colony at the mouth of the Waccamaw River, the dangers to the "virgin soil" populations of the deep interior had been brought closer to hand. Then, in 1540 under Hernando de Soto and again in 1567 under Juan Pardo, the Spanish launched aggressive probes, or *entradas*, which traced across the region and into the Appalachians. Following the *entradas*, a second wave of demographic disaster arrived in foothills and river valleys, evident in historical records, Amerindian traditions, and archaeological remains. The once-powerful neighbors of the Cherokees disappeared into the centrifugal world of the new colonial era. Because they left no records, these forgotten people are assigned labels by archaeologists—Mouse Creek or Dallas—names which derive from the nineteenth-century places where their remains were found.

While the Cherokees did not escape the harsh effects of introduced diseases, their isolated villages, far removed from the coast, may have avoided the worst impact of the political disruption and wholesale migration experienced in surrounding territories. Perhaps because the early Cherokee populations were small relative to their early sixteenth-century neighbors, their villages were not on the direct line of Pardo's march. Thus in the wake of the *entradas*, the Cherokees emerged unsteadily from their small, high-mountain settlements, by default a more powerful tribe than they had been in these twilight years.[8]

By the time whites made tentative contact with the tribe, the Cherokees had moved down the rivers to colonize the old homeplaces of their neighbors, the Creek-speaking peoples, whom the tribe had alternately claimed as enemy and kin. Especially in the western Overhill section of the tribe, village names, such as Chilhowee and Citico, appear to be Cherokee pronunciations of Creek place names. The Lower Towns Cherokee villagers seem to have lived in proximity to ethnically Creek towns in the upcountry of the Savannah and Tugaloo rivers.[9] The Conjurer, a headman of one of these villages, remembered ties to the Yamassees (who themselves spoke a Creek language); "they wer his ancent peapall," an English correspondent reported.[10]

The distinctions of dialect and political mode which separated the four divisions of the Cherokee tribe—Overhill, Lower, Middle, and Valley Towns—may thus have been rooted in individual histories of encounter with their neighbors. Small differences in hard, archaeologically recoverable materials such as pottery and bone as well as in more perishable lifeways, such as speech, of which fragments remain in early documents, reflect disparate experiences among the four Cherokee regions. For instance, Overhill pottery was undecorated, though fashioned out of a shining clay. The powder that gave the clay a glittery surface was ground out of the opalescent inner surface of the freshwater mussel shells abundant in the shallows of the Tennessee River. In the Lower Towns of the upper Savannah River, on the other hand, the pottery surface was stamped with complicated herringbone, keyhole, and "concentric cross" designs which suggest a different taste in household objects and disparate cultural influences.[11]

Just as the Cherokees were appearing on the western horizon of English colonial maps during the first two decades of the eighteenth century, a third, better documented, demographic discontinuity began. The eighteenth century also did not forgo the opportunity to retell the consoling story of Agustoghe to new audiences. Soon after the English established a permanent presence on the shell-midden-strewn Carolina coast in 1670, reports of fatal infection began to surface. The devastating effect of the smallpox epidemic of 1697 among already weakened coastal tribes was reported by John Lawson in 1700, and the same wave of infection moved west to the Creeks and Cherokees.[12] As later eighteenth-century epidemics were regionwide in scope, there is every reason to suspect that the Cherokees, who had already made tentative contacts with Carolina, were affected as well.[13]

The adult mortality from this and other outbreaks among southern tribespeople was so widespread that early eighteenth-century writers soon employed a conventional rule of thumb to estimate the loss. For John Lawson, observing the vulnerable coastal peoples, the rate of loss could be figured simply by measuring survivorship versus time: "I do believe, there is not the sixth Savage living within two hundred Miles of all our Settlements, as there were fifty

Years ago."[14] For Mark Catesby, whose own information was drawn from the southern Carolina Piedmont and foothills neighboring the Cherokee towns, the loss attributable to the "vices and distempers of the Old World" was similarly catastrophic. "It is generally believed," Catesby matter of factly stated, that the southern tribes "were at first 4 if not 6 times as numerous as they are now."[15] Adding to the toll of disease were problems created by the trade with Euroamericans, and supplemented by the near endemic political instability of the period. Though its impact was not as devastating as among coastal and Piedmont peoples, the slave trade reached into the Cherokee towns.[16] And in the west and north of the Overhill villages on the upper reaches of the Tennessee River, traditional warfare with the Five Nations was made more damaging by gun-ownership within the tribes.[17]

This diffuse and long-lasting third major episode of demographic disruption culminated, just before Catesby made his observations, with the forced upcountry displacements of the Yamassee War during 1715–16. On a South Carolina map of 1722 the "dispeopling of the Savannah-Altamaha country" was presented in a series of quick map notations[18]: "Salude. deserted," and near the center of the map, "Hogolaguas and Apalaches, deserted 1715," and "Ochese Indians deserted these towns 1715."[19] The map documented the destruction of these trading centers during the Yamassee War and the disappearance of many native communities throughout Carolina.[20]

The Cherokees themselves remembered the disappeared people of Oakmulgee, a broker-town through which they had channeled their first trade to the English port at Charlestown. "Especially at Oakmulgee," trader and historian James Adair wrote, "which the South Carolinians destroyed about the year 1715, they strenuously aver, that when necessity forces them to encamp there they always hear, at the dawn of morning the usual noise of Indians going down singing their joyful religious notes, and dancing, as if going down the river to purify themselves, and returning to the old townhouse."[21] The land itself offered a reminder which could not have escaped their eyes. When William Bartram visited the site of the abandoned Oakmulgee trading center in 1774 he noted that the blue-green young forests marking "old fields and planting land extend up and down the river, fifteen or twenty miles," a reminder of once-extensive cultivation for vanished villages.[22] And among the northern Iroquois nation the Cherokee country had a reputation for being "surrounded with extensive Deserts" which were the legacy of prior distress.[23]

It was in 'new' towns, many of them still with the Muskogean, or Creek-language, names given by their former inhabitants, that the English first encountered the Cherokees face to face. By the second decade of the eighteenth century, the partial buffer provided by the old fall-line trading settlements which had screened the tribe from direct contact with the English colonies had become a casualty of the Yamassee War. In the wake of the war, the best English estimates indicated a Cherokee population reduced from the prior levels, but sizable enough to become nervous about—sixty towns with a total population of over eleven thousand.[24]

The Cherokees first faced the English as a people in recovery from a succession of severely taxing episodes of disruption. Their own numbers had been more than cut in half, from approximately 32,000 in 1685 to roughly 12,000 in 1715.[25] At the same time, the Cherokees had only to look around them to see that they were the survivors in a country where their neighbors had vanished. Whether in border towns or older core settlements deep in the mountains, eighteenth-century Cherokee villages could not ignore the new frontier created out of the displacements of the Yamassee War on the east.

Cherokee Women and Men at Work

Through the middle of the eighteenth century, Cherokee village life remained intensely local. In the villages Cherokee society maintained its traditional egalitarian politics and matriarchal kinship. Consistent with kinship descent organized along the female line, Cherokee women held strong roles in politics, joining men in the council house and being honored for their exploits in battle as "War-Women" who fought alongside men. However, village work provided separate economic identities for Cherokee men and women: women were the tribal farmers; men, the hunters. While this division of labor was never perfect—men assisted and sometimes took the lead in field-clearing and planting, and women joined in on the hunt—this split, which was as much vocational as occupational, provided a measure of certainty about the conduct of Cherokee life and an economic underpinning to Cherokee authority.

Even the Cherokee marriage ceremony made reference to the different work the new partners could expect. A white woman, a captive among the tribe, recalled one marriage:

> there were a number of both sexes convened; they arranged themselves in two rows, with a space between them, the males in one row, the females in the other, the groom at the end of the row, the bride at the other. At a signal the two advanced between the rows, till they met in the center. He presented her with a leg of venison, and she gave him an ear of corn, denoting that he would keep her in meat, and she would keep him in bread, ending in loud laughter.[26]

Farming was not only women's work; men, even visiting traders, were sometimes handed hoes and led to the corn. Agriculture was put in the care of women by the female corn-god Selu, but aside from pride in this legend, field work, like hunting, had a day in-day out inevitability that could stand laughing about.

The bride's corn had not always been with the ancestral Cherokees, and her gift recalled a revolutionary event in proto-Cherokee agriculture: the long arrival in the mountains of dry country crops from the southwest. Corn-farming, the keystone of the second Appalachian agriculture practiced by indigenous upland farmers across the South, was preceded by an earlier farming pattern based upon the exploitation of locally domesticated herb and tree species.[27] By the beginning of the eighteenth century, a third Appalachian agriculture had been created through exchanges of new crop plants—watermelons, peach trees, and sweet-potatoes—from African and European sources which were conveyed to the mountains.[28] For instance, black-eyed peas, originally African in origin, were cultivated in Creek gardens along the Tallapoosa River before 1700. The villagers called them "Appalachian Beans" and explained that "we received them from a nation of the natives of that name," the Apalachee of northern Florida.[29]

The garden crops and domestic animals finally selected by the tribe were as distinctly female as the gardens in which they were grown. Even village names, such as "honey-locust place" or "mulberry-grove place," had an economic significance which carried over into the gender-basis of Cherokee village work and governance, as mulberry and other useful trees were part of the semi-domesticated forest encouraged over hundreds of years near the villages as a source of food and fiber.[30] Like the village gardens, this forest was a distinctive landscape of the female descendants of Selu. In 1724, Mark Catesby returned to Charlestown from a trip up the Savannah River with "an Indian apron made of the bark of wild mulberry."[31] The Cherokee women of one town were themselves sufficiently confident of their craft, and of the political and economic status which it implied, to ask another early eighteenth-century Carolina traveler to send "that good Woman," Queen Anne, "a present from them viz a large carpet made of mulberry bark for herself to sit on and twelve small ones for her Consellours."[32]

In opposition to the garden-centered world of Cherokee women, the economic status of Cherokee men was centered in hunting territories. When John Stuart, the Superintendent of the Southern District, wrote a memorandum to his superiors attempting to explain the reality of life for the tribespeople he dealt with every day, he began with a maxim: "their whole business is war and hunting."[33] The business of hunting was, like farming, something more than base-level subsistence activity, for it had a direct connection to the life of Cherokee men, particularly the warriors. Warfare was a qualification, a step toward maturity. Sachetche of Tocologia was careful to define his standing to a Carolina audience: "though I am but a young man I have been at war."[34] War, politics, and hunting were all expressions of power in Cherokee manhood, red forces which could not be easily separated out into discrete economic or political activities. And for Cherokee men, trade was the moral equivalent of war.

The basis of this was more elusive than the consumption or the accumulation of wealth in the manner of Euroamericans. In the early eighteenth century village, headmen rewarded achievements in warfare with gifts of beads and deerskins. "The king calls the head Senator," Alexander Longe observed, "that has the public store which consists only of beads and dressed deerskins. He brings to the King some of each Sort. The king stands up if it be a great warrior and gives each of them a war name and a present." [35] Though the role of the king in rewarding his townspeople may have declined during the remainder of the century, the gift (or acquisition in other ways) of goods continued to confirm the standing of warriors.

The clothes, guns, ammunition, and deerskins which were part and parcel of both the intercultural (as well as intervillage) commerce, and the demand for such items, thus stemmed partially from the ambitions of Cherokee warriors. Many of the petitions of Cherokee headmen to the English for increased trading were not cries for material aid from villages dependent for their well-being on trade, but were instead motivated by a desire for the expression of status. Old Hop's conversation with Raymond Demere is suggestive of this underlying motivation: "I see you and your warriors are well dressed in red cloaths; I am naked and ragged. I hope to be enabled to appear like a man, that I might sit with you without disgracing you." [36] This recurring protest of "nakedness" often (though far from always) related more to conspicuous consumption among warrior peers than to material impoverishment. Male politics within the towns contributed significantly, furthermore, to the interest of Cherokees in bargaining to keep markets open, and to "inveigle thereby more traders to come in." [37] In this way the violence of Cherokee warfare was paralleled by a form of consumption motivated by dual economic and political goals. In at least the first years of the century—and probably much longer—the egalitarian politics of the towns were not altered by trade but, at least in warriors' lives, were instead enhanced by the influx of Euroamerican traded goods. Cherokee men used new goods to express their older roles with new emphasis.

The Many Faces of Cherokee Village Authority

Throughout most of the eighteenth century the Cherokees resembled less the tribe mentioned in the treaty books than an assembly of "village egalitarian societies." [38] In the village, political authority and influence were earned rather than ascribed to individuals, and limits to personal power were enforced by kin, peer-groups, and village opinion. When consensus failed, as it often did, those who disagreed with a decision remained silent or simply withdrew from the council. [39] Diffusion of power preserved the freedom of the Cherokees by fractioning authority. Whether asserted in the guise of elders or of priests, the exercise of power was fleeting. Cherokee society was built upon such conflicts, and authority was maintained by successfully counterposing "tendencies toward egalitarianism" with an impulse toward hierarchy.[40]

This tension cut across the face of Cherokee society along lines of age and gender. Authority was often in the hands of elders—both men and women who took on passing roles, at one moment leading in the council-house and then slipping out of temporary office in a succession of "structural poses."[41] Young men and women challenged the many faces of authority, and this opposition cut across other divisions within Cherokee society. Power was earned from village constituencies—warriors, young men or women, elders—and holding power depended upon approval.[42] Much hinged on who spoke and who listened. "Frequent communication with these Indians, both by word and writ," an English agent reported, "is a great heartening to them."[43] Goods, whether shell-beads or cloth, often took the place of words as a form of political communication, and for this reason individual leaders were interested in keeping channels open, even to their enemies.

Success as an intermediary earned risk. Some Cherokee leaders, particularly mediators and diplomats such as Old Hop, were accused by more ideological rivals of listening and speaking too freely. For instance, another village leader complained that Old Hop "was an old fool, that he would hear anybody that brought him a small string of beads."[44] Yet bead messages were as much a key to power for Cherokee leaders as were interoffice memoranda for their counterparts in the British Colonial bureaucracy.

Wherever power flowed, Cherokee politics stirred an eddy of control. While the following of Cherokee leaders was dependent upon the "eloquence and abilities" of the speaker, "civility and decorum" demanded that everyone be listened to in attentive silence.[45] The Cherokees complained that the same privilege was not extended in colonial meetings. The Cherokee spokesman Skigunsta upbraided his Euroamerican hosts during one council by reminding the contentious crowd that it was "not our custom like the white people to talk altogether, but when one is done another begins."[46] Colonial agent John Stuart faulted the English who (unlike their French rivals) never mastered the ability to "put on a solemn and grave air, at the same time to appear open and without reserve. This the Indians look on as respectful and treating them like men, but the least levity they interpret as proceeding from contempt."[47] "Treating them like men," Stuart believed, was a Cherokee precept of diplomatic communication directly derived from the egalitarian life of the villages. This dimension of political life was to be increasingly challenged as the volume and velocity of communication between widely different cultures increased with the passage of the eighteenth century.

From the perspective of a colonial Euroamerican society, village authority was slippery and hard to get a handle on. It lacked the clear markers of power—

land wealth or overlording—familiar to colonists. "In riches they are much upon an equality," John Stuart wrote, acknowledging a strong current of economic commonality maintained by the tribespeople. The exercise of authority was kept under close watch as a result; "no Indian whatsoever, let his influence or power in his own country be he ever so great, can give away any more than his own right in any piece of land, which in the Cherokee nation," John Stuart wrote in the 1760s, "would be no more than as one to 13,500." Furthermore, when the "Principal Warrior and Beloved Man measure[d] a certain proportion of land to each family," any error or favoritism was quickly spotted. "The greatest among them would through the least partiality forever forfeit the good opinion of his townsmen upon which alone his influence and power depend." [48]

Cherokee authority roles were distinguished, especially on the male side, by the colors red and white, symbols of war and peace. Within the village councils white roles had to do with peace and civil authority and red with the conduct of war or assertion of political power. Though the colors symbolized actions which could be taken by both men and women, red and, to a degree, white functions were exercised most conspicuously by men. Red was the flag of the warrior and white of the peacemaker. [49] Euroamericans quickly learned the symbolism of these colors. When George Chicken's troops came into the town of Chota in 1715, Chicken brought two "flaggs, ye Red and ye White" and the town "sett them up on ye top of ther Round House," in this way signaling both his treaty-making intentions as well as English power. [50] Complex activities were carried out, each involving the temporary participation of men and sometimes women, under each color, and these activities in turn overlapped with the competing interests of tribespeople both as individuals and as members of kin-lineages, clans, and towns. Within this matrix of social control and village freedom, political and economic distinctions often dissolved for a time, just when whites such as Chicken felt that they understood them.

Priests had a special place in Cherokee governance. Priestly power had obscure and ancient sources but, if historical traditions are to be believed, had always been a burden for the Cherokees themselves. The conjurers were tolerated because they provided rituals of certainty for events out of tribal control. Hunting and war expeditions were planned with consultations and dream-interpretations and illnesses treated with physick. Magical formulas employed by priests were commissioned by the "tithes" of women to stave off the work of a trickster "black petty God," the north wind, who true to his symbolic color "sometimes at night . . . sends out cold without wind and blasts the fruit trees and the water and muskmelons and pumpkin vines and the first small corn that we plant called rosripe corn. But he is forced to do it very stealth-ily." [51] Against disorders of weather as well as of war the Cherokees attempted a magical control of the world.

Even the power of the priests had not escaped the history of political and demographic disturbances affecting the tribal regions. The power in the hands of the eldest of the group of men which James Adair lumped together as "old Majii" had, according to Cherokee myth, originally been that of a priestly "class," or hereditary lineage called the Ani-Kutani, the members of which were killed in a popular uprising.[52] The rejection of the Ani-Kutani was linked to the resistance of most Cherokees to coercion, whether in the rituals of priests or in the strictures of Beloved Men and elder women. Furthermore, whether the tradition of the killing of the Ani-Kutani represented an actual event or a lasting tension in Cherokee society, both young women and men—warriors as well as farmers—would have repeated the story with an inflection of freedom in their voices.[53]

The structure of priestly and other authority in Cherokee society was both an inheritance and an indication of adaptiveness. The oppositions of Cherokee society—men's versus women's work, Conjurers versus women, young versus old—played against each other to contribute to a stable but resilient structure within the Cherokee villages, one which could accommodate tensions growing from the assertion of communal control over individual actions.

Beyond the Village

The Cherokees were mountain dwellers, but this fact did not imply isolation. From their villages the Cherokees followed gravity west, north, and south along the branched headwaters of the Tennessee, Kanawha, and Savannah rivers. There are no flat bodies of water in the southern Appalachians, no natural lakes. For the Cherokees, the river was the "Long Man, Yunwi Gunahita," anthropologist James Mooney recorded, "a giant with his head in the foothills of the mountains and his foot far down in the lowland, pressing always, resistless and without stop."[54] Townhouses—the centers of village affairs—were often constructed near river banks to allow convenient access to the running water which was part of many Cherokee purification rituals. In this way the river buffered contacts between the interior and the exterior, wider life of the town. Cherokees who had been taken captive were sometimes required to undergo a ritual washing in the river in order to make them fit to rejoin their town. The river also provided an escape valve for villagers dissenting from policies decided in council. In one instance the Cherokee leader Old Hop faced ridicule in his home town for the failure of a diplomatic initiative, and, in order to regain face, suddenly one day "took half a bag of the Town's ammunition and in his canoe went alone down the river" to an unstated destination.[55]

The Cherokees occupied a central place in the river and land routes which spiderwebbed across the South and the Ohio Valley. The Overhill Towns were located on the Tennessee headwaters, to the west of the Appalachian crestline. By following the Tennessee River's arc west and then north to its confluence with the Ohio, the Cherokees could arrive within a short journey to the outlets of the Wabash, Cumberland, and Illinois rivers and the Ohio's confluence with the Mississippi. From the Overhill Towns the Tennessee followed a great loop around the southern edge of the Cumberland Plateau and passed carrying spots where short portages linked to headwaters of the Coosa and other rivers emptying into the Gulf. The French fort at the "Alabamas" was only seven days by this land and water route[56]; "Fort Cususkia," the mid-continental trading hub of the French at the Mississippi-Missouri confluence, was twenty-six days away by boat.[57] And east, twenty-one days from the mountains, lay Charlestown.[58]

The long canoes cut from the smooth limbless trunks of forest-grown tulip-poplar trees, drew only "ten or twelve inches of water all the way up" and were ideal shallow-draught craft. These vessels efficiently brought the best and worst aspects of the colonial exchange into the mountain towns.[59] European and African-derived diseases, seedstocks new to the Appalachians, slaves, and trade goods were all materials of the trade.

In times before the Euroamerican contact, these autochthonous trade channels had carried favored goods such as yaupon holly in a trade web that tied the narrow coastal zone, where the plant naturally grew, to the mountains. The "sower faces" of Cherokees and other tribespeople when deprived of daily yaupon suggested to Mark Catesby that the "paines and expenses they are in procuring it from remote distances does not proceed from luxure (as with tea from China) but from its virtue and the benefit they receive from it." While tribespeople in the "maritime parts" supplied the "Mountain Indians" with it, the Cherokees themselves seemed to have used their central position in the trading system to broker it, for, Catesby continued, "the inhabitants of the north and west are supplied with it by the mountain Indians in exchange for other commodities."[60] Colonial commodities—especially guns—found a rapid transit along the same lines; according to Mark Catesby, writing in the 1730s, "there are very Few Indians," he wrote, "(and those very remote) that retain the use of bows and arrows."[61]

The Cherokees in the Greater Southeast

One early map places the Cherokee villages and their trade in the regional context of early colonial and indigenous trade. In 1723, an English colonial governor obtained a bit of cartography, most likely Chickasaw in origin, which depicted a region stretching from Kansas to New York on the north and Texas to Florida on the south.[62] The geographic information sought by the governor was there, labeled in words reflecting the mixture of specific tribal tongues, Chickasaw and western Muskogean, into trade languages such as Mobilian. Rivers, designated with the Muskogean term "Oakhinnau," had a special prominence on the map; only partly legible on a surviving copy was the Tennessee River—"Ta[]canuck Oakhinnau"—near the center of the map.[63]

While the lines denoting rivers and trails were drawn in black, the circles which located thirty-two tribes on the map were filled with a margin of red paint. This red vision of the world was consonant with male transactions in which the routes of war, peace, and trade were fused. Lines of alliance were also represented on the map and paralleled the existence of institutions meant to maintain peace between the tribes. "In every town in the Cherokee nation," John Stuart noted, "are beloved men appointed by the Creeks, Chickasaw, Catawbas and other nations with whom they are at peace . . . the person so approved ever after and on all occasions interests himself in the affairs of his constituents."[64] During the late seventeenth and early eighteenth century, however, the activities of these official mediators were often overruled by conflict.

The design of colored, spoked circles is broken only once near the center, by a figure of a man, a trader or a warrior or both, leading a horse and holding a bow and arrow. The circles of the Chickasaw map were emblematic not only of trading patterns but also of the changing politics of the interior. For instance, Cherokee and Six Nations, or Iroquois, migration legends, language affinities and similarities in dance suggest a deep rooted cultural kinship between the tribal groups, as well as a history of "stable" conflict.[65] During the seventeenth century, Iroquois raids against such tribes as the Delaware on the east, the Shawnee of the Ohio, the Creeks—and perhaps the Chiscas of the upper Tennessee River drainage—had rearranged the political configuration of the region displayed on the map. The Chickasaw mapmaker documented this expansion by applying the label "Senottova Oakhinnau"—Seneca River—to the Ohio, south of which the Iroquoian Seneca warriors followed the "Kenocolu path" to their hereditary adversaries among the southern tribes. When the Cherokee villages came into the view of English colonists, the tribe was "miserably harassed by the Iroquois."[66] At other times the Cherokees provided a safe-harbor for the northerners, a stopover for the "Sennagouns," Senecas, who raided all the way to the "Geulph of Florida."[67] Similar vectors of long distance trouble crossed the Cherokee country in all directions, fed by earlier regional demographic and political shifts and intensified by colonization.

This heritage of instability had uneven effects. For instance, the Middle Towns (which were perhaps the highland source of the compensatory Cherokee expansion during the seventeenth century) remained relatively isolated and unaffected. Geography was most important where town centers were also ancient land and water route junctions, points of contacts for a region in desperate motion. The Lower Towns in the upper Savannah, the Valley Towns along the foot of the Appalachian escarpment, and the Overhill Towns on the Tennessee faced different exposures to change. One view on the map would remain particularly dominant. From the Savannah River on the east, newly established Cherokee towns such as Keowee looked out across country emptied by the war of 1715. The English port was labeled on the Chickasaw map with a circle already as large as that depicting the Chickasaws themselves.

On another map of about the same age (this one made by a South Carolinian), at the foot of "Nunie, the greatest ridge of Mountains," lay the thickly inked trunk of a river called "Tisundigo."[68] Along this river was a village called "Chiowee" and other nearby villages such as Estatoe, Chauga, and Tugaloo also on the map. These eighteenth-century towns were built on the troubled soil of the village sites of powerful Mississippian-era chiefdoms of Ocute and Cothiquithi and presaged trouble again in the eighteenth century.[69]

Before full engagement with Euroamerican colonists, the life of every Cherokee town, no matter what its location, had undergone radical change. The villages were filled with new things—iron hoes and axes, peach trees and watermelon vines—but the Cherokee country itself was also transformed. Memory tempered the tribe's first encounter with the English colonies. The view down the river valleys and eastern trade routes from the headwater towns remained sobering: the land between the Carolina colonists and tribal towns, on the Carolina map described as "void of pines," had been emptied of people as well. The look of the new-green old-fields in the countryside which lay between them and the English was a saddening confirmation of the mass death which had visited their neighbors. Nevertheless the villages were confident; after all, the eastern view was a red direction—the direction of trade, warfare, and power.

2

Carolina's Appalachian Promise

I N 1674 Henry Woodward opened trading relations with the Westoes, a broker tribe which had recently sought out the trade of the new English toehold at Albemarle Point on the Ashley River. As he traveled west toward the Savannah River town newly colonized by the Westoes, Woodward saw signposts of willing sellers: "these Indians had drawne upon trees (the barke being hewed away) the effigies of a bever, a man, on horseback, and guns." While he was at the Westoe town, Woodward looked forward to a trading visit from the tribe in the next season, "wth deare skins, furrs and younge slaves." Woodward's reconnaissance had taken him only just beyond the fall-line from Charlestown, and the Westoes alluded to the promise of further frontiers beyond. His hosts told him that eight days' travel beyond their outpost "inhabit the Cowatoe and Chorakae Indians wth whom they are at continual warrs." This first notice of the Cherokee presence to the west was followed by sporadic contacts, including a treaty of 1684, perhaps initiated by the tribe to staunch the slaving activities of the Westoes themselves.[1] However, the Cherokees for years remained a distant presence, even though their goods—and at least some of their own folk—were sold in Charlestown markets.

Cherokee Appalachia and Carolina Ambition

Henry Woodward was among the first of the Carolina entrepreneurs who fixed on intercultural trade as a way to tap the indigenous wealth in the west.

They soon found partners. Tribes such as the Savannahs, Yamassees, and Westoes claimed the economic watersheds of the interior as their own and soon skimmed handsome middlemen profits by brokering trade to the English. Only the most ambitious English adventurers penetrated this economic and political barrier to the Cherokee west, and then only occasionally. After the seventeenth century, the ranks of men such as Woodward expanded, but though western contacts were still relatively infrequent, the image of profits and the prospect of alliance in the West remained. (Fig. 1)

Unlike the balanced, closed circles of the Chickasaw map of 1723, another map, drawn by a Carolina expansionist, John Barnwell, presents the interior as a series of open-ended, east-west corridors.[2] Barnwell was a principal of a colony on the move, attempting to pre-empt the initial steps of the French into the continental interior. His map has as much the look of a hurried report as of finished cartography, small enough to be unrolled on a desktop, its contents not quite jelled. During the wartime emergencies of the Tuscarora War in 1711–12 and the Yamassee War that followed, Barnwell had commanded troops of slaves, colonists, and tribal allies, including Cherokees.[3] Barnwell's troops and his compatriots won, if by the narrowest of margins, the Yamassee conflict, and, after decades of clash with the Spanish and tribal neighbors to the south, they looked westward with a somewhat premature confidence in their own destiny. Barnwell charted the vanishing of the coastal tribes that the Carolina colony had grown up with since its establishment in 1670, and captions such as "exceeding good land," inked in expansive hand across a band of land corresponding to the Piedmont region, served as an encouragement to expansion.[4]

The flat, marsh-bound Atlantic seacoast seemed particularly to inspire westward ambitions. Taking shape first as fledgling military and commercial ventures to the west and south, moves by Carolina expansionists such as Thomas Nairne and Price Hughes successfully countered the trade dominance of Spanish mission-trading posts by the first decade of the eighteenth century and even established a tentative trading presence among the Quapaw and Chickasaw villages along the Mississippi.[5] Yet from early on the colonists were aware of a potential obstacle to the west, a chain of mountains. Though poorly defined on Spanish and French maps and in scattered latter-day English travel accounts of the seventeenth century, the mountains were already a formidable, though compelling presence.

But the English were latecomers. The name by which the mountainous interior region first became known to the English colonists was inherited from nearly two centuries of prior Spanish-Creek Indian encounters in northern Florida. Until its destruction by the English in 1704, the northwestern outpost of Spanish Florida officialdom was known as Fort San Luis of Apalache.[6] Gradually, during the mid to late sixteenth and the seventeenth century, as trading contacts with the Creeks and other tribes grew and as military expeditions ranged farther north, the name "Apalchen" or some variation on it (most preserved the Muskogean objective ending *n*) was applied on Spanish as well as French maps to the distant mountainous regions north of the Spanish colonial province of Apalache and its fort.[7]

Similarly, rumors of wealth waiting in these mountains were as old as Spanish travel accounts and maps. In the early sixteenth century, reports of mining among the Chiscas, who lived along the upper Tennessee River tributaries, locally corroborated the traditions of gold to the west which in part motivated the Spanish *entradas* of De Soto and Juan Pardo. Mica sheets and native copper had long been mined and traded from the Appalachians, and during the mid-sixteenth century the Spanish may have also engaged in mining operations of their own with conscripted native labor.[8] European mapmakers of the early colonial period gave great graphic specificity to what were never more than vague reports of indigenous or Spanish metal-mining. On LeMoyne's map, "Floridae Americae Provinciae" of 1565, the village of "Apalatci" is nestled in ranked mountain ranges. Nearby a lake is given the Latin legend "in this lake the natives find silver grains of sand."[9] Theodore deBry's engraving provided a striking illustration of the "mode of collecting gold in streams running from the Apalatcy Mountains," an after-image of the first century of Spanish conquest and exploitation to the south.[10] This half-imagined feature of the American interior became a lodestone for ambitious colonists. In spite of a lack of clarity about the actual lay of the Appalachian land, belief in its potential richness remained. The Appalachian gold mines were an inviting signpost on the late-sixteenth-century maps archived in the research libraries of European expansion. (Fig. 2)

A century later the first legitimate information explosion concerning the mountain region took place. The establishment of the Virginia colony gave impetus to first hand fact-finding. The published reports of the journeys of John Lederer, who claimed to have been guided to the foot of the Blue Ridge, stimulated a series of ventures by Virginia traders to the west during the 1670s. His dramatic narratives provided essential intelligence and encouragement for the Carolina Proprietors, the colony's developers, as they began their southern settlement.[11] While in the planning stages, the informal cost/benefit calculations made in London concerning the Carolina colony figured in the prospective wealth of the Appalachians. Lederer served to confirm earlier Spanish reports by noting that:

> could I have foreseen when I set out, the advantages to be made by a Trade with these remote Indians, I had gone better provided . . . Some pieces of Silver unwrought I purchased myself of the Usheries, for no other end than to justify this account I give of my Second Expedition, which had not determinated [terminated] at *Ushery,* were I accompanied with half a score resolute youths that would have stuck to me in a further discovery towards the Spanish Mines.[12]

More enticements than precious metals and inter-tribal trade were involved, however, in Lederer's travel writings. The English translation of his journal, dedicated to Carolina Proprietor Lord Ashley, made clear the strategic position open to the proposed Carolina colony. "From this discourse it is clear," the translator added,

> that the long looked-for discovery of the Indian Sea does nearly approach; and Carolina out of her happy experience of your Lordships success in great undertakings, presumes that the accomplishment of this glorious Design is reserved for her. In order to which, the Apalataean Mountains (though like the prodigious Wall that divides China from Tartary, they deny Virginia passage into the West Continent) stoop to your lordships Dominions, and lay open a Prospect into unlimited Empires.[13]

By colonizing Carolina, the Proprietors would have an advantage over the established Virginia colony, as the passage through the Appalachians lay to the south and west of Virginia—closer to the fledgling southern settlement. However, the meaning of the view west was ambivalent and the prospect still raised serious question marks. Before La Salle descended the Mississippi to the Gulf of Mexico, speculation was strong among Europeans about southern rivers that might yet be found flowing east-west, perhaps as far as the Pacific.[14] While silver and a passage to the South Sea, or the Pacific, beckoned the Carolina projectors, the formidable ridge of mountains presented obstacles. Lederer's own description of his first sighting of the mountains conveys the awesomeness of the range:

> From the top of an eminent hill, I first descried the Apalataean Mountains, bearing due West . . . their distance from me was so great that I could hardly discern whether they were mountains or Clouds, until my Indian fellow travellers prostrating themselves in Adoration, howled out after a barbarous manner, *Oke'epoeze*, i.e. *God is nigh*.[15]

Travel accounts such as Lederer's and those of his successors struck their intended mark. The speculative geographical placement of the passage to the South Sea directly contributed to the founding of the Carolina colony and continued to inspire post-establishment ventures there and in Virginia. The image of the Appalachians—offering precious metals as well as river passages west— encouraged projector William Blathwayt and a group of investors to send prospectors west from Charlestown.[16] However, by 1698, when Blathwayt undertook his venture, clear geographical fact was just beginning to supplant rumor about the interior.

In 1690, James Moore, following on the earlier Virginia missions of Gabriel Arthur, and Batts and Fallam, had crossed the "Apalathean Mountains" in a journey beginning in Charlestown. Moore's objective was to open a trade relationship with the Cherokees; however, stories told by his native guides of bellows and furnaces lured him onto the track of ferreting out former Spanish mines. Though Moore was prevented from reaching "the place which I had gone to see . . . due to a difference about Trade . . . between those Indians and me," the ore samples taken by Moore and his partner were sent to England and analyzed. In spite of the prospect of gold, the Proprietors, dismayed by the news that Moore's company had "fallen upon the Cherokee Indians in a hostile manner and murdered several of them," ordered a halt to Moore's adventuring.[17]

Despite the hesitation of the Proprietors, Moore's trip fueled the hopes of colonial expansionists. At Savannah Town, an old fall-line trading center on the way to the mountains, Blathwayt's investors encountered Jean Couture, a *coureur de bois* and veteran of LaSalle and Tonti's explorations who had deserted the French to become a free-lance trader. Couture had cultivated the reputation as the "greatest Trader and Traveller amongst the Indians for more than Twenty years," and had encouraged Moore's party with political intelligence concerning the interior.[18] After a chance meeting with Couture, Blathwayt's prospectors gained a strong impression of the strategic importance of the Tennessee River to continental competition with France, a geographical idea which was to firmly graft itself on the minds of both colonists and English officialdom. To prove that the Tennessee linked up with the Ohio, and to demonstrate its importance in driving a "wedge" between the French territories in Louisiana and Canada, Couture in 1700 led a group of Englishmen down the Tennessee River to its confluence with the Ohio and then west to the Mississippi. A year later, alarmed by the news of the English incursion, Iberville in France commissioned a "reverse reconnaissance" of the Tennessee River. Eventually the French party found a portage near the Cherokee Valley Towns linking the Tennessee with the Savannah drainage, and progressed downriver to Charlestown, where they discussed with Governor James Moore the possibility of establishing a trading pact.[19]

This river road was scarcely traveled in the years before 1715, because of the intercolonial and intercultural hostilities—especially in the direction of Spanish Florida—which engaged the English during the first decade of the century.[20] An equally important reason was the presence of the Cherokees themselves, who lived at the junction of the waterways.[21] Though John Lederer had a few decades earlier suggested that the Appalachians were "deserted of all living creatures but bears,"[22] the reality of a powerful Cherokee people, long intimated by native American traders in the Piedmont, was emerging just as the geopolitical centrality of the western region was being verified. The concern of first-generation expansionists such as Thomas Nairne lingered and focused on the western region where the "English American Empire" could be "unreasonably cramped up." In the mountains, Carolina's westward growth could be impeded not only by French actions but also by the undefined disposition of the Cherokees.[23]

However, the Cherokees were still to remain outside of the English trade network. Until the region-wide intercultural war of 1715, most Carolina western trade was routed to the west overland across the Upper Creek Path and approached the Cherokees only along a spur off the main track. The English trading axis was south of the tribe, running west on the Upper Creek Path past broker towns at Chatahoochee and Savannah Town, and the Cherokee towns were not directly intersected on this route, even though they contributed to the flow of goods along it. From the perspective of early eighteenth-century Carolina, the Cherokees were a tribe which, unlike the Chickasaw, Creek, and Piedmont peoples, remained a relative unknown. The Virginians, colonial competitors of the Carolinians, who dominated the trade from the Catawba towns north along the Piedmont trading path, trafficked with the Cherokees indirectly, but the merchants of this colony were also largely out of direct contact with the Cherokees before 1715. However, for the French, the Cherokees were critical players in their hopes of empire, and, as in the past, the English coastal colonies shaped their own world partly out of the perceptions of the world of their rival.

The differential importance assigned by the French and the English to the Cherokees stemmed in part from the alignment of trade routes and rivers. However, the French also encountered the Cherokees first hand, as formidable pirates of the tenuous water-borne commerce between Louisiana and Quebec. The weakest section of the French commercial network tying Louisiana to Canada lay along the Mississippi, where the French interior port of Kaskaskia was established in 1703 (roughly midway between the Mississippi River confluences on the north with the Illinois and on the south with the Missouri). The tribe had easy access to this pivotal region from both the Cumberland and the Tennessee rivers, which join the Ohio within fifteen miles of each other and close to the Mississippi-Ohio confluence. The first two decades of the eighteenth century saw an increasing volume of traffic to New Orleans (including some originated by the Cherokees themselves). The Cherokees made raids against French shipping on the Ohio and the Mississippi along this critical section of the river. In what was perhaps the worst of these incidents, two French officers and perhaps forty soldiers were killed in 1717 near Kaskaskia.[24] French strategists argued most forcefully for an "Ouabache" fort in order to protect the north-south link between the French territories, by citing geographic as well as geopolitical advantages related to the Cherokees. "The communication with Canada," one observer noted, "is as easy as by the river of the Illinois, and the way much shorter. A fort with a good garrison would keep the savages in awe, especially the Cherokees, who are at present the most numerous of this nation."[25] The poorly executed *politique de paix* of the French colonial administration, as well as the migration of the French-allied Shawnees away from the

Ohio region, caused the French to ignore this pressure point until the 1750s. But the Cherokees continued during the early years of the century to present a decisive challenge to the interior stability of French water communication.[26]

Salvation at Tugaloo Town

Even though contact was minimal, the weight attached to the Cherokees by the English colonists in South Carolina grew, largely as a result of second-hand reports. The relative importance given the tribe—and its mountain territories—by French accounts of the interior (such as the map "Carte d'Amerique" of Guillaume Delisle, which first appeared in 1703 and conspicuously labeled "gros Villages des Cheraquis"), by intelligence concerning French ambitions from sources such as Couture, and through information supplied by a growing number of Angloamerican traders, added to English impressions of Cherokee power.[27] By the end of the first decade of the eighteenth century, the English colonists had become well aware that the Cherokees possessed enough power not only to influence their plans of expansion but also to affect their lives. Their strength was demonstrated in the regional revolt against the English by coastal tribes under the leadership of the Yamassee tribe.[28]

The first attack by the Yamassees, at a trading town on the Pocotaligo River, came on Good Friday, 1715, and was soon followed by the capture and killing of nearly 100 colonists closer to Charlestown. In May of 1715 "the Southern parts which include a fifth of the Province" were abandoned in panic. Sporadic engagements continued into the early summer and, though the Yamassees began to gradually withdraw, the Carolinians feared that they were facing a war of much wider scope—a conspiracy of the western tribes beyond the horizon of the trade brokering towns. From the beginning the Coweeta Creeks were reported to have inspired their Yamassee kin, and the Cherokees were implicated in the damaging assault on Schenkingh's Cowpen near the Santee River.[29]

This and scattered other reports of Cherokee hostility were counterbalanced by reassurances from traders during the summer of 1715 that the mountain folk would not sponsor a second wave of violence against the settlements, but Carolinians still feared that a Cherokee alliance with the Yamassees would tip the scales against the English. Thus, when the mission of two English traders to win over the Cherokees appeared to succeed, and news arrived that a Cherokee legation was on its way to Charlestown, a desperate city was relieved. An Anglican missionary reflected the sentiment of the colony when he noted that our "hopes are increas'd by the expectation of the Cherokees, a very populous & warlike nation entering into alliance with us."[30] In October a group of Cherokees led by the pro-English intercultural powerbroker Caesar of Echota arrived at the town and appeared to agree to alliance with the English against the Creeks.

The courage of the South Carolinians was buoyed by this diplomatic initiative of the Cherokees; Anglican missionary Francis Le Jau remembered later that the tribal representatives came "in a most submissive manner" and offered promises of peace and cooperation to weary Charlestown. Still, though Charlestown welcomed its strong new allies, the town was impressed with and perhaps intimidated by their strangeness. "The Cherokees," Le Jau wrote:

> made peace with us with their wild ceremonies of grave dancing wherein they stripped themselves and put their cloaths by parcels at the feet of some of our most considerable men who in return must do like for them. Their exchanging of cloaths and smoaking out of the same pipe is a solemn token of reconciliation and friendship.[31]

Convinced finally that a turning point in the war had been reached, planters began to return to their houses.

This hope, however, was quickly undermined by the failure of the Cherokees to follow through. After the Charlestown conference, and on the assumption that the Cherokees would join the colonial forces for a Creek campaign at the end of November, Maurice Moore, a Carolina adventurer, had led an expedition to a preappointed place of rendezvous. When the Cherokees failed to meet their new allies at the end of November to carry out the campaign against the Creeks, colonial fears were re-aroused. In an urgent attempt to regain the initiative and to hold the Cherokees to their promises, Moore set out for the Cherokee towns with a force of "100 Negroes and Indians" and with perhaps two hundred white men.[32]

The hoped-for Cherokee action again failed to materialize. Unlike the western Cherokees who had visited Charlestown and promised assistance, the Lower Towns were of another mind, and hesitant to make war on their neighbors. Moore's uncomfortable stay in Tugaloo and neighboring Cherokee towns was prolonged by the routine pace of Cherokee diplomacy. The second day after his arrival at Tugaloo, the town's leader, the Conjurer, firmly laid down ground rules by which the village was willing to join with the English. The Conjurer flatly rejected the suggestion by the English that the Yamassees be pursued by the tribe, on the disconcerting grounds that his people and the Yamassees were related. Similarly, Tugaloo was unwilling to engage the so-called northward Indians (an amalgam of Iroquoian people who routinely moved through Cherokee territories to attack the Catawbas). The Conjurer was willing "to ware ageanst none botte ye Sauonose and Yutsees and Apolaches."[33]

The negotiating position of the Conjurer of Tugaloo reflected not only recent shifts in tribal territories but also a political landscape further destabilized by the events of the Yamassee War. Significantly, each of the tribal groups named by the Conjurer as potential adversaries had had a fresh history of violent encounter with the Cherokees. In 1713 men from the Overhill Towns had attacked the nearby Yuchi settlement of Chestowe, a venture which may have been triggered by two English traders who had just prior to the attack fled to the Cherokee villages.[34] Cherokees had also been among the tribal allies of the English in raiding Spanish mission Indians in Guale as early as the 1680s.[35] The repeated assaults of slaving campaigns led against the remnants of the Franciscan missions at Apalachee by Thomas Nairne and James Moore between 1702 and 1706 involved some Cherokees, as did the Tuscarora War.[36]

In most of these campaigns Cherokee cooperation with the English simply overlay continuing and much older conflicts between the mountain tribe and their Muskogean neighbors to the south. During the period prefacing the Yamassee War, tensions along the diffuse and changeable Cherokee-Creek border seem to have been strong. Tugaloo—the Conjurer's town—was itself a border settlement on the Chatahoochee headwaters and was often used as a conference place between the two tribes. The region of the upper Piedmont and Appalachian foothills into which the colonial troops marched had long been unstable country; for example, "Tacowe," which was also visited by the Moore expedition, was "a place newly settled" by the Cherokees,[37] thus, the Carolinians faced the task of winning over persuasive town leaders to a fight against people viewed in some respects as their own.

While the South Carolina troops of 1715 sat nervously during the Cherokee deliberations, they were

> informed by ye Congerare that abought ye latter end of Augus ther weant out 50 of ye Charrykeese to goe agenst ye Coeakeas [Coweeta Creeks] . . . in ye fitte they killd 50 of ye Coeakees and 16 frinch men and toucke all ther women and cheldern slaves with aboondnce of goods that ye frinch was going to Trade with all among them.

While this action would have justified Creek retaliation for the killings, the Creeks seem to have postponed confrontation until the intent of the unexpected English colonial expedition was gauged. A formal diplomatic fact-finding process was initiated by the Cherokees, and the Creeks "excepted the flag of trouce that was seant to them."[38]

However, as in all Cherokee political decisions, there was dissent in Tugaloo. The Cherokees were divided. Among some Cherokee warriors, especially those from the Overhill families who had been represented by the Caesar in Charlestown, anti-Creek sentiment ran strong. When the Creeks seemed to stall, these Cherokees "threatened to send ye Ride Stacke [red stick] trow the Nashon and geatt all Ridey one day to goe and fitte with [alongside] the English."[39] The Conjurer worked to delay the hostile ambitions of these western people as well as those of the English.

As the English observed the village debate, they became increasingly un-easy about the eagerness of some Cherokees to have them join them in combat against the Creeks. While the English had hoped to incite the Cherokees to attack the Creeks singlehandedly, they themselves did not wish to fight. To do so would have been to hazard head-on warfare hundreds of miles from their base of supply. On the other hand, the Cherokee anti-Creek faction under Cae-sar, sensing the hesitation of the colonial force, refused to take up the invitation of the English to fight unilaterally against their neighbors. The Cherokees con-tended that they expected the English to participate. They maintained that they had agreed to English entreaties "to warr against any nation of Indians that were our Enimies" only with the understanding that any action would be jointly undertaken.[40] The Cherokees had earlier made this mutuality clear in Charles-town, when the tribal emissaries had instructed the English by example, putting their "cloaths by parcels at the feet of some of our most considerable men who in return must do like for them."[41] The last phrase, "do like for them," was to haunt the Cherokee view of English diplomacy for the next sixty years.

While Moore and the Conjurer worked to understand each other's position, events carried the Cherokees closer to confrontation with the Creeks. The Creeks had overstepped the fourteen days "prefixt for their coming in," and Caesar's faction began to press the nervous, hesitating English to mount the attack with them. The colonial commander reported to have used "my Endeavours to per-swade them to Desist," but to no avail. The head warriors accused the English of "two talks." If the English did not join the attack or supply ammunition, as had been promised in Charlestown and in a earlier visit to Williamsburg, the tribesmen were "resolved to go to war wth there Short knives in their hands & with what amunition they had by them If not suplyed by ye English."[42] When the Creek party finally came into Tugaloo under a white flag of peace, they were killed by the most hostile of the head warriors. Sensing that the war against the Creeks which they had hoped to incite among the Cherokees, but which the colonists wished personally to avoid themselves, was about to begin, the English troops hurried out of Tugaloo.

"To Save the White People"

Moore's journey to Tugaloo was momentous for both Cherokees and Car-olinians, and was to affect future assumptions made by each group about the other for years to come. The reaction in Charlestown was straightforward: the Carolinians seized on the massacre of the Creeks as confirmation of the Cher-okee alliance which they had long wished for. The importance of this decision on the part of the Cherokees was strengthened by the fact that the message of the Creeks to the Tugaloo Cherokees had proposed the massacre of the English force. The Carolina Assembly reported the surprising turn of events to London in glowing words: "as Providence order'd it they Chang'd their minds and fell upon the Creeks and Yamassees who were in their Towns and kill'd every man of them."[43] The role of the Cherokees, formerly an ambiguous presence in the distant mountains, had finally been clarified. To desperate white Carolinians, the Cherokee promise to take hostile action against the Creeks seemed a "wonderfull Deliverance" for a besieged city, and though conflict continued off and on, the war was deemed to be over with the return of Moore's force in early 1716.[44]

At the most practical level, Charlestown residents felt safe against a future combination of allied tribes in the west: "we have nothing more to do," Francis Le Jau reflected, "but send some of our men to head the Cherokees against the Crick if they think fit to stand against us."[45] On a deeper plane, the dramatic culmination of the war made a lasting imprint. As a result of the Cherokee "rescue" of the colony from a broadened second phase of the Yamassee War, the western mountain landscape began to cast a longer shadow over the Carolina lowcountry. The "vivid tradition of the crucial character" of Moore's expedition was to persist as a touchstone of Carolina policy and trade in the West after the war.[46] The Cherokees had become a part of the political landscape of Carolina, and afterwards the colonists could not afford to undertake diplomatic initiatives without at least a glance west.

The Cherokees drew different, cautionary conclusions from the experience, as their assistance to the English rekindled an older pattern of conflict in the region. The Cherokee Lower Towns would pay a high price for violating the "punctillioes of form" in killing Creeks traveling under a white banner of peace. Their act of violence was returned to the Cherokees by their neighbors immediately, and was to constitute the beginning of an episode of inter-tribal war which would continue over the next thirty years.[47]

The Cherokees later noted the failure of the English to fulfill the basic obligations of allies to fight together. The residents of the Cherokee town of Noyoowee told a Virginia trader with some bitterness that the origin of severe Creek attacks in 1724 lay in the favor that they had done the South Carolinians earlier. "In the first place," they said, "South Carolina was involved in an Indian war . . . [the colonial governor] sent up to the said Nation some hundred men, white and blacks, . . . and at the same time a body of Cricks or southern Indians came to them in order to cutt off the army." When the Cherokees killed the Creek legation, "it brought upon themselves and their families a continued war . . . Their wives and children have been killed and taken and they have told me that if it had not been to save the white people they would have been at peace and quietness."[48]

The war engendered by the Tugaloo incident was intense, and the pain it caused in the Cherokee villages, extreme. In its wake, Muskogean-speaking villages as far south as Apalachee joined in actions against the hill people. The impact of the hostilities was apparent in the reports of the military column sent north in 1716 from Florida to "Apalachee and Apalachicolo" in order to reassert a Spanish presence in the area. While the troop was resting at a Creek town, word came from the Cherokees that they wished to make a peace with the Spanish themselves. Their chief motivation, according to Peña, the commander, was to dampen the slave-raiding which the Creeks had directed against their towns after the massacre of the Creek ambassadors to the Cherokees.[49]

The mixed peace which followed this expedition failed to staunch hostilities, and raiding continued into the 1720s. When faced with latter-day English requests for assistance, the Cherokees often objected. After a Creek raid in which a trader had narrowly escaped death, the complaints by the Carolina agent against the Cherokees for failing to retaliate were met with a pointed reminder that

> the papers you brought up [to] us that the Governor says, if the Creeks will not be good and mind what the papers say to them, that they [Charlestown] will send us white men to joyn us and go to war to fight them . . . that if they [the Cherokees] had been guilty of doing half so much to the white people as the Creeks had done, they was sure we should soon come to warr upon them and that they shoud expect no other.[50]

Furthermore, the agent noted that the townspeople were resentfully and "continually putting us in mind of the former promises that was made [to] them how that we should always stand by them against their enemy which has ever since been neglected."[51]

The continuing breach of faith by the English in their treaty relations would condition Cherokee attitudes toward alliance with the English in the decades to come. Nearly forty years after the Tugaloo incident, a veteran of the early century wars, Tittigunsta of Tennessee, accused the English of disloyalty to their friends; "in the last war," the Yamassees, he reminded the South Carolina governor,

> the Creeks, Chickasaws and Catawbas killed a great many whitemen . . . yet embrace them now as friends, but they [the Cherokees] are slighted and forgot; in the Tuskororo' War this nation joined with the white people, that he himself was among the white people at that time, but now all is forgot.[52]

The political memories of the Yamassee War persisted in the Cherokee villages, as, like other political events, lessons learned became part of village traditions, "imprinted in our memories . . . always amongst us from Father to Son."[53] The persistent memories of the intensified Creek war, added with the rapid decline of population, sharpened the lessons taught in the villages about the English.

The View West

The continuing Cherokee-Creek conflict was not without advantages to South Carolina. Carolina governor William Boone echoed earlier arguments against attempts by Carolina to weld alliances between tribes, a policy which many believed had brought on the Yamassee War. Boone and other Carolinians shared the opinions of a correspondent during 1720: "The warr continues still between the Creeks and the Cherokees which I take to be good news for us." [54] And the outlook of at least some Carolinians who had come through the Yamassee War was baldly, "to assist them in cutting one anothers throats without offending either." [55]

Among other, less aggressive, white Carolinians the plastic heat of the Yamassee War and the apparent intervention of the Cherokees on behalf of Carolina, reformed attitudes toward the western people. Official political initiatives such as that of George Chicken in 1723 seemed to solidify relations with the mountain villages. The unofficial negotiations conducted by Alexander Cuming (a land investor "led by a dream of his wife's to undertake a journey into the wilds of America") and a group of Middle Towns during 1729 resulted in a treaty which was cited as the basis of relations between tribe and colony until the 1760s. [56] Prospering trade also kept the connection alive; John Barnwell's map was careful to ink the term "English Factory," or official trading post, alongside several of the Cherokee towns. Though this was a provision of the trade law passed in the wake of the war, many of these towns had seen only a small trading presence.

The South Carolina colony had early begun to exploit the products of their tribal neighbors in the deerskin trade and, as demands for export of indigenous slaves rose, had aggressively planned to mine away at the lives of tribespeople in the interior. A 1710 population estimate showed a two-thirds majority of "Indian subjects," a striking admission of minority status by white colonists which reflects the pre-Yamassee War perception of the tribes more as royal subjects or potential slaves than as independent or hostile neighbors. [57] The Carolina trading system from the beginning made the assumption (though disputed by the behavior of its clients) that commodities were a route to control. During the first years of colonization, faith in political seduction through trade had been encouraged by invitations to trade, such as the bark pictures observed by Henry Woodward. Although the Yamassee experience dramatically contradicted this early optimism, the demand for commodities in the years after the war continued. Thus the Cherokees played two crucial roles in the eyes of post-Yamassee War Carolinians: guardians of the little known and unsecured western flank of the colony and a large and little exploited market which beckoned commercially minded men.

These assumptions continued as political realignments turned the Cherokee settlements into a major commercial destination of the Charlestown trade after the 1730s. The routes west changed in a way which signaled the increasing prominence of the Cherokees. The path to Keowee—the Dividing Paths—was used more and more in order to avoid the upper Savannah waterway and the contested no-man's-land which had been created by the war. Much more was involved than potential commercial profit on the English side, however, and whatever the commercial shift toward more direct trading brought by the war, other subtler changes in political perception came along as well.

The Barnwell map, made soon after the crisis had passed, projected a new Carolina geopolitical perspective in which the Cherokees occupied the strategic center. The land between Charlestown and the mountain was dramatically foreshortened, and the exaggerated Cherokee settlements seemed to dominate the smaller space occupied by the English plantations on the seacoast. This warping of perspective displayed the deepened colonial consciousness of the new Carolina-Cherokee relationship. Considered as a graphic statement of perception as well as geographic fact, it revealed a terrain of both unease and expectancy concerning Carolina's western neighbors and recent saviors.

The dense detail concerning the Cherokee settlements also stemmed from the rapid increase in information yielded by the war about the Appalachian tribespeople and their mountains. Barnwell even abandoned the designation "Appalachian" (the standard label for the mountains for more than a century) and provided Cherokee names for two distinct ranges. In the place of what had been randomly placed ridge lines, Barnwell described territory "which goes along the back of Virginia and being impassable [to] the head of the Santee River." [58] The name of this region—Nunie—was authentically Cherokee in origin, perhaps derived from the Cherokee adjective "Nuniyu'sti" or "potato-like," which well describes the shape of these mountains.[59] West of the Nunie mountains was the "high Ridge of Mountains called Cheuee," at the foot of which lay the Overhill Towns. This broken country was for generations afterwards familiarly called the Cherokee Mountains, a tacit recognition of tribal control of its topography.[60]

Beyond the Cheuee ridge and across the Appalachians, Barnwell filled a blank space with the caption "level country according to the statements of the Savages." During the 1715 expedition the commanders had taken a side trip across a "way verry mountannas and stoney." The goal of the short venture was to observe a tributary of the "Chattahouchey River," and to get a glimpse of "ye hade of a nother River that Rones into masashipey." The view to the "verry brode" "hade" of the Tennessee River tributary of the Mississippi was significant.[61] In the wake of a regional war, Carolina had finally staked claim to the river road to the west with the cooperation of the Cherokees. The new geography bounded by the Cherokee Mountains—west to the Mississippi—would fix itself in the political consciousness of the colony.

The westward prospect confirmed the mythical geography of John Lederer as well as the on-the-ground tracings of Jean Couture. The experience also cemented in the minds of the coastal Carolina elite the intimate connection between the geopolitics and geography of the interior. The Cherokee mountain people were the key to both. Control of the rivers and land surveyed in trans-Appalachia required the acquiescence, if not the friendship, of the Cherokees. And in the experiences of the Yamassee War and Moore's expedition Carolinians perceived a confirmation of the willingness of the tribe to stand for the English and against Euroamerican rivals staking out their own bits of sandy coastal soil.

3

The Early Cherokee–Carolina Trade, 1700–1730

T HE first colonists who came to the Cherokee villages were clearer about their entrepreneurial ambitions than their ultimate destinations. The Cherokee towns were stop-over points along the way west or north, wherever the fuzzy maps of the interior led these questing and often anonymous individuals or officials. Only after the 1690s did the deerskin trade begin to expand dramatically along the rivers which drained the east face of the Cherokee Mountains, bringing the tribe face to face, on an irregular basis, with Carolinians. The distance from the Lower Towns to Charlestown was a serious obstacle to sustained encounter. There is no indication, however, that the tribal villages were uncomfortable in those early years with their isolation, or that they sought rapprochement or even regular contact with the colonists, then barely occupying the fringe of the Atlantic coast. Instead, the early pattern of middleman trading persisted in which broker tribes, often situated at the fall line, buffered the Cherokees from direct contact—whether with the Spanish in the first years of trade, or their eighteenth-century competitors, the English.

This middleman-run trade restricted Cherokee-Carolina encounter, for the most part, to the fall-line settlements such as Savannah and Manakin Town, or the Catawbas, which were marketplaces from the 1680s on.[1] European goods were exchanged at these sites for leather, medicinal herbs, chestnuts, and cane mats. Once in the hands of trade-broker communities, trade items were sometimes treated like raw materials instead of finished goods, refashioned into forms which suited the tastes of the ultimate purchasers among the Cherokees or other interior tribes. The Cherokees appeared infrequently to the colonists at these spots, intermittent trading partners only, before 1715. According to historian Verner Crane, the Cherokees "long occupied a subordinate position in the Carolina Indian System." As late as 1708 the Cherokees were still described as "a Numerous People but very Lasey," a phrase which seems consistent with only sporadic trade.[2]

Nevertheless the circulation of Cherokee village-made goods in early eighteenth-century Carolina suggests that villagers—women as well as men—were soon increasingly active behind the scenes. Though deer leather and pelts were the bulk commodities of the early trade to Charlestown, the split wood and cane baskets made by Cherokee women were from the beginning among the highest value trade items regularly offered by the tribe.[3] The meticulous design of Cherokee basketry required time and concentration. "They divide large swamp canes," James Adair recorded, "into long, thin, narrow splinters, which they dye of several colours and manage the workmanship so well, that both the inside and outside are covered with a beautiful variety of pleasing figures." Accordingly, baskets, sold in nests of up to "eight or ten," commanded high prices in Charlestown; "so highly esteemed even in South Carolina, the politist of our colonies, for domestic usefulness, beauty, and a skillful variety, that a large nest of them cost upwards of a moidore,"[4] a Spanish gold coin prized in the colonies. The Indian Commissioners were aware enough of the importance of this aspect of the trade that in 1716, when the first Cherokee trade manager requested "Liberty for a private Trade in Baskets," they concurred with a negative ruling of the Assembly, and added that "such a License will infringe the Trade."[5]

Though by the time of the Yamassee War trading initiatives had penetrated to the heart of the village economy—drawing out baskets, deerskins, and even chestnuts from village stores—the process had taken decades. In the beginning years of contact there were compelling reasons for avoiding Carolina traders or their agents. The early subsidiary role that the Cherokees held in the pre-Yamassee War colonial trade must have been envied by those tribes exposed to the harshest colonial demand—for native American slaves.[6] The reach for slaves was extended beyond the colonial settlements through the cooperation of tribal peoples in capturing slaves from their neighbors in the interior. The Cherokees themselves seem to have occasionally participated.[7] For the most part, however, the Cherokees were victims. As early as the 1670s Henry Woodward realized his hope of receiving "younge slaves," some of whom were inevitably Cherokees, from Westoe middlemen. In 1681, a permit was issued for the export of two "Seraquii slaves" from Charlestown. Just over a decade later, the Cherokees unsuccessfully petitioned the Commons House to punish the Savannah people for slaving raids against the mountains.[8] The 1723 escape from slavery in Virginia of a Titisane, or Cherokee, man along with two Creeks (one a "carpenter by trade") was cut short when the men were captured. The stress of the escape had taken its toll, and one of the men told his captor that "being starved so much he was not able to walk and he told them he should dye."[9] This single Cherokee man was among the handful of visible casualties in a generation of uncounted indigenous men and women who disappeared into slavery.

Face to Face: Post-Yamassee Commerce

The fall-line trading network managed by middlemen was destroyed by the Yamassee War and the conflicts which accompanied it. The war also, unexpectedly, changed the terms of intercolonial rivalry for the trade of the broker towns. For many years the Carolinians and Virginians had been in intense competition for dominance at these towns. Virginians held the advantage in the Piedmont centers, at the Catawba and Occoneechi towns, because of their easy access to the north-south running Great Trading Path. Though in 1698 the Carolina Assembly had prohibited Virginians from trading in their province, the legality of this action was contested for decades, and the colonies continued to share in the trade.

The Yamassee War rerouted the trade of the prewar era. Though Carolina at first appeared to be the loser compared with Virginia (suffering direct attacks from both the Yamassees and, eventually the Catawba), in the end, the southern colony profited. In the wake of the war, trade renewed, but on different terms. The Carolinians continued to share the Piedmont market with the Virginians, where traders from both colonies married into the kin-lines of their native trading partners and established stores which controlled local trade.[10] However, this localization of trade into the hands of a few Euroamerican colonial trader-brokers was accompanied by shrinking markets in the now depopulated Piedmont. The new commercial potential lay to the west, with large tribes such as the Cherokees. At the same time, the war had freed access to the markets of the Cherokee towns—towns which were accessible across the well-known but underdeveloped northwest routes opening to the Carolinians.

While Virginians also came in numbers to the Cherokee towns, and the rivalry continued, they were now a minority.[11] Whether from Carolina or Virginia, however, these men came to stay. Some followed contacts made in the older trading centers back toward the mountain villages. Important linkages were made not only by white traders and black factors, but also by intermediaries like the town leader Caesar of Echota, who had worked to turn Cherokee sentiments against the Creek villages near his town, and who after the war turned his cooperative energies toward brokering trade between the English colonies and a handful of villages.[12]

The early century influx was not entirely Carolinian. Traders loosely associated with the French in the Tennessee River Valley moved more or less freely to the Cherokee towns. The French also made an official overture soon after the establishment, in 1717, of Fort Toulouse. Robert Bunning, an English trader among the tribe, noted that the French had previously

> brought some Petiaugers up the River from New Orleans or Mouthkill within 30 or 35 miles of Great Taraqua laden with large Presents of Goods and Ammunition in order to draw the Indians to their Party and to have Leave . . . but after Deliberation and Consideration of the head Men and Conjurer, whose name was Jacob, commanded them to be knocked in the head and thrown headlong from his Scaffold on which they were sitting and their bodies to be dragged into the River.[13]

In spite of this setback, the *métis,* French-Creek population surrounding Fort Toulouse was eventually to become more important in politics than in commerce as French prestige gradually recovered from the Conjurer's rejection just after the Yamassee War.[14]

The aftermath of the Yamassee conflict left colonial Carolina society sharply divided. The planter interests, determined to cut off the free contact with the tribes which had proved so painful, overruled the merchant faction in the Assembly in the summer of 1716 by creating a public monopoly to take the management of trade into government hands. The "resolution and sense of the whole Country" was to end the practice of establishing stores in the villages, "but by degrees cause the Indians to come to our Forts and purchase what they want."[15]

Neither the Cherokee trade brokers nor the "self-ended," self-employed traders who had formerly lived in the towns were pleased with this arrangement.[16] The immediate mandate of the trade was to transfer war material (in July of 1716, "400 pounds of fine Gun Powder . . . 1000 flints") for a campaign of retribution against the Creeks that the Carolinians hoped their newfound allies would carry out as their proxies.[17] In order to encourage trade, particularly at the Savannah Town "factory," rum was sold freely and prices on goods were lowered. However, this did not overcome initial Cherokee reticence about entering into formal trade, especially at a distance from their towns. Theophilus Hastings, the early agent of South Carolina to the tribe, argued that "the Charikees utterly dislike coming down to the Garrisons, to deal, and will not agree to that Proposal on any Account (except for rum)."[18] Under pressure from Charlestown's powerful merchant community (who saw profits fall), competition from Virginia's unregulated traders (in the very Cherokee towns from which the Carolinians had backed off), and complaints from influential tribal town leaders, the trading act was to go through a series of reforms over two decades, privatizing measures which de-emphasized public control in favor of free trading.

Trade Regulation and Colonial Social Agendas

Government policy sometimes backfired and created problems which proved to be ungovernable. The ambitious statute of 1717, spurred by the feeling that traders' abuses had triggered the Yamassee War, was an attempt to exclude colonists—whether white or black—from the Cherokee villages. The progressive dismemberment of these restrictions over the decades following their passage only confirmed their lack of success. However, the growing openness of covert trade as well as government-endorsed structural changes, such as the shift to horse-carrying and the subsequent recruitment of packhorsemen, white and black, in the colony, worsened the problem faced by the Charlestown merchants in controlling the actions of colonists among the tribal towns. George Chicken's visit to Elijay in 1725 was an expression of nervousness about the renewed influx of colonists into the Cherokee country brought about by state policy as well as an attempt to regain control of a deteriorating English position.[19] The statute of 1731 thus broadened the restrictions on multiracial trade and attempted to limit lower class white as well as black participation.[20]

The early efforts at trade regulation by South Carolina not only reflected a desire to manage better the business of the trading but also, and even more important, had a hidden social agenda. The rules legislated by the colony reflected anxieties about the social risks of an interracial, as well as intercultural, Indian trade. Afroamericans had been essential personnel in the trade from the beginning, not only because of their labor but also because of their shared experience with tribespeople. During the Yamassee War, red and black troops were housed together in non-white camps, and this experience, as well as encounters between Afroamericans and Amerindians working in the white settlements, created ties of language and understanding between the two groups.[21] In peacetime blacks worked alongside tribespeople at the English trade factories, or trading posts, and in leather-carrying operations. As a result, blacks filled essential intermediary jobs in the trade as translators and boat-pilots and worked far into the interior.[22] Because they were indispensable, the initial proposal for a complete ban was modified to allow a black presence halfway into the backcountry, to Savannah Town or Fort Moore, though at a safe distance from the Cherokee towns. Furthermore, both white traders and their agents could no longer enter towns other than designated "factories." Racial prohibitions were broadened in 1731 when native Americans were excluded from the ranks of sanctioned traders.[23]

The common experience of blacks and native Americans also proved to be a liability for white Carolinians concerned with political control. During Maurice Moore's visit to Tugaloo in 1715 there occurred just the kind of independent action by blacks which whites feared. "Ye 2 Rogues of negroes run away from ye English," Moore recalled, "and came and told them [the Creeks] a parcell of lies, which hindered their coming."[24] Such fears of fellow feeling between two potentially dangerous groups had been reinforced at the close of the Moore expedition. When white commanders prepared to withdraw from town, they suggested to their Cherokee hosts that a force of fifty whites remain at Tugaloo; however, the Conjurer and his "gritte men" had other plans. Instead, "they were for having 30 nigrous left with a briske white man to command them thinking they would be very serveeas abell in Roning after ye Enimy." [25] The trade reform legislation passed the year after Moore's expedition reflected a consciousness of the dangers posed by the familiarity of blacks with the Cherokees.

Though formal participation by tribespeople in trade was effectively curtailed by the statute of 1731, the broad effect of colonial rule-making was limited. Cherokees continued to participate both as buyers and as sellers in the deerskin trade, roles which had expanded with the post-Yamassee boom. For several decades independent Cherokee factors, or agents working with traders, continued to be a feature of the towns. For instance, the Cherokee town leader Raven of Hiawasse suggested in the 1750s that an errant group of towns be punished by depriving them of their white traders and that "no Indian nor Half-breed should be a Factor from any white Man among them." [26] A licensed and established Carolina trader, one of a group that had counted only twenty in 1751, was pushed to hyperbole in complaining about the growing use of tribal factors later in the century. Indian hunters returning from the hunt, he wrote, hardly had time "to dress their skins [before] a neighboring trader and sometimes one at great distance, would either appoint an Indian factor or send one of his Pack Horse Men into his town." [27]

"A Burthen Not To Be Born"

During the first half of the century, the Cherokees continued to exercise their own, less conspicuous, control over the trade. The most obvious strategy of indigenous power brokers sympathetic to the English, such as Caesar, was to threaten to take their business elsewhere; for as colonial trade lobbyists noted, "Caesar assures me that if they cannot be supplied with what Goods they want, up at their Towns, having now a great number of Skins, They will be forced to go to those that will seek their Friendship." [28] The Virginians as well as the French both offered commercial alternatives, which the tribe continued to exploit. However, because of the most-favored-nation terms (relative to other tribes) extended by South Carolina, the Carolinians gradually became the chief trading partners of the tribe. [29]

The Cherokees, perhaps taking a lesson from the hard experience of tribes who had traded more openly with the English and been penalized by the Yamassee War, leveraged trade wherever they could. For instance, in an agreement with colonial military leader James Moore in 1716, the Conjurer insisted that Cherokee burdeners exclusively carry goods from the Congaree Fort, the building of which the Conjurer had requested, to their own villages.[30] And for a time, at least, this request was respected and seems to have agreed with the opportunism of some individual Cherokee carriers, especially men. One observer noted that traders "sustained great Losses and Damages in ye said Goods and Skins, Several of ye Burtheners each time they went down to ye Settlements usually made away with whole Packs of Goods even to very great Quantities sometimes amounting to one third part of ye Cargo." Adding insult to this injury was what the burdeners did with the stolen items: "They thought it no crime but would go away by ye Catawbas and game away their Packs of Goods and come home without any of it as unconcerned as if they had an authority to do so."[31]

Still, a generation of Cherokee men and women burdeners, sometimes involuntarily, shouldered heavy bundles of skins with the help of carrying straps.[32] The interests of both sides quickly turned against burdening, especially after the transportation revolution brought about by the arrival of the horse in the Cherokee towns. Villagers quickly reasserted at least a semblance of control over this commercial activity by supplying horses for traders' packtrains. While the early movement of horse stocks to the Cherokees from native peoples to the west is largely unrecorded, the post-Yamassee War period saw the delivery of horses in large numbers by Virginia traders in 1717.[33] The news that Virginians had stopped a few years later in the Catawba towns on their way to the Cherokees with "2 or 300 horses" carrying goods, which the Virginians promised to "sell to them much cheaper then those from Carolina," brought immediate recriminations against the Carolina agent who was then in the towns. He reported an anti-Carolina pitch from the Virginians

> that we imposed upon them, and made Horses out of 'em to carrie Skins, but they should not do that, they had brought Horses abundance to eas them . . . This News so Elevated them and so overjoye'd They was thereof, that they looked as cheerful and apear'd like Men eas'd of a Burthen not to be born. Orders was ishued out imeadiatly throw ye Nation for ye building of Houses and Stores for them.[34]

The horses which packed the Virginia goods from the commercial hub at the Catawbas may well have seemed as valuable to the Cherokees as the trade items themselves.

Cherokee men and women shared an initial enthusiasm for horses, but for different reasons. Horses were closely adapted to the male activities of hunting and warfare, but at the same time they eased the burdens of village women carrying skins from the hunting ground. Though this advantage was at first offset by the problem of fitting a large grazing animal into the farmscape of the towns, a substantial number of horses began soon afterwards to be raised. The enthusiasm of the neighboring Creeks for horse-keeping is suggested by the ruling of the Indian Commissioners in 1720 which required a record of each horse purchased by traders.[35] Abundant pockets of grass and winter browse such as cane ("provision the hand of providence has made for the horses," one observer later would call it) and other fire-dependent forage enhanced by regular burning, probably led to a rapid increase in horse population in the southern mountains.[36] By the 1750s a "prodigious number of excellent horses" was a feature of the Cherokee settlements.[37]

For twenty or thirty years before 1750, some Cherokees acted as suppliers of horses to the colonial trade. The demand was substantial; by 1735 as many as 800 horses were used in the deerskin trade alone.[38] Horsetrading and a desire on the part of villagers not to return to the hard work of carrying leather probably increased the strong opposition by the Cherokee headmen to the proposal by George Chicken, the colonial agent, for a return to the burdener system at the Elijay conference in 1725.[39]

Even though the Cherokees' favored position as horse traders to Carolina did not last long, most tribespeople were tolerant of that eventual loss. Because of its unique fit to the distinctly male activities of raiding and hunting, horse-owning became an end in itself. Traders soon took over the job of raising stock for trade, and the Cherokees did not contest their activities. For instance, at the town of Cowee, James May's horse corral was a local landmark; ties of friendship led the "Siniwaska Jonney, the Prince, and the Raven of Cowee," three leaders of the Middle Settlements, to tend them when the trader was forced to flee a fight in another town. Though the Cherokees were willing to care for the horses for a time, however, their patience eventually ran out. They wrote to the governor, requesting that "their Father . . . not stop these Men from coming up to take care of their own Horses themselves." In the end, May was allowed to return, and he and then his successor in the town continued to send off "a troop of them every year" from the town's "horse-stamp."[40] This kind of small economic passage—entailing a shift from human burdening to Cherokee brokering of horses, and then the ultimate loss of both of these tribal roles—encompassed a complex mixture of indigenous and colonial ambitions.

"Willing to Sleep and Parch Their Corn Where the Cattle Dunged"

When Cherokees entered white settlements—whether at designated trading sites such as the Congaree Fort or at undesignated, informal trading locales—they came into an unfamiliar land. Their experiences as burdeners or in following the horse-caravans deep into the colonial settlements proved to be a powerful fixative of attitudes toward white society. The leadership of the colony was sharply divided in the post-Yamassee years between a pro-trade merchant faction and a planter alliance which saw the renewal of trade to be another glimpse into Pandora's Box. The see-sawing between open and restrictive trade regulations during the first half of the new century gave the Cherokees contradictory signals of colonial loyalties.

One journey of conciliation organized by the Carolina agent to the Cherokees in the 1720s allowed a group of Cherokees to witness a charged display of disunity and animosity among the very colonists who claimed to be their allies. Conveying a gift of 130 deerskins to the governor, sixteen "head men" and the Cherokee "king" proceeded with a train of burdeners to the Congaree garrison. There the commander of the fort, William Russell, snubbed his rival, probably William Hatton, the Cherokee agent, because he believed that the agent had accused him of cheating burdeners of their pay. Personal vendetta quickly became political incident. Russell denied food to the party and, "would not suffer the old King nor any of the Head Men to set their foot so much as within ye outward gate." "Such abuses I rec'd from him," wrote the agent, "that I never Rec'd from any man in all my life." Eventually, in keeping with tribal etiquette, the burdeners along on the trip shared their food with the agent. "If we had not found a little more humanity among the Indian Burtheners who spared us each man a little out of his allowance," the beleaguered escort wrote, "we might have starved in the path."[41]

The disasters of an ill-fated diplomatic mission quickly multiplied. While waiting to leave the fort the Cherokees "took a great deal of notice of" the invidious friendliness shown to Catawba arrivees, who had instant access, "and at their coming in orders was given to get them some victuals to eat, while ye Cherikees was all most starv'd."[42] However, what was to occur later at Charlestown would cause the Cherokees to think even further about the civility of their neighbors and about their relationship with South Carolina as well. Upon entering the town limits,

> they was not suffere'd to sleep there but was ordered to encamp without ye Gates, and the Person that own'd ye land where they was sent his Servants to drive them from thence and that little Rotton wood which they had pick'd off ye Ground to Boyle their Corn with they took it from them and throw'd their things about ye Camp and drove them away in ye night when they was a Sleep . . . drove them 4 or 5 miles from ye Town.

The former owner of the property where they had finally settled asked the agent,

> in a huffing manner . . . why I put the Indians upon that land, I bid him to go and ask the Governor, and the Governor be Damm'd and Indians too for he got nothing by none of them . . . there was at this time besides ye King some of the most Leading men in the Charikee Nattion and men very sinceer for ye Interest of Carolina, that in ye War would never come against ye White

people nor ever had been down to ye settlements before, when they saw all these things told me that this was ye first time that ever they was down to see ye English Governor and it should be ye last for they never come no more . . . Saying they was willing to sleep and parch their Corn where ye Cattle Dung'd but ye English would not suffer them to do that.[43]

The bitter taste of this visit must have lasted. In spite of the conciliatory efforts of government officials, the Cherokees swore upon leaving that they would from then on favor Virginia trade over Carolina. From their perspective, one of the intercultural rules which John Stuart would later set down as an axiom of conduct, had been broken. "No people," Stuart warned, "are more offended by contemptuous treatment."[44] This and other incidents led to a gradual increase in Cherokee dissatisfaction with their trade partners. Like the painful lessons brought by their cooperation with whites in the Yamassee War, the story of the embassy to Charlestown, and the snub which they had faced, was to be repeated in the council houses.

4

Colonial Minority: Traders in the Village

EXACTLY how many colonial traders passed through the Cherokee towns in the early years is impossible to say. Certainly there was an ample supply of declared "Indian traders" in Proprietary-era South Carolina. By one accounting, over 10 percent of the white male population fell into this category, and continuing immigration into the colony soon added significantly to their ranks.[1] While most of these men never ventured directly into the Cherokee towns, a few took the risk. Traders and the merchants who backed them were at the top of the income ladder, and factors, or agents, of the Charlestown trading houses could make nearly twice the wage of "those who oversee Plantations." "Self-ended traders," unaffiliated with merchants, occasionally found the trade to be even more lucrative, while others came in order to put a comfortable distance between themselves and the colonial authorities.[2] However, the growing populations of the seaboard colonies had, by the 1730s, increased sharply the number engaged in the trade. In Georgia alone by 1740, "the traders, pack-horse-men, servants, townsmen, and others depending on that business," arriving in the spring to do business at newly established Augusta, were "moderately computed about six hundred white men, who live by their trade."[3]

During the early 1740s, men came from Savannah and Augusta following old rumors, seeking gold and silver. Two prominent traders claimed to have obtained a title to 30,000 acres—with a silver mine included—from the Cherokees (a claim never affirmed). When this news broke into the newspaper a small land rush seems to have taken place.[4] Carolinians with merchant interests agreed with Robert Pringle, who noted that the venture would "certainly Ruin the trade of the Province and the Province itself if it should go on and prove a silver mine as is thought and may engage the Province in a war with the Indians as well as the French.''[5] In the end, the claim of the would-be developers was negated, though incidents such as this continued to lure colonists west and into contact with the tribe. The silver mine incident perhaps left a lasting memory. More than thirty years later, William Bartram was struck by the degree to which the Cherokees ''are extremely jealous of white people travelling about their mountains, especially if they should be seen peeping in amongst the rocks, or digging up their earth.''[6]

Whether occasional interlopers after compact metal or traders in bulky deer-skins, larger and larger numbers of colonists soon came into the Cherokee lands. Some traders, such as Alexander Longe, James Adair, Cornelius Daugherty, and Ludovic Grant, maintained a high profile due to ethnic ties (many prominent traders were Scots), scale of business, or longevity. However, these men were only a handful of the total, and small or part-time traders were far more numerous. When traders appeared in the record books because of legal problems, affidavits often briefly listed several partners, acquaintances or rivals who afterwards disappeared, unknown except for a single mention. Others were remembered because their names stuck to the geographic landmarks, for instance, ''Branon's Horse Range'' near the town of Cowee, by which whites navigated the Cherokee country.

Friendship, Kinship, and Commerce

In transactions with traders, whatever their race or nationality, the Cherokees proved to be shrewd bargainers. In one early instance, a group of unwilling burdeners had walked to the garrison at Savannah Town with seventy bulky pounds of trade leather on their backs. Once there, each received a blanket in payment, but suspecting that they had been cheated, brought the blankets to the factor, a colonial agent, to be measured. The blankets measured ''half a quarter of a yard'' short, and the agent was ''called a thousand rogues and liars, and they told me they would never more Carrie a skin for us of Carolina unless I paid them in ye Nation before they went away.''[7] On another occasion the headmen of two Overhill settlements refused to use the scales (which had been mandated to be used by colonial officials to protect the seller) because they lacked half-pound weight marks and argued at length over the edge given to traders in negotiations by various rules for trimming the hides.[8]

Cherokee trading behavior was more than savvy sharpened through years of brokering between villages and towns. It was also guided by social obligations within the towns. The relationships of towns and traders were understood by the Cherokees to involve not only the back-and-forth flow of goods but also more personal considerations. Some traders became fixtures in specific villages, bound by ties of marriage as well as debt. This attachment was so well known that Edmond Atkin, writing a brief for the reform of the trade, expressed concern about limiting traders to towns of a certain size. He argued that this action would alienate the Cherokees and the Creeks, "who have been always used to have the Convenience of a Trader in most of their Towns."[9]

The Cherokees did not compartmentalize commercial, personal, and political relationships. While Charlestown merchants bankrolling factors in the distant western towns may have had some loyalty to long-time employees, business was their principal tie. Cherokees associated in the trade seem to have viewed participation in a different way, and made selective distinctions between commerce and kinship. Little Carpenter, a prominent Overhill region townleader, was puzzled by and complained about the way a trader named Elliott had conducted business, adding that "he has heard that Elliott was related to Governor Glen and that he was concerned in the Trade with him."[10] This sense of personal connection to individual Englishmen was as important as debt in tying some Cherokees to the trade.

The familiarity which the connection of traders to specific villages implies, however, did not get in the way of disagreement, whether in the family or at the trade house. And as the century approached the mid-point, the white presence in and around the villages became more strained. Abuses occurred on both sides. Beatings seem to have been commonplace. Often the victims were Cherokees who failed to live up to their obligations to pay back debts to traders.[11] Reports of traders' abuses often occurred in the context of political disturbances, which suggests that more was involved than credit problems or personal affronts. Atkin related that "Many Traders were killed from time to time in the Nation," and their trade goods stolen, even though it was unclear whether the Cherokees or raiding parties from their northern tribal allies, the Savannahs or Nottawagas, were to blame.[12] Sometimes violence against whites was too quickly ascribed by the witnesses to trade debts when the real cause of the disturbance was political, for instance, dissension in the towns over a perception of English favoritism to the Creeks in setting prices for trade goods.

Goods with the Power of Things

An incident at the town of Nayowee in 1724 suggests the indifference which the Cherokees were capable of showing their colonial trading partners—and their goods. Although the character of John Sharp, a trader from Virginia living in Tugaloo town, has been forgotten, he inspired strong enough antipathy to be taught a lesson by his Cherokee hosts. When a Creek party attacked the house where he was living alone, the Cherokees refused to come to his assistance. Firepower was not spared, and after a fusillade lasting several hours, "the house was like a Cullendar, so full of shot holes and ye yard perfectly plowed up with ye bullets.'' [13]

Cherokee inaction in the attack against Sharp was more than a diplomatic concession to the Creeks or warning to the English. Instead the incident suggests how straightforward colonial perspectives on why the Cherokees or Creeks wanted guns could be off the mark. Bullets were spent in hunting and war, but guns were also fired as, in the Sharp incident, for noise and smoke. That Sharp survived the Creek assault unharmed suggests that the intention was not to hurt him; had this been the case Sharp would certainly have been killed. Instead, the assault directed by "Gogel Eyes" made a symbolic statement about the strength of Creek men to the onlooking Cherokee villagers.

Firepower was also magic and the new force was orchestrated by the "old majii," controllers of another largely male domain of village power. Alexander Longe recalled that

> when the sun is in eclipse these Indians will run up to the tops of the high hills . . . and sets up the hidiousest cry and shouting as if hell was broke loose and with their guns keeps firing up of bullets up at the sun and others that has no guns with their bows and arrows. [14]

Firearms were also incorporated into Cherokee greeting ritual. For instance, when Maurice Moore's Carolina column approached Noucouchee in 1716 his troops were met by "a boundances of serimoneys as is usual" including "fireing ther guns as wee went up." [15]

The manner in which presumably precious lead was expended not only against Sharp but routinely in ceremonies, raises underlying economic issues concerning Cherokee participation in the trade. Though trade has usually been envisioned as simply an exchange of goods—Cherokee or Creek raw materials for manufactured items—the question of why the tribes wanted the goods in the first place is still largely ignored. [16] The usual explanation of Cherokee demand, offered by most historians, writing out of a world of assumptions more closely related to those of the colonial traders than of the Cherokees, has attributed village desire for trade goods to the technical advantages of the objects themselves rather than to other motivations of the buyers.

The Cherokees of course valued guns for what they could do on the hunt. But when European goods were suited to Cherokee demands, no matter how obscure such demands seemed to Europeans, these goods were eagerly sought. For example, instead of replacing pottery with iron pots for cooking, Cherokee women broke up the cast-iron trade pots and used the fragments in hoes for tending fields. Mirrors and glass fragments became symbols of empowerment and were substituted for the magic crystals of the magi. And decorated Delftware and faience pottery seem never to have been used to hold hominy mush for village meals; the fired clay pots served for this, and continued to evolve new forms (only a few of them inspired by Euroamerican example) during the century. Fancy trade items survive as buried shards, fragments (perhaps broken for this purpose) incorporated into necklaces and pendants found as burial goods.[17]

In some cases, direct substitutions were made of trade objects for tools crafted from traditional materials: bullets for arrows, iron for bone cutting edges on hoes, iron tomahawks for stone, and colored cloth scraps in the place of traditional plant dyes. Such replacements occurred throughout the Cherokee village economy, in both men's and women's realms. For instance, the reddish-orange plant dye obtained from bloodroot and other plants was partially abandoned in favor of the starker red coloring which could be derived from trade cloth. "The very elegant scarlet colour with which the Indians dye the different substances is made in the following manner," William Bartram observed, "they purchase of the traders the shavings, or shreds, of fine scarlet cloths: from these by boiling they extract the scarlet tinge or color." Mark Catesby reported that, by the third decade of the century, "since the introduction of Iron hatchets which they still call Tomahawks they have wholly laid aside their stone ones."[18]

What the Cherokees actually traded for will always be clearer than *why*. Substitutions, transformations of pottery into magic shards, technological advantage are all part of the equation, but not the full solution. "Goods," anthropologist Mary Douglas writes, "are neutral, their uses are social, they can be used as fences or bridges." In abstract, they can be viewed as "information," or as communication passing from hand to hand, owner to owner.[19] There was, above all, a great volume of this material exchange. And it can be marked into periods that roughly follow the course of political exchange as well.

For the most part, the most obvious substitutions visible in either record books or excavations seem to have been well under way, perhaps virtually completed, by the end of the first quarter of the eighteenth century.[20] Thus the strong demands for some European goods—guns and cloth for instance—which were new to the towns early in the colonial period, dwindled more rapidly than is usually suggested in historical accounts stressing the dependency of the Cherokees on Euroamerican goods. Certainly the demand for goods based on technical superiority continued if for no other reason than the need for replacements. But after the novelty wore off, and ownership became widespread, a kind of second stage in consumer demand for trade goods was reached in which picking and choosing was more the rule. Just where to fix the turning point in demand is difficult. However, at least by the Yamassee War the majority of Cherokee men already owned the most costly trade item, a gun.[21] After the first quarter of the century, access to trade goods was easier as the backcountry economy progressively diversified and Cherokees found alternatives to officially sanctioned trade paths with the colonies. Perhaps reflecting this slackened demand and more open market, prices for guns, hoes, and the whole range of officially listed articles fell by half over the period between 1715 and 1762.[22]

One indication of this second stage of lessened reliance on the official trade comes from within the village economies themselves. By the 1750s, and perhaps earlier, the trade in high technology Euroamerican goods seems to have been largely subordinated to a Cherokee demand never completely understood even by the most perceptive of colonial trade reformers. Part of the difficulty in uncovering this dual Cherokee pattern of consumption lies in the fact that some trade items were used in more than one way; for instance, the desire for guns and ammunition, noise and smoke, coexisted with a market for the same items based on their utility in war and hunting.

Adding to the complexity is the fact that Cherokee demand reflected the values of both village men and women. In general, the items most valued by the Cherokees were what whites were likely to discount as trinkets or fail to understand the value of at all. The "value of an Indian's effects," James Adair observed, could be judged by "the quantity of red paint daubed on his face and by the shirt above the collar, shoulders and back, should he have one."[23] In the eyes of Cherokee consumers, especially young men, paint, mirrors, and physic were as potent in war as was the tool representing the technology of firepower.

A Trading Vernacular

When they bought and sold guns, deerskins, or corn, Cherokees behaved according to their traditional rules of economic conduct—but with an eye open to the perceptions of their white partners. A trading vernacular, which combined cross-cultural civilities and specific accommodations, had begun to develop well before the Yamassee War.[24] Much like the trade language Mobilian, which eased commercial transactions through the lower South, this marketplace idiom facilitated Cherokee trading goals at the same time that it protected traditional patterns of village exchange. And much like the reality of consumer demand for European-made items, this two-sided behavior was rarely made specific to whites, and thus allowed the Cherokees much flexibility in negotiation.

An incident just over three decades after the Yamassee War, involving a controversy over the sale of corn, provides a glimpse of the persistence of this vernacular. Corn was sometimes bought and sold to traders, visitors, or other non-Cherokees within the towns, but was also often given away in the villages in accordance with traditional subsistence ways. The reply of Connecortee of Chota, a principal Overhill liaison with the English, to a request for corn to feed South Carolina's military construction crews, throws light on the traditional conduct of gifts and sales of corn. " 'Tis true it is very hungry times here but what little we have we will share it with them and when there is a Want we will all want together," and, Connecortee said, since there was little corn available, "your people may also have part of what there is for buying as we do, one from another."[25] The conjunction of the words "sharing" and "buying" in Connecortee's talk shows the dual rationality at work in the trading of subsistence goods, and that the latter term characterized transactions with colonists. While women were enthusiastic traders in some respects—especially in the sale of non-subsistence goods such as herbs—they were cautious with respect to selling the foodstuffs grown in their own farms. When corn was sold, the price was likely to be very high, even though in other circumstances, and to others, especially native American as opposed to colonial purchasers, the same foodstuff was likely to be given away.

Euroamerican concepts of profit, credit, and debt were also gradually accommodated to Cherokee ideas of commerce. In a society in which accumulation of wealth was overridden by routines of gift-giving, and in which consumption was more important than accumulation, the notion of profit was difficult to translate. Though the Cherokees doubtlessly understood the demands of their neighbors, to colonial traders the Cherokees were maddeningly indifferent to the profits or losses on their side of the ledger.

Adair, who knew Cherokee economic concepts first hand, wrote that the Cherokees were duplicitous in their behavior: when debts between Cherokees resulted in "heart-burnings," elders settled the dispute in "a very amicable manner. They have no compulsive power to force the debtor to pay; yet the creditor can distrain his goods or chattels, and justly satisfy himself without the least interruption."[26] For most Cherokees, debts remained a kind of moving gift which served to tie the creditor to debtor. However, when the Cherokees failed to pay debts to colonial traders, more often the villagers applied another maxim to their business relationships: " 'An old debt . . . of nothing.' "[27] An old debt is nothing.

Debts and the economic well-being of their trade partners became important to the tribespeople only when whites insisted on them, or when a particular need was pressing. And those times when debts needed to be settled in order to keep the traders coming were, at least in the second phase of trade contact, far fewer than usually imagined.[28] This double-sided trade vernacular, accommodating colonial traders as well as tradition, buffered the sometimes destructive impact of trade goods. Cherokee business idiom allowed villagers the latitude to either respond to or ignore, as political and economic circumstances varied, traders' demands for satisfaction of debts and other obligations.

"'twas Rum Did It"

Just as the complexity of Cherokee consumption patterns and their intimate relation to gender and economic roles, have been underestimated, so also has the impact of the introduction of new goods been oversimplified. Alcohol is a particularly important case, since from the beginning colonial commentators identified it as a source of social pathology and political breakdown among their neighbors. While drinking contributed its share of tragedy, alcohol's destructiveness within the villages was greatly different from in Charlestown or Savannah.[29] Often, especially among young men, drunkenness was a political statement. Drunken deportment obliquely challenged the control exercised within the village by local Cherokee authorities and also played a role in violent behavior—such as revenge or warfare—away from the village. Among the Cherokees, drink was called by the same name as physic, Nawohti, and the consumption of both ritual potions and alcohol was a part of preparation for war.[30] The linkage between drinking and aggression on the part of young warriors was underscored by a request from the warrior Mankiller to the British commander at Fort Loudoun. "All the paint is gone you gave him," a messenger from Mankiller suggested, "and he desires a little more to paint himself when he is drinking."[31] As suggested by this connection between body-painting (an act usually associated with aggressive acts) and alcohol, drinking was distinctly connected to the missions of young manhood.

In a society in which reserve was highly valued and in which confrontation outside rules of decorum was discouraged, drunkenness loosened inhibitions of political behavior. Drinking was a way of not socializing, of removing oneself from control, and for this reason hard drinking was much more common than casual consumption. "The Indians in general do not chuse to drink any spirits," James Adair wrote, "unless they can quite intoxicate themselves."[32]

The authority of Cherokee elders over drinking was imperfect, and just as in the case of unsanctioned raiding, responsible Cherokees leaders simply shrugged their shoulders at the misbehavior of young men. Except for murder, drunken acts were excused and exempted from retribution; only for this extreme crime were "Drunkenness, accident or self-defense" . . . "not considered as any attention."[33] Edmond Atkin noted that when confronted with any "mischief or outrage," the village leaders were "sorry for what hath happened, But that it was not they that did it, 'twas Rum did it.' "[34] At the worst, as in an incident at Keowee, most drunken infractions of village rules were punished by "scratching." In this way village authorities imposed rules indirectly, placing the blame on a third party, rum.

Though alcohol consumption posed a serious health problem in the villages, Cherokee drunkenness resulted less in aggressive anomie than in an exaggeration of traditional male behaviors. Young men had always strained against but rarely broken the rules. Though drunkenness by the end of the seventeenth century was already a severe affliction for coastal tribes driven to near-extinction or among fugitive tribes settled at trading nodes such as the Catawbas, the full negative impact of alcohol consumption on the Cherokees and other large interior tribes appears to have come later.

The ability of Cherokee authorities to accommodate the challenge of alcohol was underestimated by the special lens through which colonial bureaucrats viewed the tribespeople and the trade. The social concerns of the administrators themselves for the well-being (or control) of their own society—for instance worries over drunkenness as well as social and racial drift—biased their perception of tribal culture.[35] Colonial traders were often victims of their own wares, and their behavior created problems in the villages almost equal to those posed by tribal alcohol abuse. As Fort Loudoun commander Raymond Demere noted, "they are worse than the Indians themselves and are all Drunkards."[36] Partially because of this reform outlook, South Carolina was receptive to the request of some village headmen to limit the trade in alcohol, and in 1755 totally (and completely ineffectually) prohibited the sale of rum to the Cherokees. However, colonial bureaucrats attempted to interdict the importation of rum, even though the proliferation of rum traders and the increasing backcountry production of spirituous liquors during the middle years of the century made this virtually impossible. Instead, the most effective control of a very real problem for village health was asserted in the villages themselves, by indigenous authorities.

Colonial Traders and the Challenge to Village Governance

The life of the towns was changed but not revolutionized by the presence of traders and trade goods within them. As with the case of alcohol, Cherokee authority was challenged, and Cherokee town leaders were quite vocal in their complaints against the problems the influx of colonists brought to their towns. However, Cherokee authority—whether represented in the old magi, the old women, or the warriors—was constantly, and traditionally, challenged. Only in the most stressful times did the consensus and group control out of which Cherokee authority arose break down. Even when disturbances brought on by the actions of whites appeared to erode authority, older guidelines of restraint and of acceptable tension were respected.

Trade goods were more easily managed than the traders themselves. In a long memorandum, John Stuart attempted to bring home to the desk-bound bureaucrats of the Board of Trade a sense of the reality of the country he attempted to keep under control. In his report Stuart described the misconduct of a trader and the Cherokee reaction:

> I begg your Lordships leave to communicate the following anecdote . . .
> An English trader who resided in Tannassee had a Dog which he valued much killed by an Indian. He went to the Town House and complained of the injury, to the Beloved Man, who ordered him a pound of leather in value of 2 [pounds] Sterling as a compensation and which he deemed a sufficient price for any dog. The trader was far away from being satisfied and determined to show the

injustice of the decision. The next day he loaded his horse with leather, took his gun and as he passed through the town began to kill every dog that was unlucky to fall in his way, saying [here is] a pound of Leather. Amongst others the Beloved Man's dog fell victim to whom when he complained the trader offered a pound of Leather also putting him in mind of the preceding day's sentence. The Indians immediately entered into the Trader's hut and altho' they were sorry for their faithful doggs They blamed the Beloved Man more than him for the loss of them.[37]

In this instance, people could identify with the trader and his contemptuous protest against the "Beloved Man." The authority of the headman was challenged by the trader indirectly, in the Cherokee way. In this and other instances traders found themselves drawn into the traditional Cherokee face off between young and old, and forced to play by its rules.

This and other episodes brought to the villages, and especially to their white inhabitants, a reputation for disorder and even endemic violence. However, among men and women of both societies, associations went beyond simple hostility or business conducted at arm's length. Over the years the residence of English traders also produced a kind of familiarity reflected, for instance, in the sympathetic protest offered by townspeople to the trader in John Stuart's story. Other personal relationships produced reliable friendships. James May, the trader of Cowee, could depend on the Raven to look after his stock of goods when he was forced to leave the village. The Cherokee-Carolina trade often appears to have been less an unbroken field of commerce than an exchange in the broadest terms, a realm of transactions in which goods simultaneously built "bridges" and tore down "fences" between colonist and mountain villager. Among the Cherokee towns during the first half of the century, traders and their goods were simply accommodated, though with increasing difficulty, to the world of their hosts.

5

"We Should be Well Set to Work to Take Notice of Women's Actions"

T HERE were many private as well as public crossings of the cultural line
separating colonist from Cherokee. " *'There's one frontier we only dare
to cross at night,'* the old gringo said. *'The frontier of our differences with
others, of our battle with ourselves.'* "[1] Many 'frontier' crossings were made
by women. Since nearly all colonial-period documents were written by men,
they have given an artificial, distinctly male cast to many intercultural events.
The official testimony, the surviving records (whether from colonial trade-
reformers or Cherokee headmen), has left a lasting, but superficial, impression
of Cherokee villages as wide-open frontier outposts and provided little evidence
of the economic life of both women and men. And, unlike colonial seaports or
interior trading stations, where men were long in a clear majority, Cherokee
women outnumbered men in the villages during most of the eighteenth century.

Women appear at the edges of the paper records of commercial transactions
and friendships, a pervasive though still marginal presence. This marginality,
however, at least in the trade economy, was partly the result of female choice.
Tribal women sometimes chose not to participate fully in the colonial trade by
holding their agricultural products off the market. They were blocked from
entering the well-documented deerskin leather trade by the strong associations
of this business as man's work on both the colonial and Cherokee side. Because
colonial papers reflect the bias of a Euroamerican culture in which women were

pushed to the side, the story of the economic lives of tribal women—especially elements of women's self-determination—can be told only in outline.[2]

It is impossible, however, to read the documents, even those bearing on the most overt economic relationships of the trade, without finding traces of a female presence. For instance, the warning words of a woman "who had come over from Stecoe on Tucosigia River" were enough to cause James May to flee his home village; in this act the woman had clearly been as loyal as May's friend the Raven, though neither May nor the Raven gave her a name.[3] This and other instances of support shown by native American women toward traders and soldiers garrisoned in the villages have often been assumed to have been motivated simply by sexual liaison. Similarly, the erotic side of culture contact has most often been reserved for women, and usually with an implication of surreptitiousness—the economic and diplomatic side left to men. In an early colonial account of Cherokee life, trader Alexander Longe takes great pains to play to his reader's fascination with the proported permissiveness of tribal women by providing suggestive observations; "sometimes," Longe wrote, "the young maids come and steal away women's husbands." In this stress on the sexuality of Cherokee women, Longe's writings echo similar themes in early colonial travel accounts and natural histories. John Lawson, for instance, had words on the subject: "as for the Indian Women, which now happen in my Way . . . they are of a tawn complexion; their Eyes very brisk and amorous; their Smiles afford the finest Composure a face can possess . . . nor are they strangers nor not Proficients in the soft Passion."[4]

In his hyperbolic account of "Indian Matrimony," however, Longe touched on another dimension of indigenous domestic relationships—the family dominance of Cherokee women over men:

> I have this to say that the women rules the roost and wears the breeches and sometimes will beat their husbands within an inch of their lives. The man will not resist their power if the woman was to beat his brains out; for when she has beat one side like a stalk fish, he will turn the other side to her and beat till she is weary. Sometimes they beat their husbands to that height that they kill them outright; but then the husbands parents assemble and kill the woman.[5]

This and other paragraphs in Longe's "Small Postscript" presaged much of what was to come as Cherokee women developed a reputation for power in domestic relations. This information, conveyed by Longe and other writers, must have discomfited audiences in Carolina, where racial demographics and tensions were rapidly reinforcing inherited Euroamerican patriarchal tendencies. Longe's final remark in "Indian Matrimony" perhaps signified his own realization of this important intercultural distinction. The trader's advice to the reader: "we should be well set to work to take notice of women's actions."[6]

"Petticoat Government"

Cherokee women crossed both sexual and economic boundaries in the light of day as well as in the night. Such crossings had implications not only for their own economic activities or political status but also for the basic management of village life and the preservation of tribal identity. Cherokee women, confident in their own matriarchal world, came face to face with Euroamerican men who had brought with them (and reinforced in their colonial situation) a history of male inheritance and family leadership. Cherokee women bolstered by their central place in the kinship system shifted mates with ease and informality. Colonial commentators reported this degree of female freedom as exceptional even among the other major and matriarchally organized southeastern tribes:

> the Cheerake are an exception to all civilized or savage nations, in having no laws against adultery; they have been a considerable while under petticoat government, and allow their women full liberty to plant their brows with horns as oft as they please, without fear of punishment. On this account their marriages are ill-observed, and of a short continuance; like the Amazons they divorce their fighting bed-fellows at their pleasure, and fail not to execute their authority, when their fancy directs them to a more agreeable choice.[7]

Colonial observations of Cherokee family relations must also be read cautiously. The consciousness of many commentators of implicit comparisons between the Cherokees and southeastern colonial society, with its "politest" behavior in this regard, created a kind of reflected glare which must be filtered out to get a clean picture of Cherokee domestic life. What can be said is that, at least compared with the seaboard societies, sexual freedom was, within limits, publically sanctioned. Widespread practice of abortion (and perhaps infanticide as well) gave Cherokee women an added measure of independence in marriage by reducing the demands of childbearing.[8] Given this, it is not surprising that at least some village women chose to enter into sexual liaisons and even marriages with colonial traders.

In the Cherokee towns as late as the mid-point of the eighteenth century, indigenous women continued to choose to live with colonial traders. However, a gradual change had taken place in the same villages which had witnessed the first interaction between Cherokees and colonists. The slow learning about Euroamerican society—and vice versa—which had brought a degree of alienation in diplomacy and even in trading was also reflected in the politics of gender relationships. Intimate interaction resulted in a rejection by some indigenous women, not of colonial men as individuals, but of colonial expectations of behavior.

A confident, somewhat critical stance toward the colonial rules of liaison with white men survives in trader-historian James Adair's account of the marriage of Dark-lanthorn. This woman, "no stranger in the English settlements," married a white man "according to the manner of the Cheerakee." However, Dark-lanthorn's new husband, "observing that marriages were commonly of a short duration in that wanton female government," hoped to tighten his hold on his bride with an English ceremony. "He flattered himself of engrossing her affections," Adair continued, "as to get her sanctified by one of our own Beloved Men . . . and taught the conjugal duty." The attempt to overcome the rules of female government failed when the minister at the Congaree post attempted to instruct the woman on marital fidelity and the proper subjection of women in marriage by "urging her to use a proper care in domestic life." "You Evil Spirit," Dark-lanthorn sharply replied, "when was I ever careless at home?" "Tell him his speech is troublesome and light," she instructed her new husband.[9] Far from being intimidated by colonial attempts to put Cherokee women in a proper, colonial place, Cherokee women such as Dark-lanthorn were willing to attend to the rituals of white society but rejected the cultural instruction of white men.

Other incidents spotlighted domestic difference in the mountains. Newspaper reports of the mysterious Frenchman Christian Priber's efforts in the 1730s and early 1740s to plan an intercultural utopia at Coosawattee aroused anxieties among the colonists about sexual (as well as racial) revolution. "He enumerates many whimsical Privileges and natural Rights, as he calls them, which his citizens are to be entitled to"—the *South Carolina Gazette* highlighted—"particularly dissolving Marriages and allowing Community of Women and all kinds of Licentiousness."[10] While reports singled out Priber as the inventor of this risky sexual agenda, his own precepts squared with basic Cherokee ways. The popular press figured in a quotient of alarm about the intentions of both Priber and Cherokee villagers.

Economic and sexual relations were often intertwined. Yet the assumption that all such relationships were largely sexual has discounted the economic life of Cherokee women. Freedom in marriage—and in the marketplace—was consistent with the early century independence of Cherokee women; village women remained the arbiters of their own conduct. Though reports of wide sexual latitude among the tribespeople captivated colonial observers, village women themselves could put strong brakes on such behavior. A Virginia-based trader named Hunt, residing in a Cherokee town just after the Yamassee War, became embroiled in tribal controversy over his relationship with the wife of a Cherokee and faced problems which went far beyond the usual commercial issues of fair weights and prices. It seemed that "said Hunt" had

gotten another man's wife (with his leave) to make his bread and look after his house and for which he sometimes gave her a flap and other small trifles which made the other women reflect upon her and said Hunt as being too familiar, tho' her husband was not aggrieved. But these reflections of Women made the Indian woman to go to another town, her husband being then out hunting, after which the young men comes to the said Hunt's house to jeer the said Hunt about his house-keeper leaving him.[11]

Cherokee social relationships were maintained through the opposition of freedom with restraint, of tolerance with exclusiveness. When colonial and indigenous society mixed, as it did in Hunt's village, Cherokee women faced much the same kind of implicit regulation of their behavior as that faced by young men during drinking bouts, warfare, and disputes over compensation of personal injury. In all cases, a clear generational pattern of authority was apparent. Just as Beloved Men blocked violence among young men, the pressure of female elders, old women, and village peers caused Hunt's hired woman to flee. In the face of this, Hunt was "jeered" by Cherokees. He had somehow stepped over the line and was, like his housekeeper, exposed to the pressures exercised to mold conduct in Cherokee society.

Even after the mid-point of the century, when economic and demographic events eroded some of the traditional female roles like that of war-woman, other less visible political power remained in the hands of tribal women. Female lines of authority are much less commonly portrayed in the colonial documents than rules enforced by men. Still, the rule-making of both men and women seems to have been similar in at least one respect, a deference to age. And elder Cherokees, female and male, seem to have been especially united in their attempts to shame young men and women into conformity in areas of sexual behavior.

Disasters such as drought, often attributed within the village to sexual misconduct, brought recriminations. These small dramas reveal women in specific and sometimes opposing authority roles. After one particularly dry summer, a failed rainmaker turned his criticism to the young people of the village, attacking "with bitter reproaches, for their vicious conduct in the marriage state, and for their notorious pollutions, by going to the women in their religious retirements." After being upbraided, the young villagers were filed out; "the old women, as they go along, will exclaim loudly against the young people and protest; they will watch their manners very narrowly for the time to come, as they are sure of their own steady virtue."[12] Women seem to have had the last word here, indicating a special responsibility for surveillance of both harvest and village behavior. And older women exercised some of the special authority bestowed by old age.

The "Wave of a Swan's Wing"

Women were the gatekeepers of Cherokee society and in this role were an important force in sanctioning war and keeping peace. Cherokee warfare, like that of many tribes, was "either inspired or rationalized by the obligation to avenge dead relatives."[13] The murder of their own people could be set right through revenge-killings or, more commonly, through the replacement of the dead by the adoption of captives.[14] Women played a key role in setting the stage for war, since they mourned intensely and publicly. Determining the fate of captives among the Cherokees was also clearly the prerogative of women, and their decisions had both diplomatic and demographic significance. That women enjoyed a range of options in consigning the lives of their captives was made clear to the Carolinians from the beginning. As early as 1716, a Cherokee woman appeared in records delivering a captive to the Carolinians for a price. In this instance, the "Indian Woman, Peggy," was paid with a "suit of Calicoe Cloaths, for herself, and a Suit of Stuff and a Hat, for her Son . . . for Satisfaction for a French Man belonging to her."[15]

A darker reputation shadowed other, less humane actions by women. The Senecas, traditional enemies of the Cherokees, portrayed this female Cherokee role in a nightmarish legend. Ganogwioeoñ, a Seneca war chief, was captured in a raid on the Cherokee towns and was carried to

> two women of the tribe who had the power to decide what should be done with him. Each of these women had two snakes tattooed on her lips, with their heads opposite each other, in such way that when she opened her mouth the two snakes opened their mouths also. They decided to burn the soles of his feet until they were blistered, then to put grains of corn under the skin and chase him with clubs until they had beaten him to death.[16]

Historical accounts concerning the authority of war-women to condemn or reprieve captives confirm the myths of the Cherokees' adversaries. "They can, by the wave of a swan's wing," Henry Timberlake noted, "deliver a wretch condemned by the council and already tied to the stake."[17]

Though the torture described in these stories occurred with some regularity, adoption was a more frequent outcome of captivity and meant a secure (though often temporary) residence among the mountain folk. During the population crisis of the colonial period, adoption also became a means of replenishing a lost labor force. During the seventeenth century, as many as two-thirds of the Oneidas were adoptees; among the Senecas entire villages were assimilated. The Cherokees also accepted fugitive groups in the early eighteenth century such as groups of Natchez and, perhaps, Creek peoples such as the Taskagis, and in this way further augmented their own strength.[18]

Nor was the process of establishing Cherokee citizenship restricted to captives of war. Perhaps because of their own role in controlling access to the tribe, tribeswomen returning from either captivity or peaceable residence among other tribes underwent ritual purification on their arrival home. Thomas Griffiths, in the Cherokee towns as a clay-purchaser for Josiah Wedgwood, re-

ported finding that his "old Consort the Queen" had, like other women, been
forced

> to undergo Eight days Confinement in the Town house, after Returning from,
> or being a Prisoner to any Enemy whatsoever, and after that to be strip,d,
> dip,d, well wash,d and so conducted home to their Husband, wife or friends.[19]

Child-rearing and Politics

In lasting intercultural marriages, indigenous women and traders confronted
basic issues, such as child-rearing, which further pushed the maternal authority
of Cherokee women against the paternal governance projected by white male
reformers. This confrontation may partially lie behind the limited success that
the Society for the Propagation of the Gospel missionaries had in bringing
indigenous children into their mission schools. Cherokee females perhaps formed
a front line of this indifference, for as Alexander Longe wrote, child-rearing
was conducted by the women of the family:

> All of the female relations looks on the child to be their proper daughter. If
> the mother dies before the child has left off sucking, any of the woman's
> relations that gives milk will take the child and give it suck and they will
> make no distinction betwixt that child and their own children. They will rather
> be more kinder to it than to their own proper children and the husband of the
> woman must show more kindness to that child than to his own or else he must
> expect but little quiet of his wife. Moreover from the time that she begins to
> suckle it for the space of one year she will not let her husband bed with her
> for fear that it should spoil the child's milk and cause it to die. So you may
> see that the man has the worst of it on all counts.[20]

By the middle of the century, several incidents suggest a growing, uneasy
awareness among the Cherokees of the Euroamerican treatment of children.
Cherokee children were spared the rod. Even though she was an assimilated
Cherokee, Ann Matthews was punished only twice during her captivity of several years

> first for refusing to go for water. She was shut up all day without anything to
> eat. The second offense was going for water (as they used gourds) she rolled
> the gourd down the hill and broke it, for which she was taken by the two
> hands and plunged into the river three times, without giving her time to breathe.

Ann, a teenager during her forced residence with the tribe, was subjected to
harsher punishment than her Cherokee friends; she observed in her "Memoir"
that the "Indians never use the rod of correction."[21]

A Presbyterian missionary encountered a firm opposition toward his proposals to send Cherokee children to school in the colonies when he first arrived among the Overhill Towns in 1759. William Richardson uncritically recounted the silent rejection given by the Cherokee leader Great Warrior to his initial proposal for the education of Cherokee youth. Richardson recalled that the Warrior

> said they were all rogues and would not learn. He told me that he had seen children at school among the English, and that the master loved them that read well but corrected them that did not with a rod; now they never corrected with a rod, but pour'd water upon them or threatened them with physic which does as well. I told him he need not be affraid for them for they should not be wipt with a rod and so he went away without telling me anything whether he would have them learn or not.[22]

By walking silently away, the Great Warrior had left little doubt about his own child-rearing preferences. Another missionary with broad ambitions for the teaching of native children may have been discouraged by a brief visit to the Cherokees. John Hammerer believed that boarding schools in the white settlements would never attract support because "the fondness the Indians have for their children will always prevent them from . . . sending any into the colonies to have them educated."[23] The permissive parenting of Cherokees, in which discipline, when it came at all, was likely to come from the mother's family at the hands of a female relation or uncle, could hardly have come up against a more striking opposite than the paternal discipline designed into Protestant theology and its educational precepts.

These differences had to do with cultural assumptions.[24] What mattered was not solely kinship—whether mothers or fathers were in charge—but how authority was discharged. Because the handling of dependents—especially children but also anyone in the charge of another—went to the heart not only of the Cherokee family but also of Cherokee political life, the debate over child-rearing practices was not at all irrelevant. The cultural issues which lay behind the debate anchored the politics of adulthood as well as childhood. Authority and dependency, in contexts ranging from child-raising to warfare, were to become the points of reference against which Cherokee society would measure its own distinctiveness from, and ultimately its opposition to, colonial society.

Race and the Tensions of Personal Identity

Though some Cherokee women were open to colonial partnerships, tribal society as a whole remained diffident and protective of its singularity. In spite of its rituals of greeting, hospitality, and gift-giving, barriers to outsiders were far from insubstantial. And the presence of white and black colonists in many Cherokee towns from the first decade of the eighteenth century quickly raised issues of ethnic boundaries. The intermarriage of Cherokee women and colonial men posed an immediate challenge to these limits. The paradox posed for Cherokee society at large did not stem from these interactions themselves. Traditional lines of authority and governance, except in the most stressful times, were strong enough to have resisted the potential for disintegration growing from relationships between tribal women and colonial men. The real difficulty faced in the villages was due to the children born to bicultural marriages. The conventional solution was consistent with matriarchal kinship: "when they part," Henry Timberlake observed, "the children go with, and are provided for, by the mother."[25]

Some children slipped out of the hold of Cherokee mothers. Scattered references crop up even before the Yamassee War to mixed-blood children, including one Cherokee "mustee," born into captivity, who was taken into custody by an Anglican missionary in 1714.[26] Male children are retrospectively more visible because at least some seem to have followed their fathers into the leather trade—or their mother's side into warriorhood. The timing of the 1731 Carolina trade statute, which banned tribal or *métis* participation in colonial commerce, may have reflected the coming of age of a generation of *métis* youth, and white anxieties about their increasingly high profile in the trade. More direct confirmation of the presence of such children, and their integration into the economic world of their colonial fathers, comes from personal records. For instance, the will of Robert Gowdy, for many years a Carolina trader in the Overhill Towns, left a "small sum of money" for each of his Indian wives and children.[27] However, the rules of racial ranking developing in the colonies kept *métis* individuals on the margin, confined to trading communities far removed from polite towns such as Charlestown, literally middlemen between the world of their mothers and that of their fathers.

Racial gradations prevalent in colonial society, such as "mustee" and "mulatto," either did not exist or were subdued among the Cherokees. The most important and lasting distinction was not whether men or women were white or black, but whether they counted themselves Cherokee or not. However open Cherokee society was, at least superficially, in racial terms, in ethnic terms the villages were closed societies. Only native born or assimilated Cherokees had standing; non-Cherokees were guests of the villages at best, and at worst, strangers who were merely tolerated. Racial identity, however, sometimes overruled individual self-choice—whether or not one had been accepted into a Cherokee town or clan. Male warriors made blanket racial distinctions and, in their rhetoric at least, were equally contemptuous of all non-Cherokees.[28] The political openness extended by the tribe to those willing to assimilate was countered by a strain of exclusiveness among male warriors, particularly as the middle decades of the eighteenth century approached. When

Buck, a mixed blood native of Nuquose, died, "none of the warriors would help bury him," James Adair related, "because of the dangerous pollution they believed should necessarily come from touching such a white corpse; as he was begotten by a white man and a half-breed Cherokee woman."[29] Even though Buck had been a warrior, perhaps because the mother of Buck was of mixed blood (and thus of uncertain kinship status), he was excluded from full equality in warriorhood, the most restrictive, radically Cherokee male status.

Cherokee women, however, continued to keep open the door which, in times of war, the warriors wished to slam shut. At least through most of the century, colonists taken captive often had the chance to become Cherokee just as could Afroamericans or members of other groups, but it was not captives or visitors—outsiders to the tribe—who felt the tension of ethnic identity most directly. Instead it was *métis* children born within Cherokee villages. As the first generation of these children became adults, the middle ground confidently crossed in the first decades of the century by their parents had become a kind of quicksand.

These abstractions became intensely sharp by the middle decades of the century for young male Cherokee mixed-bloods who had grown up confident in their mothers' lineages. Like Buck, they aspired to full rights in warriorhood but found obstacles in their way. As raiding became more focused on white settlements rather than on other tribes, *métis* children confronted profound questions of cultural and personal allegiance. For some mixed-blood men, the tensions of proving their Cherokee allegiance were shown in harsh, hostile acts of cultural disavowal. For example, a trader from Keowee reported the extreme behavior of "a half-breed Fellow, called Andrew White." In the company of a group of Cherokees, Andrew White had been a part of a raiding party which had killed a party of traders to the south of the Cherokee Lower Towns. The same young man threatened James Maxwell, and when he was confronted by Maxwell, "the half-breed answered, I have killed a white Man. Do you think the Governor will be cross? He may if he will. I wish I could see an Army of Whites coming down that Hill. I would be the first to stick my All [awl] in their heads."[30] While this hypertribalism was to some degree a motif of the intensely individualized Cherokee fighting style, Andrew White's hostility was driven by the conflicts of his mixed-blood status.

Under growing white-red confrontation, psychological stress could also push Cherokee *métis* (and their mothers) toward loyalty to the English. Thus "Indian wenches, half-breeds and others" became a familiar line-up of informants to backcountry officials. Though some mixed-blood males appeared as mediators in times of conflict, women much more often played that role, sometimes acting in concert with "war women." "Half-breeds" caught in the middle were vulnerable, and, like women, were often singled out as victims of violence.[31] Confusion about the victim's ethnic identity was a common excuse given by Cherokee warriors when non-combatants and allies were killed in war. When

Cherokee town leaders apologized to colonial authorities for the killing of a white hunter, they explained that the young killer had believed that the victim was a "half-breed with his head shaved in the manner of other Indians."[32] A *métis* appearance could be a fatal liability, and the violence directed at these men was felt by both the children and their kin.

During the first half of the eighteenth century, Cherokee villagers, male or female, young or old, learned much about the neighboring society whose traders and diplomats had pushed their way into the mountain villages. The political warning signs were clear in retrospect to the Cherokees: the war with the Creeks which had followed on the heels of a tentative alliance with the English in 1715; the repeated unwillingness or inability of Carolina to play fair according to indigenous rules of political conduct; and the influx of traders and their goods which both enriched Cherokee life and challenged its older routines of authority.

Yet, Cherokee attitudes toward their colonial neighbors also hinged on less tangible and more poorly documented events. Images of colonial society were partial, whether derived from brief glimpses on trade or diplomatic missions, or from sustained encounters of marriage or commercial partnership. Within the villages themselves the Cherokees' image of their own society was also challenged by the growth of a *métis* Cherokee population, and the residence of these "new people" illuminated basic tensions of gender and ethnic identity within tribal society. This kind of personal experience, and the variety of lessons drawn from it by Cherokees, depended on an individual's perspective, whether that of male or female elder, trading factor, or *métis* warrior.[33] The most profound change in attitude—one relevant to diplomacy as well as mixed marriages—had to do with the distance between Cherokee and Euroamerican stances toward individual freedom and social authority.

The poet Octavio Paz suggests the linkage between the political and personal in a passage which is relevant to the complexity of the experience of the Cherokee villages in the first decades of the eighteenth century. "Love's connection with politics," Paz writes, "is the concept of 'person.' A more or less civilized society has to be based on a minimum of respect for the person. The destiny of the person is linked to the destiny of love and the destiny of politics."[34] Traditional Cherokee marriage guarded the personhood of women. Dark-lanthorn spoke for other Cherokee women in protesting the intrusion of outside authority, alien to her own precepts of marriage. Dark-lanthorn was not the only Cherokee woman who encountered the political side of personal decisions. And *métis* children felt the connection between love and politics as they sought to fuse their own individual political and cultural identity.

By the 1750s the most politically and commercially active of the Cherokee villagers and Carolina colonists had images of the other roughly faceted along the angles of personhood, humanity, and even decency. The first eighty years, between 1670 and 1750, of encounter in the Appalachians between colonist and mountain villager had contributed to judgments about the civilization of the other which, together with events in the crucial decade of the 1750s, would recast Cherokee-Carolina relations.

PART II

An Unstable Margin

6

"Their Country is the Key of Carolina"

D URING the decades of the 1720s through the 1740s, official contact between the colony and tribal mountain towns had been sporadic, and intercultural politics had for the most part been overshadowed by the ebb and flow of trade. On again off again hostilities between the Cherokees and the Creeks sometimes interrupted steady routines. The Carolinians at times attempted to mediate or exacerbate this conflict—depending on their reading of the costs and benefits to themselves—while always looking for the French behind the scene. However, there was a constant logic in their western policy beyond opposition to the French. The Carolinians, in this and other contexts, still hoped to gain the prize they imagined would secure them the interior: a firm alliance with the Cherokees. During the Yamassee War the English had sought out village brokers such as the Tugaloo Conjurer and Caesar, but by the late 1720s they were increasingly concerned with formally cementing their connection with their tribal neighbors. When Cherokee authorities could not be easily identified, the English attempted to create for themselves Cherokees of rank worthy enough to negotiate with the King's representatives.

During his quixotic journey to the Middle and Lower Towns during 1730, Alexander Cuming, a utopian land speculator and minor Scottish official, named the Cherokee village leader Moytoy as the "Cherokee emperor." Cuming sought Cherokee alliance with a biblical fervor that made a mystical connection between peace with the Cherokees and the King and the redemption of other 'lost' peoples: Jews, Jamaican Maroons, and his own Scots. The Cherokees he visited tolerated Cuming's behavior but the traders considered him erratic. "He seldom staid above two or three hours," in any town, Ludovic Grant stated, "never above a night at any place, whenever any Indian met us, as it is their Custom to shake hands—Sir Alexander would take his name down in his pocket book saying that he had made a friend of him."[1] While their standing among their peers was unchanged by Cuming's action and fell far short of Carolina expectations, Moytoy and his kin-lineage were able to operate as liaisons between the Cherokee Middle Towns and Charlestown.[2] Cuming conducted seven Cherokee warriors to London, where they stayed for four months in the summer of 1730. Though any other aspect of Cuming's mission was subsumed in the spectacle which the visit afforded the public, English officialdom used the opportunity finally to put on paper what they viewed as the implicit promise of alliance made during the Yamassee War.[3] This Cherokee tour came twenty years after a Mohawk delegation had been eagerly received by the court, and the provincial leaders who supported the treaty were also anxious to obtain similar courtly approval for their handling of tribal affairs.[4] During the warriors' visit the Board of Trade sealed a treaty with the tribe.[5] (Fig. 3)

Trade seemed to the English to provide the closest and most dependable binding with the tribespeople. This assumption had its roots in the self-assured ambitions of first generation Carolinians like Thomas Nairne. "May it please your Lordships," Nairne wrote in 1708, "the Indian trade for Cloath always atracts and maintains the obedience and Friendship of the Indians."[6] Even during well-orchestrated state visits from Moytoy or his successors, the colonists tended to interpret the relationship in material terms. A British officer serving as a military consultant to the colony cast a cynical eye on the intentions of the Cherokees during one such visit in 1745:

> We had a visit at this time from a war captain or king as they called him, with about one hundred Cherokee Indians in his retinue, under the pretence of renewing his alliance with King George; but the real object, I believe, was to receive the customary presents . . . after the ceremonial part of their visit was ended, they shook hands with every one in the room, took their leave, and were conducted back to their camp, in the coach that brought them; they [the king and his "principal officers, and three women"] were neither painted nor adorned with feathers, as the rest, but were decently clad in blue cloth, and each a gold-laced hat.[7]

Bruce's assessment of the Cherokees' motive underscores a prevailing outlook of colonial Euroamerican diplomacy from the first years of contact: that trade goods had the power to buy the economic dependency of the tribes. In Bruce's view, it was as if the goods themselves—fancy hats and clothes—had the effect of taming and tying the tribespeople to Carolina; dressed properly, the Cherokees were suddenly reliable. The ledger-keeping mentality of Charlestown merchants was thus transposed easily into colonial diplomacy. Whereas gift-giving for the Cherokees was a political act that demanded reciprocity, the Carolinians saw it as outright purchase.

Some perceptive colonial politicians, most prominently Edmond Atkin, challenged this narrow interpretation of political exchange between the tribe and colony. In his *Report* of 1755, Atkin couched his criticism in an ethnographic perspective which drew on the expanding global trade contacts of the British. "According to the practice of the eastern nations of the World," Atkin wrote, "there was an exchange of presents, (however small on the part of the Indians on Account of their poverty), yet as expressive of a true footing upon which they met, a mutual friendship."[8] Atkin's argument remained a minority viewpoint, however, as most colonial policymakers saw in gift-giving none of the mutual obligations and expectations such transactions carried in the villages. A colonial military commander expressed the prevailing view bluntly: "Indians are a commodity that are to be bought and sold . . . Indians are but Indians and are very little to be depended on; the highest bidder carries them off."[9] Tribespeople were aware of this over-simplifying tendency on the part of colonial agents and used it to their favor. In one incident, a Creek warrior parodied English perceptions, and in a near-holdup attempt demanded goods by shouting, "give me your shirt for I am a King. Don't you know . . . I am a King."[10]

There is not an abundance of candidates on which to test out the great man theory of history in mid-century South Carolina. However, Governor James Glen stands out as Carolina governor between 1743 and 1756. His actions set the course of Carolina's Indian policy well beyond his long tenure. Glen, a student of history, diligently sought to apply its lessons, and his policies were footed in hope and fear centered on Cherokee Appalachia. Though he was to oversee a remarkable escalation in intensity of contact with the tribe, James Glen essentially continued the pattern of diplomacy and acted on the intercultural assumptions set during the post-Yamassee War period. Some of these assumptions proved at times to be hazardous. Glen's career as governor is important in this respect because it exemplifies, even personifies, the fragility of the political culture of the colony during this period. The mentality which experienced Carolina officials brought to their dealings with the tribes became critically important by the mid-point in Glen's governorship. By then the first stirrings of the continental war for American empire between the English and French, a conflict which drew in the native peoples of America, were about to be felt in the South. For Glen, this slowly escalating conflict would provide a critical test of Carolina's geopolitical future.

Glen himself acted on the idea that the Cherokees could be controlled effectively by turning the valves of trade open or shut. He alienated influential villagers during the early 1750s by abruptly cutting trade shipments of ammunition in an attempt to force an end to hostilities between the Cherokees and Creeks.[11] The Cherokee response reflected an independence Glen had not counted on. Cherokee leaders first threatened to request the traders residing in their towns to leave. "If they agreed to go," they argued, then the towns would have "their leather to make them some shoes."[12] "As to the powder and bullets of Carolina," the Nottewezo Warrior and Headman of Chota replied, "they can make arrows serve instead." A Cherokee-drawn map of the period suggests that the Cherokees had taken steps to establish their independence from not only the Carolina but also the entire colonial trade. The notes on the map record that some tribesmen had visited a "large Rock of Ore as Big as a House" on the Mississippi, "and made Bullets."[13]

Though the colonists may have overestimated the bindings of trade, there is no doubt that joint Cherokee and Carolina trade expanded greatly, along with the burgeoning commerce of Charlestown, right up to the 1750s. Though rice had supplanted deerskins in export value, deerskin loadings remained high at the Charlestown docks, and a significant percentage of these were of Cherokee origin. During 1747–48 the value of shipments of deerskins (and other tribal commodities) roughly equaled the combined total of indigo, beef and pork, lumber, and naval stores.[14]

Thus, when James Glen came to take over the reins of the Royal governorship, Charlestown had all the appearances of prosperity, if not freedom from economic and political anxieties. The decades after 1730 were profitable for fortunate Charlestown planters and merchants, who reaped returns on investment nearing 30 and sometimes 50 percent and believed that the colony was on the way to becoming the richest in America.[15] Planters built blocky rural "power houses" to anchor plantation complexes.[16] As its agricultural catchment basin expanded, Charlestown itself also spread out along the water, its low slung profile punctuated by St. Michael's Church. But the sea was an avenue of danger as well as prosperity. The War of Jenkins' Ear, in the late forties, continued to pull South Carolina into direct conflict with Spanish Florida. However, even during this conflict, the direct exposure of South Carolina to the Spanish had eased (because of the establishment of Georgia in 1733) from the high level of the early years. But interior threats continued to preoccupy the colony. The Stono Rebellion in 1739, a slave insurgency, had reminded propertied Carolinians of the price of the prosperity that rice-cultivation had brought to the low country. Nearly two-thirds of the Carolina population were black, and the desire of these men and women for freedom posed a real threat to the stability of the colony. (Fig. 4)

Diplomatic affairs with the western tribes were calmer during the thirties and forties, though not totally unclouded. The raids of northern tribes such as the Six Nations had kept the western backcountry settlements "under one almost continued state of alarm and uneasiness," and individual Cherokee towns were sometimes implicated in harboring these attackers.[17] However, Glen's agenda was too grand to be preoccupied with the upcountry concerns. He looked forward to the continued growth of trade—and more—with the mountain people. He had some reason for optimism in diplomatic precedent. The English had received Cherokee help in Oglethorpe's campaign against Saint Augustine in 1740.[18] The apparent cooperativeness of the Cherokees encouraged Glen, the ambitious western expansionist, when he wrote in 1754 that the Cherokees were the "key of Carolina."[19] He fully expected to be able to turn the key.

Glen's thirteen-year term (the longest of any colonial South Carolina governor) saw resurgent expansionism, based on "large scale planning," from South Carolina toward the west.[20] His own program had had, at least in his eyes, its own early successes. The Carolina governor had actively sought to mediate the sporadic but damaging clashes between the Creeks and Cherokees during the 1740s and 1750s. He would, with great overstatement, claim to have settled the conflict, thus opening the door for unimpeded diplomatic initiatives.[21] Glen's interest in the west was made more urgent by European warfare and by the contest of France and England for the interior of the continent. By 1755 outright confrontation among the French, English, and tribal groups in the north grew world-wide into the Seven Years' War, or as it was known in North America, the French and Indian War. This made quickly restaking the pre-Yamassee War trans-Appalachian land claims an urgent part of the South Carolina agenda. Citing Cuming's treaty as legal precedent for relations with the Cherokees, Glen would even attempt to use its provisions in order to leverage concessions from the tribe. However, in the neighboring province, Virginia, the Carolinians faced a challenge for influence in the west, nearly equal to that of the French. Virginia continued to be the major competing claimant to the Cherokee trade—which, in Glen's view, translated to Cherokee loyalty and access to western lands.

The governor had an almost legalistic faith in earlier precedents for Carolina's claim to the Cherokees. Glen's memoranda on the subject were filled with historical minutiae, so much so that one Board of Trade bureaucrat sarcastically penciled, in the margin of one of his letters, "Gentle Shepherd, tell me where you lodge at noon your fleecy case in."[22] Although Glen was disliked in Charlestown by the elite of the city and grew increasingly isolated from other colonial officials toward the latter part of his term,[23] he worked with great energy to fulfill his vision.[24] In this respect, his ideas were less a new political analysis than a restatement of wisdom received from the brief but traumatic history of Carolina and the Cherokees.

After the declaration of war against France by George II in 1756, the British began to invest money to defend their holdings, and this brought Virginia and South Carolina into renewed competition. During a squabble with Virginia over the allocation of funds for fort construction, Glen highlighted the strategic importance of the Cherokee country and its rivers. While he would be "sorry to see the French permitted to settle the Ohio river," Glen wrote, "he would be "infinitely more so to see them settle and build forts on the Tennessee River."[25] This argument had a detailed exposition in Edmond Atkin's *Report* of 1755, which put Glen's fort-building proposals in a wider context.[26] However, it was the political strategy of expansion mapped out by Atkin and Glen which interested the Board of Trade, and not Atkin's insights or Glen's historicism. Glen's geopolitical argument was persuasive to English officials for whom Carolina and Georgia provided a second front in which operations could be undertaken against French expansion and fort-building in the Ohio and Mississippi valleys.

Even though men such as Glen and Atkin were unabashed advocates of Carolina's manifest destiny, their own arguments often concealed a provincial vulnerability. The troubled history of the colony yielded a lesson to Glen and others that the "key of Carolina" in the hands of the Cherokees opened a back door to the province, which could favor the future or lead to disaster. If allied with the French, for instance, the Cherokees would be an unbeatable foe, "several thousand gun men all acquainted with every inch of this province," Glen pointedly observed: "they may the Day after be back at their Mountains which may be said to be inaccessible, as ten Men will defend some of the Passes against a thousand."[27] On the other hand a Charlestown alliance with the tribe would finally give Carolinians access to the long-sought Tennessee River road to the Mississippi.

Like many Carolinians, Glen was self-conscious about the position of South Carolina relative to the faster-growing, more prosperous, and better protected colonies to the north, and fearful of the consequences of weakness during wartime. "Carolina is the country that has reason to fear the force of France in case of any rupture," Glen wrote in a letter to the Virginia governor which enumerated the disadvantages of the southern colony vis-à-vis its northern and more centrally located neighbors: "it is thinly inhabited; it is a frontier Province, and consequently weak by situation. It may be easy to cut off a corner, but it would be madness to attempt the center where the English are remarkably strong, rich and populous."[28] Carolina's weakness was not only its location, but extended as well to its financial standing relative to other colonies. Although when measured in terms of simple shipping volume, the city of Charlestown was a major port, its commerce was not self-supporting. It remained painfully dependent on Britain for credit, the prices of its exports on protected markets, and decisions affecting its business were often made in the home country.[29] The Charlestown leadership was acutely aware that Carolina was the borderland of the seaboard colonies, but they also feared another marginality—the fact that they constituted a racial minority in their own colony.

The Terrain of Fear

Uncertainty concerning Cherokee intentions (whether the tribe would or would not ally itself with its trading partner should the French invade South Carolina) paralleled equal anxieties about the ability of white Carolina to defend itself against enemies within. An immensely profitable agricultural economy had been established on the base of forced black labor. Black hands and skill had modified the coastal wetlands of South Carolina into a rice machine.[30] The bargain made by white slave-owners—prosperity bought with the lives and labor of black slaves—came, however, at a grave cost of personal security. Soon after the Stono Rebellion in 1739, a frightened white wrote:

> On this occasion every breast was filled with concern. Evil brought home to us within our very doors, awaken'd the attention of the most unthinking. Everyone that had a life to lose, were in the most sensible manner shocked at such Danger daily hanging over their heads. With Regret we bewailed our peculiar case, that we could not enjoy the benefits of peace like the rest of Mankind; and that our own Industry should be the means of taking from us all the sweets of life, and rendering us liable to the loss of our lives and fortunes.[31]

Fear had many permutations. Anxiety guided the defensive reconstruction of the Carolina countryside. Enslaved workers drained marshes and inland wetlands and built mile upon mile of dike[32] to open areas to cultivation, and also to tame the wild places in which hit-and-run attacks from Indians or escaped slaves could originate. The gentle dendritic curves of wetlands were replaced by linear roads and straight-shot waterways—cut-offs and thoroughfares.

Native-born member of the Provincial Council William Bull admired the manner in which the agricultural transformation of the countryside solved simultaneous social demands facing white planters:

> The introduction of Rice hath proved very fortunate circumstance in this colony . . . many large swamps otherwise useless and affording inaccessible shelter for deserting slaves and wild beasts have been drained and cultivated with such banks as to keep out torrents of water in planting season and by reservoirs supply artificial rain when wanted.[33]

It was within the power of the planters to provide "artificial rain" by remaking the level coastal marshes and higher islands into a grid of canals, dikes, causeways, and fields—a reassuring landscape image of control. Pennsylvania naturalist John Bartram wondered in 1765 at the Carolina penchant for open avenues running across the marshes to the houses of planters. "They think its ye beauty of A road to have A very extensive prospect endway with large vistoes near A mile to some gentleman's seat."[34] Gentlemanly seats visually elevated in this way also gave gentlemen a head start in seeing who was coming.

The rice-land itself with its impoundment, channeling, and redirection of brackish blackwater mirrored the control of forced labor. However, Bull's technological vision of nature and society reflected more image than reality. In spite of local clearing, bay and riverine forests continued to provide safe havens for slaves. During the colonial period, South Carolina harbored more reported colonies of maroons, or slaves who had settled into refugee communities, than any other colony.[35] And northern tribespeople utilized the same cover for raids near Charlestown in the early 1750s.[36]

Illusions of control were proven perishable during the 1750s, on both the mainland and the island colonies. The homeland memories of the white Barbadian settlers who had first emigrated to the colony, and continuing family contact with the Caribbean, kept alive a particular topographic context of fear. In Jamaica, where as in most Caribbean colonies deforestation had been an instrument of social policy, the mountains remained an escape hatch for fugitive slaves, who regrouped themselves into permanent maroon societies and from these secure places launched raids against planters.[37] South Carolina had its own potential Jamaican Blue Mountains in the Blue Ridge of the Appalachians.[38] This geography also presented an analogy for William Bull, who wrote, that should the Cherokees be destroyed, "an almost inaccessible country would be laid open," which would provide "a plentiful refuge to the runaway Negroes from this province who might be more troublesome and more difficult to reduce than the Negroes in the mountains of Jamaica."[39] News of Christian Priber's activities in the mountains, with his reported plans for a new nation at the "Foot of the Mountains among the Cherokees, which was to be a City of Refuge for all Criminals, Debtors, and Slaves who would fly thither from Justice of their Masters,"[40] doubtlessly had contributed to Bull's anxieties.

Planters, already burdened, perceived another nagging danger in the intertribal trade and political rapprochement with the western tribes encouraged by state policy and merchants' lobbying during the Glen administration. Whites in the English colonies responded to this red and black double threat to their lives and prosperity by reassuring themselves that "a natural dislike and antipathy" existed between tribespeople and Afroamericans, all the while insisting that a similar dislike on the part of the tribes did not apply to the colonists as well.[41]

The reality of the new continent was, however, quite different for Euroamericans from that of small islands with vanished native American populations. There was a record of tribal cooperation with the Spanish and fugitive slaves to harass Carolina in the Yamassee War era.[42] Incidents in the 1750s replayed this combination, minus the Spanish. For instance in 1751, a "half-breed . . . a subtil fellow," a resident of a Cherokee town, "seduced" six blacks to run away with him to the mountains, "from whence he promised to conduct them to some place where they might depend on their freedom."[43] Once in Keowee, the black runaways played to Cherokee fears by telling the Old Warrior that the "white people was coming to destroy them all." This news "obtained belief and more," for the Old Warrior "said some Negroes had applied to him, and told him that there was in all Plantations many more Negroes than white People and that for the sake of Liberty they would join them.''[44]

With a history of this sort of incident, which increased concern for internal security, the news during the summer of 1755 proved particularly disquieting. Braddock's campaign—meant to recoup colonial dignity after the embarrassing Virginia campaigns led by George Washington—had failed, and the repercussions went beyond a blow to colonial ego. "Negro slaves," Lt. Governor Dinwiddie wrote from Virginia, "have been very audacious on the defeat on the Ohio. These poor people imagine the French will give them their freedom."[45] And the South Carolina leadership could not take any malicious comfort in the problem of their rival colony, as "the wonderful art of communicating information" practiced by slaves at the time carried news "several hundreds of miles in a week or fortnight," leaving Charlestown to wonder if a communications network of such potential breadth could also include the Cherokees.[46]

The Saluda Conference as Ritual and Reassurance

James Glen felt left out of British strategy during the initial phase of the Seven Years' War in the colonies and yearned for a fair share of appropriations for defense and public works.[47] Irritatingly, Virginia was actively using the wartime emergency (and British funds) to advance its territorial claims westward by planning its own fort for the Overhill villages. It temporarily seized the diplomatic high ground by conducting unilateral negotiations with the Cherokees at Winchester in May 1754. There the Cherokees gave tentative approval for Virginia to build its fort.

For Glen's constituents in the backcountry the early stirrings of the war brought home more immediate concerns. Far western anxieties were accelerated by the killings of twenty-one people assembled for a marriage celebration at Buffalo Creek in the fall of 1754. According to the local justice of the peace:

> It seems the white people that first discovered the affair, which was the new married couple and etc had not a force sufficient to follow the Indians, but were themselves in such a panic that they could not wait to bury the dead but by flinging them into a well on the said plantation . . . this affair, sir, has caused a great Dread in these parts.[48]

Thus, the summer of 1755, when Braddock's doomed expedition was launched, reflected the counterposed hopes and fears of the Carolinians and their government concerning western affairs.

In the spring of 1755 Glen planned a conference at Saluda which he hoped would cement a strong presence for his colony in the west. However, the Cherokees sent mixed signals. Though Glen had succeeded in obtaining Cherokee permission to construct a fort at Keowee in 1753, now only two years later their mood had become more hesitant. The Cherokees had first refused Glen's invitation to come to Charlestown in 1755, excusing themselves by pointing out how many of their leading men had "left their bones upon the path" to and from the city.[49] Instead, they offered to meet the Carolinians halfway, an offer which reflected both practical considerations and their view of the colony as a diplomatic equal. Glen put the offer in the best possible light, as a go-ahead for the building of another fort farther west, the long desired concrete Carolina presence among the western Overhill Towns. As planning for the conference that would make or break his plan was under way, the governor learned that a replacement for his post had been named. This news may have spurred him to attempt to demonstrate, finally, his own competence and the rightness of his vision of alliance with the Cherokees.

Once under way, the Saluda Conference was impressive to Cherokees and colonial onlookers alike. Glen stage-managed the meeting; his advance men had been working to make sure that enough backcountry citizens were present to "prevent a mean opinion" of the colony among the Cherokees. At least five hundred Carolinians did attend, spectators as interested as the Cherokees themselves in a glimpse of the government. Elaborate exchanges of gifts (including presents of "furniture laced with gold" to the leaders of the 500 or 600 tribes-people present) prefaced the negotiations. A feast served on silver bowls and cups outdoors, in steamy July, "under an harbour" marked their close. The correspondent of the *South Carolina Gazette,* himself impressed, reported that the

> Indians expressed great surprise and satisfaction adding that they had few such things to treat strange Indians with who came into their country.[50]

Expansive Cherokee imagery of alliance misleadingly inflated Glen's private hopes for Cherokee concessions.[51] The chief Cherokee speaker at Saluda, opened

> a small Leather Bag, in which was contained some Earth, laid the same at his Excellency's feet, adding that they gave all their Lands to the King of Great Britain; and as a token of it they desired that this Parcel of Earth might be sent to the King, for they acknowledge him to be the owner of all their Lands and Waters.[52]

Glen happily construed the rhetoric as an absolute fee-simple transfer, in the English sense of land rights, rather than what the ceremonies actually meant to the Cherokees: a symbolic gesture of alliance.

The Scots traders among the Cherokees (many of whom were facing bankruptcy and desired a bail-out promised by the fort-building project) had lobbied hard for Glen's meeting. And the most ebullient, Ludovic Grant, later swelled the accomplishments of Glen by recalling that:

> when Connacautee the Chief returned to his nation . . . he gave very good talks to all his people telling them that they must no longer have any complaints against the English for settling on their lands for they had no longer any lands they properly call their own, they had given them all to the English.[53]

Less self-interested backcountry whites in attendance must have taken note— even though perhaps remaining a little skeptical, and rightly so—of the apparent generosity of the Cherokees at Saluda. Even the governor appeared to sense before the end of the conference that the Cherokees had a more limited agreement in mind than a sweeping land transfer, since Glen insisted on the Cherokees receiving token payment for the land. They refused it at first, and then accepted it only out of politeness.

Yamassee Memories and the Saluda Outcome

Once the Cherokees had accepted token payment, Glen believed that, in one stroke, he had defused the prospect of Cherokee allegiance with the French, secured a foothold of unknown size in the trans-Appalachian land for the English, and one-upped rival governor Dinwiddie of Virginia. Charlestown greeted the news with ebullience. The *South Carolina Gazette,* in an unusually detailed story taking up the entire front page (rarely did the political news of the colony displace the latest reports from the Continent), gave a lengthy account of the ceremony and the speeches and noted the implications of the land cession. Equally impressive was the coverage of the treaty in England.[54] The London *Historical Chronicle* reprinted the *Maryland Gazette*'s article on the Saluda Conference, and parenthetically added that the meeting was "not only very interesting to this province, but to all His Majesty's colonies on this continent."[55]

Adding greatly to the symbolic impact of the Saluda Conference were other events of 1755. The news of Braddock's defeat just after the Saluda meeting was made more disturbing by the conjunction of that disaster with the fortieth anniversary of the Yamassee War. Glen issued a proclamation remembering the dire condition of the colony. "It is probably owing to that March," recalled Glen with reference to the Moore expedition to Tugaloo:

> that we have this opportunity, so long after, of commemorating that Era; for had the Cherokee and Creeks joined at that time, which nothing prevented but

> the resolute Behaviour of our Militia; it might have proved fatal, it must have
> been at least very dangerous to the Province.[56]

In the 1750s the events of the Yamassee War were lodged just a generation back, on an edge of public consciousness, in historian C. Vann Woodward's words, in the "twilight zone which lies between living memory and written history" and within the recall of many Carolinians.[57] In 1755 the same configuration of twilight dangers reappeared. Thus it was no accident that Edmond Atkin began his primer on the handling of tribal affairs with a passing reference to lessons learned during the "fatal experience of the Indian War in 1715."[58]

Glen's remarks were particularly pointed in that danger, ominously, seemed to be appearing in the west again, this time with the French as the instigators. "The People of most Experience," James Glen wrote, "in the Affairs of this Country have always dreaded a *French* War, from an Apprehension that an *Indian* War would be the Consequence of it."[59] And the *South Carolina Gazette* cited an early eighteenth-century French commentator, Père Charlevoix, to validate the wisdom of Glen's focus on the west, and most particularly on the Cherokees as the vehicle of expansion.[60] Furthermore, the newspaper noted, the size of the tribe was impressive as well, making the Amerindian population of the northern colonies seem insignificant in comparison. "The Cherokees," the newspaper reminded its readers, "are computed to be three times the number of the Six Nations put together."[61] Carolina allies again, they were celebrated as the "best barrier" to the French and any threatening native American group.[62]

James Glen played out the received wisdom of Carolina history in his courting of Cherokee allegiance. However, no matter what the root of his thinking, Glen brought a coherent design to provincial western policy. By the time Glen left his Charlestown office for the position of hanger-on waiting for the recognition that never came, he could look back on three accomplishments: the building of Fort Prince George near the town of Keowee in 1753, the Saluda Conference in 1755, and the setting of a timetable to begin Fort Loudoun in the Overhill Towns in 1756. The Saluda Conference had been decisive. Cherokee alliance was necessary in order for Carolina to compete, particularly with rival Virginia, for engagement in the trans-Appalachian west. Carolina's western destiny could now be reclaimed, and the colony could begin to take its rightful place among Britain's most important American colonies. Glen took comfort in the words of like-minded supporters. One backcountry resident wrote to Governor Glen a thankful note congratulating him on the personal energy he had put into western Carolina affairs. "I think your Successor has nothing to do but follow your Footsteps," wrote Moses Thompson, "for you have paved the plainest road that can be taken which I think will keep your memory in remembrance when you are dead and gone."[63]

Yet, even after the Saluda Conference, other Carolinians had concerns about the reliability of the governor's best barrier. Glen's achievement at Saluda had after all reaffirmed Carolina's uncomfortable dependence on the Cherokees. In signing the treaty, Glen had reset the stage for energizing anew the powerful connections in South Carolina between geopolitical ambition, homegrown racial anxieties, and private and public recall. The Carolina expansionism of the seventeenth century had always been fueled by fear as well as ambition, and a similar mix underlay Glen's policies during the early 1750s. These doubts were to reappear more intensely later in the decade as Glen's successor continued to follow the plainest, but increasingly hazardous, road west. Somewhere along the road, Glen's vision of mingled destiny was to be transformed into shared fate.

7

"Rumble Parts"

W HEN the Cherokees told James Glen that they would meet him halfway at Saluda, rather than Charlestown, they were proposing to gather
at a traditional intercultural crossroads. Yet the Saluda country was changing
rapidly, as was the entire region between the mountainous Cherokee core and
the colonial coast. At places such as Saluda, on the margins of both Cherokee
and colonial societies, great changes were taking place—some prefacing the
Saluda Conference and others coming after. Rapid regional demographic and
economic change was creating a new western political constituency for Carolina and reshaping Cherokee political agendas. Radical change is often visual-
ized as emerging on a single social margin—a frontier—and working its way
back toward the center. In this case the social margin was in a shared geographical middle ground *between* the Cherokees and Carolina that gradually became
the center stage.

By the mid-1750s the world outside the Cherokee villages was very different from that which the tribespeople had encountered in the first years of the
century. While official diplomatic relations continued to reflect the strategic
importance of the Cherokees to Carolina expansionists, the backcountry folk of
the southeastern colonies now viewed the Cherokees, depending on place and
time, as business partners, competitors, or, hostile enemies. A time of chronic
unsettledness and, increasingly, of direct conflict between the towns and colony
ensued.

Tremendous demographic change during the decade of the fifties remade
the outlying colonial settlements. Some of the increase in population had been

fervently hoped and planned for in Charlestown, the colonial upcountry having been the object of intensive settler recruitment and economic development efforts by Charlestown since the 1720s. The western regions were beginning by the 1750s to contribute to a long-awaited colonial self-sufficiency in grain production. By 1759 the government would be able to contract with "backcountry residents" for "70,000 weight of flower" and feel confident of delivery.[1] The population increase which fueled this agricultural production had been quite rapid under a system of land grants and bounties. On the way to the Saluda Conference in 1755, James Glen's secretary was impressed with the effectiveness of these policies: "the back settlements of this province are crowded with people from Pennsylvania, upwards of 300 families have come down since last fall and many others are still arriving."[2] Many arrived illegally as indentured servants on paper, with the masters releasing them from service after claiming the land.[3] Though from a Charlestown perspective the whites in the interior were country people, these settlers—whether rural elite or red clay farmer—had ambitions of their own which had to be reckoned with.

As the population center of the southern colonies shifted west, more and more colonial guests, many now unwelcome, wandered into the tribal towns. Trader Anthony Dean complained about the growing number of irresponsible colonists among the towns, and argued that solid traders were facing danger from other colonists as they ventured into "these rumble Parts, through so many Dangers."[4] But the "rumble" in the west stemmed from dynamic changes within both Cherokee and colonial societies, and it found expression in mounting, and often troubling, changes in the borderland between the two.

Cherokee Resettlement

The demographic flow into the colonial backcountry was matched by a continuing ebb in the forecountry of the Cherokee towns. A tribal population eroded by the progressive toll of disease and episodes of inter-tribal warfare and raiding, declined to around 8000 in the early 1750s.[5] The 1739 smallpox epidemic, which struck from Charlestown to Chota, had been most severe among the Cherokee villages, where it had caused "a most depopulating shock."[6] Four traders, forty-year veterans of the villages, testified in 1751 to the disaster. "The nation," they reported, "in our time has been greater than at present. We remember since there were six thousand stout men in it. They are not now half."[7] The undercurrent of population decline had an uneven effect on the distribution of Cherokee settlements. In some areas the towns were diminished, while in other regions new ones were formed. In this changing geography of both colonial and Cherokee country lie clues to elusive shifts in economic and ethnic relations which were to remake the relationship between the tribe and colony just as decisively as treaty-making or war.

The gradual diversification and expansion of the colonial economy was paralleled by change on the Cherokee side. By the 1750s the Creek population was putting pressure on the common lands of the western Piedmont. In the best of times, both Cherokees and Creeks seem to have shared these lands as hunting grounds, a subtle cooperation which tended to maintain a reserve of deer for hard times. Border towns such as Estatoe and Tugaloo, nominally Cherokee, had long preserved kinship with the Creeks as a kind of insurance against aggression. However, in the wake of long Cherokee conflict with the Creeks, which ended in 1751, these communities saw increasing competition for their loyalty between the two tribes. After more than two decades of instability, in 1750 the Creeks seem to have held the upper hand.[8] In the late 1750s, a growing Creek population resettled the site of Estatoe on the Savannah headwaters, thereby reclaiming land which their Muskogean ancestors had abandoned forty or fifty years before.[9] And in the west, backcountry reports gave credence to the establishment of a new "Indian Town," probably Creek-Cherokee, "in the midway between the Alabama Fort and Telliquo."[10]

Cherokee population movements were also under way in the early 1750s in the main western Cherokee settlement core, in the headwaters of the Tennessee and Cumberland rivers. In several cases, the temporary abandonment of the Lower Towns seems to have forced small groups of Cherokees north into intersections with the emerging colonial settlements. One particularly important destination for this Cherokee migration was the upper reaches of the Holston, Clinch, and Powell rivers, upstream from the Overhill Towns. This territory, like the southern fringe shared with the Creeks, an important regional "cultural crossroad," had been abandoned late in the seventeenth century.[11] During the early eighteenth century it had been intermittently occupied and hunted by the Cherokees.[12] Because the upper Holston remained an important intersection of western and northern indigenous trade and travel routes (including the extension of the path from the Virginia valley)[13] it took on great strategic importance. During the 1750s, Cherokees and colonists converged on this ancient hub.

Approximately one hundred Cherokee refugees from the Creek war moved to the "old fields" along the Holston in 1751, seeking, they said, "better land and fresh hunting ground."[14] Located at the junction of the North and Holston rivers, this transient Cherokee settlement was called Aurora "in the Lower Tongue."[15] At Aurora, Cherokee village life intersected briefly with the life of an outlying white community which provided foodstuffs and other services to tribespeople, travelers, and hunters. The Cherokee colonists were soon followed by a Virginia trader named Daniel Murphy of the Augusta Company, who had been "run out of Canutry . . . and designed to settle with his Slaves, Horses and Leather which he had taken at the New Settlement called Aulola . . . to supply that Place with Goods from Virginia."[16] James Patton, the Shenandoah land speculator, also capitalized upon the arrival of the Cherokees (and perhaps a Shawnee group which had "enforted" itself nearby in 1753) to bolster his community at "Indian Fields." There, Patton opportunistically courted the larger-scale trade of the Cherokees for his home colony.[17] Aurora and other short-lived settlements, along with the Overhill Towns just down river, provided a new market for colonial corn. Settlers such as Samuel Stalnaker and his neighbor Erwin Patterson grew trade corn on the "corn lease" Patterson obtained from the tribe.[18]

While the overtures of Virginia corn-merchants and traders were apparently not turned away by the Cherokees, the presence of colonists at the most sensitive, and at the time disordered, routes into the Overhill must have been disturbing. Life in the settlements was volatile. An incident in which "the Nor'ward Indians killed about 13 or 14 of them [Cherokees] near a small village which is newly settled" caused the settlement to break up quickly, and its people to "return to their respective towns again."[19] However, the area continued to serve both as a brokering zone for trade with the Virginians and as a key translation point for intertribal diplomacy.

Hunting and Farming in Colonial Expansion

The face colonial society turned toward the tribe was rapidly changing during the 1740s and 1750s. To the north and northeast of the Cherokee towns, a new upcountry world began to emerge. This extension of colonial influence was to be more lasting than the settlement initiatives of the tribe. Small groups of red and white hunters had long worked the area, but their way of life sharply contrasted with that of the new arrivals. A Moravian visitor in southwestern Virginia during the 1740s criticized both the occupation and hospitality of his hunter hosts: "we came to a house where we had to lie on bear skins like the rest," the minister commented, continuing,

> the manner of living is rather poor in this district. The cloths of the people consist of deer skins. Their food of Johnny cakes, deer and bear meat. A kind of white people are found here, who live like savages. Hunting is their chief occupation.[20]

In 1745 a breakaway faction from Ephrata, in Pennsylvania, had moved south to the New River and founded Mahanaim, a community called "Dunkard's Bottom" by English-speaking settlers. According to one disapproving chronicler, they were not the first arrivals, and "settled in the midst of a pack of nothing but tramps, the dregs of human society, who spent their time in murdering wild beasts." Another account stressed the extent of the German Brethren's hunting activities, writing that hides "lay in such heaps that we slept on piles which could not have been purchased for one hundred pounds or more."

Unfortunately most accounts of these settlements are flawed by either sectarian or ethnic prejudices and the complexity of their economy (along with its ties to tribespeople) has probably been underestimated. For instance, Thomas Walker noted that the Ephrata Brethren in Virginia already had a grain mill operating in 1750. Nevertheless, market hunting soon became less an uncouth activity than an acceptable, well-integrated venture in many western communities.[21]

The colonial commercial lines anchored in the Shenandoah Valley extended to the south along the New River Valley, where they intersected with another line of population expansion following spur routes from the Great Wagon Road in North Carolina. In North Carolina, the migration into the backcountry was substantial enough to merit the formation of a new, open-ended western county called Anson in 1749. The map of Anson soon began to fill in with the growth of the "Irish" and "Trading Ford" settlements on the Catawba and the establishment of the "Bryan settlements" on the Yadkin.[22] (Fig. 5)

The Blue Ridge foothills and the North Carolina Piedmont also felt a new intensity of exploitation.[23] Leather rapidly became a major cash crop along with wheat in the emerging agricultural economy. As a result, these points of growth, and the expansion of hunting which they sustained, brought white and Cherokee hunters into either partnership or collision. By the middle of the 1750s, business between the towns of Moravian Wachovia and the fall-line commercial centers like Camden and Cross Creek seeded a new regional economy.[24]

The outcome of these intersections shadowed the future course of back-country ethnic relations. When they actively associated with whites near new provincial settler communities, Cherokees were targets of the small farmers' resentment of tribal lifestyle. Along the South Fork of the Catawba, a group of established settlers in western North Carolina complained of the "large quantity" of Cherokees, perhaps from the Lower Towns in South Carolina, who in 1752 had moved next door to the Davidson and Long Creek settlements on the main branch of the Catawba River. A trader named John Anderson was reported to have instigated the unwelcome settlement by following the Cherokees "up and down our Rivers," the upstanding petitioners wrote, "and come and traded with ammunition and other goods." The Cherokees, interested in more than just trading with Anderson, began to build houses and plant corn along the Catawba. The Cherokees were frightening enough to the growing settler population, but also disturbing was the report that "there are white men that live with the aforesaid Anderson."[25] Anderson and his friends, in living with the Cherokees, had violated an ethnic boundary which was becoming increasingly guarded by the responsible citizens of South Fork settlements and other influential men in the western territories.

South and west of South Fork, in the borderland between South Carolina and the Cherokees, new arrivals tended to cluster around older meeting grounds. Thus, relations between provincial settlers and tribespeople were governed there by traditional, far more complex, and seemingly more stable modes of contact and exchange. Well before the 1750s, clearly defined contact points between native American society and colonists were in place. In the westernmost reaches, traders and storekeepers such as Robert Goudy, James Francis, and others had established what were in essence *métis* trading communities, united through kinship and commerce with both societies. By the middle of the century, the backcountry commercial centers where they lived such as Ninety-Six, Saluda, and Waxhaws were being transformed into settler communities by colonial immigration. In this sense, the new settlers' 'frontier' of the 1750s was not new at all, only diversified beyond the Indian trade-based beginnings of most of these communities.

Robert Goudy and Herman Geiger, for instance, had both profited from trade with the Cherokees in the upper Savannah River basin before white settlements provided a new market for their stores. Eventually both became merchants and large landowners, but, as in the careers of other prominent men, profitable intercultural trade connections figured in their rise.[26] This double-sidedness appears in the career of James Francis, another prominent backcountryman. Francis was a trader and later farmer in the region west of Ninety-Six that was to become a focus of migration. Francis's trading partners had included Chickasaws and blacks, people who were often the subject of complaints by more respectable neighbors.[27] However, by the early 1750s he was a justice of the peace and Ranger captain with close connections to James Glen. Roughly paralleling Francis in his climb into respectability was Moses Kirkland, who operated a store selling to the Catawbas during the 1750s, and who in the 1760s moved to the lower Saluda and Broad River valleys where he expanded his business and landowning interests. Still others used upper South Carolina as the jumping off point for far-flung trading expeditions to tribal settlements on the Mississippi.[28]

It was at places like Saluda and other nodes of trade that the first steps toward the major economic growth to come were taken. Towns with diversified economies such as Ninety-Six and Saluda, which had flour mills by 1749, suggest the early symbiosis of intercultural trade and the commercial domestic economy.[29] Geiger's store was built at Saluda, and another was established at nearby White Hall Creek by Andrew Williamson. Yet another was started by Goudy at Ninety-Six. These stores soon became economic landmarks of the surrounding countryside.[30] Storekeepers, traders, and landowners in these prewar settlements would emerge from the decade well positioned for the future evolution of the backcountry.

Long Cane

The Long Cane settlement—and the small, nearby communities on the Little and Saluda rivers with which it was associated—was one of the most important intercultural settings of the 1750s. Long Cane was the uppermost colonial community along the trail to Keowee Town. For this reason its history can serve as a small case study of intercultural dynamics of backcountry life in the upper Savannah River region, the southwestern section of the South Carolina backcountry. It throws a stark light on the tensions created in the lives of the entire community, and most especially in the careers of important or leading men, by intercultural realities.

The story of Long Cane, like that of the Cherokee Lower Towns due west, is one of both accommodation and rejection of its neighbors and has more than one violent outcome in its telling. Positioned along a major tributary of the Savannah, Long Cane developed near an early point of intercultural intersection in the pre-Revolutionary-period south.[31] It was located sixty miles southeast from Keowee, near the junction of the two forks of the Dividing Paths. Though the native peoples no longer lived at Long Cane in the eighteenth century, the Cherokees still hunted there, and their recent use of the area was clearly revealed to colonial settlers in the landscape they inherited. Even the name of the place reflected its environmental history. Called "Long Grass" by the Cherokees, the creek bottom canebrakes present during the early days of settlement were a telltale indication of prior burning by indigenous hunters. "The region composing the district was in a virgin state," John C. Calhoun recalled hearing as a child, "new and beautiful, without underwood, and all the fertile portion covered by a dense cane brake and hence the name Long Cane. The region was full of deer and other game, among them Buffalo."[32] Other prior environmental modifications turned to the advantage of the new colonists. Settlers repaired the weir-dam across the Little River, used in capturing runs of fish migrating upstream, and brought cattle to the still open and muddy salt licks previously frequented by deer and woodland buffalo.[33]

This productive landscape inheritance, along with its incipient commercial infrastructure, soon enticed a group of Virginia immigrants to the upper Savannah. In 1746, the Glen administration received a petition from several families who had moved from Northern Ireland only seven years before. When soon afterwards the Cherokee Lower Towns transferred ownership of Long Cane (at least in Glen's eyes) to the colony, the settlement began slowly to materialize.[34] The first land claim in the region, on the bottomland flats of Little River, a Savannah tributary adjoining Long Cane, went to John Chevis, a free Negro carpenter, in 1751.[35] Chevis was by no means the first of his race to visit the area, given the involvement of blacks in the local deerskin trade for decades. But the settlers who followed Chevis were prosperous, white, largely Presbyterian farmers.

At first, delays frustrated the would-be migrants. Not long after the arrival of John Chevis, the first group of Presbyterian families followed this black pioneer into the upper Savannah. While the Calhoun family was the first to establish itself in Long Cane proper, soon others would arrive, friends of the Calhouns first in Paxton County, Pennsylvania, and later in Augusta County,

Virginia.[36] Other prosperous farmers, bearing the Calhoun, Caldwell, and Alexander surnames, soon established large claims around Waxhaws and Long Cane in the late 1750s. Many were Dissenters, acquainted with or related to the Calhoun or Pickens families,[37] who had moved to the Waxhaw settlement (on the Catawba River and northeast of Long Cane on the North Carolina border) with another group of prominent Augusta County families. Like Long Cane, the Waxhaws had been a place of long prior settlement and similarly took its name from a plant, in this case the haw, which, as in other Piedmont "hawfields," had achieved its prominence as a result of human-directed fire. Resettled, the Waxhaws and Long Cane communities were yoked together by a fire not on the land but in the spirit.

The Tensions of Patriarchy

These interrelated families reached upcountry South Carolina after several decades of residence first in Pennsylvania and then in Virginia. "Locational instability"—a collective urge to move on—was characteristic of Dissenters, especially the tight-knit Presbyterians who came to Long Cane.[38] Because of their religious identity, the Calhouns and their friends carried with them a sense of alienation from the Anglican leading citizenry of the districts in which they had put down shallow roots. The Presbyterians had encountered special opposition from the Shenandoah Valley's Anglican elite, and the apparent isolation of Long Cane must have seemed a solution to this problem. Their initial petition to South Carolina for land had grown out of such tensions, and it did not mince words about the urgency felt by the settlers in looking for new land: the "want of such a purchase has caus'd a War and Bloodshed where we now live."[39]

Church members and ministers alike had experienced marginality in Virginia, and a generation of Presbyterian ministers worked in each of the new northwest Carolina settlements to ensure a hoped-for hegemony in the new country. The traditional authority of family members (perhaps bolstered by vestiges of clan social organization) was abetted by colonial appointment. William Calhoun, the most senior of the Calhoun men in Long Cane, was made justice of the peace and recorded the arrest of a relative, Hugh Calhoun, "for cursing and swearing 10 oaths and curses in my own hearing."[40] Religion further reinforced local solidarity among the northwestern Carolina settlements which grew so rapidly after the war. The Long Cane Presbyterian church, along with the other large congregations at Waxhaws and Saluda, was established in 1755.[41] A feeling of religious kinship was increased by intermarriage between the friendly families who had made first settlement.[42] Adding to the pressures felt in South Carolina by the Presbyterian congregations was the growth of Separate Baptists churches in their communities, a religious presence which exceeded the Presbyterians in number by the mid-1760s.[43] There were internal splits between "Old Side" pastors who held to older clericism and the evangelical "New Light" preachers caught up in the Great Awakening. However, among the ministers of Long Cane and Waxhaws these divisions were for the most part overridden by a sense of denominational apartness from their neighbors.

As the leaders of the denominational community of these backcountry settlements, ministers were protectors of their flocks. In western settlements during the 1750s this often translated into terms of protecting both family and the community at large, as the clerics often functioned as, or were closely related to, the political leadership of the community. Inward-facing but united by overlapping family and religious ties, leading men faced the heavy burden of responsibility for the well-being of their dependents—whether wives, slaves, or congregations.[44] The backcountry war of the 1750s in Virginia put these men at risk. The threat was not only from the attack of French allies. In the Shenandoah Valley, towns like Winchester boomed with the business of assorted British expeditions. John Craig, a pioneering minister of Augusta County, with family and denominational ties in western South Carolina, complained that the "Heathen" (and the Cherokees were implicated by others) "must be supplied at any home they call at with victuals or they become their own Stuarts and Cooks sparing nothing they chuse to eat or drink . . . which was trouble and sometimes dangerous for they go all armed for war in this way." Craig took a "leading role" in frontier self-defense after Braddock's defeat. The tensions of wartime disorder were compounded by the personal grudge of the local magistrate, land speculator James Patton, against Craig. Late in his wife's pregnancy Craig was taken into custody; and his wife "took unease immediately." On his return, as the birth of his child approached, Craig fell into a "stupid Dullness and pressure of the spirit" so that he "could not connect two sentences." While his wife was giving birth, Craig was possessed: "utmost bitter hatred arose in my mind against the wife of my bosom and object of my tenderest love and the women all of them that was with her" and he imagined the house "and all that was in it in one flame but . . . knew not for what reason or cause." When day came he walked away and his "anguish" lifted as "suddenly as it came" and he returned home. The sanity of John Craig broke under the same threats that sent his neighbors and relatives south. There, in South Carolina, these men found a degree of refuge from the denominational tensions of Virginia but at the same time they stood alone with their families, exposed to new dangers and new personal demands. They were private: "none know of it but myself which I was well satisfied with ever after," John Craig wrote of his breakdown.[45] Thus, in many respects, the emigrations of the prominent families that founded the Long Cane and Waxhaw settlements were attempts to protect and renew a core of spirit—and kin-community—damaged in Virginia. And the manner of this restoration in large part depended upon the regeneration of paternal authority in secular as well as sacred society.[46]

For many of the residents of Long Cane the decision to move to South

Carolina had been triggered by a real emergency—the panic which followed Braddock's defeat in Augusta County.[47] Though western South Carolina provided a haven from religious harassment, the intercultural life of the area must have provided the migrants with unsettling reminders of threats in their collective past, and, for some leading men, of their inability absolutely to control their lives and those of their dependents in this new place.

In the first years of the Long Cane settlement, the migrants overlooked the risk posed by doing business with their tribal neighbors. Cash flow provided by trade with the Cherokees fueled land purchases and deflected attention from the latent threat posed by their neighbors. The mixed subsistence and trading economy of Presbyterian-dominated Long Cane during the 1750s grew as naturally out of the older regional pattern of trading as from the ethnic and economic traditions of the Scotch-Irish as well as their recent involvements in the backcountry economy of Pennsylvania. Whatever the source, their activities were marked by economic opportunism and flexibility.[48]

One commodity—distilled spirits—may have been of higher value in the trade with the Cherokees than any other product. William Calhoun, the elder brother of Patrick and community leader at Long Cane, was, for example, a substantial liquor producer. Sales and exchanges of liquor were entered frequently in his diary, and alcohol appears to have been a commonplace currency of the western Savannah economy. Liquor sales in turn paid for, among other things, the purchase of horses from the Cherokees, which led a British official to complain that "the people Inhabiting the Frontiers of this Province carry on a trade with the Indians by bartering Rum for Horses."[49] Travel between the upcountry colonial settlements and the Cherokee towns was unimpeded and routine. Because he had been in contact with tribespeople through trade, Patrick Calhoun was able to travel into the towns in the tense months of 1759, to observe freely "a private meeting of their old men in the woods as I rode between two of their towns," and even to reconnoiter into the more remote Middle Settlements.[50]

The seasonal arrival of trading parties in the colonial upcountry settlements, along with the regular flow of deerskins and herbs from the Cherokee villages to backcountry stores, carried with them an undercurrent of women's trading. Contact between the two female-run domestic economies was focused on subsistence goods, unlike the rum, horse, and leather trade carried on by men. Dealing in foodstuffs, and bypassing colonial stores, exchange was on a smaller scale, from household to household, and it formed a bond between women in the two societies. The memoirs of Ann Matthews, a niece of Patrick Calhoun, throw some light on this connection, and on its eventual disruption. Matthews relates that "a squaw, a young woman," overheard a group of warriors planning to attack the settlement in 1759, and that this Cherokee woman,

> disliked very much to think that the white women who had been so good to
> her in giving her clothes and bread and butter in trading parties would be

killed, she became determined to let them know their danger, she started after night, when all was still, and walked ninety six pmiles [roughly the distance from the Lower Towns to the edge of colonial settlement] in twenty four hours . . . spreading the news as she went.[51]

This extraordinary warning was an act of friendship built up in years of trade and casual encounter.

Just as relationships between native American men and indigenous women are too often construed as reflecting only sexual contact, parallel female-to-female relationships have often been interpreted as reflecting charity given by sympathetic white women to less fortunate tribal women. Rather than detailing straightforward ties in commerce between women, nineteenth-century editors seem sometimes to have interjected "charity" into the Matthews narrative as well as other sources. An incident in 1761 near Fishing Creek, on the upper Catawba, reflects friendship between Cherokee and Carolina women. In this incident "Indian women" from a Cherokee spring fishing encampment ran toward a nearby farm in order to warn the woman, Katherine Steel, and the children in the house of an impending raid. "The assistance rendered by the Squaws, whether given out of compassion for a lonely mother, or in return for a kindness shown them proved effective."[52]

Such meetings during the 1750s grew naturally out of shared female roles and shared viewpoints. For instance, there is more than a hint of economic commonality in the critical remarks of the "Chickkasah female" who assisted James Adair in writing his *History of the American Indian*. The woman, who was living in the Saluda trading community during the 1750s, pointedly corrected Adair's description of corn mortars which he had written for inclusion in the *History:* "She bids me not to mark the paper wrong, after the manner of most of the traders; otherwise it will spoil the making of good bread, or hommony, and of course beget the ill-will of our white women."[53] The Chickasaw woman chose a uniquely female image—a corn mortar—to communicate the foundation of a kindred feeling for white women in shared work. And this bond seems to have extended beyond sympathy and into ties of trade between women on both sides of the narrow cultural border in far western South Carolina.

Leading men at Long Cane and other similar communities, as they observed this trade and learned more of their neighbors, must have been reminded of the political as well as economic independence of tribal women. Pushed by ambition and events into community and family dominance, they may have been wary of the loss of control that threatened if their wives and sisters achieved economic—or political—autonomy. While female trading was submerged within the far more extensive business and contacts of the Cherokee trade, these encounters threatened the hard-won but fragile authority of backcountry men.

Though this subtle challenge to the economic authority of colonial males was mainly a family matter, and business continued, the new migrants to the west also lived with an uncertainty about the dependability of Glen's Saluda alliance with the Cherokees. Incidents such as the massacre of the wedding party at Buffalo Creek in 1754 were deeply disturbing, and occurred at intervals. And traditionally urban anxieties about black rebellion spread west with escalating slave ownership. But local troubles seemed small in respect to what was happening to the north. In the late fifties, the Carolina settlements could reassure themselves that they offered safe havens for refugees from the "French and Indian" War-stricken western counties of Virginia and Pennsylvania. However, even this sense of reassurance, for refugee and host alike, was to disappear.

8

"At Peace with All Kings"

D
URING the late 1750s, South Carolina and Virginia still vied for Cherokee alliance. And this competition for Cherokee sympathies snugly fit
tribal notions of diplomatic relations, which thrived on pluralism. Often there
was no united Cherokee policy, only an addition of reactions at the local level,
where the bottom line was town politics. Thus, when Tistoe, the Wolf of Keowee,
met a Catawba on the trail who inquired of his home, asking "what nation we
were," Tistoe answered simply, "of Keowee." [1] Accordingly, the Cherokees
were guided in their dealings with the English by a basic rule of diplomacy—
which treated the English colonies as separate but equal political entities—
afforded the same privileges and considered vulnerable to the same hostilities
as any tribe or village with which they had dealings. When a Cherokee headman addressed Lt. Governor Dinwiddie in 1756, he was not overawed by the
status of Virginia as a colony. Instead he was careful to pause in the talk to
note that "The Governor of Virginia's Thoughts are good, so likeways are the
Governor of Chota's." [2]

Some Cherokee towns were, in certain respects, more equal than others,
and this fact skewed Euroamerican perceptions of political power within the
tribe. Chota, Kituwa, and Keowee, among other villages, enjoyed the particular status of mother towns which had an independence of action not afforded
less ancient settlements. Furthermore, most town-level debates were purposefully out of sight; the political maneuverings kept a "profound Secret." [3]

Undeterred by these complications, the English scrambled to vest the willing voices of a succession of mother-town leaders with authority for the Cherokee tribe as a whole. The faces, and thus the emphasis of their communica-

tions, changed through the period with the ascendence of particular villages.[4] After the Saluda Conference, for instance, power brokers such as Old Hop from the Overhill villages speak strongly in the records, both for the tribe as well as for their own aggrandizement. Other mother towns sometimes protested the nearly exclusive attention given by the Carolinians to the Overhill Towns. For instance, the Prince of Jore, in the Middle Settlements, wrote after the Saluda Conference to remind Governor Glen that "there was such a people as the Middle Settlements people. We think you do not believe there is."[5] Nevertheless, Cherokee town authorities often did nothing to resist English proposals of alliance that excluded villages other than their own. The objections of excluded villages ensured that unilateral agreements would not be binding on other towns. Instead of exclusivism, Cherokee diplomacy encouraged multiple contacts with their neighbors, fostering a complex diplomacy which the colonists often misunderstood, and which contributed to mounting differences within the tenuous alliance of the 1750s.[6]

The complexity and sometimes apparent chaos of Cherokee village politics forced the English and French to oversimplify as they struggled for measurable diplomatic results to include in year-end reports. Both colonial powers found themselves grasping for signals and hints of momentous interior events. Relations between the Lower Creeks and the Cherokees, which had during the late 1740s swung in a hostile, red direction, provide a telling example. Traders reported that "on account of the war betwixt them and the Creeks all the Lower Towns excepting three is broke up and moved further back."[7] Because these two peoples were Carolina's western trade base, the Carolinians worried about the commercial disruption that would arise from continuing conflict. The French too were concerned, and through the *métis* settlement at Fort Toulouse and surrounding Coweeta Creek towns related to the Cherokees could exercise some leverage over the Cherokees' kin.[8] In 1751, after the battle of Taliwa (reportedly a Cherokee victory), the Cherokees and Creeks settled their differences.[9] The Cherokees reported finally to Glen that, on their own, they had "met and smoaked in the hunting grounds" to make peace with the Creeks.[10] While the peace between the Creeks and the Cherokees had little if anything to do with European mediation, the French commander at Fort Toulouse wrote a memorandum claiming to have brought about the conciliation in 1756.[11] James Glen, unaware of his French counterpart's claims, submitted to the Board of Trade that he himself had "reconciled the differences that had so long subsisted betwixt the Creeks and Cherokees and had happily extinguished the flame of war."[12]

"When We Build New Towns"

The most pressing problem of Cherokee diplomacy in the early 1750s lay not in responding to the Euroamericans but in reconstructing their own political relations after the recent episodes of warfare with the Creeks—and others. During the 1740s, scattered Cherokee towns attacked and were in turn assaulted by the Illinois and other mid-Mississippi tribes,[13] including the Choctaws and Chickasaws. Regularly, the Iroquois and Shawnees, moving south on the Great Valley routes, intruded as well; Cherokee ritual, dance, and legend bore witness to this traffic.[14]

The surprising invitations by the Cherokees to the Virginians, French, and Carolinians to build forts, each at different towns, must be considered in light of the Cherokee need to repair the unsettledness of the prior decade.[15] The first of the English forts—Prince George—was built at Keowee town in 1753, perhaps to send a warning to the Creeks about Cherokee-Carolina friendship. The building of Fort Prince George provided a precedent for the Overhill leaders present at Saluda to acquire a Carolina fort in order to send a similar signal north.[16]

Though there was an element of pragmatism in the Cherokee response, the English request to build a fort was understood by the Cherokees to be as much a symbolic confirmation of English alliance as military aid. The English would join representatives from other tribes. For instance, when Old Hop learned that James Glen intended to build a fort at Chota, in the Overhill villages he spoke for, he expressed happiness that the governor had "built his house among their houses, and there to take him by the hand."[17] For Old Hop, there was never any doubt that the English would share their Chota with other allies. When the commander of the Virginia fort-building expedition, Andrew Lewis, initially requested that the Carolina colonies be given a joint site, "they would by no means hear of it . . . they insisted on our building a fort at Chotte and told me they had laid off a spot for the Carolina people to build another."[18] The Cherokees in this way made no special concession to the English colonies, beyond other southeastern peoples, indigenous and colonial. The alliances sealed by fort building were simultaneous and various, at least in the minds of the Cherokees, with the Virginians, Creeks, "Nuntaways," and South Carolinians all having a presence within the Overhill villages.

Both the Carolina and Virginia commanders made their separate agendas clear, when their construction forces arrived in the Overhill Towns. The South Carolina troop leader Raymond Demere told Old Hop that the Overhill fort was a favor to be repaid with Cherokee raids against the French. The influential village leader, sometimes called the Emperor, countered by criticizing the English for demanding unilateral loyalty.

> The Emperor and his Lady came soon after us and brought me some bread, watermelons &c. The first words he spoke to me was, "What do you think of our having given up one of our towns to the French?" I said I was very sorry to hear it. Then says he, "have you not got a great many French amongst you at Charles Town? When I was last there I saw a great many myself." I told

him that those French People he saw had been there from their Youth and that they came for the sake of their Religion and were good subjects to King George. To which he said that it was good to be at Peace with all Kings.[19]

The Cherokees were eager, after the conflicts of the 1740s and 1750s, to lay a foundation for peace through the building of new towns or forts by *all* their allies—the French as well as the English, Carolinians as well as Virginians. To seek a new balance in diplomacy was in accord with Cherokee precepts, but ran counter to the unitary alliance demanded by the Carolinians. As the English forts began to be built, it became apparent to the Cherokees that a permanent English presence in their villages was not in the interests of the balance they desired.

The Virginians, who had pressed their case for assistance first, raced to throw up quickly a palisaded fort just after the agreement at Winchester in 1754. The fort was to be a down payment in kind for badly needed Cherokee help in the colonial expeditions hastily planned for the north, where conflict with French-allied tribes was escalating. However, the efforts of the Virginians to collect Cherokee warriors in time for Braddock's march in 1755 came to a disappointing end.[20] The Cherokees were hesitant to go north for the British without deliberation on Cherokee objectives. Andrew Lewis, the Virginia commander, split his time between building supervision and recruiting in the villages and quickly became frustrated, writing home that the Cherokees "were like the Devil's pigg, they will neither lead nor drive."[21] Lewis, the South Carolina governor smugly reported, "complains bitterly of [Cherokee] perfidity . . . and says that until he had finished the fort they made him the fairest promises imaginable, but as soon as it was completed they excused themselves from sending any men with him."[22]

It was in this context of squabbling between Virginia and Carolina that Cherokee troops were finally raised in 1756 by trader Richard Pearis. Under the leadership of warrior Outacite, they were to participate in the abortive Sandy Creek expedition against the Shawnee towns on the Ohio River which was sent to retaliate for Braddock's defeat. After a disorganized and unsuccessful march, the Virginians abandoned the pretense of their fort. Never permanently garrisoned, it lay "quite abandoned" just months after its completion, and soon a few Cherokee houses were built within the walled perimeter.[23] The nearby South Carolina fort then became by default the focal point of recruitment efforts by both colonies.

The Fort in the Village

The single recorded Cherokee word for fort—*chizowi*— may derive from ancient Mississippian-era village palisades. In talks and conversations, however, the Cherokees used several words as English equivalents of fort: house, strong house, and even town.[24] These terms suggest that when the Cherokees invited the English or French to build forts, they expected something in many ways at odds with the timber and stone European fortification.

The construction of the substantial fort built by the South Carolinians near Toskegee and Tommotley aroused apprehension.[25] Village concerns were perhaps not so much about the structure itself as about who had taken up residence in it. A colonial official was told in no uncertain terms that "the greater part of the Indians . . . look upon the Words Fort and Slavery to be synonymous Terms." The underlying fear was that the forts were not proper towns—occupied by men, women, and children—but were instead staffed only by men, numbering a threatening 200 or even 300 in the case of the Carolina troop. "A few men not exceeding 15 or 20 would be a sufficient number at first, and among them some women and children which would alleviate their fears greatly of being made slaves."[26] Cherokee political wisdom also raised a red flag. The Cherokees had a tradition, perhaps rooted in their Yamassee War experience, warning against the coming of a white army. "Some old Men have said that how soon an Army of white People should come amongst us," the Mankiller of Highwassee told the English commander, "our Women and Children would be taken and made Slaves, and that our Land would be taken."[27] As a result, it was only with much lobbying that the Carolina commander, Raymond Demere, was able to reassure the village headmen—at least temporarily—that his intentions were not hostile.

While the villagers worried about the military presence, they also welcomed the availability of trade and diplomatic channels it brought. Elders spoke for young men interested in broadening access to goods useful in the earning of warrior rank. In a talk expressing his hopes for the English garrison, Old Hop addressed Raymond Demere, noting that, "I see you and your Warriours are well dressed in red Cloaths; I am naked and ragged." Furthermore, Old Hop continued,

> I hope when your fort is built that our young Men will always have a place to go for a supply of Necessaries in return for their Deer Skins . . . and likeway expect that our Warriours and Headmen will have a Store where they can go and cloath themselves that they may look like Men, and not be ashamed to show themselves for an empty House looks but poorly.[28]

Cherokee women were also interested in exploiting the commercial opportunities the forts presented. When, on their way over the hills to build Fort Loudoun, the South Carolina troops passed through Keowee, they were ceremonially greeted by the men of the town, and on the following day welcomed by village women who presented Demere with "a great Number of Cakes of

Bread of their own make and green Peas and Squashes, every Woman bringing something of this Kind in a Basket and laying it before [him], notwithstanding Provisions are now scarcer amongst them than ever was known.''[29] Furthermore, the town requested that Demere allow them to hire the blacksmith at the fort, not solely to repair their guns, but also to mend agricultural implements, "Hows, Hatchets and other Trowels when they want repairing.''[30] Within a few months Demere wrote that the fort had begun "to have the Appearance of a Market" rather than a fortification, as women sold corn and other "Eatables" to the troops.[31]

Women eventually became (along with colonial traders) suppliers of foodstuffs to the Carolina and Virginia troops. "The wenches, as usual, brought corn,'' became a kind of refrain in messages from the forts dealing with the provisioning of the troops.[32] The wenches sometimes brought food as a gift, but more often to sell at inflated prices. Demere congratulated himself on purchasing corn in Keowee, one of the Lower Towns, at a bargain price, particularly since "people says that they had rather go from here to Charlestown than over the Hills to buy it.'' Corn cost more in the villages' than in the seaport's markets.[33] Without the ability to raise their own provisions in gardens the troops "could not live,'' Demere wrote, for "their Pay could not afford it.''[34]

Although colonial officials had assumed that their troops could grow their own food on fields near Keowee, the Cherokees (and perhaps, especially, Cherokee women) worked instead to guard the new market represented by the troops. In 1754 at Keowee, the commander of the colonial troops complained that his men were denied access to a "corner" of land purchased for raising the garrison's food. Further, he reported that the town leaders had "denied me the privilege of planting anything for some time . . . the Raven denys that he promised any more land than what the Fort stands on and a road to it.''[35] In spite of this precedent, the Carolinians continued to profess that the Cherokees had offered an unrestricted gift of the Keowee fort site, but when a similar problem arose two years later at Toskegee, the Cherokees remembered differently.[36] "Old Hop gave me to understand that the land we are building on is a present from them to the Province, but that they must be paid for all the planting ground,'' the English commander wrote after the village elders had halted his plans for raising corn outside the fort.[37]

The Cherokee stance was not surprising. Corn ground, productive bottomland rotated in and out of cultivation over generations, was the most valuable shared property of the villages. At the same time, women's interest in keeping the village foodstuffs trade thriving required shutting off the English from alternative supplies. Just as warriors sought trading opportunities for the deerskins they traded, female farmers also sought to keep their farm-produce market open. Eventually the garrison at Keowee was, after many official requests, allowed to plant a small cornfield outside of its walls, but even then the harvests were inadequate to support the troops. Each of the Carolina and Virginia garrisons remained strongly dependent, at a high price, on the villagers around them for the basic goods of subsistence.

Uninvited Guests

By the time Fort Loudoun was completed in 1756, events beyond the garrisons were contributing to a growing Cherokee discontent with the English. The Cherokees confronted unwelcome numbers of colonists living on their land during the 1750s, and the war in the north sent more south. Their presence created a constant reminder of the opportunities—but also of the costs—of their relationship with the English colonies.

This influx had several sources. The issuance of "general licenses," part of the South Carolina trading statute of 1752, allowed merchants to send more agents into the Cherokee towns. James May reported to Governor Glen that within only a few years "a parcel of idle people" had moved into the small villages around his town of Cowee; "at Echoee and Elejoy which is the two outside towns of the middle settlements, no less than 12 traders, Pedlars, and Idle fellows" had taken up recent residence.[38] Such a number of lewd, idle white savages," James Adair fumed, "are very hurtful to the honest part of the traders . . . by heightening the value of vegetables, especially in the time of light crops, to an exorbitant price."[39] A few came with entrepreneurial ambitions. For instance, a white trader reportedly proposed the establishment of a "tanyard and shoe and harness factory," outside one of the Overhill Towns.[40]

War sent others, voluntarily or not, into the Cherokee Mountains. Some colonial troops, who had been recruited for the campaigns of the period with implied promises of western land bounties, either deserted along the way or were stranded at the end of the campaign. Some may have moved close to the Cherokee fringe, but others, deserting militiamen and regulars, came directly into the towns.[41] In 1756 Ludovic Grant wrote concerning "one Irish (a young man who it seems sometime ago run from one of the Men of War) and his wife" who had taken up residence in his town.[42] In another incident related to the disturbances of colonial war, John Burn, a "deserter from Col. Washington's expedition in Virginia," set up "an outlaw camp" and in 1756 near-fatally assaulted a village headman whom he "knockt down with a grat Billot of Wood." The headman, Chuchecha, requested that the governor send "a Power to the White-Men to have him taken so as he may suffer the Law according to his Deserts."[43] Chuchecha was joined in the petition by six white traders, who reported that there were, including the outlaws, twenty-four white men in the vicinity of the town. Not only were they unable to raise enough funds to pay an Indian to take action (they made an offer of sixty-four deerskins to "take" Burn, but it had been refused), but they lacked the authority to do so themselves. The traders had to petition for the "power" to take action against one of their own. Even when the authority to make arrests was in hand, white residents interfered. When James May "commanded Ambrose Davis, Alias Collier," to assist him in taking an accused criminal into custody at Cowee, "his Reply was I might be dammed and my Orders too, I might wipe my back Side with it."[44]

The incident with Burn and other similar happenings revealed to the Cherokees the powerlessness of the white authorities to control their own kind. Personal as well as social divisions between village whites were sharply, and disconcertingly, presented to the tribespeople. When most of the whites fled the villages near Great Tellico, seasoned trader Anthony Dean observed, "I never found Indians in my Life civiler, than what they are to me since the white people went down."[45] By the end of the 1750s, the Cherokees were becoming increasingly dissatisfied with the manner in which colonial society failed to govern itself.

Troubles like these also sensitized the Cherokees to colonial violations of what they themselves viewed as the rules of diplomacy. A hasty strike from Fort Loudoun against a French-allied Shawnee band added to the resentment felt by the tribe toward the provincial forces in the towns.[46] A handful of Cherokee warriors were incited to attack through promises of scalp bounties and urgings that "now is the time . . . to show their zeal, affection and true friendship for the English."[47] Old Hop afterwards criticized Raymond Demere severely for this breach of protocol in the towns, and complained that his village's relations had formerly been "a free path, clean and neat, without any danger, but now that I [Demere] had sent the White people in it and hooped and hallowed in it, they [the Shawnees] had made it dirty and bloody, and very dangerous."[48]

"Neither Lead Nor Drive": Lessons from the English Expeditions: 1756–58

At the same time that troubles in the Cherokee towns were increasing, colonial requests for assistance in their faltering offensive to the north were mounting. Braddock's defeat and the Sandy Creek fiasco made the colonial leadership more desperate for Cherokee help, but their initiatives were by and large strongly resisted. In 1758, the Forbes campaign brought renewed demand for warriors to join an all-out British military initiative. The Cherokees never directly said no. Instead, they stalled for more time to make travel rations of "parched corn flower and bread." The village conjurers delayed as well: "They told me that several bad omens had appeared in their conjurations," a colonial recruiter reported, "and they were threatened with Sickness and Death to many and vast Fatigue to the Whole."[49] Other Cherokees refused to cooperate in a quieter way, but the conjurers' warnings reflected the awareness of many Cherokees of a widening divergence in council talks and dreams between their own agenda and that of the English.

Three hundred or more young warriors did, however, eventually accompany Colonel Byrd of Virginia in the 1758 campaign and there fulfilled the conjurers' warning. On the trail through Virginia, the country was charged with hostility and fear, compounded by confusion on the part of settlers about who the enemy was, who the ally. The British commanders tried to solve this problem by giving the Cherokees a "yellow piece of stuff which they tied about the head and flung down loose."[50] Such attempts, however, did not deter the killings of Cherokees returning to their villages. In the vicinity of Winchester, Virginia, for example, at least thirty Cherokees were murdered by farmers on their way back from fighting as English allies in the fall of 1758.[51] At Bedford Courthouse, Carolina historian George Milligen reported, a band of returning Cherokees lost six horses, and accusations quickly turned to confrontation: "The white people all rose up . . . and ordered the Indians to ground their arms which they did and the white people fired on them." Milligen put the consequences squarely on the Virginians' attacking

> small parties of the unsuspecting Indians, killing at different times about 12 or 14 of them; the Savages were not backward in taking Satisfaction for their slain countrymen; and this was the beginning of a war . . . there is no acquitting those people who attacked the Cherokees of ingratitude; the Indians had gone to war in their defense.[52]

A lengthy affidavit concerning another incident involving a troop of Virginia rangers from Mayo Fort, on the headwaters of the Dan River on the North Carolina and Virginia border, provides an eye-witness to white-on-red violence.[53] Unable to draft enough men to supply the regular militia, Virginia had opened up the problem to private, profit-motivated solutions. "Associations" of local settlers were sanctioned, such as the one which marched from Mayo Fort. Though the men went without pay, the government provided other incentives: £10 for every scalp or prisoner taken from French-allied tribespeople and full rights to any "plunder." Ironically, the same defensive program was behind Virginia's simultaneous attempts to recruit the Cherokee warriors which the Mayo rangers would soon confront.[54]

"Capt. Rot. Wade marcht from Mayo fort with 35 men in order to take a range to the New River in Search of our Enemy Indians," began troop member John Echols's account of the events during the expedition. After several days of traveling, a man "in the crook of the Little River" sent news of Indians "a Catching horses at Draper's Meadows," and finally there was a surprise, but far from unwanted, confrontation:

Some of the men spyed 5 Indians very near to us, for the place was grown up weeds so that we could not see them, nor they see us 'till they came very near . . . I raised up and presented my gun at one of the Indians, but I heard some of our company that was in another house cry out don' shoot—I stopt at that and askt them what they were, and I believe they said Cherokee, but stood in amaize and reason they had for I suppose there was 20 guns presented at them, we went up to them and examined them—they said they were Cherokees, I made signs to them to show me their pass but they had none—they had with them 5 head of horse kind, and skelps, that appeared to be white mens.[55]

After a bit of on-the-spot negotiation the Indians attempted to leave, but Echols held them, since "some of the company insisted to fall upon them and kill them for they said they believed they were Shaunee and that they were spies." The Captain was called, and after "he heard the opinion of the people, he past sentence of Death upon them." However, to the pain of the would-be executioners, a hunter who happened to be present, Abraham Dunkleberry, intervened saying that "they were Cherokees, yet he agreed they were Rogues,

which seemed to put the captain at a stand . . . the next morning . . . [the captain] let them have their guns and let them go off—which displeased some of the Carolina men—so much that they swore if they were not allowed to kill them, that they never would go ranging again—which you must think is very hard for us to be compeld to range and then let the enemy have liberty to kill some of us before we dare kill them-at that rate we may all be killed, and never kill an indian: for if there is enough of them to overcome us then they are enemy, but if we are too numerous for them then they are friends.

Echols goes on to report that when Dunkleberry "packt up his skins to go off" the Captain told the troops to "be easy . . . we would go after them and kill them." They did finally overtake the Indians in "a peach orchard—jest as they were a leaving it and we waited our opertunity and fired at them and followed them up 'till we kiled 4 of them and wounded the other—he bled very much, he went into the river and to an island—but we could not find where he went out."

On returning home after this small victory, all the men "were sworn—the words of the oath I do not remember exactly, but the intent of the thing was not to tell that we ever heard them say that they were Cherokees."[56] These random killings were grounds for Cherokee retaliation. The Cherokees who escaped the ambush must have been startled by the anti-tribalism which made no firm distinctions between ally and enemy and which jumped to class all red people as foe.

"Like a Child and No Man"

The Cherokees' encounter in backcountry Virginia was paralleled by other insights into the differences which set their own life apart from that of the colonists. Their participation in colonial military operations gave many Cherokees a chance to observe Euroamerican military regimen and reflect on its basis in power relationships within colonial society. During the 1758 march, General Forbes treated his tribal participants with a coldness and hostility which violated Cherokee notions of the proper conduct of allies toward one another. The Overhill leader Attakullakulla, Little Carpenter, was particularly stung, when he tried to quit the expedition (a right of any Cherokee). Forbes responded by ordering Little Carpenter to be intercepted, treated as a deserter, and the presents issued earlier to the rank-and-file warriors to be seized.[57] Little Carpenter's message to his home town put the offense in distinctly Cherokee terms: "that his arms had been taken from him; that he was like a child and no man."[58] In the colonial armies with which the Cherokees fought at intervals between 1690 and 1768, the Euroamerican and imperial military leadership exercised sole power over the troops, whose martial efforts—and lives—were in essence a property of the state.[59] Among Cherokee troops, individuals remained as autonomous—with as little fear of punishment for dissent—as in village council discussions.

General Forbes's attempt to force Little Carpenter into the dependent position of colonial troops was, from the Cherokee perspective, a stinging personal affront. The by-then former governor Glen, on a trip north, accidentally heard that Little Carpenter had been placed under guard. According to his own account, he intervened "at the critical moment" and averted disaster by gaining the prisoner's release.[60] Perhaps Glen saw in the warrior's deeply offended face the slippage of the Cherokee-Carolina detente which he had struggled so long to achieve.

This and other incidents were as much cultural as personal. Whereas English troops were powerless to resist commands, Cherokee warriors retained the option to fight or not. Backing away had consequences in the eyes of other warriors; "a young fellow who deserts or disobeys a leader under whom he goes to war cannot be punished, but he certainly loses his reputation," John Stuart observed.[61] But backing away was not desertion.

During the disastrous Sandy Creek expedition against the Shawnees in the winter of 1756, William Preston, a Virginia landowner and officer, nervously recalled in his journal the Cherokee reaction to the discipline meted out by colonial gentlemen-officers to their troops. "I had occasion to switch one of the soldiers for swearing profanely for misbehavior," Preston noted, "which with Lt. McNeal and [myself] divertying ourselves by playing very much incensed the Indian Chiefs then present."[62] The next day the party of Cherokee allies abandoned the expedition in disdain.[63]

Contributing to the angry response of the Cherokee war-leaders was a dislike of the manner in which white commanders imposed harsh discipline on their troops during war—a time of unencumbered male self-expression among the Cherokees. On one occasion, village leaders who had taken a runaway from the colonial army into custody answered official demands for his return by stating that they would agree to his return only if "you may not make his flesh smart by beating him."[64] They went on to inform the governor of South Carolina that "if we lose a man we are uneasy and when he comes back we are glad, so we hope that you will be glad likewise. I desire that you may not hurt their flesh in no place for we are all of one flesh and blood."[65] In another incident involving a military runaway, the town leaders acquiesced to his return only after they were assured that "the man should not die."[66] The Cherokees were not alone in leveling criticism. In a pointed response to the South Carolina governor's complaints about the raids of the tribe on backcountry farms, a Nottoway delegation replied that "we value our men as much as the white people do their cattle."[67]

The manner in which power was deployed in colonial armies, especially during the heightened tensions of the 1750s, provided a distasteful lesson to the Cherokees in the cultural distance which separated them from their allies. Colonial martial discipline violated the protections afforded warriors, 'troops,' or even captives in Cherokee society. The underlying issue was not the propriety of beatings or other physical abuse but the interpersonal context. The most basic Cherokee right was that of autonomy, prized enough to be maintained against the counter-pressures of coercion within tribal society. The Cherokees themselves staged ritual beatings of captives which sometimes (though less often than usually portrayed) led to death. The reserve and pride in which the beatings were suffered by warriors has been the subject of caricatures but involved much more than vanity. Such behavior stated independence in the face of death. A newspaper report of the treatment of white prisoners among the Cherokees in 1760 suggests how ceremonial beatings, and even killings, celebrated radical autonomy. The prisoners were taken "to their junker [ceremonial] yards and beat and abused . . . in a most inhuman manner and likewise obliged to dance. That dancing continued for several nights but not the beating . . . the Indians were very liberal of their provisions to the prisoners, gave them of the best and told them they were not slaves."[68] Thus, the liberty of the prisoners—even the freedom to suffer defiantly or, potentially, to die—was not breached by the tribe: the prisoners were not slaves. The Cherokees carefully made this reassurance explicit to men and women from a slave-keeping society.

For the Cherokees, the radical dependency forced by colonial society on its own people, not only soldiers but also slaves, was progressively more disturbing. Prior Cherokee observations of slave-master relationships added to the broad cultural context of their critiques of military discipline. In the treaty negotiations between Alexander Cuming and the tribe in 1730, the Cherokee headmen balked at a provision requiring them to return runaways. Though the tribal representatives finally agreed, they hedged their agreement. "This small rope we shew you," the headman at Nuquasee spoke, "is all we have to bind our slaves with, and may be broken, but you have Iron Chains for yours; however, if we catch your Slaves, we shall bind them as well as we can, and deliver them to our Friends again, and have no pay for it." [69] The talk counterposed metaphors of coercion, the "small rope . . . which may be broken" and "iron chains." Even though the treaty was signed there are few records to indicate that the Cherokees actively participated, as did other tribes such as the Catawba, in slave catching. It was no accident that as tensions grew in the Cherokee villages near Fort Loudoun tribal spokesmen used images which echoed those utilized in their own critiques of slavery in colonial society. At the beginning of the fort's construction, they wondered if the iron brought up by the fort-builders was to be "imployed in other uses than to make Hand Cuffs for them." [70] The vast fatigue predicted by the conjurers grew closer.

9

"The Plainest Road": The Coming of the Cherokee War

IN the late 1750s, the Cherokees' impatience grew toward the colonial allies who had ventured to build new towns within their settlements. The troubled stay of a Presbyterian missionary among the tribe during this period opens a window on Cherokee displeasure with colonial society and the escalation of tension in the villages.[1] Missionary William Richardson had come into the distant Overhill Towns late in 1758, while Little Carpenter and his warriors were still away on the Forbes expedition. During Richardson's visit Cherokee disillusionment increased with each round of bad news filtering back from Virginia.

Richardson's mission was brief—only three months—but was long enough for the minister to set down in his diary the deteriorating mood of the towns. While Richardson moved around freely as a guest, Old Hop repeatedly denied Richardson's requests to speak publicly. Finally, after Old Hop wondered out loud if Richardson could "not be satisfied with one answer as well as a thousand" did he get his chance at preaching. But too late. Richardson noticed a palpable change in his audience. "Tho never much inclined," he jotted, "now they shew the greatest Indifference."[2] Rumors of Cherokee deaths in Virginia were circulating in the towns, and at the same time French agents and their Creek compatriots were making overtures to the tribe from Fort Toulouse.

As Richardson observed a dramatic shift in Cherokee political sentiment, he also found a deepening dissatisfaction with colonial culture as a whole. In fairness, the ground for his proselytizing had been poorly prepared by his pre-decessor, William Martin. The Cherokees early told Richardson that Martin, "having preached scripture till both his audience and he were heartily tired, was told at last that they knew very well, that, if they were good, they should go up; if bad, down; that he could tell no more; that he had long plagued them with what they no ways understood, and that they desired him to depart the country."[3]

The Cherokees were unwilling directly to confront Richardson, who was lodged in the town of Chota on what the Great Warrior described as the white, or peace, mission of an English beloved man or ambassador. At times, even Cherokees who could speak English refused to talk with him, feigning igno-rance of his language.[4] The Cherokees found room to maneuver playfully against their earnest guest even within the ground rules of politeness. Old Hop point-edly reminded Richardson to respect the Cherokee custom of offering food to visitors, and then sent such a steady stream of hungry drop-ins that Richardson could not afford to feed them. The missionary discouragingly noted "that I am obliged to eat by stealth or I should not have Provisions for half a year, my salary not affording it."[5]

By late winter "they talk bad," Richardson wrote, "appear in general dis-affected; are jealous of us that we will take their land from them; now they don't want to go to war, for fear we sh'd take their wives & children for slaves w'n they are gone." Then, the insults offered to Little Carpenter during the Forbes expedition brought this issue to a head. In the council at Chota, Rich-ardson listened as Old Hop "began to introduce the affair of his men being sent in naked & and got into a great passion; on this I left him," Richardson wrote, "when he said he knew not but his Friends might be in prison." With an unsuspecting understatement, Richardson concluded, "there appears to be something going on among them."[6]

Anxieties concerning the already strong force at Fort Loudoun surfaced within Richardson's hearing, and he continued, "what confirms them in this opinion, is a reinforcement lately come to this Fort." The Carolina commander of the Overhill garrison had, with reason, been on edge. Early in his residence, the commander heard distressing news from a female Cherokee friend: the Emperor of Tellico (recently returned from Fort Toulouse) had advised attacking the Carolina troops. "While the Emperor was speaking," Demere wrote,

> the Wench Nancy . . . took the Emperor's wife aside and got from her the news aforesaid, which may be the more depended on as these two women are remarkably intimate. The Emperor's wife was seen to cry several times in the day. It is supposed out of compassion for the white people. The Wench Nancy aforesaid when she gave Captain Demere this intelligence apprehended great concern and cried also.[7]

The Emperor's speech had only confirmed the worst fears of the women; ear-lier, the "Old Woman" had been heard to ask "what will become of our white people, for I know not who will take their Part,'' and added ''that Old Hop being very pensive, said, 'who would have thought it would have come to this, must we throw away our white men at last?' ''[8]

An incident in the Lower Towns soon added fuel to the smoldering fire set by the Virginia killings and brought Old Hop's words closer to reality. ''Three light-headed, disorderly young officers of that garrison, forcibly violated some of their [Cherokees'] wives, and in the most shameless manner, at their own houses, while the husbands were away making their winter hunt.'' Furthermore, when the husbands returned, the offenders ''took pleasure in insulting and abusing the natives when they paid a friendly visit to the garrison''[9] and brought anger toward Carolina to a new pitch.

William Richardson eventually sensed that his hosts were about to ''throw away'' their alliance with the English. He fled to the Presbyterian settlement at the Waxhaws, and the Cherokees began to act on the news from the Virginia backcountry by taking revenge for lost relatives. An underlying hostility gathered its strength from the sum of many small disillusionments. When the war came, Cherokee actions reflected not only the strict price—life for life—called for by Cherokee notions of justice, but also a deepening estrangement from their neighbors.

While Cherokee discontent built slowly like a thunderhead at the foot of the mountains, political events in Carolina moved along with a momentum of their own. James Glen had been replaced by the aristocrat William Henry Lyttelton in 1756. Glen stayed in the colonies long enough to see the storm at the foot of the Cherokee Mountains, rather than the clear western view which he had always expected. Lyttelton would follow Glen's hopeful western initiatives but with different motivation. Unlike Glen, he hoped to claim British celebrity rather than fulfill the imperatives of South Carolina's short history. But his personal agenda, influenced by a home-office outlook, jibed by chance with Glen's policies.[10]

Lyttelton had depended on the cultivation of family ties to obtain his governorship. And events in Britain would soon serve Lyttelton's power in the colony. A year after Lyttelton's arrival in South Carolina, William Pitt, a friend of Lyttelton's family, assembled a governing coalition in Britain with Pitt himself acting as the Secretary of State.[11] A half-joking letter from Richard Lyttelton, his brother, flippantly underscores the governor's ambitions. The news in London, his brother wrote, was that the tide was turning in the war and that a large campaign might be brewing in the Caribbean. The letter continues: ''it is not impossible that you may have your share of glory, and as same is the basis of every profession, I know not why your name may not be added to those of Marlboro and Clive.''[12]

For the leadership of the colony, the appointment of a well-connected governor was a promising sign of commitment from the crown. In contrast to the governorship of James Glen—an outsider to the cousinhoods and patronage of the colonial bureaucracy—Lyttelton's appointment seemed a kind of restoration to home country favor. It provided a badly needed comfort during the mid-1750s, when political tensions in the interior were climbing. James Grant, a member of a visiting battalion in 1757, found this unease to be almost palpable. He wrote that, "The people here are rich and were much alarmed for fear of a visit from the French, who probably would have taken the rice and indigo at a low price, which brings in large sums into the province." [13] Echoing Carolina worries, the Georgia upper house wrote its fears into the record in early 1757, stating what members perceived to be the two "approaching dangers that threaten the destruction of this his Majesty's Province." They foresaw, on the one hand, "an invasion from the French at Sto. Domingo," coordinated, on the other hand, with an attack by "the Indians on our western frontiers." [14] The Georgia Commons House took concrete defensive action six months later by obliging all white males to "carry fire arms to all places of public worship." [15]

During Glen's tenure, the South Carolina Commons House had chafed under what it regarded as the unwarranted executive control of diplomacy, especially "Indian affairs," and had succeeded in limiting the funds allocated for that governor's projects, including the Cherokee forts and tribal conferences.[16] From the outset, Lyttelton's increasing preoccupation with western affairs brought him into conflict with the Assembly. However, Lyttelton won most such disputes, and his firm stands against the Assembly for better or worse, "went a long way toward restoring the executive's power over Indian diplomacy and won him the praise of the Board of Trade." [17]

Lyttelton's Western Agenda

After an initial hesitation, Lyttelton continued Glen's program by garrisoning the Overhill fort. Word of French activity in the Alabama Fort on the Coosa River had raised the specter of a revived Creek-French alliance against the English [18] and plans for seeking Cherokee and Chickasaw alliance as well. Concerned about the reliability of the flow of trade goods from Carolina and persuaded by the arguments of Creek and Savannah kin, Overhill Town leaders had traveled to Fort Toulouse in the fall of 1756 and signed a preliminary document of alliance with the French,[19] witnessed by as many as 600 tribespeople (roughly the same number as had attended the Saluda Conference with James Glen the year before). A copy of the treaty fell into English hands and was transmitted to London by Lyttelton.[20]

This material was summarized for the court in order to provide a rationale for the southern war theater desired by Lyttelton and Pitt. Earlier secret correspondence between the two had already mapped out in some detail a southern strategy which had awaited this kind of trigger. Pitt wrote that attacks on Mobile and Fort Toulouse, through the instrument of tribal allies, could begin at "His Majestey's pleasure," as soon as victory was assured in Canada.[21]

In spite of contradictory signals concerning Cherokee allegiance to the English, Lyttelton assumed that their cooperation could be coerced. Lyttelton encouraged the Creeks to "fall upon the Fort at St. Augustine, which fort is garrisoned by Negroes whom they hope to bring away in order that they might dispose of them to the English as slaves."[22] Lyttelton's overconfidence in his ability to use the tribes as tools of his private policies continued as he persisted in planning provocations against the French well into 1757. In one letter to his Overhill chief of staff, he wrote,

> I have instructed Lieut. Coytmore to endeavor to engage a body of Indians in his neighborhood to go and drive away the new [French-Creek] Settlers at the forks of the Coosa River . . . if the Indians are eager to have any soldiers of your garrison to accompany them you may send a small number, but they must be dress'd and painted to look like Indians; for I would wish to conceal the part that I take in this business that the Creeks may not consider it as an attack made by me upon their countrymen in the new settlement.[23]

Backcountry News

Lyttelton's sanguine view of Carolina's western policy was gradually diminished by unfavorable reports from the backcountry. Unlike Glen, who had gathered information from a broad network of traders and storekeepers throughout western Carolina and the Cherokee country, Lyttelton depended for news mainly on a handful of military officers under his command. The chief officer of Fort Loudoun, Raymond Demere, was Lyttelton's most important correspondent, sharing and shaping confidential policies. However, as Demere's post became the lightning rod for growing tensions in the Cherokee towns, his mood changed from optimism to frustration to near desperation between 1756 and 1757. The tenor of his letters, consequently, made a distorting impression on the policy-making of the young executive.[24]

Raymond Demere's warm initial reception in the Overhill Towns had early run into difficulties. Demere ignored Old Hop's continued defense of the occasional visits to his town of French emissaries and the semi-residence of French-allied Shawnee bands and Creeks. Demere's unprovoked raid on one such French-allied Shawnee legation at the town of Tellico produced scalps ("of three big, large fellows") which he forwarded to his commander in Charlestown, "drest and done up the way that the Indians do."[25]

Demere sent these in the hope that they would be the first of many trophies taken by English-led Cherokee allies. Instead, incidents in the backcountry began to take a toll on Demere's ambitions. Soon after the Tellico raid he reported to Lyttelton the tragic story of a white woman, apparently insane, who had run away from the troop coming to relieve the garrison in 1757 and was murdered by a group of Cherokees in spite of the efforts of her husband ("several people have been employed . . . to bring her up" to safety in the fort). The violence of this incident shocked Demere; the woman was reportedly betrayed by a Cherokee woman, wife of a pro-Shawnee tribesman, who

> gave her to Savannah Tom and he executed his inhuman, cruel, and barbarous Will on her Body by stabbing her several times with a knife, scalping and opening her Belly, and taking out a poor infant Creature that she had in her body.[26]

Another casualty of the tension in the area was trader Thomas Ross, "a superannuated and very improper person," who upon hearing of the killing of other traders by Creeks near Oakfuskee, "turned perfectly lunatick . . . gave away all his cloaths to Indians as he met them in the path and strolled away from the Handsom Fellow (who took him in charge)." Ross feared that Handsom Fellow would kill him, yet his intentions were, "so far . . . from that, he took a great deal of care of him and made him sleep with his head in his bosom to secure him from the apprehensions he had of being murdered."[27]

Facing disorder on all sides, the conflict became dangerously personalized for Lyttelton's chief operative. His lieutenant Robert Wall deserted and was captured on his way to Fort Toulouse, carrying "a large tin pot on the side of which was laid down the Path to the said Fort."[28] Earlier, the mercurial engineer, William DeBrahm, had departed abruptly and near "mutiny seemed to prevaile amongst the Provincials" assigned to labor at the fort.[29] As a result, Demere faced ridicule from Cherokee men, who viewed such setbacks as a loss of face. As his situation worsened, his words picked up the overt, taunting tenor of the Cherokee warriors he confronted daily. In an unusually candid and desperate letter to Lyttelton, Demere wrote that the warriors

> mistake very much their way of thinking, for as long as I can craul about and shall have a drop of warm blood in my veins, I shall fight. I flatter myself to have much courage as any man that ever wore a head.[30]

Demere's reports, like missionary Richardson's diary, communicated the seriously deteriorating British position.

While the disturbing content of the governor's correspondence from the Cherokee country was privately troubling, other threatening news was abroad and public knowledge in Charlestown. Sporadic published reports from the backcountry, as well as local news items, were frightening in their implications. Charlestown was constantly reminded of its vulnerability both to French-inspired attacks and to slave revolts. These tensions came to a head in the summer of 1759, when the *Gazette* reported that Creek and Shawnee warriors, under the pretext of taking a "ramble," had held "frequent private conferences with the Cherokees in the woods." The "plot," as the *Gazette* termed it, was accidentally uncovered and was quite serious, "to break out a war with the English; to begin it by a general massacre of our traders at their great Busk or Green Corn Dance . . . and to follow to immediately after falling on all our poor Back-Settlers."[31] The report concluded that when the Creek plotter "opened to the Cherokees"

> they rejected his proposal [for immediate attack] and consented conditionally only that the Creeks should strike the first blow. And that one part of their agreement was not to show the least dislike, but to make the strongest outward professions of friendship to the white people, til the very day appointed.[32]

Two paragraphs down, on the same page as this dire intelligence, the editor placed a not unconnected report of the "seditious practices" of two Negroes, Phillip Johns and John Pendarvis: "Johns manifestly appears to have had very wicked intentions; some of the evidences he told, that the Indians were to be concerned in the extermination of the white people from the face of this Earth."[33] The fuller story of the plot of Johns and Pendarvis was suppressed and emerged only in the minutes of the closed Council and most completely in Lyttelton's subsequent report to the Board of Trade. The plot revealed how old racial fractures—focused on the western tribes and the resident slave population—had traveled through the city. Though the *Gazette* reported that the conspiracy was confined to "two Negroes," the event had far wider implications. The account sent by Lyttelton to the Board of Trade is worth quoting at length:

> In the month of February last the Reverend Mr. Clarke, rector of one of the parishes of this town, a clergy man of much learning but of an overheated imagination preached some sermons in which he asserted that the world would very soon be at an end. And that this month of September a great calamity would befall the Province. At length his enthusiasm rose to such a height that he let his beard grow and ran about in the street crying, Repent, Repent for the Kingdom of heaven is at Hand, . . . his conduct and doctrine made an impression upon some weak minds, not long after his departure one Phillip John[s], a free mulatto was tried, whipped and branded for endeavoring to stir up sedition among the Negroes, by telling them he had seen a vision in which it was revealed to him that in the month of September the white people be all underground that the sod would . . . shine with their blood, that there should be no more white kings, Governors, or great men but that the Negroes should live happily and have laws of their own.[34]

The Council minutes underlined the seriousness of the conspiracy by noting that Johns' partner was "reputed to be a person of credit and property . . .

[who] had laid out the sum of seven hundred pounds currency for arms and ammunition for that purpose.'' Johns had delivered to co-conspirators

> a written paper and charged them to carry it to all the Negroes and show it
> them . . . [which said] that the 17th day of June was fixed upon for killing
> the Buckraas [whites], but afterwards told him that it was agreed to wait til
> the corn was turn'd down and the Indians were then to be sent to and they
> would come and assist in killing all the Buckraas.[35]

What was most disturbing about the plot to propertied whites sensitized to such dangers was its cross-racial and cross-cultural dimension, involving black, red, and mulatto together, an enactment of what white Charlestown had long feared.

Adding to the distress created by this incident were doubts about the loyalties of recent arrivals to the colony. In Charlestown, the stay of several hundred French-speaking Acadians, was taxing and alarming given the course of the war.[36] In the backcountry, the large population of recently settled German-speaking farmers gave even more reason for worry about loyalty. Thanks to farmer-recruitment successes, Germans constituted a substantial non-English presence.[37] Furthermore, these new settlers kept to themselves in communities like SaxaGotha, founded by Swiss immigrants, and in the smaller farming enclaves geographically, socially, and even economically segregated from English-speaking areas.[38]

Isolation created suspicions among the Angloamerican governing elite about the allegiance of these industrious settlers. A letter (perhaps a forgery) which circulated through governmental channels suggested that the German backcountrymen were potential recruits for the French. The author, ''Filius Gallicae,'' warned of the prospect of French recruiting from Pennsylvania to Georgia, where lived ''vast numbers of Germans . . . who are very poor and would be glad to do anything for a living,'' including, the author suggested, kill the English.[39] Whether this letter was bogus or not, that it was ever written suggests the increasing nervousness of the seaboard colonies, especially Carolina, about the demographic imbalance between Angloamerican and black, red, and other non-English populations within their borders.

The accumulation of bad news moved James Glen, then living in Philadelphia, to write independently to Stanwix, the British commander, urging assistance to his former subjects and reminding him that

> whatever danger threatens Carolina from the Indians they are greatly increased
> by the number of Negro slaves there, whose behavior of late has been sedi-
> tious. They will undoubtedly be invited by the Indians to join them and will
> be incited to it by the hopes of Liberty.[40]

As Governor Lyttelton and the decision-makers of the Council faced western unrest, the danger there took on the familiar look of social anxieties long faced by Carolinians.

Lyttelton's Decision for War

Lyttelton's yearning for engagement in the west increasingly intersected with popular anxieties about the danger posed by the Cherokees and by events at Carolina's own back door, but the Assembly at odds with his increasing power (and still stung by the forced appropriation for the Overhill Fort extracted when the governor first arrived) continued to balk at financial backing for Lyttelton's ventures. Lyttelton attempted in the summer of 1758 to ready the colony by raising funds for a Carolina regiment, and even offered to contribute his salary.[41] When the Assembly finally turned down his initiative a year later, Lyttelton was bitter. While attributing the Assembly's hesitation to "a spirit of excessive parsimony and some fractious humours that unfortunately prevailed,"[42] Lyttelton's condescension was responsible for alienating some of the Assembly's members. In commenting on the reply of the Assembly to one of his speeches in the following year, Lyttelton noted that "they presented to me an address in which they omitted the common form of giving thanks for the speech, I received the address but made no answer to it, and I have reason to believe that silence was a better reproof to them than any other I could have used."[43]

More and more, however, the popular climate seemed to offer Lyttelton encouragement. Alarmed by what was going on around them, Carolinians cast an eye on the military news from the north. A letter from the backcountry to the *Gazette* provided an example of this oblique connection between the northern theater of war between the French and Indian allies and the British and the homefront: "it is to be hoped that we may not be incredulous SHEPHERDS . . . 'til the wolves in the shape of Indians swarm on flocks and desolate our back settlements."[44] Furthermore, there was a spirit of volunteerism in the backcountry; the same letter offered "100 good men . . . ready and willing to serve for common pay, less than is allowed to rangers." If the Assembly was unwilling to support this patriotic spirit with appropriations, volunteers could be found to build a defensive line of backcountry forts ("log forts, 8 or 9 feet high, 3 or 4 inches thick and musket proof") similar to those strung out along western Virginia.[45]

As Lyttelton began to take matters into his own hands, his condescension became outright indifference to the sentiments of the Assembly. Guided by the tense advise of his beleaguered commanders in the mountains, he took incremental actions against the Cherokees. The English traders at Settico were withdrawn and eventually, in August, of 1759, ammunition sales to the towns were stopped.[46]

However, for the Carolinians, and especially for their governor, a reaction temperature had been reached. War was the decision; the timidity of the provincials had delayed the governor long enough. On the fifth of October, 1759, Lyttelton announced his unilateral decision to "take command of the forces myself and carry the war into the Enemy's country." Lyttelton's western agenda was finally in motion. Though the Council vote for war was split, Lyttelton claimed that it was unanimous when he informed the Commons House of his decision after the fact.[47] Initially, Lyttelton had simply given notice of his intentions to the lower house without making a full statement or speech, curtly noting that to do so would "occasion a delay," though he remained in town for two more weeks.[48]

The reaction of the Commons was at first understandably negative. It asked the governor to reconsider and expressed fears that Lyttelton's march would be "attended with the greatest evils and calamities and be productive of the most dangerous and fatal consequences."[49] The Council continued to behave passively. However, its members were careful to remind him of the paramount need to ensure "the interior safety of this province."[50]

The offended Assembly worried that South Carolina itself was too vulnerable and too weak to undertake such action on its own. Furthermore, there was the continuing feeling that the colony was being forced to carry a fiscal burden which should have been shouldered, or at least shared, by the British colonial administration. The *South Carolina Gazette* put up a half-hearted brave front, reporting that "not withstanding our immense taxes our spirits are not depleted; on the contrary, that they are (as they have always been) as zealous to exact ourselves in His Majesty's Service as any more powerful colony on this continent."[51]

Two weeks later a delegation of Cherokee town leaders entered a Charlestown gearing up for war. The delegation, which included fifty-five men and women, of whom seventeen were headmen, had come to apologize for Cherokee raids in the Carolina backcountry, particularly one raid by the young men of Settico.[52] The Cherokee peace mission presented a diplomatic embarrassment for Governor Lyttelton because he had earlier tentatively encouraged the Cherokees to reaffirm the peace, but they now arrived too late. When they were interrogated in Council, Lyttelton used the opportunity to browbeat the conciliatory headmen, hoping thereby to keep the momentum for his proposed action strong. In reply, Oconostota, a leader of the group, offered a metaphor of peace: " 'it is just like a cloudy morning which looks dark but it clears away again,' " and added, " 'I am endeavoring to clear all that is bad.' Here some deerskins were produced," the Council notes added, "and thrown down at his Excellency's feet."[53]

However, the hearing was *pro forma*. In closed Council session later Lyttelton discussed taking the leading men hostage, an idea rejected at first because the governor admitted that they were in town partly at his behest. But, by the time the public Council session reconvened, Lyttelton had changed his mind. Noting that the headmen had not formally responded to his invitation, he said that they were "not strictly entitled to protection according to the words of my Talk."[54] Just how little protection they would receive would become evident: the three headmen were soon afterwards put under house arrest.

During the dry fall of 1759 the news from the north impelled Lyttelton to seize the initiative. William Johnson had succeeded in capturing Niagara. Lifted up by northern successes,[55] Lyttelton found the moment finally to initiate his long deferred secret southern strategy. "We hear that our Excellent Governor," the *Gazette* approvingly reported,

> is determined to go in person to the Cherokees as well to humble our perfidious enemy and to reestablish the peace, serenity and prosperity of our province, which no one has ever appeared to have more sincerely at heart, and we hear a great number of Gentlemen will attend his Excellency as Volunteers.[56]

Just two weeks after this announcement the governor's advance entourage set out on the operation "to repel the invasion of and humble the Cherokee."[57] With the growing support of the formerly stand-offish colonial politicians, and with the Cherokee peace legation under house arrest, Lyttelton began the first colonial expedition of what was to become the Cherokee War.

PART III

The Cherokee War
and Its Aftermath

10

Anatomy of a Conflict

THE Carolinians, assigning blame, called it the Cherokee War. There is no record of what the Cherokees called it. We do know that for both sides it was more than an incident of border warfare. The conflict, bracketed between 1759 and 1761, saw three separate campaigns launched into the Cherokee towns.[1] On the surface, its causes were straightforward. The Cherokees, particularly certain kindred families living chiefly in the Overhill town of Settico and the Lower Towns, had returned the injuries they had received in the Virginia backcountry in the western settlements of South Carolina. Governor Lyttelton retaliated by organizing an expedition to intimidate the tribe back into the British camp. Two more campaigns followed, conducted by British regulars and backed by colonial troops. In the end, neither society seized satisfaction from the other.

Yet, only in the narrowest interpretation are the colonial campaigns the sum of what took place. The fighting escalated by an ambitious colonial governor would continue off and on for the next two decades. And the broader war, fought on the margins as well as at the center of both societies, reflected a sense of continuing Carolina-Cherokee confrontation. It was a game—a man's game for the most part—where political stakes on both sides hinged on remembered notions of prestige and place and destiny. The consequences of the persistent warfare and confrontation pulled in everyone—women and children, hostages and slaves, warriors and soldiers.

Perhaps because no one of the expeditions was militarily decisive, the three campaigns have too often been subsumed into one episode. However, the three initiatives, like acts in a play, were distinct, with each moving toward the same ending. A kind of public drama for Carolina society, the Cherokee War moved from near-failure in 1759 to half-success a year later, to the achievement, at least on paper, of military objectives under James Grant's leadership in 1761. Behind many events was a shadowing of Carolina history, both imagined and quite real parallels to the experience of the generation of 1715, and a relearning of Yamassee War lessons concerning tribal society in general and Cherokee society in particular.

Writing about another conflict distant in time and place, the Easter Week uprising in Ireland, William I. Thompson stresses the importance of understanding this revolt "in terms and shapes of imaginative experience," and, he continues, "over and over one is struck by a sense of drama." Fought in the theater of colonial imagination, the Cherokee-English war was also not without its interpreters. Contemporary writers and historians saw in the war—its broken progress—dramatic significance for the colony's story itself, and the presentation of the war here has attempted to follow their view. The following three sections retell the colonial side of the unfolding of the war, stage by stage, and the homefront and backcountry events that distinguished each of the three campaigns, the realities and illusions skirmishing behind the lines.[2]

Lyttelton's "Wild and Ridiculous Parade"

In William Henry Lyttelton's 1759 expedition against the Cherokees there was more at risk for the Carolinians than high military expenditures or harm to the troops. The governor had placed the painful lessons of Carolina history in precarious balance: in the last Indian war, in 1715, the Cherokees had been the rescuers; for nearly fifty years the tribe had been regarded as the colony's most secure western ally, and alliance with the Cherokees was seen as the linchpin of Carolina's lingering ambitions for western territories. But the security of the homefront, as always, demanded attention, and rumors of potential slave insurrection and—even more alarmingly—tribal co-conspiracy raised the stakes of the war.

By the time Lyttelton set out late in the fall of 1759, the voices of opposition heard in the Assembly when the plan was first announced had diminished in the face of an enthusiasm for war. Part of the reason had to do with colonial pride: Lyttelton's single-mindedness had finally put Carolina at the center of conflict, with all the potential for glory which that implied, in the colonial war between France and England. The military ventures of the colony since the Yamassee War had been embarrassing failures, especially the campaigns against Spanish St. Augustine during the 1730s and 1740s, and Lyttelton's was the first major military campaign undertaken to the *west* since Maurice Moore had marched into Tugaloo in 1715. For some Carolinians, William Henry Lyttelton had become the great British hope, his expedition a potential for claiming a place of power within the empire.

The fall found Lyttelton on the road to the Cherokees with twenty-two Cherokee headmen along under protective custody. Lyttelton was at Monck's Corner when encouraging news was received, adding to his momentum. "God Be Praised!," headlined the article of the *Gazette,* "Quebec is in English hands." The troops responded by drawing up and firing volleys; "some gentlemen of the artillery company who had gone this far to see the camp also fired three rounds from field-pieces and gave a genteel entertainment."[3] The *Gazette* played up the governor's leadership in the early stages of the march, a glow that reflected the admiring fixation of the press on the successful military exploits of William Johnson in New York and of Wolfe at Quebec, events which had seemingly turned the tide of the war in a single year.

The celebration of the British local hero overcame routine newspaper copy in the *Gazette:*

> Tis Lyttelton that doth command. Then
> come my sons with sword in hand With
> him we'll fight, with him we'll stay
> Over the hills and far away.
>
> We'll teach the treacherous Indians
> how, With dire humility to bow
>
> Their savage hearts we will subdue And
> make them to our King more true . . .
>
> The Ladies too should be our *cause.* Some
> must be left to guard the *fair* To save
> them from impending harms But ready to
> stand on all alarms
>
> Inspire, Great Man, your dauntless sons
> In virtue's cause direct their guns
>
> Great Jove, all blessings on him sound
> Their country's dearest, only Friend.[4]

The image of enthusiastic troops marched on through the first days' editorial passages.

Reports from the front soon began to take the shine off the press. The reasons had to do less with the Cherokees than with the conduct of the colonial army, which started out with more than 1000 whites and a substantial number of Negro slaves. Perhaps sensing a potential problem, the *Gazette* editor was at pains to report on the happy celebration of "His Majesty's Birthday" by the troops in which:

a peculiar harmony prevailed throughout the whole Army, and no distinction
was made between the Regulars, Provincials and Militia, all were alike well-
treated and well-disciplined . . . [and] no general was ever more universally
esteemed nor more deservedly.[5]

The army was a composite, made up of "gentlemen of fortune, serving as
volunteers . . . regulars, from the Independent companies . . . provincials
. . . the others were draughts from the militia regiments."[6] Landless as well
as landed marched in the same column, though with something less than "a
peculiar harmony." Lyttelton had ordered backcountry justices to collect "vagrants" to fill out the Provincial regiment, and many recent migrants to the
backcountry arrived at camp too poor to purchase guns.[7] The expedition soon
became more and more of a confrontation between the divergent cultures of
coast and backcountry, and the social discomforts of the march increased.

By the time the army had moved beyond the rendezvous point of Monk's
Corner, nearly one hundred miles up the Savannah, the tone of the news from
the camp had changed: "some of our letters from the camp," the *Gazette*
wrote,

mention considerable desertion from the Militia assembled at the Congarees
and thence represent the necessity of having a reinforcement, but withal observe, that the deserters are people of no property and no sense of honor who
have fled from other Provinces and to whom it is never inconvenient to remain
from place to place out of danger.[8]

While apologizing for the apparent cowardice of the backcountry militiamen,
the correspondent's underlying concern seemed to be for appearances, not only
as they affected the colony's pride but also for the "consequences that might
follow our army appearing contemptible to the Indians."[9] The troops saw battle only once along the march, when the assailing force turned out to be a deer
which "broke through the line and knocked down one of the men."[10]

The army at peak strength was smaller than anticipated: with the subtraction
of "Waggoneerrs, Negroes, &c . . . not 1,200 could be called fighting men."[11]
For James Adair, who observed the aggregation as the leader of a Chickasaw
force from the perspective of the middle trading society, this "mixed body"
was unfit from the beginning, a "fine silken body [which] chiefly consisted of
citizens and planters from the low settlements unacquainted with the hardships
of a woodland, savage war."[12] The expedition's Surgeon, viewing the same
force from a city perspective, appraised the militia as "ill-armed, undisciplined
and with some reason, discontented and mutinous."[13]

Apparently undeterred by desertions, Lyttelton pushed slowly on through
the upcountry, arriving at the borderland east of the Cherokee towns in late
November. There, at the Congarees, the pretense of protective custody was

dropped, and the Cherokee chiefs were formally made prisoners, an action taken "very unexpectedly" with a "Captain's guard mounted over them." [14] Though this precipitous action may have seemed a normal wartime measure for Lyttelton, himself a former French hostage handsomely ransomed, it created immediate misunderstanding. As James Adair noted: "It is well known that the Indians are unacquainted with the custom and meaning of hostages; to them, it conveyed the idea of slaves, as they have no public faith to secure the lives of such." [15] For tribal leaders hostage-taking cut at the root of their dignity. When Lyttelton finally reached the Lower Towns and set up camp across the river from Keowee, the Cherokees were surprised. The *Gazette* reported that "the Army having so many headmen of the nation in custody had puzzled the *Indians* very much and that it was the only thing that had prevented their doing more mischief." [16] The hostages thus temporarily had the desired effect.

Encamped across from Keowee in the cold early December rain, Lyttelton seemed a captive of confusion concerning Cherokee intentions. Emerging from an inconclusive mass meeting at the Sugar Town council house, Lyttelton and his officers looked up to see "above two hundred Indians on the hills" surrounding the town. When these men began to run while firing their guns into the air, the Carolinians were unsure what to think. Some saw the demonstration as a "salute to the Governor, and others as bidding indifference." [17] However, another very real, but silent, enemy soon intervened.

At Keowee, the troops and their commander found themselves held hostage by smallpox, which had "raged for some Time before our Arrival in the *Indian* Town and killed about everyone it attacked." [18] Lyttelton stopped short of crossing the river and attempted to create a buffer against the disease by interdicting any communication between the town and camp. Quickly the conditions in the camp gave impetus to negotiations with the tribe. Though smallpox itself did not appear immediately among the soldiers, "measles, purgings and pleuritic complaints" were on the increase during the month-long encampment. [19] Robberies increased the tension in the camp, and discipline began to break down. "We are assured by a gentleman of character, a principal merchant of Mobille," James Adair sarcastically wrote,

> when he went round the delicate camp, in wet weather, and late at night, he saw in different places from fifteen to twenty of their guns in a cluster, at the distance of an equal number of paces from their tents, seemingly so rusty and peaceable, as the loss of them by the sudden attack of Indian savages could not in the least affect their lives. [20]

While the health of his fighting force deteriorated, Lyttelton was in almost continuous council regarding the hostage Cherokee chiefs. Out of frustration Lyttelton singled out Little Carpenter as the sole negotiator for the tribe—an unrealistic choice given the array of towns and families involved. [21] In a bullying tone Lyttelton finally demanded that twenty-four Cherokees be delivered up to be put to death for the backcountry losses of the whites, and he attempted to put pressure on the tribe by speaking at length on the victories of the English at Quebec and on the Continent.[22]

During these negotiations the Cherokees refused Lyttelton's demands, and in the interim smallpox flared up. At Lyttelton's request, the houses of Cherokee victims were burned.[23] Surgeon Milligen blamed the wind and smoke for what happened next: "it hurried the disease among us, by the smoke driving the infectious particles towards us."[24] By the end of December the *Gazette* correspondent estimated that "three-fourths (or more)" of the army seemed ready to desert. News from Charlestown did not help; the Assembly, for instance, had refused to continue the pay of the militia stalled at Keowee.

A settlement was quickly made with the Cherokees which stipulated that the tribal hostages already in custody remain in English hands, without requested additions. On December 28, symptoms of smallpox appeared among some of the troops. Within an hour "near 700 men had packs on their back and filed off with great alertness."[25] In the confusion, the order to return to Charlestown was given after the fact. James Adair termed the reverse march "a wild and ridiculous parade."[26]

Many Carolinians seemed eager to declare a victory even though Lyttelton had won no real concessions. The twenty-two hostages imprisoned in Fort Prince George remained the sole English prize and Cherokee loss. Lyttelton, feigning modesty, "endeavored to make his entry into town in a private manner," only to be intercepted by Christopher Gadsden's artillery company which "marched two miles up the Path to meet him where they saluted his Excellency with vollies and cheers."[27] The official British historian of the American theater of the imperial war gave an equally rousing recap of the expedition, "this quick and spirited proceeding," and devoted a section to the march.[28]

At Lyttelton's return, the *Gazette* also provided upbeat rhetoric to cap off its extensive reports on progress toward victory. It allowed its readers a moment of recaptured provincial pride, of a place in the sun:

> so ends our Account of the Cherokee expedition—an expedition we cannot forbear repeating, has been carried on by and at the sole expense of the inhabitants of the infant colony of South Carolina . . . an expedition of great importance not only to this province but also to North Carolina, Virginia, and Georgia; and *in such* a very numerous, powerful, treacherous and insolent nation of SAVAGES has been compelled to submit to such terms.[29]

But the hoped-for redemption of South Carolina by the mother country had not come in this first phase of the Cherokee War. The following spring, as Lyttelton sailed away to take on the governorship of Jamaica,[30] the *Gazette* struggled to put the departure of the colony's British hero in the best light.

South Carolina was after all a stepping stone to "the best government in America," and such a promotion was "the highest evidence of the royal approbation and merit" for Lyttelton and, by implication, for Carolina. Yet the same article expressed relief that Lt. Governor William Bull, veteran of engagements with Spain, "a native of this province," and "acquainted with Indians and their abilities and the interests and affairs of Carolina" would take over.[31] The reins of power had returned home.

The following two decades would see the colonists preoccupied with the issues of political self-definition kindled by Lyttelton's expedition. Among many Carolinians there was a lingering bitterness. George Milligen, surgeon turned historian, related how Lyttelton had immodestly accepted Charlestown's reception as a "Conqueror with Illuminations, Bonfires and Addresses from every Society and Profession." And, he added damningly: "The Propriety of their application to Mr. Lyttelton, on this Occasion, I leave to the Reader's Judgement."[32] Thus the first Cherokee campaign forced notice of conspicuous flaws in Carolina's relationship with both the British and the Cherokees.

The Homefront

The Lyttelton victory celebrations had only cooled slightly when smallpox broke out in Charlestown in the spring of 1760, spread by returning troops and by backcountry traffic from Augusta and the Catawba settlements. Four thousand town residents eventually came down with the disease. Among the sick was the young grandson of Ann Manigault, who made this spare entry in her diary for May 3, 1760: "Today my grandson's face began to break out."[33] Though upper-class households like that of the Manigault family were not spared, the infection was most serious among Negro slaves and Acadian immigrants.[34] The epidemic seemed to threaten a kind of social morbidity, a tear in the decent fabric of society, in which normal restraints and small decencies were forgotten. In a letter to the *Gazette,* a correspondent observed disturbing social symptoms:

> Hearing that many of the Negroes who died of the smallpox were buried not a foot under the ground and knowing that some days there were 12, 14 and 18 buried I went to their burial place and found more than 40 not 2 feet under the ground, many not one foot and some not six inches. I assure you that the very cows, by their pawing, had laid one coffin bare.[35]

Other evidence of decline and disruption could not be missed. The colony feared, and to a degree actually faced, a shortage of food. Bread prices in Charlestown were regulated during this period, and in 1760 legislation was passed prohibiting the export of grain or flour from the colony.[36] In the backcountry the wheat crop had promised to be good, though there were not enough mills to grind it, and harvest and delivery seemed jeopardized by tribal raids. Beef was also in short supply, "seldom at any market," during 1760.[37] The inflation of commodity prices not only was an index to the stress felt in urban and backcountry districts but also reminded older Charlestown residents of the prohibitions of the Yamassee War, when the export of foodstuffs had also been banned.[38] The scarcities of 1760 served as a painful reminder of the still-fragile lines of supply within the colony.

All along the permeable boundary of settlement at the backcountry of the southern colonies, fear—already high—soon surged to a near-universal nervous intensity. Fort Prince George near Keowee was the epicenter of the first wave. After the fort was "close blocked-up" by a virtual barricade in February, an English officer, lured out on the pretense of talking to a Cherokee delegation, was killed. The garrison, in near mutiny, in turn killed all of the Cherokee hostages. So quick were the troops to seek revenge that the garrison commander was later to write simply that "I was obliged to put up with the Massacre."[39] George Milligen provided a straightforward analysis of the events:

> the soldiers of the Garrison were permitted to kill the innocent and unfortunate Prisoners, called Hostages; who were butchered to Death, in a Manner too shocking to Relate. By this Massacre, for I can give it no softer Name, most of the Head-Warriors lost Relations and Friends.[40]

Two days later the commander reported cutting a new port hole, and discharging one of the fort's "Great Guns" toward the town of Keowee, "through their Town House, and particularly the old Conjurer's House which put what Indians was in the town to flight, and went and took refuge under the cover of the hills."[41]

A second wave of fear centered on reports of impending alliance between the Creeks and the Cherokees. While negotiating with the Creeks, Edmond Atkin confirmed the deep-seated hostility toward the colony of the faction of the tribe led by the Mortar, a group united by kinship as well as recent agreements with the Shawnees, the French, and some Cherokee Lower Towns families. Atkin and his colleagues reported the troubling news of the arrival at the Creek council of a "Cherokee fellow and three women . . . [the man] carrying a war spear having 300 notches on it, denoting the deaths of so many of the white people."[42] The colonials began to search for clues to the allegiance of the Chickasaws and Choctaws, widely reported to be the recipients of Cherokee invitations to war.[43] These diplomatic probings were not reassuring. By the summer of 1760 the Assembly stated for the record the "impossibility of defending our properties against a united force of the Creeks and Cherokees."[44] At the same time reports began to circulate in Charlestown of the extreme difficulty in which Fort Loudoun found itself. Charlestown also felt itself in crisis. "A great cloud seems at present to hang over this province," Eliza Lucas Pinckney wrote early in 1760 to a friend, "We are continually insulted by the Indians on our back settlements and a violent kind of small pox rages in Charles Town that almost puts a stop to all Business."[45]

Under pressure, provincial distinctions between tribal friends or enemies were increasingly overshadowed by the perception of a generalized red threat. In July the *Gazette* carried an apocryphal story which reflected the shift. A French officer in Canada, the story ran, had been charged with the safety of a wounded English officer. The guardian turned away long enough for "a few straggling Indians" to scalp the prisoner and horrify the returning Frenchman, who swore he would withdraw from the war, "declaring that he would not stain his honor any longer under a man who countenanced such horrid barbarities."[46] Whereas the Cherokees, as foes, had once stood as a kind of proxy for the French, now it was clear that Euroamerican men—no matter what their political allegiance—were tied by decency to oppose what was beginning to be regarded as an indecent enemy.

The Spring of 1760: A "Tourrant" of Refugees

In the early spring of 1760, the Keowee hostage-killing was revenged by the Cherokees in the young backcountry settlements.[47] Relatives of the victims were "fired . . . with an implacable Desire of Revenge; they set out immediately in small parties against the Settlements." Westerner John Pearson wrote of the "tourrant" of white and black refugees, "they being chiefly killed, taken prisoners, and drove into small forts" hastily thrown up during the first panicked days.[48] One hundred and fifty settlers attempting to reach Augusta from Long Cane were working to free their wagons from a "boggy Place" in the road when they were attacked by "100 Cherokees on Horseback."[49]

The *South Carolina Gazette* headlined the subsequent report from the upper Savannah:

> Mr. Patrick Calhoun, one of the unfortunate Settlers at Long-Canes, who were attacked by the Cherokees on the 1st Instant, as they were removing their Wives Children and best Effects, to Augusta, in Georgia, for safety, is just come to Town, and informs us, that the whole of those Settlers might be about 250 Souls, 55 or 60 of them Fighting Men: that their Loss in that Affair amounted to about 50 Persons, chiefly Women and Children, with 13 Loaded Waggons and Carts; that he had since been at the Place where the Action happened, in order to Bury the Dead, and found only 20 of their Bodies, most inhumanely butchered.[50]

Random and isolated acts of violence broadcast terror. In a petition to the North Carolina legislature, William Shaw asked compensation for "feet cut off

by the Indians in 1759.''[51] Blacks, perhaps because they were exposed in field-
work, were a common target. The body of one black man was left "hid amongst
the feathers" pulled from a mattress; "the tick was carried away."[52] Nor were
the Cherokee young men alone in their inventiveness. At Rabl's fort on the
Congaree River colonists gained the upper hand after deflecting a Cherokee
attack: "the bodies of the savages were cut to pieces and given to the dogs."[53]
In Georgia, "where the late alarm had done incredible injury to the Province,"
panic spilled over into the coastal district. Settlers at Halifax, Briar Creek, fifty
miles from Savannah, and Augusta had "left the Forts which they had constructed with Swivel guns, arms and ammunition . . . many substantial planters, settled near the Coast abandoned their Plantations."[54]

The dislocation was massive, and the self-conscious response from the
weakened colony disastrously ineffective. "Many who fled into the Woods, for
Safety," Milligen remembered two years after the fact,

> lost themselves and miserably perished . . . the luckiest, who escaped the
> Indians and gained the lower Settlements, were reduced, from Affluence, Plenty
> and Independence, to Poverty, Beggary, and Want. This Desolation extended
> upwards of 100 Miles; every Hour brought to *Charles-town* Accounts of Rav-
> ages, Depredations, Scalpings, and Ruin; the unhappy Sufferers calling aloud
> for Assistance and Support: but alas! the Province (distressed by the Expenses
> of the late Expedition, and at the same Time afflicted with the Small-pox)
> . . . was unable of itself to manage this War, unwisely brought upon us.[55]

Many of the most economically marginal backcountry settlers were recent
migrants forced to run from war in the Virginia backcountry, only to face
renewed danger in Carolina from both smallpox and warriors. The Cherokee
raids of 1759–60 caused them to backtrack, "travelling for safety to the northern colonies with their effects."[56] For those who stayed in the forts dotting the
backcountry, conditions were desperate. Patrick Calhoun implored Governor
Lyttelton for relief for the four hundred "men, women, and children, white
and black," who had taken refuge with prominent trader John Tobler at New
Windsor.[57] Writing from the Waxhaw settlement, ex-missionary to the Cherokees William Richardson envisioned social disintegration if help did not arrive:

> if some speedy assistance is not afforded the frontiers will, we are afraid, be
> immediately deserted with the prospect of a famine as our crops are poor,
> scarce able to maintain ourselves and other frontier inhabitants that have been
> flying in make our condition fitful.[58]

Profiteering was commonplace; Calhoun reported that though "there is provisions sufficient in that neighborhood . . . it is in the hands of those who will
not part with it without money or a certainty of it in a little time, neither of

which is in the power of these poor people." And Calhoun added, "without such relief is granted them they will be under the disagreeable necessity of dispersing over this and the neighboring provinces in the hopes of subsistence."[59]

The Second Expedition

Just as Lyttelton left South Carolina and the backcountry dissolved into chaos, the southern border campaign he had wished for finally began to materialize. Successes in Canada and the persuasion of colonial lobbyists freed a troop of British regulars commanded by Archibald Montgomery to take up Lyttelton's abortive mission.[60] At their arrival on April 1 from Canada, William Bull declared a "DAY OF FASTING, HUMILIATION, AND PRAYER TO ALMIGHTY GOD for averting the Evil which at present threatens us . . . not only with a pestilential and contagious distemper the SMALLPOX, but likewise a war."[61] However, there was an air of insecurity. Perhaps reflecting the uncertainties of the moment, militia recruitment lagged. A powerful lobby pushed militia pay levels higher than those of any other colony, but a backcountry sheriff believed that this incentive might not be enough:

> I am much pleased at the increase of the Rangers' pay as I am almost convinced that not one company would ever have filled but now hope they may. As to the Regiment, I believe they will go slow and I must confess I can find in my mind not one proper person that I think will take Commission.

The hesitation among backcountry residents was shared by potential native American allies, such as the Catawba. The same sheriff, also negotiating with the Catawbas for help, observed that "they have no relish for going against the Cherokees."[62] Carolina also received little help from neighboring colonies.

Once on the trail, accompanied by seven troops of South Carolina Rangers, Montgomery's 1200 Highlanders made a rapid march. Official silence was imposed, in sharp contrast to the free flow of news from Lyttelton's expedition. The first meager report was: three lines of type noting their arrival at Ninety-Six near the Cherokee border.[63] Afterwards, the conspicuous absence of news required a round-about disclaimer from the *Gazette* editor:

> as no person in this province is yet legally appointed by authority sole vendor, publisher, collector of authentic intelligence, we flatter ourselves that the public will not suppose us excluded, precluded from such nor disregard the advises we shall give them from the Army marching to the Cherokees . . . altho' they should not be dated from the camp.

The same notice hinted darkly at another reason for the blackout—one so familiar to the elites in all Atlantic slave societies in times of external crisis that it scarcely needed to be named: "Good reasons have been suggested for not inserting in this paper any accounts of Insurrections especially at this time." [64]

There were to be no further direct communications from Montgomery until his second in command, James Grant, wrote a letter reprinted ("for the information and satisfaction of the public") in the *Gazette* at the conclusion of the march.[65] The censorship, however strategic in military terms, rankled the readership of the *Gazette* because it seemed to underscore the inferior status of the colonials in their own war. This feeling was sharpened by the preface to the Montgomery mission. Arbitrary decisions made by an invisible bureaucracy, such as the surprise transfer of Lyttelton to Jamaica, had lessened the colonial sense of control and heightened the impression of dependency in their relationship with the Crown. Colonists such as Christopher Gadsden, who had cheered Lyttelton, began to write in the *Gazette* directly to the issue of the tie between Charlestown and London. "At a time such as this," Gadsden wrote,

> when the greatest misfortunes seem ready to overwhelm us; when we seem likely to be destroyed because we do not act like FREEMEN; when our understandings seem to be so blinded and our spirit is so debased, as to suffer us to love evils; indignation makes a man break that silence which prudence would persuade him to keep, if not to work upon the minds of his countrymen, yet to ease his own.[66]

Though Gadsden's prose was hyperbolic, the underlying sentiment—of a damaged colonial pride and humiliation—reflected a painful ambivalence toward the British rescuers of 1760.

When the full story emerged after Montgomery's return, it quickly became apparent that there was little reassuring to tell. Montgomery's troops had encountered insignificant opposition in the Lower Towns. Marching sixty miles in forty-eight hours they had arrived at the first town, Keowee.

> The surprise was complete; and the Indians so terrified that their resistance was trifling, and we could plainly observe them on the tops of their mountains tamely stand by and see us destroy all before us . . . Doubtless numbers perished in the flames and the smallpox was in their towns and we came upon them like lightening. The neatness of those towns and their knowledge of agriculture would surprise you; they abounded in every comfort of life, and may curse the day we came among them.

The Lower Towns of Estatoe ("a pretty village"), Toxaway, Qualatchee, Consatche were all burned; at the last named place the townhouse was "stockaded round,'' an ineffective preparation for the kind of threat suddenly facing the townspeople.[67]

In the Middle Settlements steep mountain trails slowed the march. Near Etchowee, or Echoe, a hamlet on the sinuous road to Cowee, the Cherokees ambushed the English expedition, firing on it from the cover afforded by the tightly packed hills along the Little Tennessee River. The surprise was complete: "We were suddenly fired upon from all quarters by the Cherokees," reported a participant, admitting that

> the Cherokees . . . shewed some judgement in taking possession of ground that was most advantageous to them . . . they had vastly their advantage of us with their rifle barreled guns, which did execution at a much greater distance than our musket; besides they fought in their usual way and we gave them our fire by platoons. Some of the Indians spoke English and gave us very insulting language, the Raven of Estatouih was with them, the Young Warrior seemed to be their commander in chief; his voice was distinctly heard the whole time, calling loudly to his people to fight strong.[68]

First reports held Creeks had joined the Cherokees, validating the fear of Creek alliance. Later the Cherokees, with an uncanny insight into the psychology of the English troops, would simply call out "Coweeta," (meaning Creek) during skirmishes, in order to evoke buried fears of collective tribal assault in the colonial lines.[69] After the battle at Echoe, the Cherokees bragged that because the English warriors had stood in "heaps," that they had been able to shoot them down "like turkies."[70] During the fight the army answered Cherokee yells with "three whirra's and three waves of our bonnets and hats which they did not seem to relish."[71]

In spite of their bravado, the English suffered. Over twenty were killed, nearly seventy wounded. Captain Williams of the Royal Scots fell near the Cherokee line; Ensign Munro of the Highlands was wounded in the groin attempting a rescue. The *Gazette* readership was told in detail how the body of Captain Morrison, the leader of the colonial rangers, was abused: "his arms, legs, and head were cut off and his body cut in two, and shockingly mangled."[72] Morrison died unsupported by his own men. Lieutenant Grant reported in an official letter to the *Gazette* that the laxity of the colonial rangers contributed to his death:

> I am sorry that I cannot say anything in their favor . . . they behaved most infamously; near fifty deserted the night before we marched, and they ran off to a man the moment they heard the firing begin at which time poor Morrison was killed when he was advancing and doing his duty like a gallant good officer.[73]

Following this disaster, the British troops regrouped briefly and marched into the abandoned town of Echoe. A British officer assessed the damage in strategic terms: "Echoe cost us dear. The killed I look upon as a trifle, people are then provided for; but the wounded in a remote frontier is a distressing circumstance."[74] As had been the case a year before, when Lyttelton's troops had fled before smallpox, cowed rank and file soldiers pressed for a retreat. After the turnabout of the British troops at Echoe, "not a man of the Rangers or the new raised Regiment could be prevailed upon to remain [in this country], alleging that their time was up."[75]

Within a day Montgomery abandoned the dual objective of relieving the Overhill garrison and scouring the Cherokee towns. He ordered a retreat in the night.[76] Once received, this was not happy news for Charlestown. The *Gazette* feared once again arbitrary abandonment by their protectors: "The unexpected return of Col. Montgomery from the Cherokees is a matter of very great concern to us and will be more so should the forces under his command suddenly embark for northward."[77] The destination cited by the paper, northward, is significant; to the north lay the theater of war that had been the focus of British efforts while Charlestown's needs were unmet, to the north lay the colonies to which Carolina felt it had too long taken second place in the mother-country's affection.

The Third Expedition

British military officials immediately attempted to put the Montgomery expedition in the best possible light. "The greatest stroke the Indians have felt," General Amherst wrote to Pitt of the campaign (doubtlessly keeping in mind the special attention Pitt had given the affairs of Carolina while Lyttelton was governor).[78] Charlestown commentators were less sanguine about the war and disturbed by the rapidity with which Montgomery left town. Only a month after the about-face at Echoe, Montgomery and his troops managed to "cross the bar" and sail out of Charlestown harbor. Alexander Hewatt contrasted the mood in Charlestown at Montgomery's arrival and departure, sounding almost apologetic when he discussed the context of the decision:

> Great was the joy of the Province upon the Arrival of this Gallant Officer: but as the Conquest of Canada was the grand object of this year's campaign in America, he had to strike a sudden blow for the Relief of Carolina and return to headquarters.[79]

Montgomery's retreat created a new paranoia in Charlestown. The city had pleaded for the four companies which remained though even they were believed to be inadequate to check the danger facing the colony. "It is well known," a letter writer to the *Gazette* pointed out, "that the services of a whole detachment was thought necessary."[80] Eventually, with strong lobbying, such a force was promised for the coming year by Lord Amherst.

At the same time the Assembly, at the urging of William Bull, was taking steps of its own to meet a new emergency. "For the poor unfortunate people in Fort Loudoun and self-preservation," enlistment bounties of 50 pounds sterling were offered and scalp bounties worth half as much were continued. Captive tribesmen would be vested as the slaves of their captors. In initial discussions, the Assembly had proposed that any live captives be shipped "to some of the West Indian Islands," the same destination to which the Yamassees had been deported forty years before.[81] An artillery company was created, and financial measures were passed both to pay off the debt created by Montgomery's expedition and to fund ten companies of soldiers.[82]

So great was the terror among the western population that the commander at Keowee could not find any white person willing to travel from Augusta to Orangeburg: "if I was to give one hundred Guineas to a person to cross the country . . . I could not get any person to undertake it."[83] Midsummer questions about the fate of the Fort Loudoun garrison, which had been under siege since Montgomery's march, were answered at last by Abram, a black messenger who had become the primary link between the Overhill fort and the colonials after no white colonist had been willing to volunteer for the duty.

Abram's news shocked Charlestown. The garrison, leaving Fort Loudoun under truce, had been attacked by a band of Cherokees and Creeks while being led to the safety of the Virginia encampment northeast of the backtowns. The commander, Paul Demere, and thirty-two of the colonial troops were killed, the rest shared among the participating tribal towns as slaves. "We have just learned that a war party of Cherokees, commanded by Wolf, has captured Fort Loudoun, belonging to Great Britain," a Frenchman privately reported to his superiors, "and that the commanding officer, Mr. Demere, was killed by the Indians. They stuffed earth into his mouth and said, 'Dog, since you are so hungry for land, eat your fill.' They treated several others the same way."[84] Urging resistance after hearing the news, a writer from besieged Fort Prince George, the last remaining colonial outpost among the tribe, grasped for the emotional touchstone of the Yamassee War: "If it is my lot to die by inches here, I can only regret . . . that my countrymen have not exerted that spirit which prevailed amongst and did honor to their ancestors in the last Indian war [against] . . . savage nations 5 or 6 times more numerous than now."[85] After the failure of Montgomery to save the colony, and as subsequent crises escalated, the Carolinians began to personalize the Cherokee threat as a test of colonial manhood. When certain of the Cherokee town leaders, such as Serowih, the "commander in chief" at the Echoe battle, sent peace overtures to Charlestown, the colonial reply had a new and different pitch. "I confess I don't like the Young Warrior's talk, it looks more like dictation than begging the peace," wrote a correspondent from Fort Prince George, "tho' by an illiterate hand it has too much the language of a conqueror."[86]

Colonial Disunity and Disappointment

The attack on the retreating Fort Loudoun garrison by a French-sympathizing tribal faction galvanized the frustrated colonies into a long-delayed action. Lt. Governor Bull, now in charge, hoped to reassemble a joint colonial initiative from the pieces of the failed Montgomery campaign. Bull proposed a winter offensive in which the newly formed South Carolina regiment would thrust against the Lower and Middle settlements while the Virginians, who had arrived too late to assist Montgomery in 1760, would converge on the Overhill Towns. The Virginia army's hesitation to engage the tribe sooner had angered the Carolinians, who felt that, except for the "accident" of Little Carpenter's bringing the Fort Loudoun survivors to Byrd's camp, "the Cherokees had never heard of Mr. Byrd's Armament."[87] The North Carolina troops now showed a similar lack of resolve. Governor Dobbs of North Carolina summoned the Assembly to three meetings in a two-month period before funds were earmarked for a force under Hugh Waddell, but strings were attached. North Carolina soldiers were instructed to march to the Holston to rendezvous with the Virginians only if they were not needed for direct defense in North Carolina. Even then some of the troops refused to go "on the pretense it is out of the province."[88] By the time that the North Carolina commander finally arrived at Byrd's army on the Holston, half of his force had deserted.[89]

Disappointed by the failure of North Carolina to vote sufficient funds to create a credible joint-colonial offensive and by similar indecisiveness in Virginia, Bull nevertheless sent the newly formed South Carolina regiment to a winter camp at the Congarees, where the troops awaited James Grant's arrival from New York. South Carolina thus waited in anger at uncooperative sister provinces, at unreliable British help, and at their own inability to get basic information concerning the backcountry. But a growing energy for war grew in coastal Carolina, fueled both by anxiety as well as frank enthusiasm for the coming fight. An exuberant interest in martial fashions had manifested itself from the beginning, especially among the upper-class members of the colonial military forces—the "fine silken body" of the Lyttelton expedition.[90] While Montgomery's troops slogged over the hill trails, John-Paul Grimké, "Jeweler in Broad Street," held a close-out sale on "suitable swords and belts for Gentlemen troopers and others from 6 to 60 pounds . . . now on sale to be disposed of (extremely cheap) for ready money."[91] Less than a year later, Grimké found a new market in the regiment forming to go against the Cherokees. The recruiting notice touched on matters of style:

Many gentlemen of character and very considerable property propose to go as volunteers . . . The dress will be the same as that of the Regiment, except as to colour, which they have agreed upon shall be altogether a deep green.[92]

However well dressed, the members of the "deep green" regiment, commanded by Thomas Middleton and with the impatient Henry Laurens second in authority, spent a hard winter. The ineptitude of Middleton's preparations "must have been early perceiv'd by every Regular Officer of the least discernment from the Apparatus . . . provided for that purpose on a Winter's Campaign, as well as from the pompous & Cumbrous equipage for accommodating his own person, well enough indeed for a Campaign in Flanders."[93]

Provincial momentum was slowed during the long winter encampment, and problems that had dogged Lyttelton's mission re-emerged. Keeping peace among the troops brought to the surface social tensions between commanders and their recruits. The residents of Charlestown outfitting for war were aware of the prominence their efforts were gaining by default in a pause in the larger, Continental war during peace negotiations in Canada and the Caribbean. As Thomas Mante, official early chronicler of the Seven Years' War, would point out in his account of the Grant expedition, "this was the only warlike expedition which distinguished the year 1761 in North America."[94]

Conditions in the camp at the Congarees contradicted the glorious campaign which would be extolled in postwar histories. Even though the payments promised to Carolina soldiers by the Assembly were quite high, they were not high enough to quell discontent, and desertions remained commonplace.[95] During the extended bivouac the colonial commander kept strict discipline, but he himself was often absent. Laurens provided a stinging indictment of his superior, who "hastily mounted his Horse and retired to his family and to his business, leaving scarcely four days provision for the camp." At the Congarees encampment, Laurens disapprovingly wrote, the recruits were

turned out night and day to constant duty in the exercise of cannon . . . and other branches of regular and "artificial fighting" Where they were severely Flogg'd, hors'd and hang'd!? That Camp from whence they (except the parsimonious ones) therefore notwithstanding their "double pay" march'd pennyless depending upon future wages for future drink.[96]

Many others deserted rather than face service at Congarees.

"Mac-La-Moor": Colonial Fears and the Cherokee Image

The arrival of Grant's troops in January 1761 did little to stem doubts about the ability of the colonies to mount an effective campaign.[97] The forays of

Lyttelton and Montgomery had uncovered not only a lack of resolve among recruits but also worrisome insights into the loyalty of the backcountry. During the official news blackout of the Montgomery campaign and the confusing period that followed, the Carolinians had been forced to depend for news of Cherokee intentions largely on the most marginal of backcountry residents. The Overhill fort had looked to more than thirty "Indian wenches," as well as "half breeds and others" to keep the garrison alive, the *Gazette* disparagingly noted.[98] Further, in the face of the breakdown of standard channels of military intelligence, colonial authorities had been required to trust men and women for whom they had little but contempt. The names Samuel Terron, Nancy Butler, Abram, George Downing, Charles McLamore appeared regularly in the *Gazette,* but the newspaper frequently expressed misgivings about the dependability of its informants—misgivings which often centered on race.

In the eyes of the Charlestown elite, the backcountry had always provided an environment for a dangerous racial mingling among red, white, and black, and three years of war fused racial and cultural hatred into a new and strong amalgam. The shifting characterization in the *Gazette* of Charles McLamore, a packhorseman in the deerskin trade and important intermediary during the war, suggests the manner in which racial fears hybridized across cultural lines. After Montgomery's retreat, questions began to be raised about this man's allegiance and possible treachery. Though McLamore was valuable because of his knowledge of the Overhill villages, the *Gazette* noted he was "by most . . . thought to be a consummate villain, a perfect Cherokee, and a spy."[99] Within two months the threat posed by this "perfect Cherokee" had transmuted. The *Gazette* noted that McLamore is "so called as he was never known by any other name . . . if the reading of it was of any importance, it might appear that McLamore derived his name from being a mulatto and that it should be written 'Mac La Moor.' "[100]

The flow of news to the provincial capital also fueled concerns about more explicit racial threats than the confused public identity of backcountrymen such as McLamore. Even help offered by blacks was suspect. For instance, Abram, the loyal messenger, was a runaway slave; the week before he delivered the message of Fort Loudoun's fall, a reward had been offered for his return to his owner at Stono.[101] Though Abram's freedom was later gratefully purchased by the colony,[102] this was a near-unique gesture. Some slaveowners remained more interested in safeguarding their property than in rewarding runaways. For instance, an advertisement for the return of "Phillip, 16," "gone with the army" appeared during Grant's march.[103] The disruptive passage of the army had created an opportunity for blacks to free themselves. The difficulty posed by these events in Charlestown was brought home during discussions of whether to put into force the Militia Bill provisions that allowed "trusty Negroes" to be armed to fight for the defense of the colony, and which budgeted fifty black "pioneers" for the upcoming Grant expedition.[104] In Charlestown, more usual racial worries thus continued to crop up as the situation in the west deteriorated.

Alarming as well to the residents of Charlestown was evidence of loosening social control in the backcountry. The most conspicuous, the so-called Webber heresy, played on the anxieties of the Angloamerican colonial elite concerning the potential for revolt on the part of white, but non-English, countrymen. The Webber sect, which fused New Light religion and apocalyptic vision, had flourished for a time in the late 1750s; its intensity may have been heightened by tribal raiding broadcast through upland communities. Though its origins are unclear, the trial of the Webber leadership by colonial authorities revealed what they certainly viewed as social pathology. "Some Dutch People were brought to Town and confined to the Gaol for the most extraordinary piece of Enthusiasm I ever heard of," Christopher French recorded in early March 1761 as Grant marched to the colonial camp at Congarees. "One of them," French continued,

> took it into his head to believe that he was God Almighty, or, at least equal to him, another said he was the Devil and desir'd he might be put to Death which was accordingly executed; a third these mad People seized & put between two feather Beds and smother'd him, 'tho they only intended to warm him saying he was come from the Moon & must, consequently, be very cold.[105]

Though this incident was downplayed by authorities as the work of a few deranged men, the Webber heresy appears to have been less a local anomaly than a broader movement related to German spiritual and political consciousness under the pressure of the Cherokee War. According to a Lutheran cleric who investigated the heresy, the message of Webber and his followers had spread "from South to North Carolina, thence to Maryland and Virginia among the German and English population," and even "left some seeds" in Charlestown.[106] The public hanging of Jacob Webber and his compatriots in Charlestown suppressed the movement by reminding Germans of the willingness of the English-speaking majority to act against them on ethnic grounds. A Moravian leader traveling in northwestern South Carolina attributed the reticence of German settlers during the late 1760s to this event: "I found several awaken'd souls who speak in their own words," he observed in a letter to Henry Laurens, "but the impression of Moses and Sinai appears more in their countenance than Christ and Golgotha; they are very timorous and shy on account of the affair of Jacob Webber and his associates."[107]

No one in Charlestown could escape ill-ease about other events. During May of 1761, Halley's Comet was overhead, and a large waterspout barely missed destroying ships anchored in the harbor. The *Gazette* recorded the unnerved Assembly's thanks to God for "miraculous interposition in diverting the course of a most formidable and complicated meteor, which, by its most direct

and sudden approach seemed to threaten us with immediate and sudden destruction."[108] Looking back to this perilous era nearly twenty years later, historian
Alexander Hewatt juxtaposed his account of the Grant campaign with celestial
disturbances, especially the "whirlwind." "As it approached the inhabitants
were alarmed with an uncommon sound . . . which brought number of people
to witness the dreadful phenomenon . . . the town narrowly and providentially
escaped."[109] The madness in the sky on the eve of the Grant campaign seemed
to confirm insanity on the ground. Natural disaster seemed to forebode social
peril.

The Colonists Under Grant's Command

James Grant mounted a spring offensive from the Congarees jumping-off
point. Discipline problems inherited from the Congaree camp led to the desertion of nearly 40 percent of the Carolina regiment by the time it reached Ninety-
Six.[110] A few British regulars also tried to flee; near Ewsaw Spring seven were
tried for desertion. Two were shot the night of their conviction "at the head of
the army."[111] Together under the general authority of Grant, with Middleton
commanding the provincial regiment and rangers, the troops continued to Keowee.
Like Montgomery, Grant chafingly ignored the colonial need for full partnership. Even Henry Laurens, who would later defend Grant in the controversy
that grew out of the expedition, would admit that "Col. Grant, 'tis true, does
say that he never consults anybody."[112] Grant, however, did seem willing to
give the colonial troops the benefit of the doubt in spite of their timidity at the
battle of Echoe.[113] His outlook toward the provincial soldiers serving under
him improved as the march progressed.

The combined force marched without opposition from white communities
to the Cherokee towns, past the landmarks of earlier conflict. Abandoned early
in the century, though recolonized from time to time, Saluda Old Town was
again empty: "an abandoned settlement and a pretty one."[114] On the road
beyond Fort Prince George, the town of Ocunnih showed signs of more recent
damage from another source—"destroyed by the Creeks," an officer wrote in
his journal. After Grant's troops had passed through, the Lower Towns and
most of the Middle Towns also were burned by the white troops, their stores
of corn and beans ruined. Grant's major bragged "we build our Wigwams of
the materials of the [Cherokee] Houses."[115] (Fig. 6)

Just beyond the site of the ambush of Montgomery's troops, a large body
of Cherokee warriors, perhaps the entire fighting population of the Middle Towns,
engaged the English force in the "Battle of Cowhowee."[116] Casualties on the
white side from the three-hour exchange on June 10 were substantial enough
to slow the army—ten men and officers killed and another fifty wounded. After
a twenty-four-hour march the army stopped at Noucassih. Here the "Town

House which is a large Dome, surrounded with resting places made of Kane & pretty enough . . . we converted into an Hospital.'' [117].

Frustrated by his inability to gain a clear victory, Grant pressed on. ''At three the army marched again toward Echoy, keeping [to] the mountains as the Road led to another pass.'' Echoe, where Montgomery had turned back, ''stands in a large plain commanded by Hills, this we tore to pieces and set fire to. Here we halted for about two Hours, when the Light Infantry, Royal and Burton's march'd to surprise a small town call'd Tase, 2 miles.'' After Echoe, with English casualties, the pitch of violence increased: ''I had orders to put every Soul to Death. I sent a platoon to each House but found them Deserted. We then march'd with Intentions to surprise Noucassih but found it deserted also.'' [118] Grant's order to ''put every Soul to Death'' represented an escalation from the Montgomery campaign, where some effort was made to shield women and children.

As Grant had nothing but contempt for what he regarded as his unsoldierly enemy, he provided a detailed chronicle of domestic destruction proficiently practiced, a narrative of bushels of corn destroyed and houses torn apart, but the satisfaction of direct engagement was missing. ''Destroying an Indian town may be credible,'' Grant himself admitted, ''but 'tis in fact a matter of no great consequence, where the savages have time to carry off their effects.'' [119] Ultimately, the terrain slowed the march and the troop ''near a thousand men . . . absolutely without shoes'' were forced to turn back. [120] In retrospect, the Cherokee Mountains impressed the veteran officers, who agreed that ''no such march was ever made by Troops . . . even those who had been at Pitsbourg . . . Colonel Grant declar'd our march was much worse than the passage of the Alps, which he had seen.'' [121]

After spending thirty-three days raising havoc in the Cherokee settlements, Grant turned around his troops. The Cherokees had quickly made peace overtures. An Overhill peace offer, carried by Little Carpenter to William Byrd (perhaps because of Little Carpenter's experience with negotiation in Virginia) was received while Grant was still on the march, but Byrd turned it away saying that it was more appropriately directed to the Carolinians. While these negotiations were proceeding, the Virginia force, finally bolstered by North Carolina reinforcements (including fifty Tuscarora warriors), refortified Fort Henry on the Long Island of the Holston and independently began to step up pressure on the Cherokees. [122]

The fall peace treaties signed by the Cherokees represented a compromise. The initiative taken by the Cherokees, and the ultimate acceptance by the colonists of much of their position, reflected both their negotiating skill and the contention within the British-colonial army. Grant demanded the execution of four Cherokee leaders, ''one or two from each of the main regions.'' [123] Further, Grant insisted that all vestiges of French alliance be erased and that the sovereignty of the English courts over offenders in the villages be recognized, and a line twenty-six miles east of Keowee be respected as the Carolina boundary. Though there were differences in the Virginia treaty, both Grant and Byrd confirmed Little Carpenter as Emperor, a political ploy designed after the precedent of Alexander Cuming's crowning of Moytoy, and accepted with the same indifference on the part of most Cherokees.

Though the other provisions were agreed to with little more than paper cost to the tribe, there was no compromise possible over the issue of hostages—something that the tribal negotiators could not compel their people to do. Henry Laurens watched the councils from the inside as the Cherokees successfully talked the English out of this clause, saying, "that they had talk'd and consider'd very much of it, they had look'd all round them and could not distinguish which should be the four persons to be put to death." [124] As a result of Little Carpenter's "very artful Speech which show'd they were by no means inclined to kill the four People requir'd of them," Grant conceded the point. [125] Instead, both sides would exchange. Against the urging of Middleton and the Commons House, the first revengeful article was dropped, beginning a long process of trading prisoners that was to take years to complete. Thus, Little Carpenter accepted Grant's terms in October, and made a separate peace with the Virginians. [126]

11

Postwar Colonial Society, 1761–1768

THE immediate aftermath of the three-year crisis found Carolina wrestling both with the unavoidable reflection on its wartime performance and with recovery. The evidence was far from reassuring on the old, sensitive issue of the colony's vulnerability. The smallpox epidemic had killed 650 people, 300 white and 350 black, 12 percent of the town's official population. There was little evidence that the steps taken by the authorities to control the spread of the disease, including inoculation, had been effective.[1] The record also showed an inability to cope with food shortage and the strain of suppressing domestic unrest by blacks and white minorities.

Moreover, the colony had been hobbled by the cost of the war and was struggling just to pay its bills. The Lyttelton expedition alone ("from which much greater things had been expected") had cost the colony 25,000 pounds sterling.[2] The long residence of the Provincial regiment at Congarees during the winter of 1760–61 and the staffing of the Ninety-Six and Fort Prince George garrisons had also been costly. Public debt incurred in the creation of the Provincial regiment and the Artillery company, in contributions to the British forces engaged in the campaign, and in the establishment of a "watch" in Charlestown was large and, for the most part, uncompensated by Britain.[3]

The war's end also saw a push for domestic legislation aimed at slowing the worrisome growth of South Carolina's black majority. The renewal of the Duty Act of 1751, which placed a surcharge on imported slaves, was heatedly discussed during the war and finally passed over British objections in 1764.[4] The previous decade had seen only a slight decline in the ratio, still nearly two to one, by which blacks outnumbered white colonists.[5] A letter writer to the *Gazette* offered the emerging lessons of war in support of a 1761 proposal to limit imports of slaves by reminding merchant and planter interests (which had long opposed the measure):

> I am not so old or so weak . . . as to suffer myself to be surrounded with fears and suspicions, or startled at distant dangers, yet I think our situation alarming; Heaven knows how our military capacity is not very great; and our numbers are so inconsiderable that should a general desecration happen, we might easily be served, as Gulliver did geese and turkies when he lived among the Liliputians.[6]

The letter appeared during Grant's march, and at the end of a flurry of discussions of the forced reliance of the colony on black forces ("trusty Negroes, good gun men") in support of its war effort, as provided for in the Militia Act. Other arguments for the import duty bill were less roundabout. Whites had seen their numbers diminished ("cruelly murdered by the Cherokee Indians"), and colonial forces had been stretched too thin, divided between the need to "defend their country against the encroachments and barbarities" of the Cherokees and the need to patrol the homefront.[7] Even while the bill was under public debate, the *Gazette* carried terse hints of danger. In mid-June, for instance, the editor reported the capture "of no fewer than 13 Negroes, several of whom were on horseback and one of them armed with a bayonet."[8]

The war had left a lingering sense of inadequacy and a growing impression that Carolina was, after all, a margin of the empire. British approbation had visited Carolina under William Henry Lyttelton and then faded away. The powerful British armies which had fought the conclusive battles to the north in Canada had stopped in Carolina as an afterthought, fought inconclusively, and were gone as quickly as they had come, sailing away to protect more vital British interests in the Caribbean.

Even more upsetting to the colony was the realization that this marginality was more than a private suspicion. There was to be no day in the sun for the Carolina elite.[9] A bitter status lesson was driven home as outsiders assigned Carolina its place in the proceedings of the war. The British press during and after the war tended to downplay the contribution of the colonists to the war effort. For instance, the official military history of the American theater of the Seven Years' War, published in 1769, must have been especially stinging in its careful attention to the hardships suffered by the Royal troops and its effusive congratulations to William Henry Lyttelton. Episodes relating the colonial side of the war focused on dramatic and, for the colony, embarrassing failures, such as the siege of Fort Loudoun. Much to their discomfort, the Carolina colonists were presented almost as victims in such postwar appraisals.

Also disconcerting were the press reports of the visit of three Cherokees to

London in the summer of 1762 to "pay their respects to the King of Great Britain, for whom they express the greatest veneration." [10] The four young warriors were cordially received by the Earl of Egremont, then the British Secretary of State, who wished to bolster ties with the tribe. [11] The warm reception by British officialdom was bested by the riotous greeting of London working people. Ten thousand people were reported to have waited at Vauxhall Garden to catch a sight of the Cherokees and inspired the Ministry to issue an order banning further excursions. [12]

For the South Carolinians, the reception shown their recent adversaries in London must have been viewed as another grating slight from home-country public opinion. The English press tended to blame the civil disturbances— drunkenness and pick-pocketing mainly—brought by the Cherokee visit, on their own citizenry. [13] However, the colonial press, if the remarks in the *Boston Gazette* are a guide, chose to condemn the Cherokees themselves and complained that the "Ministry is not a little embarrassed in regard to these Indians." [14] The war seemed to have advanced Cherokee, rather than Carolina, standing in the empire. And more was at stake than hurt feelings. British observers had found much to admire in Cherokee egalitarianism. On the arrival of the entourage the *London Chronicle* informed its readers that "the Cherokees are the most considerable Indian Nation with which we are acquainted and are absolutely free so that when we call any of their chiefs Princesses or Kings it is to accommodate their manners to our ideas." [15] (Fig. 7) The implicit praise given to Cherokee egalitarianism touched a nerve with Carolinians. While the Cherokees met with British ministers as equals to reaffirm the peace, the Carolinians were increasingly unsure of their own place within the empire—the Cherokee visit to London seeming to suggest that their own citizenship remained second-class—and perhaps wondered who really won the war.

Battles, Duels, and Debates

The issue of colonial standing and competence was replayed, in the most personal terms, just after the Grant campaign. The feud between James Grant and Thomas Middleton, the colonial commander, had actually begun on the march, after Grant arrived at the Congarees, when Middleton abruptly returned to Charlestown on the lame excuse of tending to business. Then, the colonial commander-in-absentia in a series of letters impugned the motives of the British commander. [16] Middleton publicly insulted Grant by writing in the *Gazette* that as far as he was concerned the "noble ends" of the campaign were less to humble the Cherokees than to embarrass "those petty Provincial Officers who have presumed to censure of the Conduct of the Commander of the Expedition." [17]

Grant remained in Charlestown after his troops moved on, and by December 1761 had challenged Middleton to a duel. He described the event in a letter to General Amherst:

> Upon my coming to Town after a Campaign of nine Months, I was insulted every time I appeared in the Streets, a trifling Accident has made everything Quiet & People in general begin to have a favorable Opinion of me, because I did an Idle thing, which you'll no doubt hear of, & I flatter myself will Excuse as it was attended with no bad Consequences and as I was under a sort of necessity of doing it. In short, the Provincial Colonel & I went out together & tho he had used me worse than any Man ever did another, I gave him his Life, when it was Absolutely in my Power.[18]

The political theme of the Grant-Middleton duel was picked up in a print war between two young Carolinians, veterans of the Cherokee War, Christopher Gadsden and Henry Laurens. Their debate, carried on in the coarsely printed pages of the Charlestown press during the early 1760s, disturbed the uncertain but valued "harmony" which was a motif of colonial South Carolina politics.[19] Laurens, using the pseudonym "Philolethes," urged Gadsden's "Philopatrios" to "repent of having officiously and busily taken upon himself so great a [role] in spreading the flames of party disputes to the total subversion of order and decency, the prejudice of the public and to the detriment of private families, persons, and characters."[20] However, Laurens's own replies to Gadsden, also riled the usually calm surface of Carolina politics.[21]

Their bitter exchange suggested the degree to which the war had sharpened issues relating to the rights and responsibilities of the British and the colonists. The Grant and Middleton duel fired the two commentators. Gadsden's "Philopatrios" indicted both Grant's supposed deceptions and tactical failures. Laurens defended the actions of the British command and strongly criticized Middleton's desultory leadership.[22] Unlike the colonials, according to Laurens, the British officers were "well acquainted with" all the different "ways," "systems," and "sciences of Fighting."[23]

It was, however, Gadsden's vehement voice which was heard most loudly in the debate over colonial ability in "sciences of Fighting." The commander of an artillery company formed in 1759, Gadsden had himself led new recruits into the mysteries of the most potent technology of warfare. The *Gazette* noted that the company was "so zealous . . . in what they have undertaken that there is already a Scarcity of Books upon Gunnery."[24] The re-training undertaken by British professionals under James Grant, who felt that such colonial self-education had fallen short, irritated Gadsden. In his "Second Letter of Philopatrios," he critiqued Grant's operation with a systematic analysis of time, motion, and destruction. The tabular format, borrowed from accounting, served to illustrate Gadsden's, and symbolically the colonial army's, competence in the business of war. (Fig. 8)

In this debate, issues of technical competence often fronted for arguments about control. For instance, Gadsden criticized Grant for usurping Montgomery's command. Gadsden thus pointed to a lack of principle among the *British* command of the Cherokee War. By arguing that the British commander himself had betrayed traditional, home country values, he signaled his own incipient political alienation. Eventually, Gadsden's rhetoric was to become both frankly anti-British and anti-Cherokee, with vehement postwar calls in the Assembly for retribution against the tribe.[25] Gadsden's reactionary turn away from allegiance to the crown was first impelled by the Cherokee War, a course that would eventually be paralleled by fellow colonists who had fought both wartime and postwar battles.

Class Identity and Young Charlestown Men

The lives of both Laurens and Gadsden were clearly marked by their experience in the Cherokee War, as were those of so many other colonial men. The initial recruitment for the Lyttelton campaign had netted many young members of prominent lowcountry society. Among the names of the Charlestown volunteers who had arrived at Congarees in addition to Gadsden were William Moultrie, Francis Marion, George Milligen, Thomas Middleton, Isaac Huger, Barnard Elliott, and Owen Roberts.[26] Many of these same men would later join the Revolution as prominent Whigs.

The Cherokee War thus served as a field school for young "military leaders"[27] with an impact on graduates far beyond the realm of tactics and training. One of the school's most important lessons had to do with class identity. The officers' ranks of the Artillery company and the Provincial regiment brought together upper-crust planters with Charlestown tradesmen, who together all advertised and conducted themselves similarly as "gentlemen of character and considerable property."[28] In tone, aspiration, and bearing (if not in strict occupational status) the Provincial regiment of 1759 was "silken."[29] In 1761, Grant's second-in-command was impressed with both the social standing of the Provincial officers and their earnest interest in warfare; "their officers," he wrote, "are Men of very considerable Property & give great application to their Military Profession." And as the same officer later noted, the £600 sterling per year paid to the Captain of even a troop of rangers made the campaign no financial hardship for the colonial officers.[30]

The South Carolina troops were also youthful and inexperienced. Henry Laurens, a commander in 1761, reflected on the collective experience which the campaigns had held for Charlestown's future leadership:

> scarcely one man in 50 under his command had ever seen the 'Cross Lines Legible' in a Cherokee face or heard one Gun fired in Anger. The Inferior

young officers were in General very young gentlemen. Many of them had not
travel'd beyond the clear'd land of Carolina & some hardly without the Gates
of Charlestown.[31]

There was innocence and enthusiasm for war among them. "During the war
with the Cherokees in 1761 and 1762," wrote Andrew Pickens, "I was young,
fond of a gun and active life and was much out in that war, and was intrusted
for some time with a small detachment of men on the frontier . . . I served as
a volunteer."[32] Another, a young officer from Virginia, joined the "company
of gentlemen," because "arms had been my delight from my infancy, and I
now resolved to gratify that inclination."[33]

The Cherokee War campaigns created a certain solidarity, especially among
the Carolinians—among these impressionable young men, solidarity developed
through marches and battles and through shared encounters beyond the "clear'd
land" of the city. Marching to the Cherokees these young men passed through
the red clay country, ethnically and economically distinct from the tightly controlled lowlands, and the homeland of many of the colonial conscripts. The
punishments—floggings, and executions—meted out by British and colonial
commanders to errant, mainly backcountry troops must have impressed the young
officers.[34] In fact, disdain for the backcountry and its people surfaced during the
war with new vehemence. Contemptuous words were heard in the Assembly:

> those back settlers or Rifle-men are a parcel of Riff-Raff. They are a collection
> from all the Northern provinces and care not a straw what Country they are
> in, & must be compel'd by severe Laws if we ever hope for any good from
> them. I know that within a Little time past since the Cherokees have been
> troublesome to us again, as many of those people have cross'd . . . the Pee-
> dee river & gone away to the Northward as there are Gun-men in the Cherokee
> Nation.[35]

Some postwar commentators found them worse than Cherokees. Even as
he put tribal villages to the torch, Henry Laurens emphasized that "we found
their habitations convenient and comfortable in every respect better entitled to
the name of Homes than hundreds that I have seen in the occupation of our
White Brethren, the backsettlers upon North and South Carolina."[36] Men such
as Laurens also found an affirmation of their self-importance in the behavior of
the Cherokees themselves, who tended to view only officers as accomplished
warriors and equals. The Cherokees "are extremely proud," wrote self-distin-
guished gentleman Henry Timberlake, "despising the lower class of Europeans, and in some athletic diversions I once was present at they refused to match
or hold conferences with any but officers."[37] With this sort of observation
developed a shared sense of class.

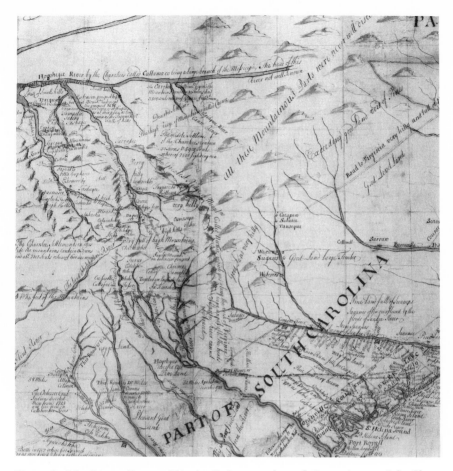

Figure 1. John Barnwell created his detailed map and population estimates of the Chero-kee villages by drawing on information from French and Carolina traders and missionary censuses. The "souls in all" reported in the Society for the Propogation of the Gospel figures were joined with other information and converted to "gunmen." Portion of John Barnwell's Map of Southern North America, 1721. Courtesy, Yale Center for British Art, Collection of Paul Mellon.

Figure 2. DeBry's engraving "Mode of Collecting Gold in the Streams Running from the Apalatcy Mountains" presented stylized, tropicalized indigenous laborers known from the Spanish entradas—*and perhaps from actual mining activities. 1591. Courtesy, Special Collections, New York Public Library.*

Figure 3. The Cherokee headmen who accompanied Alexander Cuming back to England in 1730 to affirm "Articles of friendship and Commerce" posed among exotic plants, including tobacco (on the left). The caption notes that they were clothed with "These Habits out of ye Royal Wardrobe . . . They were remarkably Strict in their Probity and Morality . . ." Courtesy, National Anthropological Archives, Smithsonian Institution.

Figure 4. "Charles Town the Metropolis," June 9, 1739. An engraving dedicated in later printings to James Glen, its view is reminiscent of secure Dutch harborscapes, exhibiting a commercial panorama, man-made relief along a flat coast. Just months after the engraving was issued, the Stono Rebellion would rock the serenity of the view. Courtesy, Winterthur Museum.

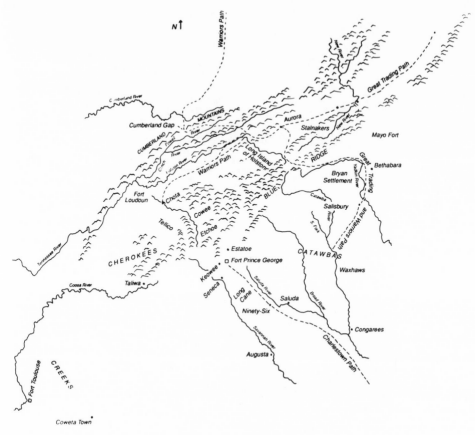

Figure 5. Map of the Middle and Cherokee Country during the 1750s.

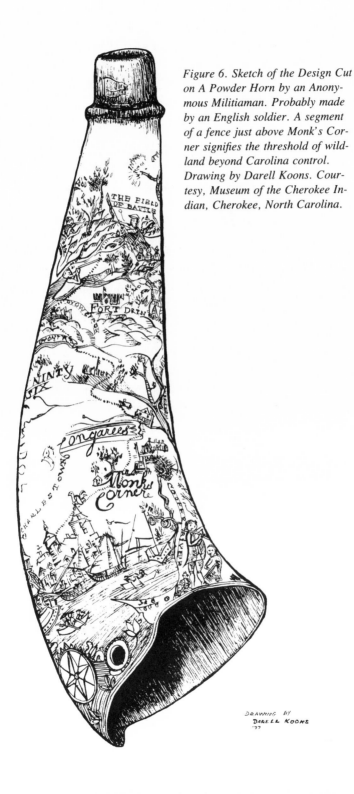

Figure 6. Sketch of the Design Cut on A Powder Horn by an Anonymous Militiaman. Probably made by an English soldier. A segment of a fence just above Monk's Corner signifies the threshold of wildland beyond Carolina control. Drawing by Darell Koons. Courtesy, Museum of the Cherokee Indian, Cherokee, North Carolina.

Figure 7. This 1762 engraving, which in separate versions appeared in two London magazines, Royal *and* British, *depicted "Austenaco, Commander in Chief of the Cherokee Nation," in court regalia. Courtesy, National Anthropological Archives, Smithsonian Institution.*

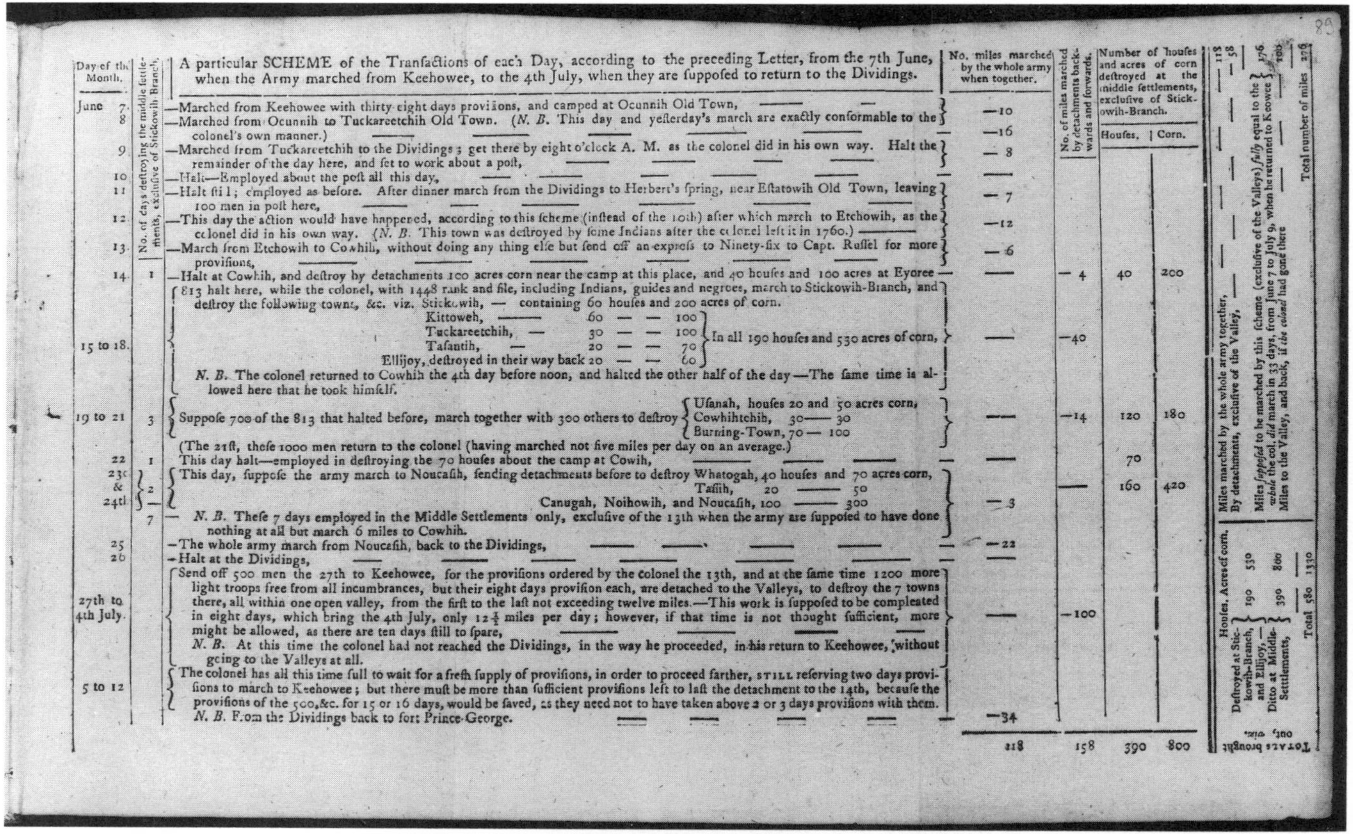

Day of the Month.	No. of days destroying the middle settlements, exclusive of Stickowih Branch.	A particular SCHEME of the Transactions of each Day, according to the preceding Letter, from the 7th June, when the Army marched from Keehowee, to the 4th July, when they are supposed to return to the Dividings.	No. miles marched by the whole army when together.	No. of miles marched by detachments backwards and forwards.	Number of houses and acres of corn destroyed at the middle settlements, exclusive of Stickowih-Branch. Houses.	Corn.
June 7.		—Marched from Keehowee with thirty-eight days provisions, and camped at Ocunnih Old Town,	—10			
8		—Marched from Ocunnih to Tuckareetchih Old Town. (*N. B.* This day and yesterday's march are exactly conformable to the colonel's own manner.)	—16			
9.		—Marched from Tuckareetchih to the Dividings; get there by eight o'clock A. M. as the colonel did in his own way. Halt the remainder of the day here, and set to work about a post,	— 8			
10		—Halt—Employed about the post all this day,	—			
11		—Halt still; employed as before. After dinner march from the Dividings to Herbert's spring, near Estatowih Old Town, leaving 100 men in post here,	— 7			
12.		—This day the action would have happened, according to this scheme (instead of the 10th) after which march to Etchowih, as the colonel did in his own way. (*N. B.* This town was destroyed by some Indians after the colonel left it in 1760.)	—12			
13.		—March from Etchowih to Cowhih, without doing any thing else but send off an express to Ninety-six to Capt. Russel for more provisions,	— 6			
14.	1	—Halt at Cowhih, and destroy by detachments 100 acres corn near the camp at this place, and 40 houses and 100 acres at Eyoree	—	— 4	40	200
15 to 18.		813 halt here, while the colonel, with 1448 rank and file, including Indians, guides and negroes, march to Stickowih-Branch, and destroy the following towns, &c. viz. Stickowih, — containing 60 houses and 200 acres of corn. Kittoweh, — 60 — — 100; Tuckareetchih, — 30 — — 100; Tasantih, — 20 — — 70; Ellijoy, destroyed in their way back 20 — — 60 } In all 190 houses and 530 acres of corn. *N. B.* The colonel returned to Cowhih the 4th day before noon, and halted the other half of the day—The same time is allowed here that he took himself.	—	—40		
19 to 21	3	Suppose 700 of the 813 that halted before, march together with 300 others to destroy { Usanah, houses 20 and 50 acres corn, Cowhihtchih, 30— 30, Burning-Town, 70— 100 }. (The 21st, these 1000 men return to the colonel (having marched not five miles per day on an average.)	—	—14	120	180
22	1	This day halt—employed in destroying the 70 houses about the camp at Cowih,	—		70	
23d & 24th	2	This day, suppose the army march to Noucasih, sending detachments before to destroy Whatogah, 40 houses and 70 acres corn, Tassih, 20 — 50, Canugah, Noihowih, and Noucasih, 100 — 300	— 3	—	160	420
	7	— *N. B.* These 7 days employed in the Middle Settlements only, exclusive of the 13th when the army are supposed to have done nothing at all but march 6 miles to Cowhih.				
25		—The whole army march from Noucasih, back to the Dividings,	—22			
26		—Halt at the Dividings,	—			
27th to 4th July.		Send off 500 men the 27th to Keehowee, for the provisions ordered by the colonel the 13th, and at the same time 1200 more light troops free from all incumbrances, but their eight days provision each, are detached to the Valleys, to destroy the 7 towns there, all within one open valley, from the first to the last not exceeding twelve miles.—This work is supposed to be compleated in eight days, which bring the 4th July, only $12\frac{1}{2}$ miles per day; however, if that time is not thought sufficient, more might be allowed, as there are ten days still to spare, *N. B.* At this time the colonel had not reached the Dividings, in the way he proceeded, in his return to Keehowee, without going to the Valleys at all.	—	—100		
5 to 12		The colonel has all this time full to wait for a fresh supply of provisions, in order to proceed farther, STILL reserving two days provisions to march to Keehowee; but there must be more than sufficient provisions left to last the detachment to the 14th, because the provisions of the 500, &c. for 15 or 16 days, would be saved, as they need not to have taken above 2 or 3 days provisions with them. *N. B.* From the Dividings back to fort Prince-George.	—34			
			118	158	390	800

TOTALS brought out, *viz.*

	Houses.	Acres of corn.
Destroyed at Stickowih-Branch, and Ellijoy, —	190	530
Ditto at Middle-Settlements,	390	800
Total	580	1330

Miles marched by the whole army together,	118
By detachments, exclusive of the Valley,	58
Miles *supposed* to be marched by this scheme (exclusive of the Valleys) *fully* equal to the *whole* the col. *did* march in 33 days, from June 7 to July 9, when he returned to Keowee	176
Miles to the Valley, and back, if *the colonel* had gone there	100
Total number of miles	276

Figure 8. *Christopher Gadsden's tabular rebuttal of James Grant's claim to military efficiency: "A Particular Scheme of the Transactions of each Day . . . from the 7th June, when the Army marched from Keehowee, to the 4th July, when they are supposed to return to the Dividings." Courtesy, Beinecke Rare Book and Manuscript Library, Yale University.*

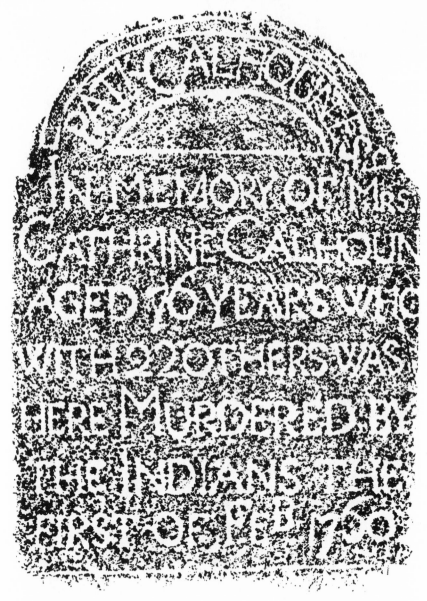

Figure 9. Memorial to Mrs. Cathrine Calhoun and the Long Cane Massacre Victims. Erected by Patrick Calhoun, ca. 1761.

Figure 10. General Andrew Pickens, ca. 1800. Pickens, born in Paxton County, Pennsylvania, in 1739, died at "Hopewell on the Keowee" in 1817. Courtesy, South Caroliniana Library, University of South Carolina.

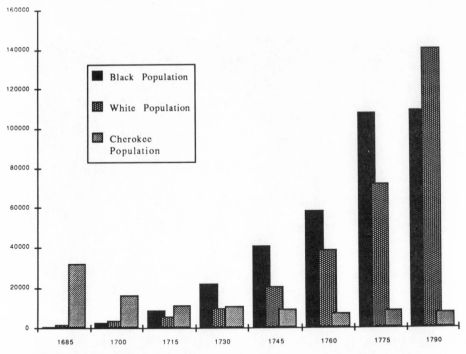

Figure 11. Estimated Cherokee and South Carolina (Black and White) Populations, 1685–1790.

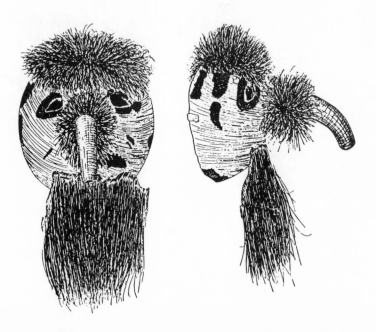

Figure 12. Gourd Booger Mask Representing a White Man. From Cherokee Dance and Drama *by Frank G. Speck and Leonard Broom. New edition copyright © 1983 by the University of Oklahoma Press.*

The colony's gentlemen officers shut the door not only to their fellow colonists but also to the British command. And this development had external manifestations. During the Cherokee campaign the young Carolinian men had ambivalently borrowed from the styles of both the British and the Cherokees. The colonial officers of the Carolina company or Virginia's "Patriot Blues" had achieved the appearance of solidarity—through uniforms, equipage, and other trappings—and thus created a separate identity from that of the English troops.[38] A small but highly visible minority had expressed its own political distinctiveness from its British commanders by mimicking the dress of its adversaries. In an expedition from Fort Prince George in 1760, nearly seventy of the 550 colonial rangers "left their horses, desiring to go on foot, in a light Indian hunting dress."[39] The colonial-Chickasaw force which joined the Montgomery campaign included thirteen white men "dressed and painted like Indians," and another similar contingent was along with Grant.[40] Even after the war, Thomas Sumter, a member of the Patriot Blues who had accompanied Henry Timberlake and four Cherokee leaders to England in 1762, disembarked on his return "dressed in scarlet," the badge of a warrior, like his indigenous fellow-travellers.[41]

While only a few colonial men actually made this flamboyant fashion statement, others admired its connotations. The dress of southeastern warriors was a statement of virility, and such display was part of the folklore of the warrior prevailing in colonial society. "They have a great aversion to the wearing of breeches," James Adair wrote about the tribal men, "for to that custom they affix the idea of helplessness and effeminacy . . . the Indian women discreetly observe that, as all their men sit down to make water, the ugly breeches would exceedingly incommode them; and that, if they were allowed to wear breeches, it would portend no good to their country."[42] Dressing for war with a hunting shirt rather than a uniform had little to do with frontier egalitarianism. Rather, it enhanced for some a provincial identity separate from the British and from the riff-raff in their own army.

And the manhood of the colonial troops became an issue after the war. The first two campaigns had raised questions about their courage; in one of the few newspaper reports published from the Montgomery expedition, Grant had reported that the backcountry rangers had run away from the Cherokees at the battle of Echoe. Later, Grant would report that the colonial rangers "seem now to despise the Indians, as much as they were suspected to fear them before." Grant made these remarks in a letter which was, much to the chagrin of colonial partisans such as Gadsden, reprinted in the London newspapers.[43] Even though Grant later complimented the conduct of the colonial regiment in his final expedition, the sting remained.[44]

Strong Women and Proud Victims

The war left Carolina's elite uncertain about more than just their own society. It also reshaped the colonial image of the Cherokees. The manner of this reshaping suggests a conflicted, simultaneous cultural embrace and personal rejection of Cherokee warriorhood. Postwar reflections, newspaper reports, and imaginative accounts of the wartime action also indicate a deeper cultural ambivalence toward indigenous women, and by implication, toward colonial women as well.

The young men who had engaged the Cherokees knew their enemy mainly through the popular natural histories, almanacs, and newspaper accounts. All of these sources emphasized the strong position of women in Cherokee society.[45] And the surviving print sources may mirror a more widespread but unrecorded oral tradition, in which Cherokee women were viewed simultaneously as attractive and threatening to white men. These women could take care of themselves; a telling contrast to the newspaper sloganeering—"Ladies too should be our cause"—which had launched the first Carolina campaign against the Cherokees.

A view of tribal women as both sexually easy and at the same time dangerously domineering in tribal marriages pervaded colonial "natural histories" and travel accounts and also appeared in more widely disseminated print forms, such as almanacs and immigration tracts. For instance, John Tobler's German-language pamphlet, published in 1754 in South Carolina at the height of German migration into the backcountry, devoted a section to Tobler's tribal neighbors at New Augusta. Tobler recounted that Indian men were often jealous of their women's extramarital activities (if helpless to control them) since "their women are very desirous of new fare . . . the women do not stay all the time with one man . . . in old age their temperament grows cold in other respects."[46] According to this view, tribal women, while willing sexual partners for their men, possessed a freedom that could chill even warriors.

Bits of news from the front reported in the colonial press suggest that village women began to trouble the colonists by challenging proper authority. During the siege of Fort Loudoun in the Cherokee War in 1760, female farmers willingly sold their corn to the colonial garrison for ribbon and other goods. When the headman Willenawa, hostile to the whites, threatened the women with death, they simply laughed and "boldly told him, they would succour their husbands every day, and were sure, that, if he killed them, their relations would make his death atone for theirs."[47] (Eventually, the frustrated warrior attempted to hide the corn in order to keep it from reaching the enemy.[48]) Facing white troops, women showed the same spirit. Like captive warriors, they remained confident even in the face of death; "it is to be observ'd," wrote Grant's Captain, "that the Sqwa we brought to Camp Smil'd at us even when she must have expected to be put to Death every Instant."[49]

Both during and after the Cherokee War, colonial participants began to question the political legitimacy of Cherokee women. Henry Laurens expressed hostility toward Cherokee women who by "their own natural treachery and deceitfulness create jealousy and suspicion of other people."[50] Christopher Gadsden carried the generalization even further; "the Cherokees," Gadsden wrote, "are known to despise their wenches, and disregard all they say."[51]

A rumor afoot among the towns during the Grant campaign suggests that Cherokee men were themselves startled by this newly articulated prejudice. The news troubling the villagers was that Grant had built "two strong houses, in which he designed to confine all the Cherokees that should come there on their way to town, their Men in one apartment and the Women in the other; so that they should neither go up nor down the Country, and more such stuff as this!"[52] The metaphor is important here. The image of confinement, isolating men and women, voiced fears that at least one of the military objectives of their neighbors was to forcibly break up the equality at the root of Cherokee domestic relationships. Attakullakulla underscored the same point less figuratively during a peace council in which no women were present among the colonial negotiators: "White men as well as red were born of Women," and he "desired to know if that was not the Custom of the White People also," to admit their women into the Council. Governor Lyttelton answered later that "The White Men do place a Confidence in their Women and share their Counsels with them when they know their Hearts to be Good."[53]

The way that men such as Gadsden, Laurens, and others misread the context of Cherokee male-female relations is less striking than the intensity of their misconstrual. Expressing contempt for tribal women themselves and searching for validation in the opinions of Cherokee men, they soothed their own anxieties. Women were often victimized by red and white men alike during the war, and colonial observation of and participation in these acts served, they believed, to show the weakness of "petticoat government."

However, the postwar period saw old anxieties reemerge, sometimes closer to heart and home. In one incident a white woman taken hostage by the tribe in the raids which sparked the 1759 campaign seemed to have "become so habituated to the Indian manners," that she refused to return to the English with a group of other captives after her ransom had been paid. "Among those prisoners," Henry Timberlake wrote in his account in *Gentleman's Magazine,* "was also a woman whose husband had been murdered and who had afterward married his murderer. The Indian though reluctant, was disposed to comply with the terms of the treaty, but she absolutely refused to return with her countrymen."[54] This woman had made her own choice in Cherokee fashion and thus disturbed the basic sanctity of marriage. Her betrayal in marrying her husband's killer was both familial and cultural. She had turned her back not only on her husband's memory but also on her society.

The high profile of Cherokee women during the Cherokee War brought to the breaking point a long standing tension in colonial attitudes toward native American women. On the one hand, such women were viewed as sexually receptive and free in fantasized natural history accounts. On the other, women appeared to some colonial men as dangerous controllers of matrimony and as alarming women warriors. Juxtaposed against white images of their own domestic relations, imagination and selective vision were turned by the war toward deeper issues of male competence and control within Carolina society.

Cooks of Hell

This cross-cultural tension was reflected in the first captivity story proper to emerge from the Cherokee War. While such fictionalized narratives were common in New England, in the Southeast they never constituted a "distinct literary genre." The New England captivity story was by and large a woman's form—with female captives, victims and heroines—with themes of wilderness, sexual threat, individual faith and striving.[55] However, the captivity story told by David Menzies, a surgeon connected with the Lyttelton expedition, substituted a male protagonist and victim. Instead of a helpless woman, a man was captured by the tribe and faced the hostility of a Cherokee woman. Though "A true Relation of the unheard of Sufferings of DAVID MENZIES, Surgeon, among the CHEROKEES, and of his Surprising Deliverance"[56] was not published until 1778, accompanied by a long essay by Alexander Kellet, the themes of gender, sex, and power which run through Menzies's narrative are consistent with the changing colonial view of tribal life just after the war. Its Cherokee War setting is significant, for the Menzies story is a leading indicator of a changing popular consciousness in the decades after the war.

In the story, Menzies, who had been captured during a trip to northwest Georgia to treat "a gang of Negroes," reports that he was able to speak some Cherokee, though this failed to exempt him from torture. Menzies begins his story with his introduction to the "chief's mother,"

> at which I was overjoyed, as knowing that I thereby had a chance not only of being secured from death and torture, but even of good usage and caresses. I perceived however that I had over-rated much my matter of consolation as soon as I was introduced to this mother of heroes. She sat squat on the ground with bear's cub in her lap as nauseous a figure as the accumulated infirmities of decrepitude, undisguised by art, could make her.

Instead of courteously inviting her captive to replace by adoption her slain child, the woman "fixed first her blood-shot haggard eyes upon me, then riveting them to the ground, gargled through her throat my rejection and destruction." Menzies was "larded" with fat and roasted and brought "stark naked before a large fire,'' but, luckily, the torturer, "the diabolical heroine," became intoxicated and fell asleep long enough for an escape to Augusta. Menzies reported that he afterwards lived with a "paralytic complaint" on the roasted left side of his face.[57]

This story plays upon surprise at the inventiveness of the torture—worse than the unexpected tomahawk blow—and thereby offers something new to readers worn out with stale reports of conventional mistreatment. More important, however, is the dramatic sexualized depiction of the barbarity of Cherokee women. In this way, Menzies plays on earlier and more favorable images. At the point at which he understands that his fate is to be decided by a Beloved Woman, he believes that he has a "chance not only of being secured from death . . . but even of good usage and caresses." This image of the seductive woman, however, is pushed aside; Menzies has "over-rated [his] matter of consolation." The reality, he reports, is of a desexualized and grotesque female.[58] Menzies's Indian-hating could be discounted if it did not involve woman hating. The connection between the two provides a clue to the shaping of colonial images of women—white and black as well as red.

Like Cherokee women, but for different reasons, upper-class white Charlestown ladies were often presented as off-limits, not unattractive but either diffident wives or somehow properly distant from men. As in other aspects of cultural uncertainty, upper-class colonial men looked for signals in the lives of indigenous men to validate their own choices. During treaty negotiations in the South Carolina Council chambers, a group of Creek headmen encountered "some ladies" watching from the adjoining room. "We saw," the correspondent reported, "that beauty strikes, even upon savages, as one of these kings, advancing to take the ladies by the hand, according to Indian custom, made a sort of retreat and expressed himself so particularly as to say that *he was sensible he was not made to touch such things as these.*"[59] While colonial ladies could not be touched by native American men, tribal women were being roughly handled by their colonial counterparts.

The fragments of comment and evidence which survive suggest that the images of colonial and Amerindian women were evolving together. In effect, both were becoming unapproachable: white, upper-class colonial women because of their progressive elevation and tribal women because of their increasingly negative stereotype. At the same time, the reputation of Cherokee men after the war was becoming heightened, at least in England. A bawdy song published during the tour of the Cherokee warriors in 1763 seems to suggest that Englishmen had a new respect, and even anxiety, concerning the sexual threat posed by the Cherokees to their domain. Portions of the "Song on the Cherokee Chiefs Inscribed to the Ladies of Great Britain" follows:

What a piece of work's here, and a d——d Botheration
Of three famous Chiefs from the Cherokee Nation

The Ladies, dear Creatures, so squeamish and dainty
Surround the Great Canada Warriors in plenty . . .
Declaring no Englishman e'er kiss'd so well, Sir . . .

Ye females of Britain, so wanton and witty,
Who love even Monkies and swear they are pretty
The Cherokee Indian and stranger Shimpanzeys

By turns, pretty Creatures, have tickl'd your Fancies . . .

For weapons ye Fair, you've no need to petition
Nor weapons you'll want for this odd Expedition
A soft female Hand, the best weapon I wean is
To strip down the Bark of a Cherokee P——s
Courageous advance then, each fair English Tarter
Scalp the Chiefs of the Scalpers and give them no Quarter.[60]

However exaggerated, these British views suggest a shifting popular consciousness of the Cherokees and, by implication, of other indigenous peoples.
While the newspaper-reading colonial elite carefully followed the home-country
mood, postwar changes in vernacular word usages also suggest a parallel and
deeper shift in the colonies. During the first half of the eighteenth century,
Cherokee and other tribal women were lumped together with lower-class white
women and black women under the generic term wench. The sexual licentiousness which this label often implied had less to do with racial or ethnic than
with crude class boundaries. On the one hand, "countrywomen"—red, white,
or black—were presented as promiscuous partners; "in all companies where-
soever I have been my country women have always the praise for their activity
of Hipps," a letter to the *Gazette* explained.[61] After the 1760s wench was more
and more supplanted in the Southeast with the derogatory ethnically-specific
label of squaw. An Algonquian word more commonly in use in New England
since colonization, the word squaw separated out native American women for
special distaste on both racial and ethnic grounds, without the class connotations of sexual attractiveness or openness often associated with the term wench.
For instance, during his encounter in 1768 with the villagers of the Middle
Towns, Josiah Wedgwood's clay-prospector had made no remark about the
attractiveness of Cherokee wenches; instead, he jotted down his disgust at the
sight of "old Squaws and young Naked Vipers" in the town.[62] By the 1770s
squaw rather than wench was increasingly the popular label of choice.

The Unfinished Cherokee War

The Carolinians had faced their own shortcomings in the battles of the
Cherokee War and in the series of indecisive treaties yielded by the three ex-

peditions. While they could not change what had happened, they could argue over its interpretation. Sometimes this took a straightforward course as facts were dueled over, redrafted in Gadsden's chart of the Grant campaign, or selectively forgotten. For instance, when William Bartram reached the Cherokee country in 1775 he set down in his journal what he had heard in Charlestown about the war: "the Cherokees were vanquished and compelled to sue for peace by General Middleton, commander of the Carolinian auxiliaries acting against them."[63] In fact, Middleton had remained in Charlestown while the British troops, with the assistance of the colonists, had burned the Cherokee towns. Ten years later Alexander Hewatt also revised Cherokee War era estimates of the performance of the colonial militia in a favorable way. "All white men," he wrote, "were soldiers as well as citizens . . . ready for defense, not only against the incursions of Indians, but also against the insurrection of negroes."[64]

The Cherokee War was traumatic not only because it revealed the embarrassing military and financial weaknesses of the colony but also because it decisively challenged several public myths. One of these regarded the Cherokees. James Glen often expressed his belief in a special relationship between Carolina and the Cherokees in familial imagery. Glen observed that while in the early years of the colony the Cherokees

> have always called the governors of Carolina Brother . . . some years ago they altered that title; this was not done rashly but upon mature deliberation, and then they agreed to give him the title of father saying that they looked upon themselves to be as much as the children of the Great King George.[65]

However, the three years had reawakened a painful sense of betrayal by both the Cherokees and the British.[66] When George II died during the Montgomery campaign, the Council voted words of affection for the late king and uneasiness for the increasingly exposed position of the colony: "it is our greatest consolation in this time of public calamity, to reflect on the goodness and fatherly protection of our most gracious SOVEREIGN."[67] But even while this resolution was being adopted, Charlestown felt left in the dark by Montgomery and the Assembly was testing the protection of the British father by balking at increasing the pay of the Provincial regiment as requested by the governor.

The Carolinians could claim to have won the war, at least in marginal terms; Charlestown, after all, had not been burned as had many Cherokee towns. And outside of the arena of facts, the skirmishes of the war continued to play in the imaginations of the generation of colonials who had participated, as leaders or rank and file, in the three marches. Like herringbone brickwork in a wall, the war mortared a pattern of opposing images into memory: freeman:slave; father:son; husband:wife; wench:lady; warrior:officer; farmer:planter—

these and other pairings constituted the tense masonry foundation on which future political events would be constructed.

Because both British-colonial and British-Cherokee relationships were expressed and understood in terms of family relationships of father, son, and wife, the working out of these conflicts, as well as the varied postwar literature of the Cherokee War, often reflected these terms.[68] After the war colonial men continued to shadow box with their remembered impressions of Cherokee society by elevating and appropriating the image of the warrior while at the same time cutting away at the earlier and more positive buttressing images of the civic and domestic roles of tribal women. If even Cherokee warriors could be conquered by their women, then whites, especially the slaveholding elite of the colony, had to fight harder for control in the household and on the plantation. While Cherokee and other indigenous women had been presented in the past as inviting sexual beings, and colonists had always been aware that political and domestic freedom accompanied their sexual liberty, after the war the risks became too great even for fantasies of contact. The new image of Cherokee women provided no threat in the Carolina view to either their own warriors or the colonial men who had admired the prowess of their indigenous counterparts.

Not just military competence, but the ability of colonial society to control its own—families, allies, patrons, and by implication, its slaves—had been tested during the war. And the results were largely unreassuring. As a consequence, a generation of colonial men continued to fight for years. The issue was fought directly in political debates and duels as well as obliquely, using the image of Cherokee society and domestic relations as a kind of mirror in which the appearance of colonial society could be safely examined or criticized. But, all in all, the results were as inconclusive as the Cherokee War itself.

12

The Cherokee Village World in Crisis and in Recovery

THE war left stories of great suffering in the Cherokee towns. Postwar eye-witness accounts by white visitors are scarce; the Cherokees were themselves silent for the most part, with a silence that suggests the outsized scale of suffering in the towns and the inwardness of the struggle for recovery.[1] After the war, when questions were raised in South Carolina about whether the Cherokees had been punished enough, even Henry Laurens was moved to correct those who argued that simply burning village houses and corn had no effect on the tribe. Laurens sarcastically asked Christopher Gadsden if he believed "that the Indians were like Tortoises carrying their houses upon their backs," and added that their "women and children are as susceptible . . . of injury from inclemency of the weather as ours are."[2]

Laurens also gave a picture of a ragged starved landscape along Grant's march when the

> subsistence of at least one half of the Nation [was] rooted up and cut off. Their situation was bad enough before this, which we could discover from the meagre countenances of those who came in & surrendered to us at Fort Prince George. These creatures had been reduced to live for a considerable time upon old-Acorns, a food that we know will barely keep Hogs alive & and their hunger was so pinching that some of them were detected in grabbling up the grains of Corn and beans after they were planted around the Fort of which

several officers were witnesses. And also from the Offals of mangled Horses, slaughtered for their provision upon the path, & in all their Towns as we went along.[3]

For a decade, the upcountry between Carolina and the Cherokee settlements had been a bloody borderland, "the Indian Flanders of America."[4] This prelude weakened Cherokee defenses against the colonial armies of 1759–61. The damage done was more than the sum of the parts, more than the number of burned bushels of corn reported in English diaries. The disasters of the period possessed the destructive synergism of the crisis years of European peasant history, as the four horsemen of Euroamerican folklore visited the mountain towns. Poor harvests in the drought-ridden spring of 1759 had set the stage for smallpox, measles, and dysentery, all striking the Lower Towns as a deadly ensemble.[5] The fall of the following year, when harvests continued poor, saw several western towns depopulated by "a violent disorder in their stomach and a flux."[6] Nor were the Upper Creek Towns, at least some of which were acting in consort with the Cherokees, able to supply the bands of Cherokees who came for food. The English camp would learn that in the Creek villages a "blanket of Strouds," a valuable trade item, bought only nine ears of corn.[7]

The Cherokees were on the run, their towns abandoned or resettled at great cost. The women and children of Tussih Old Town, for example, moved seventy miles on foot to a new location out of the way of the Virginia expedition.[8] Recovery was not easy; it would take time to reclaim life. The grim staccato prose of James Grant's military reports during the summer of 1761 suggests the length of the road back. In a concluding entry Grant totaled up his results: "fifteen towns and all the plantations in the country have been burnt—about 1,400 acres of corn, beans, pease, etc., destroyed; about 5,000 people, including men, women and children drove into the woods and mountains to starve."[9] Many of the Lower Towns Cherokees fled their homes after the Lyttelton expedition and the smallpox epidemic. By the winter of 1761, a minority of these fugitives had returned to still occupied village sites to begin preparations for planting. Grant labeled these people "Neutral Cherokees,"[10] but their neutrality was forced by hunger rather than politics. In light of economic disruption, smallpox, and bullets, simply staying alive must have taken all the energy of the tribe. James Grant expecting head-on confrontation was, except for the ambush near Cowee, disappointed. The Cherokees, Grant wrote, did not really "deserve the name of enemy."[11]

War, Recovery, and Postwar Animosities

The political and personal effects of the war—as inseparable for the Cherokees as for any people—were to have repercussions long afterwards. In order to understand the war's legacy, the impact of the war must be probed from several different points of view, from Cherokee gardens as well as council houses. The manner in which the towns were drawn into the war was itself a factor not only in determining the pattern of hostilities but also in shaping diplomacy in the aftermath. The Cherokee War was from the beginning initiated on the Cherokee side by the raiding of specific families who wished to recoup the losses of relatives suffered through Cherokee participation as allies of the colonies in the campaigns of the late 1750s. Where Creeks and their French relatives urged warfare, fuel was added, but still the fire remained slow until the Lyttelton campaign. The killing of the Cherokee headmen at Fort Prince George distributed the burden of retribution for lost kin through nearly every Cherokee village.

While some towns—especially Chota, Tellico and Estatoe—sponsored hostile actions early on, others were quite firmly against attacking the English.[12] James Adair believed that in 1759 this crisis of decision had pushed the Cherokees almost to "a very hot civil war," and that the English by reacting too swiftly had lost an opening to gain the alliance of the remaining friendly towns, even in the Overhill, the center of anti-Carolina feeling. "There were seven northern [Overhill] towns," Adair counted, "opposite to the middle parts of the Cherokee country, "who from the beginning of the unhappy grievances firmly dissented from the hostile intentions."[13] Lyttelton, by imprisoning many Lower Towns leaders, sent a signal across the hills that he would treat his potential allies as slaves, and lost the political opportunity to sway the undecided.

The rapid dispatch of Lyttelton's troops in 1759 had taken the towns by surprise. After Lyttelton's withdrawal, business quickly returned to usual in some towns. The *Gazette* optimistically reported "good hunts" during the fall of 1760.[14] The successful hunters perhaps assumed that the objectives of the English war were as limited as their own and that once the transactions of revenge were over, normal relations would resume. The provisions of the treaty finally made by the colonists were mild; the Lyttelton column in retreat looked reassuringly like the disordered columns which the Cherokee auxiliaries had observed with contempt two years before in the north. All of this added to the Cherokees' surprise at the eventual turn of events.

Equally important to the village confusion was the fact that between 1759 and 1761 Cherokee defenses were not fully focused on the Carolinians. In addition to smallpox and famine, the villages faced simultaneous attacks from other quarters which prevented a coherent opposition to the English. Events along the Creek border created insecurities among the Cherokees. Even though the Upper Creek faction headed by The Mortar had courted them, awareness of the growing and potentially hostile Creek population to the south still stayed with the tribe.[15] During Montgomery's approach to the Lower Towns, the town of Keowee was abandoned and open to colonial advance partially because the Cherokees themselves were bracing for attacks from the Creeks.

Countering these fears were promises of cooperation against Carolina from the French and their allies. The French-aligned Creek faction, centered on Fort Toulouse, participated in (and perhaps even, led) events such as the 1759 back-country raids and the murder of the Fort Loudoun troops.[16] However, French promises of assistance, made before the war to sympathetic Cherokee town leaders, never materialized.[17] While colonial diplomatic and military actions hampered the French, the Cherokees hostile to Carolinia were nevertheless an-gered by this breach of promise, and on the Creek side, probably sensed a continuing indifference of the majority to their cause.[18]

No Creek involvement was better than a return to confrontation, particularly when, as the war progressed, the Cherokees found themselves involved in a multi-front war on the north and west. It was behind the mountains, out of sight of British intelligence sources, that the long conflict between the Chero-kees and the Six Nations flared up. The small contingent of Tuscarora, Ca-tawba, Mowhawk, and "Stockbridge," or Mahikan, warriors that marched with James Grant were the standard bearers of hostilities with other northern tribes which had started up again in the 1750s,[19] catalyzed by the conflict between the French and English and their indigenous allies in the theater of war that stretched from Canada to Virginia. This second front was costly to the Chero-kees; after the encounter with Montgomery's troops at Echoe, newspaper ac-counts reported that the "greatest loss the Cherokees have sustained has been in skirmishes to the Northward, where they have suffered much."[20]

The presence of tribal allies along on the Grant expedition triggered a new round of retributive warfare between the northern and western tribes and the Cherokees.[21] Raiding was to continue at a damaging pitch through the sixties, so much so that the colonists found a kind of reassurance in the hardships of their former enemy: "Cherokee gentry continue as humble as slaves," Henry Laurens wrote a fellow veteran of the conflict, "for the Northern Indians are making inroads and scalping them every day."[22]

The era after these wars saw a new focus but not new rules for Cherokee diplomacy. Shocked by the tactics in house- and corn-burning and hostage-taking, all counter to their rules of war, the Cherokees grew increasingly wary of the English. Relations with Carolina, once treated as one of many equal routes of political contact between the Cherokees and other peoples, closed down. The words of Cherokee leader Oconostota as he admonished his com-panions in council to "take particular care of your behavior toward this the English who we must look upon as ourselves; they have the French and Spanish to fight, and we enough of our own colour without meddling with either na-tion," reflected a new kind of isolationism.[23]

For the rebuilding decade of the 1760s, a similar restraint seems to have marked Cherokee relations with the Creeks, who like the Cherokees also shared the backcountry with Carolina. The Cherokees turned away calls for alliance which issued from the anti-Carolina Creek factions just after the conclusion of the Cherokee War. The Cherokees apparently refused to join the "game of ball" and cooperate with the Creeks in a series of proposals for "confederacy" against the colonies.[24] After the Congress held by the Southern Indian Department at Augusta in 1763, the Cherokees determined to remain quiet.[25] Prolonged conflict with the Six Nations and tribes further west in the Ohio Valley may have prevented the Cherokees from joining a pan-tribal groundswell in the north. While James Grant was marching away from the Cherokee villages, the first reports of Pontiac's organizing surfaced with news of trouble stirring at Sandusky.[26] When the peace was finally made between the Cherokees and the Six Nations at Albany in 1768, some Cherokees began to actively cooperate with their new northern allies in raiding the Wabash, Illinois, and other tribes which had "acted as enemies to both."[27] The Creeks lobbied unsuccessfully for more Cherokees to join them.[28] However, the Cherokees, as Oconostota had promised, diverted their young men away from areas where cooperation with the Creeks would have risked conflict with the English.

Underlying each of these decisions was a postwar logic of recovery. Sauly, a Lower Towns leader, articulated this determination in reporting to the Carolina governor that "when we had bad times, in the last unhappy war, I had repeated invitations from the Creeks to come with my whole town and settle amongst them. I answered that I loved my country, perhaps times would mend . . . upon which they were very much vexed and continue so ever since."[29] The Cherokee villages were determined to recover their health and to hold the home ground defended at great cost over two decades of war with the Creeks, Carolina, and others.

The Wartime Generation

The aftermath of the war also saw a turnover in the Cherokee leadership, as a new generation grew into maturity in a world vastly different from that of their fathers. The epidemics had carried away a part of the prior generation of town leaders most conspicuous in the English records: Round O, Standing Turkey, and Old Hop.[30] The loss of these influential policy-makers, all key middlemen between their town councils and the English, left disorganization in its wake in the Overhill and Lower Towns. Others of this generation failed to survive the immediate postwar years. For example Serowih, the *métis* Young Warrior of Estatoe, who challenged the moderation of Cherokee elders and the safety of backcountry colonists by coordinating raids in the backcountry, perished while returning from Williamsburg in 1770. He died an anonymous death, far from his mountain homeland, on the flat coastal sounds of eastern North

Carolina.[31] With these men passed the personal experience gained in fashioning the prewar world.

Thus, in the two decades following the Cherokee War, a new generation came of age among the Cherokees as well as the Carolinians, both touched by the war and its dislocations. The careers of the Cherokee men and women who would be leaders of the towns were marked by the hard times of their growing up. Dragging Canoe, for example, who was to become a leader of the tribe on the eve of the Revolution, was an impressionable young man during the Grant and Montgomery attacks. Similarly, John Watts, Jr., or Young Tassel, the son of an English trader in the Overhill and *métis* Beloved Woman Nancy Ward, was growing up at the time.[32]

This shifting composition of Cherokee town leadership, together with a changing geopolitics, set the stage for the emergence of new leaders within the tribe. In this temporary power vacuum, Attakullakulla achieved the prominence as the elder spokesman that he had long sought. He had been, by the end of the Cherokee War, singled out as the sole representative of the tribe by William Lyttelton and crowned "Emperor" by William Byrd, and from time to time he acted in a manner befitting this perceived position.[33] Elements of opportunism, colonial endorsement, diplomatic brilliance, and political lineage fueled Little Carpenter's latter-day success as a principal speaker of village opinion.[34] For example, his rise to prominence in tribal affairs may have reflected a gesture toward reconciliation with the western and northern tribes, to which he had strong ties, and which were increasingly at the center of indigenous diplomacy.[35]

A few of the prewar cohort of village leading men, such as Attakullakulla, Willinawa, Sauly, and Corn Tassel, survived the war. These town leaders had successfully fit relations with the English and French into an indigenous model and then witnessed the gradual breakup of their accomplishment. The experience of the war severely damaged this accommodation, and after the war patterns of simple coexistence, especially between the English and Cherokees, had to be reworked on the bench of Cherokee village politics.

Undercurrents of Change: The Case of Village Farming

The three years of the Cherokee War had been a strobe light on a scene of intense movement: some elements of the scene—in this case political events—were given a stark prominence, but continuity of action was lost, along with the subtler shadowing events. There was a background of substantial change, easy to ignore in the flash of war, in the villages themselves and among the generations which had survived the war, changes which would slowly but decisively recast intercultural relations.

The end of the Cherokee War signaled a return to the most basic village agenda, especially women's farming. The recovery from the crisis years was apparently remarkably swift despite occasional revisits of epidemic disease. In 1766, Cherokee town leaders described a severe disease outbreak:

> When I got up this morning I could hear nothing but the cries of women and children for the loss of their relations in the evenings there are nothing to be seen but the smoak of houses on fire, the dwellings of the deceased. I never remember to see any sickness like the present, except the smallpox.[36]

Yet in 1784 a missionary recounted that in the postwar decades the Cherokees saw the "greatest prosperity in their way" in the decades after the war.[37] Though this may overstate the case, it serves to underline the resilience of Cherokee farming. Cherokee farmers were more willing to accommodate *some* of the new crops, domestic animals, and implements that were available from their colonial neighbors. Small garden patches ("little plantations" as William Bartram called them) progressively acquired "fowl houses," pig pens, *"asi,"* or storage pits now used for sweet potatoes.[38] Bolstered in this manner, Cherokee gardening provided a cornerstone for the resistance of the Cherokee population to progressive losses after the Cherokee War.[39] The selectivity of crop acquisitions reflected not only nutritional needs but also a more political concern for the reinforcement of female, as opposed to male, economic activities. Women could take pride in the success of the changes in the fields, even if they were locked out of the men-only deerskin business. Agricultural innovation, accomplished in large part during the mid-century, proceeded selectively and cautiously at a time when Cherokee cultural stances toward their neighbors had begun to harden.

Village business reflected this alienation. Corn prices, for example, escalated, especially when traders were buying. Trader James Adair blamed the war for the altered attitude toward the traders, who formerly had had access to "everything sufficient for the support of a reasonable life, which the traders purchased at an easy rate, to their mutual satisfaction." Even though the Cherokee terms of trade had never been as "easy" as Adair suggests, by the 1760s a new diffidence was apparent among some village women who had formerly assisted traders in obtaining food.[40] "Their women and children," Adair complained, "are now far above taking the trouble to raise hogs for the ugly white people."[41] Garden economies thus reflected their own version of the disengagement from the English.

Men, especially young men and aspiring warriors, began to express more intensely a denial of white culture, even marking the domestic animals of the neighboring society for contempt. Cherokee attitudes toward the pig provide an example. Recent archaeological information has corroborated the impression left by contemporary commentators that pigs were a common feature of the Cherokee diet by at least the 1750s. Pork was the most important meat supplement to traditional white-tailed deer and bear at the town of Citico by then. Even James Adair (who, it should be noted, was attempting to prove that native Americans were a lost tribe of Israel) hesitantly admitted that hog-raising was widespread during his off-and-on mid-century residence with the tribe.

But in spite of their apparent willingness to eat pork, many Cherokee men stopped short of giving the animal any respect. The hog was as disreputable as its cousin the opossum (another omnivorous animal and significant source of meat).[42] In the Cherokee language the names for the two animals were unflattering: *sikqua* was the earliest name applied jointly to both hog and opossum, while later the hog was derisively called *sikwa utse tsti* or "grinning opossum."[43] Speaking of the opossum, Adair noted that "several old men assure us, they formerly reckoned it as filthy uneatable animal as the hog."[44] And this attitude prevailed even through the 1760s, when hog-raising, left to the women, had become an essential subsistence complement to the deer men brought home. When the commander of Carolina's Fort Loudoun sought to purchase pigs in the villages, he was informed by a trader that "the Indians do not care to sell their Hoggs because they had a bad Hunt."[45]

Though the Cherokees were willing to accept the hog, in spite of reservations, by a similar logic they rejected cattle. The absence of cattle in their towns was so conspicuous to one observer in 1762 that he suggested the situation be corrected by "breeding some tame buffaloes."[46] Part of the reason for the missing cattle was the danger they posed to the little plantations, for Cherokee women had already registered objections to horses for the same reason.[47] But the deeper objection was cultural. Since cattle were identified by the Cherokees as the 'deer' of white men, these Euroamerican animals were, from the standpoint of the Cherokee hunter, unacceptable.

Such cultural distinctions appear to have been made with increasing strictness by Cherokee men after the Cherokee War. While some animals acquired from whites—especially horses, which fit traditional male occupations—were valued by Cherokee men, other domestic animals adopted into female-controlled agriculture were signaled out for derision. However the taunting was aimed not at Cherokee women but at white men and hinged on a connection between foodways and lifeways. Thus, when young warriors readied themselves for raids in upcountry South Carolina, they promised to honor their dead by "killing swarms of white dung-hill fowls, in their corn fields and asleep."[48] The same logic led tribal warriors to pile the carcasses of domestic stock on the bodies of upcountry colonial farmers in the Buffalo Creek raid in the early 1750s.[49] Increasingly, the most radical Cherokee warriors followed the lead of the Choctaws in refusing to allow the "English the name of human creatures." They lumped them with opossums, pigs, and other "heterogeneous animals" that seemed to combine normal attributes of a variety of creatures into distasteful hybrids.[50] It was as if whites and their animals were mistakes, offensive to the Cherokee sense of regularity in nature. Cattle- and hog-killing in the colonial settlements represented an aggressive denial of the manner in which their colonial neighbors made a living—and of their humanity. And, after the serious decline of the Cherokee War years, the Cherokees seem to have been consciously determined to increase their own kind. On the return of the three Cherokee chiefs from England in 1763, Judd's Friend said that "Our women are breeding Children night and Day to increase our People."[51]

The Dual Deerskin Trade

While the towns recovered from the war, the Carolina trade continued, but on terms which were in many respects increasingly favorable to the tribespeople. The reasons for this had to do with changes on the colonial as well as the village side. Falling prices for leather in European markets, the failure of South Carolina's postwar public monopoly, and continuing village competition among a large number of traders—all of these factors depressed colonial activity. Anthony Dean was in agreement with James Adair in lamenting the "decayed" state of the Cherokee-Carolina trade even in the 1750s, and the decline in profitability for resident Carolina traders was apparent into the 1760s and beyond.[52]

While the deerskin trade to the colonies continued after 1750, its volume steadily decreased. Trade statistics provide a way to gauge roughly the amount of leather exported from the mountains to the port. When the trading paths to the Cherokee towns were closed by the Cherokee War, exports from Charlestown fell only a little. The relatively small Cherokee contribution implied by these figures suggests that the volume of Cherokee deerskins sent to Charlestown was already slipping by the time of the war.[53]

The Cherokee share of deerskin leather shipped to Charlestown from the west fell together with measurable Cherokee demand for trade goods after the Cherokee War. This decline took place even though colonial trading incentives continued on the books, such as the Cherokees' long-standing most favored nation status (which translated into cheaper prices on guns for them than for the Creeks, for instance).[54] The Cherokees enjoyed similar advantages in purchasing other types of goods. The price of woolens sold to the tribe, for example, had been set at below cost before the Cherokee War and was not raised afterwards, though traders and town merchants complained.[55] Some argued that the subsidies were the problem and that the tribespeople had too long received goods "at an under-price."[56] Even with favorable prices, the aftermath of the Cherokee War saw only a brief spurt of trading in the Overhill Towns, where Virginia traders had rapidly moved back in after the war, only to be disappointed by slack demand for their goods.[57]

Changes in village purchasing power and patterns of consumption, as well as in the geography of trade lay behind the puzzling long-term drop-off in

Cherokee demand. Cherokee hunters could still bring in surpluses of deerskins large enough to buy trade goods easily throughout the period. A tribal hunter working full time could harvest as much as 300 pounds of leather in a good year in the 1730s.[58] After the 1750s, competition with white hunters and the difficulty of finding time to travel to distant hunting territories caused hunting activities to be refocused nearer the towns, where they were more susceptible to disruption. However, overall deerskin supply within the towns seems, for the most part, to have been largely unaffected by these changes.[59]

From the outset, villagers had valued goods by their own standards, and the village stores of deerskins continued to be used to buy Cherokee goods sold inside the villages rather than ones traded with whites. Village demands still appeared to outsiders to reflect impractical tastes in goods rather than solid material values. One military observer, noting this trait, commented that "they will give no more for a thing of value than for a trifle."[60] This Cherokee demand (for example, for "looking glasses" into which Cherokee warriors "were always peeping") persisted and was in some sense intensified during the post-Cherokee War period.[61] Cherokee consumer behavior eluded the assumptions of Euroamericans involved in administering the trade. What was least useful in European eyes was the most profitable article of trade. Sometimes purchases of "trifles" involved sizable transactions. The Mankiller of Tellico, for instance, attempted to obtain "presents to the value of about £100 in currency for one of his wenches." After the war "ladies' side saddles" were, at forty skins, the most costly trade item offered by the stores sponsored under the Carolina monopoly.[62] For as sober and commercially minded a military man turned administrator as James Grant, the problem of meeting tribal demand was vexing. "The Indians know the Prices of Strouds, Blankets, Ammunition and Arms very well," Grant advised the Board of Trade in 1763; "the traders have not a very great profit upon these Articles, their principal advantage is upon Vermilion mixed up, Knives, Sizzors, Ear Rings and other Trifles."[63]

By the same token, other "trifles"—ginseng root and ceremonial goods such as eagle wings—also commanded high prices in an ebullient intra-tribal trade, far higher than that of the most valuable high-technology colonial trade item: the gun. In 1762 the prevailing price of a gun from Charlestown was sixteen skins.[64] The price of a "large eagle" was 200 pounds of leather; Cherokee sellers demanded three buckskins for a ginseng root in the Lower Creek Towns,[65] and 500 "weight" of leather bought a ton of "Ayoree white-earth" for Josiah Wedgwood's agent.[66] The prices of commodities within the villages were set by a market, still more powerful in many respects than the colonial trade. Other values were not set by any market; for instance, the cash settlements for property damage or personal injury were set by elders. John Stuart described the process:

if one man kills another's horse, breaks his gun, or destroys anything belonging to him, by accident or intentionally when in liquor; the value in deerskins is ascertained before the Beloved Man; and if the aggressor has not the quantity of leather ready he either collects it amongst his relations or goes into the woods to hunt for it.[67]

These dealings—and not the intercolonial trade—continued to absorb a large, and perhaps increasing, portion of the trade leather which had formerly been diverted east to Charlestown.

The decline in trade that Charlestown merchants witnessed was in part driven by a fall off in Cherokee demand for their goods, but also reflected the undervaluing of colonial trade offerings compared with the strong prices for village-produced commodities. It seems plausible that the high village prices for 'Cherokee goods' as distinct from Euroamerican trade stocks were driven by social rather than purely economic pressures, stresses linked to the tensions postwar recovery created for men.[68] The survivors of the Cherokee War were burdened by memories of hardship and continuing conflict on their northern borders. Further, the depopulation of the crisis years forced men to chose between assisting with collective reconstruction and hunting on their own behalf. Hunting continued, though at increasing expense to the village. Because the use of many Cherokee goods was tied to expressions of status—warriors, for instance, purchasing mirrors, paint, or even alcohol—the pressures of the times may have caused a flurry of compensatory buying, a way of regaining face through consumption. And after the severe damage of the war, public rituals may also have intensified demands for other goods tied to redemptive ceremonies and magic.

Whatever the exact cause of the difference in price between Euroamerican trade goods and Cherokee goods after the war, the net effect was clear to careful white observers. There was nothing but discouragement in the prospects of postwar trade for John Stuart, who observed that "the consumption of British manufactures by these nations is at its utmost extent."[69] Thus, Stuart acknowledged that the declining profitability of the deerskin trade could not be remedied through restructuring. The problem was in the Cherokee towns, where the demand for colonial goods had never completely meshed with village economic desires. For the remaining Cherokee trade, there was stiff competition. Those Cherokees who wished could come and go freely to official outlets, or meet itinerant traders, without limitation. When Pensacola began to siphon off the remaining leather business after 1763, Charlestown justified the Cherokee trade as a diplomatic rather than an economic necessity. The opportunistic Moravians had begun to ship deerskins from Wachovia in 1761, but by the middle of the decade were forced by falling prices to stop shipments.[70] Though the postwar trade monopoly restricted the South Carolina trade to a "factory" at Keowee, there were numerous backcountry stores willing to fill the vacuum by offering cloth, alcohol, and rifles. During this period the main source of deer-skins coming into the Atlantic ports was white backcountry settlements rather than tribal towns.[71] Although the official Cherokee-Carolina trade did not en-tirely come to a halt, the pull of commerce weakened at both ends of the trade paths during the 1760s.

Political and cultural divergence fed the slow economic alienation of the towns from the Charlestown-centered commerce. The future politics of the tribe would be less that of engagement and alliance than of disassociation. And though after the war both peoples remained acutely sensible of the importance of find-ing a way of living together, the postwar period saw the mutual bindings of trade and diplomacy loosened. For individual Cherokees, the psychological shock of the warfare had eroded the tentative respect afforded colonial society and its people. In this and other ways, the hostilities of the Cherokee War continued unresolved in the mountains. The stream of Cherokee-Carolina relations bore violence below a calm surface.

13

Pain, Profit, and Paternalism

THE war only interrupted the demographic and economic take-off in the South Carolina backcountry. With direct threats subsiding after 1761, economic growth resumed with a new vigor even in the upper Savannah River basin, where the dislocations of the war had been great. The economy of the west was bolstered in part by wartime expenditures, but mainly by the tremendous migration of small farmers into the area. Surprisingly, older, peacetime connections to the Cherokees were not completely cut off by this stream. In the modernizing Savannah River backcountry, for instance, a growing mixed farming and commercial economy blended with older business pursuits and many of the trunk roads along which wagoners carried the produce of the new colonial communities still had spurs among the Cherokees.

For centuries before the advent of Carolina, the upper Savannah had seen both trade and conflict between native peoples. The experiences of the few Euroamerican families who had made it their home prior to the war, and the rapid surge in settlement just after its conclusion, created a complicated political chemistry. In localities such as the important Long Cane community, hard hit by the war, some prominent families would retain prewar economic ties to the Cherokees. At the same time a few would establish themselves as local political leaders and as founders of the upcountry economy. This set them apart from most of their newly arrived small farm neighbors, but created community tensions and a troubling personal consciousness of the cost at which their individual prosperity had been won. The story of the upper Savannah region is, then, a story of intersections: of social divisions among the settlers; of inter-

cultural trade and colonial commercialism; of the violent past of places like
Long Cane. All of this was juxtaposed with the hopes of the residents for the
future during the decades of the 1760s.

The Sources of Economic Expansion

Encouraged by the economic allure of this expanding region, men and women
moved in great numbers to war-scarred ground. The *Georgia Gazette* reported
that "near 1,000" families had arrived at Long Cane during 1762 and early
1763, just a year after the Grant expedition, and that "near 4,000 families"
more were on their way.[1] The forward surge which was to carry western Carolina populations far ahead of their levels during the 1750s was consistent with
tremendous immigration across the South. In the backcountry of South Carolina
the white population grew by roughly fifty percent to 11,000, roughly a 50
percent increase, from a prewar total of seven to eleven thousand.[2] The black
population tracked upward at the same time, as plantation agriculture and slave
ownership expanded westward.[3] The cession of Florida from Spain to Britain
in 1763 made the Georgia backcountry safer, and townships of Queensborough
and Wrightsborough saw their total population climb to 9,000 by 1773.[4] On
the eastern and northern side of the Cherokee territories, the three westernmost
North Carolina counties saw a dramatic influx between 1761 and 1765.[5] In
southwestern Virginia the New River country across the Blue Ridge and south
of the James quickly recovered from a disastrous wartime flight and sustained
a 9 percent annual growth in the white populace between 1764 and 1770.[6]

Though the migration and the characteristics of these people on the move
have been sharply drawn, there is a lingering tendency to see the lands which
received them as open space, history-less frontier, and the migrants themselves
as people without significant pasts of their own.[7] Subsistence agriculture and
diverse, but mainly Scotch-Irish, origins have usually been viewed as the glue
that held together the experiences of this generation of migrant farmers in the
South.[8] But immigrants to western South Carolina also carried south fresh
memories of severe distress experienced during the Seven Years' War in Virginia and Pennsylvania. And they could not escape the similarly troubled past
of the country they had come to settle. Especially those migrants resettling the
upper Savannah country unavoidably came face to face with the intercultural
past and present in their new home, and discovered a degree of dark cohesion
in it.

When new settlers arrived they encountered a local establishment which had
re-emerged and prospered after the war. Inter-cultural trade still to exercised a
tremendous influence on economic patterns. The Indian trade is not usually
considered as engendering what historians have recently argued are key ingre-
dients of a 'modern' commercial-mentality/market-mindedness among farmers

or infrastructure investments in central places such as mills or warehouses—all newly visible in the backcountry. However, in the old intersection points between colonist and Cherokee, the shift after the Cherokee War fits its own pattern; it was less a clean break from a first trading stage than a checkerboard game for profit, security, and status. The Cherokees remained part of the game.

The Profitable Disruptions of War

The Cherokee War catalyzed the development of the interior. Economic disruptions were for the most part more quickly overcome in western South Carolina than three years of widespread suffering. In some cases the war powerfully benefited the prewar backcountry leadership, and the investment and business possibilities spawned by the emergency in some important respects sped the commercialization of the backcountry. Armies built up rural infrastructure; protracted campaigns funneled capital through existing backcountry channels. The cost of the Cherokee War was over £200,000 raised by a tax bill during the war five times higher than in peacetime.[9] Much of this money went west with the troops.

In several important respects the war transferred wealth to the backcountry from the prosperous coast. Although accounting for the impact of the war is extremely difficult, some results were hard to miss. For instance, troops marching to the Cherokees made substantial improvements in the backcountry road system. Near Keowee they constructed a forty-foot span bridging "Nine Mile Swamp." It was built on a "square hogsty" center pier constructed of sixteen-foot long beams, of which "the best were larger Hickery Trees split with wedges."[10] Roadwork was also carried out further west, well into the Cherokee Lower Towns.[11] Fortifications at Ninety-Six and Fort Prince George were renovated.[12] These and other improvements cleared the way for leap-frog settlement.

In addition to the contributions made by the construction labor of the Cherokee War armies, substantial amounts of money came into backcountry communities through the generous bounties and militia salaries commissioned by the Assembly. Not all the profits of the war were to be had by large holders. The payments for military service undoubtedly attracted small farmers who, like their Cherokee neighbors, were coping with serious drought in 1759. Thus, at least some payments were absorbed by the most marginal sector of the backcountry economy though probably without lasting effect. However, better-off western residents stood to benefit more directly than militiamen-farmers from the roads and protected marketplaces the war left behind.

Lucrative contracts were assigned through the colony for the provision of food and drink to the armies. Though Henry Laurens's firm was among the principal provisioners, much of the demand of the army was met from within the backcountry.[13] The success of the Congarees store of Herman Geiger—made a military depot during the war—continued to flourish.[14] And afterwards such benefits were not restricted to provisioners along the exact route of the march. In North Carolina the Moravians "furnished meal" to five hundred of the Virginia troops.[15] Alcohol probably also constituted a large, though undocumented, contraband exchange between stores and the troops.

The Cherokee War and the Careers of Leading Men

War turns the world to clay and entrusts it to the hands of a bad potter. The results in western Carolina were off-center and uneven. Some men and women lost while others gained amid intense suffering.[16] Certainly the Charlestown-centered large-scale traders in the backcountry were net losers, largely because the disruption of the supply of deerskins from the tribes added to preexisting problems. Already weakened during the 1750s, the deer-leather business between the lowcountry and the Cherokees never recovered.[17] Local stores began after the Cherokee War to compete more effectively with the commercial factors of the Charlestown houses, and Savannah achieved nearly complete dominance over Charlestown. As urban credit sources for trade goods began to dry up in the 1760s because of declining leather prices, backcountry establishments were given a further edge.

Even though the structure of the leather trade itself had changed, it was still a lucrative activity on the local level. Deerskins continued to surpass in value all other products—flour, corn, livestock—of the Carolina backcountry until the Revolution.[18] In this way the colonial settlements along the upper Savannah continued to be dominated in part by storekeepers who had long been involved in the intercultural trade, though their stores were increasingly patronized by the planters and farmers, often part-time hunters, moving into the region.

In addition to storekeepers, well-positioned landowners and community leaders also turned a profit. Patrick Calhoun, who had earlier been commissioned Deputy-Surveyor, acted as a local land broker after the war. Calhoun served in 1764 as a governmental agent in relocating first a large group of French Protestants to the new township of Hillsborough on the Savannah River and then German settlers from nearby townships into his district.[19] Colleagues such as Andrew Williamson also served as important contacts in organized settlement efforts, especially at the new township which had been delineated "athwart the trading path" between Long Cane and Keowee.[20] According to the 1761 treaty with the Cherokees, a new boundary was set at forty miles from Keowee, and settlers pushed toward this limit of western settlement.[21] For Williamson and Calhoun, settler jobbing was immensely profitable.[22]

In the most straightforward way, the careers of some leading men were made by the backcountry war of 1759–61. The Revolutionary leader Andrew Williamson was an example. Williamson began his career as a "cow driver" and first appears in the record in 1758 selling steers at Fort Prince George for the then-allied Carolina and Cherokee contingents heading to combat in Virginia.[23] His business continued throughout the Cherokee War, and he became the single most important supplier of cattle to the troops. Williamson's start in contracting was assisted by his association with John Murray and the son of Joseph Salvador, wealthy land speculators in the Saluda valley and men closely tied to the Glen administration.[24] His obviously lucrative participation in supply made Williamson rich. An English traveler in 1767 wrote that Williamson's plantation "White Hall" was:

> one of the finest plantations in South Carolina . . . abounding with fine Rich Red Loomy Land famous for Raising Corn, hemp flax, Cotton, Rice, Cattle, Hogs, . . . in the year Sixty Six his peach orchard yielded near Three thousand Bushel Baskets; which proved of great use to the poar young inhabitants of that country.[25]

Williamson had made the transition from "cow driver" to paternalistic landowner in less than ten years.

The double-sidedness of the careers of leading men, especially in the Savannah River backcountry, is exemplified by Williamson's origins as a Cherokee trader. He continued this side of his business at the same time that he took steps to realize his ambition to be looked upon as the equal of his lowcountry friends. Though Williamson's participation in the Cherokee trade is not well documented, the words of a tribal leader, Mankiller, suggest that Williamson's store was a familiar destination for Cherokee villagers: "My Old Friend Mr. Williamson has been a great trader," Mankiller recalled, "I gave [him] a great deal of land over the Savannah River to pay my debts . . . the Warriors in the Lower Towns have taken away my goods, but they cannot take away his land that is his."[26] Williamson was for many years known as a "Scotch Trader," and while he continued this line of business, his profits soon enabled him to reach for a higher social status.

More acceptable business ventures soon began to open up for men such as Williamson. Plantations "were the great investments of the period," and the upper Savannah became a favorite area for speculative investment by wealthy lowcountrymen.[27] For example, Henry Laurens was the co-owner of a 13,000-acre plantation at Long Cane and acted as an agent for the investors in the northwestern part of the colony. Laurens encouraged Williamson to back the development of churches and schools in the region in order to make his situation, and Laurens's investments, "more secure."[28] Major Charlestown capital, long pulled west by the deerskin trade, increasingly homed in on opportunities for what Roger Kennedy has labeled "Agritrade, the buying and selling of land as a commodity." [29] However, other prominent lowcountrymen continued to buy into warehouses and stores for the Indian trade as well as into land. For instance, Lt. Governor Bull had three traders operating in Cherokee towns under his license in the early 1770s, and Savannah merchants such as James Habersham were similarly involved at flourishing Augusta. [30] In this manner, links between the coast and backcountry were strengthened by money contacts which dated from the Cherokee War. And westerners such as Andrew Williamson remade themselves by succeeding in an environment of adversity.

The Long Cane Massacre Stone

Among Carolinians, the residents of Long Cane saw the worst of the Cherokee War. By 1759 some 250 families had settled the broad bottomlands of Long Cane Creek and neighboring tributary reaches of the Savannah, and all fled in an attack after Lyttelton's retreat. Returning too soon after the apparent victory, perhaps to get ready for spring planting, the settlers were caught again; on February 1, 1760, twenty-two were killed while attempting to flee, many of them women and children. This event was to scar the collective memory and life of the community.

For Patrick Calhoun, the nightmare of the Long Cane massacre in 1759 would become a transformative experience. The blow to Calhoun and the community was horrible—many victims of the raid were relatives, including Calhoun's seventy-two-year-old mother, many of the casualties were women and children. Soon afterwards Calhoun erected a stone monument, heavy and set deep enough into the ground to defy vandalism, marking the mass grave on the site of the attack. On the grainy native seyenite, Calhoun had his mother's name cut and then added his own in a line arching over the inscription. This was not only a monument to the dead but a message from the living. (Fig. 9)

The design of the stone's face witnessed to Calhoun's sheltering responsibility, first for his mother, then for the other victims, some unrelated by blood. Except for his mother, the twenty-two victims are not identified on the stone. The stone communicated the pain of his loss and justified the son's postwar assertion of family dominance. What could cynically appear personal promotion was something deeper. Calhoun was expressing both his encompassing grief and his redoubled will to prevent a recurrence of the same tragedy. The lesson cut in the stone was clear: powerful men such as Calhoun were to be the protectors of helpless women and children from the threat to the west. Failure in 1759 did nothing to diminish this impulse. Instead, it provided an impetus for the reassertion of even stronger control over community and family.

Building Postwar Community

At settlements such as Long Cane, Ninety-Six, Waxhaws, and others scattered across the southeastern upcountry, leading men were drawn together by the experience of violent encounter with the Cherokees, by commercial and family networks, and by religious faith. In those communities dominated by Dissenters, the role of leading men as guides and protectors of communal and family life was exaggerated by the shock of Cherokee raiding during the 1759–61 war. In Presbyterianism, a doctrinal belief in personal responsibility for the soul translated readily from the realm of the sacred to the civic. Coupled with memories of persecution and danger, religious instruction had a stern, urgent message for the leaders of damaged communities.

The settlers turned after the war to rebuilding their own lives and seem to have put the Cherokee threat out of their minds. However, this uneasy coexistence was charged with a tension which manifested itself in the urgent postwar task of leadership taken on by men such as Patrick Calhoun. The postwar years saw prominent families strive to solidify their identities around a new image—the planter—which could clearly set their public lives apart from the trading activities in which many of them had been, and were, actively involved.

Interpretations of political leadership and the concentration of economic power in backcountry society which accompanied the development of a rural elite have stressed the importance of economic aspirations—ownership of slaves or land, or connections to the power centers of coastal society—in catalyzing this social evolution. Becoming a farmer—a planter—was in this respect not wholly a matter of technical competence. Instead it was a manner of achieving a social style consonant with a reigning image of social and domestic authority, conformity to an icon of manhood and bearing imported into the backcountry from the slave-holding low-country.[31]

This interpretation clarifies how, in the isolated western communities of the southern backcountry, shared social ambition united otherwise "profoundly private societies of militantly independent men."[32] In northwestern South Carolina, for instance at the Waxhaws settlement, such men combined clannishness with canny financial and denominational linkages to the northern colonies.[33] Social ambition in these southern communities fed a taste for the cultivation of tobacco, as well as cattle-raising, and the establishment of facilities for processing, transport, and other value-added activities, not the least of which was brokering land, were not far behind.[34] Slave-owning was, among all of these factors, both a prerequisite for cash crop farming and a critical way to elevate one's status. This was the agriculture of legitimacy—the aim of many of the leading men of small but rapidly growing backcountry communities. However, this explanation alone leaves out other important dimensions of group experience in western South Carolina.

In the upper Savannah region, which was to produce so many leaders of the Revolution, the lives of leading men were also profoundly influenced by factors other than an interest in emulating an agricultural and class style. Other occupational pursuits of leading men carried a different kind of social baggage. For many of these men, the experience of the Cherokee War and the continuing postwar relationship with the tribe provide an important chapter in their collective biography.

The life of Andrew Pickens provides an illuminating case study of the way in which intercultural factors ranging from business dealings to cultural hostility affected individual men. Pickens's career has been usually understood as following the trajectory of other success stories from small beginnings to local dominance as major landholders, planters, and community authority figures. A hero of the Revolution, Pickens was, in his old age, to bend the facts to fit his personal myth. "I was a farmer," Pickens explained simply in an autobiographical letter written long after the Revolutionary War. The statement was calculated to communicate his social standing as a rural leader to his self-consciously republican peers.[35] However, his life was more complicated than he admitted. Pickens's career took off after the Cherokee War, when he married Rebecca Calhoun, a sister of Patrick Calhoun and a survivor of the Long Cane massacre, and took possession of the old settler fort near Long Cane, called the "Blockhouse." There he carried on trade with the Cherokees, as he had done before the war. As Pickens's grandson remembered,

> the Blockhouse in the neighborhood was a great resort for the Indians who brought their ginseng, pink root, deer and bear skins and beaver in large quantities; and he later owned afterwards a warehouse opposite Augusta . . . to which place he sent all those things obtained from the Indians. He also sent droves of beef cattle to Philadelphia.[36]

Thus, Pickens's wealth was built in part on substantial participation in trade with the Cherokees. Like other leading men in the western backcountry, he combined cattle-raising and farming with less respectable, but lucrative, trade links to the Cherokees. Late in life, reconciling the reality of his mid-career commercial participation in the Indian trade with his place as slaveowner and leading man, Pickens omitted the former.

The war had left scars which made participating in the Cherokee trade an uneasy occupation, though one still profitable enough to attract planters such as Pickens, Andrew Williamson, and others. However, upwardly mobile landowners trading for leather and herbs had company in less socially acceptable members of the community. There was still a taint to trading and the involvement of leading men in intercultural commerce, alongside disreputable competitors, may have created a concern for appearances. During the late 1760s at least two full-time Cherokee traders continued to operate in the upper Savannah area, sending mixed-blood agents out of "Long Cain."[37] Even more disconcerting was the conduct of other men, outside the family circle of Long Cane and similar communities, whose prosperity rivaled and even surpassed that of mainstream planters, but who made no effort to hide their personal ties to the Cherokees. Just west of Long Cane, men such as Alexander Cameron and Richard Pearis were prosperous competitors with Pickens and Williamson, and both had children by Cherokee women. Eventually they were both to become major landowners,[38] and in this way undermined the propriety which the leading men in the colonial settlements were working hard to project.

However, the problems of occupational acceptability were less compelling than the experience of the Cherokee War. Though important leading men pushed memories of wartime to the backs of their mind while dealing for profit with their former enemies, they could not escape a consciousness of this troubled past. As a result, a sense of unease persisted, never farther away than the abandoned town square of Keowee, as close as the periodic excursions of Cherokees into the communities.

The evolution of western backcountry settlements, like the careers of leading men within them, was different from that of the low country or even of much of the Piedmont upcountry. By striving for slaves, landholdings, and an upright two-story façade for their house, some backcountry men put distance between themselves and their small farmer neighbors. However, the prospering backcountry lay in hazardous proximity to the Cherokees, a proximity of the heart as well as the mind.

PART IV

Revolutions

14

Closing Borders and Revolutionary Stirrings, 1767–1775

D URING the late 1760s, after a time of war and unsettling settlement, the incipient elite of the South Carolina backcountry attempted to consolidate boundaries within its own society. By far the most important of their efforts was the "Regulation" which took place at scattered localities across upcountry South Carolina from 1767 to 1771, from the Pee Dee River on the east to the Savannah River on the west.[1] Early historian David Ramsay gave a capsule definition of the "Regulation" in the "Chronological Table of the Principal Events" in his *History of South Carolina:* "The peace of South Carolina [was] disturbed . . . by men who under the name of Regulators took upon themselves to try, condemn, and punish horse-thieves and other criminals. A civil war was on the point of breaking out."[2] The vigilante style of this elite-sponsored social movement was under the direction of leading men, "ambitious and commercially oriented."[3] There was an underlying political reform agenda—issues of courts, taxes, and representation[4]—and each of these factors was influenced further from place to place by shifting religious controversies and personal animosities.[5] Though Regulator rhetoric complained of governmental neglect or abuses, the Regulator leadership was also motivated by social aspirations. These backcountrymen hoped to become like their peers—planters, slaveholders, and recognized powers in the colony. In order to do so, they set

out to strengthen their hold over threatening groups within their own neighborhoods, as well as put the lowcountry on notice of their arrival.

The South Carolina Regulation was fought across social boundaries within
western South Carolina. Of course, the most significant of these was the Indian
Boundary Line mandated by the Proclamation of 1763 and approved by the
Cherokees and other southern tribes at the Congress of Augusta in the same
year.[6] This paper barrier, it was hoped, would prevent the too far westward
spread of colonial settlement and thus preserve accessible markets for English
goods as well as intercultural peace. The safety factor appealed directly to
backcountry communities stung by the war,[7] where the Cherokees themselves
were never out of mind. Young John C. Calhoun's family "returned and reoc-
cupied" Long Cane, but the Indians remained "troublesome and the whites
continued to be fated for some years."[8] Tensions resulting from the war were
also not restricted to the families of leading men but were felt as well by the
"poar young" inhabitants who gleaned peaches from Andrew Williamson's
orchard for distilling brandy or feeding hogs.[9] While the Carolina-Cherokee
war had failed to bring these people prosperity, it had left another legacy, a
growing hostility toward the tribespeople on the west. And, while only the
westernmost of the communities were, like Long Cane, most directly affected
by the Cherokee War, many sections bore its imprint.

In this light, it is perhaps no accident that the Regulation began and quickly
reached its peak during and just after the drawn-out negotiations over the territorial boundary between the western tribes and the colonies. The Dividing
Line between the Cherokees and North and South Carolina was set between
1765 and 1768, and the South Carolina Regulation began in 1767.[10] In the
upper Savannah region, which was only one of many areas which saw Regulation, once the boundary between the Carolinians and their most threatening
external adversary had been fixed, colonial leading men could address enemies
within their own society. Though there were few direct references during the
Regulation to the Cherokees, the upper-class critique of Carolina society, which
provided its social agenda, and the composition of backcountry groups singled
out for discipline—as well as the objections leveled against them—suggest that
the Cherokees were an important point of reference.

The South Carolina Regulation, 1767–71

Many of the actions of the Regulation, accentuated by class prejudices and
interest, contained reflections of older, long-standing worries. The immigration
of the 1760s had taken place under the shadow of the traditional concern of the
low country elite about the occupational and social impropriety of backcountry
hunters and Indian traders and subsistence-level farmers. The establishment of
the Boundary Line provided an apparent means of restraining what the Georgia

Assembly labeled the "disorderly and illegal practices of the back settlers and vagrants . . . [and] the clandestine trade with the Indians."[11] Laws governing trespassing, poaching timber or game, fire hunting, and squatting had long been on the books, but the late 1750s and 1760s saw a tightening of these restrictions throughout the South.[12] Many of these measures, while aimed at marginal whites, were debated and won passage in the name of protecting native rights.[13]

It was not just how the lower class, backcountry hunters made their living but how they lived that disturbed the Regulators. When the backcountry migrants were labeled white hunters or bandits, as they sometimes were, an implicit association between backcountry settlers and tribespeople was unavoidable. Domestic norms governing occupation, acceptable behavior for men and women, gender, and racial intermarriage had an underlying cross-cultural connotation. The Regulators' ill-unified and variable reform platform addressed these issues. One of the Regulation's underlying objectives, perhaps the most compelling, was to create a society safe for slave ownership and paternally governed families.[14] And it was not difficult to see that Cherokee attitudes toward both race and family now exaggerated in the popular colonial folklore of captivity stories and newspaper reports posed an invidious challenge to the values backcountry planters hoped to establish. The image of a Cherokee society in which women were dominant, and in which all Cherokees were equal, threatened the fragile paternalism of the backcountrymen who aspired to the status of planter and slaveowner. At least in western Carolina, where cultural tensions (as opposed to other civil government issues dominating the Regulation in other districts) were strongly felt, the concerns of Regulators in part represented a displacement of anxieties about the Cherokees onto the face of Carolina society itself.

Objections to the lifestyle of white hunters offered by colonial officials and the Regulators themselves echoed in wholesale judgments of the new farmer class in the western regions. Journeying in the backcountry before the Cherokee War, James Glen noted the breakdown of sexual and family codes in households where children were "naked" and "nasty" and in which "the parents in the backwoods come together without any previous ceremony."[15] Similar concerns on the part of some Regulators about the equality of men and women and the "too free intercourse between the sexes" in the evangelical churches resulted in a particular condemnation.[16] Regulator-minister Charles Woodmason's accusation that outlaw bands harbored "whores,"[17] and that "New Light" ministers were engaged in "sexual malpractice," including "Love Feasts,"[18] had invoked earlier calls for fatherly discipline. When women were criticized for stepping beyond a subservient role in church and marriage, backcountry Regulators may well have been obliquely addressing lingering fears concerning the standing of Cherokee women. Attempts to impose sexual and political, as well as religious, limits upon the behavior of white women were conditioned in part by colonial prejudices toward other women—red and black.

Regulator concerns were backdropped by social criticism reaching outside the family. In the post-Cherokee War years "horse-stealing" became the most common complaint against bandit bands.[19] Many of the colonists living on the margin of the Cherokee Mountains before the war had in fact been "vagabond horse Pedlars," according to Edmond Atkin, and some continued to carry on this trade, partly as an adjunct to carrying deerskins.[20] A Georgia statute of the 1760s complained that marginal migrant trading groups "Trafick much in horses."[21] Horse-stealing and trading by white hunter-traders and by the Cherokees themselves offended leading men who held horsemanship as a mark of masculinity and gentility.[22] For newly arrived men of rank and fortune, horse stealing was an affront to the ideas of proper gentlemanly conduct which they had just managed to embrace.[23] The suppression together of lower-class horse stealers, hunters, and freedom-loving women reflected the inner psychological struggles of emergent leading men for personal autonomy as well as material prosperity.

The vigilante actions of the Regulation in western South Carolina were aimed at marginal groups (some labeled Scovilites, or Scophilites, after an opposition leader), a few of which were dangerously close in lifestyle to Cherokees. In northwestern South Carolina, the small bandit communities living on the border between the tribe and colony came to symbolize larger fears and were singled out in Regulator actions there. These communities, which had their origin in the more extensive deerskin trade of the 1740s and 1750s, lived alongside growing farming communities in areas such as Saluda and the Congarees. When in 1751 James Glen proposed to seek the cooperation of "white hunters" in the Saluda region, he was warned that "they might perhaps exceed their orders as they are little more than white Indians."[24] In the 1760s fewer men were engaged in the deerskin trade working out of the stores of the upper Savannah, but their presence continued to arouse joint concern for racial and social boundaries. Some of Glen's white Indians, like the group headed by John Vann on the Saluda and Broad rivers, reappeared twenty years later working out of Long Cane.[25] Of the forty-six major traders operating among the Cherokees in 1765, five were identified as "half-breeds," and the surnames of an equal number of other traders may have been tied by kinship to the tribe. Of these forty-six, British agent Alexander Cameron wrote, there is not "one honest man" except the five "marked with an X."[26]

The residence of black and *métis* people within the trading communities and the lure of the west for runaways or stolen slaves also tapped fears of the potential of the Appalachians for maroon colonies. Even more disturbing was evidence of friendship crossing racial lines. An incident in the life of Jacob Williams illustrates the resistance cross-racial outlaw bands offered in defense of the social middle ground they held between colonial and tribal society. In 1767, Williams, identified as a "mulatto living in Chote," a village in the Overhill Towns, was ordered arrested by British agent Alexander Cameron and then aided in resisting arrest by several of his white friends. According to the later affidavit of Cameron's messenger, Williams had just been taken into custody when "8 or 9" men:

> insisted upon the prisoner Jacob Williams remaining with them and as the deponent proceeded on his journey with Jacob Williams some of the above mentioned whitemen pursued them and called to them to return with threats which the deponent not paying any regard to they fired at them having pursued him about a mile and a half.[27]

The anxieties generated by the presence of such men outweighed the actual size of the outlaw population. The number of bandits identified in the course of the Regulation throughout South Carolina was relatively small, and in this light the intense emotion and public discussion of the Regulation seem out of scale with the threat to the fabric of society posed by scattered communities of traders. Especially in westernmost South Carolina actions against individual bandit bands then regulated the countryside, even while the potentially more destabilizing force—the Cherokees and Creeks—remained ungoverned. Outlaws, caught on the margin of both Cherokee and colonial societies, were in part proxy Cherokees. Security, at least in name, could be accomplished through the subjugation of deviant social groups on the colonial side of the Dividing Line.

Underlying Regulator rhetoric and activities was an ultimate concern for stabilizing inner frontiers, just as setting the Boundary Line symbolized containment of the Cherokees. In fact, the Proclamation of 1763 was greeted by some Carolinians as a way to make the backcountry safe enough to attract the new immigrants necessary to overbalance the lowcountry black majority and to shut off the western escape route for slaves.[28] And, especially in the far west, the Regulation was an exercise in reassurance related both to old intercultural wounds and new ambitions.

The 'Virginians'

Charlestown authorities gave the Regulators a general pardon in 1771— nothing more than a slap on the wrist—and the Regulation as a formal movement came to a close. Yet during the period in which the western elite had attempted to smooth the rough edges of their neighborhoods, there were new arrivals in the western colonial country, men and women for whom both the Cherokees and the backcountry white elite created fears of domination.

A tragic flotsam of intercultural animosity was borne south with the migrant stream of the 1760s. The western counties of Pennsylvania and Virginia had been hurt during the 1750s, and small farmers, unable to buy themselves protection, had suffered terrible damage. Courthouse vital statistics show that in Augusta County, Virginia, the population was cut in half, from 10,000 to 5,000 thousand, between 1753 and 1758. Nine hundred lives were taken in 1758 alone in western Virginia, and though the regional population had recovered to prewar levels by 1763, residents faced more casualties as a result of the Ottawa leader Pontiac's inter-tribal offensive against the Greenbriar settlements in the same year.[29] Many of the families moving to the south during the 1760s (as in the 1750s) were refugees carrying with them the emotional burdens of the displaced. At the same time many of these migrants were also attempting to free themselves of economic restrictions and civil repression faced at the hands of a land owning elite in the north.

During the Seven Years' War in the northern provinces, small farmers in the west had seen both the colonial leadership and the British command make common cause with tribal people whom they understood to be the enemy. This was not their cause. As casualties mounted, they began to identify their enemy in racial terms and to condemn their own political leadership for dealing improperly with that enemy.

The hostile voices of white farmer/migrants can be heard raised against both the Cherokees and colonial authority in an incident in Augusta County, Virginia, in 1766. Five Cherokees were killed outside of Staunton, Virginia, at a farm lying near the Great Wagon Road; the body of a sixth was discovered later. The surviving Cherokees killed a blind man and his wife a few days later. Williamsburg officials were immediately worried about further retaliation from the tribe but also about resulting violence from their own citizenry. Lt. Governor Fauquier blamed a recent increase in militia wages, and consequently an eagerness for war, as prodding the killings, especially since the "Upper Counties" were "so inveterate to all Indians friends or foes." A distraught Fauquier wrote to Andrew Lewis that "if this is the Conduct of your young men, with what face can they complain of Indians, who are worse than Indians themselves?[30]

Both Lt. Governor Fauquier and Andrew Lewis (the same Lewis who had recruited Cherokee allies from the Overhill Towns ten years before) appear to have been genuinely afraid of their small-farm countrymen. Each saw Cherokee relations as well as issues of authority and class in colonial society threatening to spin out of control. Lewis's first report mentioned perhaps twenty to thirty "Villainous bloody-minded Rascals" involved, though many more were in sympathy.[31] Two leaders, captured and transported in secret under Fauquier's orders, were set free by "not less than one hundred armed men posted . . . round the prison, [who] with axes broke the prison Door and carried off the said Duffy, declaring at the same time that they would never suffer a man to be Confined or brought to Justice for killing of Savages."[32] Fauquier focused on taking back control; he required that the grand jury investigating the incident be called by the High Sheriff rather than the "under Sheriff who may probably

Summon ignorant men who have little or no property to lose [in] a war with the Cherokees.''[33]

The need to ensure safe conduct out of Virginia for Little Carpenter, who had come to mediate, raised the stakes considerably. An attack by the Augusta vigilantes on a tribal leader of such importance would "bring on a general national Rupture," and invite both civil and Indian war. It would, Fauquier believed, set "one part of the Colony to cut the Throats of the other, and sow the seeds of Discord which might bring on a kind of civil War."[34] The threat was moved closer to reality when a reward of one thousand pounds was reportedly offered for the capture of Colonel Lewis "that he might be brought to justice.''[35]

The Augusta Boys, as the killers and their sympathizers called themselves, extended their rhetoric to include demands for political reform much like those of the South Carolina Regulation. Complaining about the criminal laxity of men such as Lewis, they argued that they "find it Impracticable to maintain the legal rights granted us by his Majesty.''[36] By calling themselves the Augusta Boys, the Virginia insurgents imitated an anti-tribal and anti-governmental action of three years earlier just to the north in Pennsylvania. The massacre there of a peaceable Susquehannock village by the Paxton Boys had been followed by a broadly supported march of the Boys and their sympathizers to Philadelphia for redress in 1764. This provided both formula and symbol in Augusta County and aroused the fears of colonial administrators. The solidarity in spirit between the Virginia and Pennsylvania movements is suggested by reports to Fauquier, that the "Paxton Boys of Pennsylvania have sent messages offering their assistance to prevent any one of the criminals being brought to justice for they say publickly no man shall suffer for the Murder of a Savage.''[37]

The popular insurgency which had taken place in Pennsylvania and which had been threatened in Virginia made explicit the intercultural themes latent in the South Carolina Regulation. The message of support for white on red violence among out-of-power social groups was again clearly expressed in Georgia during the early 1770s. As in Virginia, colonial authorities were perceived to be in immoral alliance, this time with the Cherokees and Creeks. As a result of what they viewed as a sell-out by the colonial governor during a conference with the tribes at Augusta in 1773, a "cracker small-farm majority" in the west of the colony began to take a stand.[38] At the Augusta Conference, crackers or Virginians—both newly coined terms with the latter referring to the place of origin of the 1760s immigrants—taunted the Cherokees.[39] Though the colonial leadership attempted to quell the voices of the "anti-Indian factions" in the backcountry, the region was soon submerged in intercultural violence of the kind which had already taken place in the north.[40]

These divisions, which grew with the continuing immigration into northwestern Georgia and adjoining areas of South Carolina, were galvanized by

Creek raids in 1774. The settlers fell back into blockhouses, just as they had done fifteen years before at the outbreak of the Cherokee War. However, this time the response was quicker, "so soon as the fort was completed the people . . . organized themselves and chose their officers."[41] This outbreak also had wider reverberations: in May, Thomas Fee, a white with no provocation, killed a Creek leader in Augusta and took refuge in the Ninety-Six district of South Carolina. There he was imprisoned by authorities; however, Fee was soon set free by a sympathetic mob "who considered him a hero."[42] Alexander Cameron reported that the upper Savannah country had been filled by people "who in time of peace want to kill all the Indians on the Continent if suffered."[43]

While Carolina and Georgia authorities continued to attempt to hold the line on hard-to-govern rural residents, events in Virginia again began to presage another break in intercultural relations. After the Point Pleasant campaign of 1774, in which Governor Dunmore exploited anti-tribalism to launch an assault on the Shawnees, old social divisions again broke to the surface in western Virginia.[44] With the news of the offensive, the premise of intercultural peace implied in the Proclamation of 1763—and consequently of ordered access to western lands—began to fall apart.

"I Must Tell You, This Tea is Somewhat Like Your Black Drink"

Observers in Charlestown and Savannah during the early 1770s viewed these events in neighboring colonies through the increasingly polarized lens of a pro- and an anti-British faction. On the edge of revolution, the Charlestown establishment was more deeply divided in its attitude toward the Cherokees and Creeks than was the neighboring port of Savannah, where Whig leadership was tied to continuing free trade with the tribes—as well as to hopeful land speculations.[45] Savannah Whigs, who were often ethnic Scots, were more sincere in their efforts at accommodation with the tribe, though Charlestown's Scottish community admitted the Cherokee spokesman Oconostota to full membership in the St. Andrews Society in 1773.[46] The factional politics of the moment were equally complicated in the backcountry of both Georgia and South Carolina. In western regions of these colonies, local leaders had attempted to mute direct confrontations with the Cherokees or Creeks like the Fee incident in 1774, which risked war.

As the controversy with Britain grew into crisis, the incipient South Carolina Whig faction was uncertain about the loyalties of its own backcountry. Low country issues of political autonomy from Britain had only halting appeal in the west, which had only recently been more concerned with declaring independence from Charlestown. In the backcountry of 1775, the year after Point Pleasant, Whig and Tory agendas still had only scattered followers among leading men or farmers. Even when there were more or less spontaneous statements of sympathy, such expressions were often qualified. For instance, the Long Cane Resolves, drafted by leading men, expressed sympathy for Whig values but read as much like a contract as a political manifesto: "we propose to defend our country in her liberties from any invasion whatsoever, and all, as ready free volunteers, unless we may be called on duty, and then we expect according to the pay of the other troops commissioned and paid by the Government."[47]

Though some important leading men were strongly in the Whig or Tory camp, whether for commercial self-interest or for ideology, many others were as hesitant as the signers of the Long Cane Resolves. The western rank and file were more cautious than the elite in embracing complaints against the British. "Disaffected" men and women without any real political identity on these terms often made up the majority among the western settlements from North Carolina to Georgia.[48] Sensing this ambivalence, partisans of both sides lobbied hard in upper South Carolina to pin down commitment. William Henry Drayton lobbied the backcountry during 1775 for the Council of Safety to drum up enthusiasm for the Whigs. Reception was cool both among the "Dutch" churches[49] and among many of the ethnically Angloamerican communities.[50]

During the same time, Cherokee intentions became a preoccupation. Whigs and Tories alike were critically interested in reassuring themselves that the tribe would not intervene against them. When Loyalists and British agents subtly worked to solidify Cherokee support behind the Dividing Line, Whigs were alarmed at their activities. In 1775 the Whigs formed an Indian Department of their own to counter John Stuart's British organization and took their message on the road to the Cherokees. They received an ambivalent hearing. At a meeting at the Congarees in September 1775, William Henry Drayton confronted a group of Lower Towns leaders, and made an ungainly attempt to translate colonial economic grievances into the traditional language of the talks. "The men about the Great King," Drayton argued,

> persuaded him that he and the Men in England have a right to take our money out of our pockets without our consent . . . that if we drink tea we must pay much money to the Great King—I must tell you, this Tea is somewhat like your black drink.

Drayton went on to argue that the tea duty would raise the cost of trade goods, "and thus you see that we do not quarrel only on our own account; but that we have put on our shot pouches, not only to preserve our money, but also to preserve your deerskins."[51]

Drayton's final point touched an issue which was threatening to the tribespeople and compelling to backcountry whites listening in on conference proceedings in order to determine their own stake in the war:

> If they use us, their own flesh and blood in this unjust way, what must you expect; you who are a Red People; you whom they never saw; you whom they

know only by the hearing of the ear; you who have fine lands? You see by their treatment of us that agreements even under hand and seal go as nothing with them.

Drayton, by underscoring status of the tribe as a "red people" apart and interjecting land rights, signaled the degree to which these issues were already politicized. Even the Long Cane Resolves issued two weeks before Drayton's talk had, amid generalizations about the Whig agenda, made direct reference to the tribe's disputed ownership of an "extended tract of land, within the Limits of this Province," and the "ill-disposed minds of those savages regarding it." [52] Soon land issues would emerge more explicitly. The lessons of Point Pleasant in mobilizing small farmers with promises of captured tribal property held out new possibilities of direct action against the Cherokees for the most radically anti-tribal Whigs. [53] One backcountry correspondent raised this territorial issue as an alternative to the ineffective political agenda of the Charlestown Whigs. Since lands were the Cherokees' "only resource," he noted, "I am happy that they have those of the first quality so as to enduce farmers to take part with us." [54] The promise of land would assist in igniting intercultural animosities among newly arrived residents of the backcountry.

Shadowboxing with the Cherokees: The Snow Campaign

After the Whig mission led by Drayton in the summer of 1775, divisions between "associators" or Whigs, and "non-associators" were fueled by evidence of a real Cherokee threat. During the summer of 1775, rumors floated through the backcountry of "ministerial" provocations aimed by Loyalists and British Indian Department employees against backcountry whites. [55] As a way of countering them, the Whig Indian Department formed an umbrella strategy to win the allegiance of the Creeks and Cherokees directly. In this environment of fearful expectation, local factions—compounded by personal rivalries—soon became players in a backcountry civil war. The Council of Safety sent a shipment of arms to the Cherokees as a first step toward implementing this plan, but the weapons were intercepted by Loyalists claiming that the Whigs were attempting an alliance with the tribe. [56] After the fumbling on both sides, the Whig army captured a key Tory leader. The troops then moved against the more socially marginal group of Tories at Cane Brake, [57] across the Proclamation Line on Cherokee lands. After the successful attack, the troops disbanded and the North Carolina militia marched home to "scour" the western districts of their colony. [58] The deep early winter snowfall which had covered the ground caused this action to be remembered as the "Snow Campaign." [59]

The Snow Campaign exhibited two major motivating themes. The uppermost centered on the Whig ammunition shipment and was fed by factional

Revolutionary politics. On a second level, the Snow Campaign finished the work the Regulation had started. A Whig historian, reflecting on the second element, observed that "the names of the Scovilites and Regulators were insensibly exchanged for the appelation of Tories and Whigs, or the friends of the old order and the new order of things." [60]

The massive grassroots militia support gathered for these campaigns suggests that the revived agenda of the Regulation was still persuasive. Both leading men and their followers were strongly motivated in their opposition to those who, in their eyes, were the worst of the Scovilites, or Tory sympathizers, at the extreme—marginal peoples implicitly threatening mainstream family, racial, and political order. Among the men finally captured at Cane Brake were individuals identified in Whig reports as a "mulatto" and a "colored" captain.[61] Even some of the men taken into custody were familiar from Regulator complaints. For instance, John Pearis, James Burgess, and Brian Ward were Cherokee traders who had worked in association with the "stores" scattered through the upcountry. As in the past, the anxiety aroused by the presence of these men was overblown. The fear they inspired grew in part out of their association with the Cherokees, their cultural rather than political allegiance. The metaphors sometimes employed by the Whig forces were accordingly strongly reminiscent of earlier culture conflict. For instance, beside James Burgess's name on the list of men eventually captured was written the epithet "bloody-minded," a label usually reserved for warriors.[62]

The linkages made by the Loyalists with the Cane Brake hunter-bandits and, by implication, with the Cherokees, allowed the Whigs, after the failure of their own diplomatic gestures toward the tribe, to score a propaganda victory during 1775 by tapping deep-seated anti-tribal fears among the backcountry farmers. As a result of the connection pinned down between Loyalism and the Cherokees in the Snow Campaign, "it was the Whigs rather than the Loyalists who, in the course of the Revolution, were better able to continue the Regulator struggles." [63] The Whigs managed to emerge from the incident at Ninety-Six and the Snow Campaign as the opponents of alliance with the Cherokees, even though they had themselves courted the tribe. And the action of the Snow Campaign demonstrated Whig ability to marshal and coordinate large numbers of troops across a broad geographical front.

The Regulation, which had begun as an ordering of the backcountry in all regions of western South Carolina, had a second and different phase in the far west during the Snow Campaign, in the course of which the remaining elements of the trading settlements, living on the edge of colonial and tribal towns and economically marginalized during the 1760s, were suppressed. With the attrition of this group, one of the few surviving bridges between the Cherokees and backcountry towns was burned.

The traders and horse-stealing bands had, however, provided an easy stage for whites to act out a larger drama against a tribal adversary too dangerous to confront face to face. Even as the Regulators were ordering the country about them, their attention was drawn westward to the Cherokees. The Snow Campaign carried this focus forward toward confrontation; something lay beyond the family arguments of the Regulation. Shadow-boxing with tribal society would soon become a real match in the center ring of Carolina politics.

15

The Whig Indian War of 1776

B Y the spring of 1776, whatever Whig hopes had ever existed for continuing peaceful relations with the Cherokees had been abandoned.[1] At a
meeting at Fort Charlotte in Georgia in April the Whig Indian Commissioners
unsuccessfully attempted a last-ditch reconciliation.[2] After the meeting, the most
frightening of old rumors, that "whenever any one of the southern colonies
shall be attacked on the Sea Coast, they [the Cherokees] will attack the same
province on the frontier," took on an air of reliability.[3] And once again, there
was evidence that slaves were taking the rhetoric of freedom seriously.[4] During
the Stamp Act crisis in 1765, slaves applying the egalitarian rhetoric of the
Whigs to themselves had been heard in the streets "crying out Liberty." In
South Carolina in August 1775 a free black, Thomas Jeremiah, was "hanged
and burned" in Charlestown after being accused of distributing arms for the
British navy, and a more widespread rebellion surfaced in Pitt County, North
Carolina.[5] There were suggestions of backcountry tribal plotting in intercepted
letters, some counterfeited by the Whigs.[6] Only a few months earlier, the British had also aroused concerns in Charlestown. The Snow Campaign had been
waged while the royal governor, fearful of mob violence, was ensconced off-
shore in *Tamar,* escorted by its sister ship *Cherokee.*[7] The Whigs could not
have failed to find the ship's name unsettling.

Suddenly, the nervous colonial leadership had all the proof they needed of
collusion against white Carolina. In early May 1776, a Wachovia diarist recorded that raiders, perhaps Cherokee, had killed seventeen people, "horribly
mutilated them, scalping the entire head, and hacking the body into many

pieces."[8] And such fears were propelled further by continuing reports from Virginia, where Cherokee raiding at the Watauga and Holston settlements, recently swelled by new settlers, reached a peak in the summer of 1776.[9] A letter from the west explained the circumstances in phrases reminiscent of those used to describe the Yamassee or Cherokee War disasters: "An Indian war has absolutely taken place in all its horried consequences on the part of the Indians as they dayly comit the most crule murders on the frontiers."[10] The news from the backcountry echoed that of the Cherokee attack in 1759: " '96' is now a frontier. Plantations lie desolate, and hopeful crops are going to ruin."[11] At a time of growing western tension, the British attacked Savannah and Charlestown in the spring and early summer of 1776.[12] Their invasion was abortive, but it succeeded in galvanizing the provincial leadership. In a letter recalling the British landing in Charlestown harbor, Henry Laurens saw a poorly executed trap:

> The Active was the last of the Enemy's Fleet on the Coast—she went with a Tendor to Bull's Island landed 40 white and 20 black men, kill'd by platoon firing a few head of Cattle, augmented their black Guards by stealing Six Negroes; and went off—After the Attack on Sullivant's Island seconded by the Ravages and Murders in our West Frontier by the Cherokee Indians.[13]

The situation in 1776 replicated in important ways the circumstances facing Carolina in 1759. However, now the British were declared adversaries as well, and the colonists were on their own in a way they had never been before.

All of this triggered a remarkably rapid and vengeful response from the Whig leadership. William Henry Drayton, who had spoken of conciliation with the Cherokees at Fort Charlotte in the spring, suddenly provided instructions for genocide. *"And now a word to the wise."* Drayton wrote in bold hand to the Continental commanders,

> it is expected you make smooth work as you go—that is you cut up every Indian corn field, and burn every Indian town—and that every Indian taken shall be the slave and property of the taker; that the nation be extirpated, and the lands become the property of the public. For my part I shall never give my voice for a peace with the Cherokee Nation upon any other terms than their removal beyond the mountains.

Drayton added a cursory note to the bottom of this letter reporting "No news yet from Philadelphia; every ear is turned that way, anxiously listening for the word, independence."[14]

This juxtaposition of a wish for the destruction of the Cherokees with thoughts of independence reflected the old but always ambivalent tie between the Cherokees and the Carolinians. The Cherokees, by the renewed hostile acts of a few of their young men, had given the Carolinians the moment to erase memories of their former economic and political entanglement with, and even dependency on, the tribe. As recently as the 1750s, South Carolina's official policy toward the west had been organized around the lessons of the Yamassee War: to court the friendship of the tribe and the geopolitical key it represented. By destroying the Cherokees, the Whigs would emancipate themselves from the idea that the future of the colony was somehow, for better or worse, tied to the tribe and from the feelings of incompetence and inferiority that were the residue of the Cherokee War.

Drayton's call for final destruction of the Cherokees was heard in other colonies and amid debates and resolves for independence in the Continental Congress. In Virginia, Thomas Jefferson saw a strike against the tribe as a deterrent to others who might otherwise oppose the new nation: "I hope that the Cherokees will now be driven beyond the Mississippi and that this in the future will be declared to the Indians as the invariable consequences of their beginning a war." [15] General Charles Lee, Continental commander in the South, blamed the British for inciting the attacks, "a capital and favourite part of a plan laid down by his most excellent and clement majesty, George the third, to lay waste the provinces, burn the habitations, and mix men, women, and children in one common carnage, by the hand of the Indians." Lee welcomed the chance for action, and anticipated the oncoming game of war:

> It seems to me absolutely necessary to crush the evil before it arises to any dangerous height. . . . if we avail ourselves of the event, it may prove a fortunate one. Perhaps we ought in policy to have wished . . . [to] make a severe, lasting example of them . . . I assure myself that the game is in our hands: God give us more grace than to shuffle it away. [16]

In North Carolina the Council of Safety had cautiously held off the anxious aggressions of their commander, Griffith Rutherford. But in July, Rutherford suggested a Carolina-Virginia action against the mountain villages. If "the Frunters, of Each of them Provances," cooperated, there would be "no Doubt of a Finel Destruction of the Cherroce Nation." [17] The three North Carolina delegates at the Continental Congress suddenly joined Rutherford in visualizing the objective of the proposed campaign less in terms of strategy than cultural conquest. They declared that, were it not for "the duties of a Christian," their aim ought to be "to extinguish the very race of them and scarce to leave enough of their existence to be a vestige in proof that a Cherokee nation once was [for that] would perhaps be no more than the blood of our slaughtered countrymen might call for." And they added that "mercy to the warriors is cruelty to ourselves." [18]

Combined Expeditions Against the Cherokees, 1776

The Whig strategy was quickly pieced together.[19] The idea of an intercolonial campaign, with troops from several colonies penetrating the tribal territory, met with consensus. Andrew Williamson, the Whig commander of the
Snow Campaign, early saw the possibilities: "I understand last night, the Indians struck at North Carolina and Virginia the very day they commenced hostilities against our frontier. If these two colonies join heartily with us," victory
is assured.[20] Forces under Thomas Sumter and William Thompson were de-
tached by Charles Lee, the Continental Army's southern commander, to join
Williamson.

However, fear weighed in, and it proved difficult for Williamson to reassemble his Snow Campaign force to go against the tribe. "So general was the
panic," Whig historian David Ramsay wrote, "that in 16 days he [Williamson]
could not collect 500 men."[21] Williamson slowly began to march through the
settlements, gathering men, and making tentative probes against scattered
households of Scovilites and tribespeople. In August, with a force of eleven
hundred, he burned Keowee, the town which had served as the first station of
trade and diplomacy between the colonies and the interior towns.[22] In the
meantime, in Georgia, partisan leader Samuel Jack marched with two hundred
men and, before he was repulsed, destroyed Tugaloo, the site of Moore's tense
negotiations with the Cherokees in 1715.[23] While neither Williamson nor Jack
had sufficient strength in August to continue their initiatives, both did what
they could to eliminate the remaining mixed-blood families living between the
Lower Towns and the backcountry.[24] As Williamson's troop strength grew,
North Carolina and Virginia made good on promises of assistance. Soon four
separate coordinated expeditions, involving 6,000 Whig troops, marched from
Georgia, South Carolina, North Carolina, and Virginia.[25]

Like the colonial expeditions in the Cherokee War, the 1776 Whig campaign was marred by poor coordination and discipline, but it still managed to
damage the Cherokee countryside. The line-of-command among the North Carolina troops was confused enough for one soldier to swear that he would never
"Embark in such an Expedition Hereafter; for where Every Officer is a Commander there is no Command."[26] When the North and the South Carolina
columns finally met in the emptied Middle Towns, the troops under Rutherford
were "bewildered on account of being destitute of a pilot." The men were "fit
to Muternize."[27] The Virginia troops, independent of their southern colleagues, followed a clearer route southwest down the Warrior Path to the Tennessee.[28] Though the Whigs were able to meet Cherokees only once in a set
battle, the villagers kept up continual sniping from all sides. Random acts of
violence further splintered command. For instance, a special detachment of
men from the North Carolina troop was dispatched to capture "five or six"
Cherokees. They "pursued" one of them "Very Briskly about five miles fur-

ther and came up with sd Indian Killed and Scalped him," and in so doing delayed the march.[29]

The conduct of the massive invasion was marked by other similarities to the Cherokee War. Once again, the Cherokees offered only targeted resistance, and for the most part abandoned their towns rather than meet the armies face-to-face. They quickly offered messages of conciliation.[30] A member of the South Carolina army expressed the frustration of being deprived of vengeance against the tribe: "it grieves us that we should not have an engagement to get satisfaction of them Heathens, for the great Slavery and hardships they put us to."[31]

Denied combat, violence was redirected at tribal food stores and villages. The white farmers along on the campaign admired Cherokee fields even while they attempted to destroy them, as is evident in this eye-witness description: "cutting and destroying all things that might be of advantage to our enemies," the Carolina troops found

> curious buildings, great apple trees, and whiteman-like improvements, these we destroyed . . . we started to another town called Tilicho, a brave plentiful town, abounding with the aforesaid rarities; I may call them rarities; why so? because they are hemmed in on both sides by or with such large mountains, and likewise the settlements of the soil yielding such abundance of increase, that we could not help conjecturing there was great multitudes of them; the smallest of these valley towns, by our computation, exceed two hundred acres of corn, besides crops of potatoes, peas and beans.[32]

The destruction of this abundance was increased by the pilotless wanderings of three separate armies.

The collaborative expeditions were eminently successful punitive actions. "It was reported," a participant wrote of his enemy, "they were reduced to a state of the most deplorable and wretched, being often obliged to subsist on insects and reptiles of every kind."[33] And though, as Joseph Williams noted, the expedition of 1776 was "unattended with the grandeur of war, with brilliant exploits and sanguinary scenes,"[34] each column of troops faced sporadic, alarming opposition and themselves returned random acts of harm.

Themes of race and class which had been integral to the Cherokee War and to the Snow Campaign resurfaced as well during the course of Williamson's first probes against the residences of Cherokee traders. After an engagement with "Indians and Scopholites," the capture of four Tories "painted like Indians," aroused anger still fresh from the Regulation.[35] At the outset of the war, Andrew Williamson had asked that captured Indians "become slaves and the Property of the Captors."[36] Williamson's proposal reflected the need to entice troops to undertake a dangerous mission, and played on the preoccupation of many men with becoming slave owners. The legislature issued a "slave bonus'' for captured Afroamericans living freely in the tribal lands or taken from Tory households, and South Carolina troops under the command of Thomas Sumter took the greatest advantage of this offer.[37]

An incident along the march of the North Carolina column as it moved down the Pigeon River headwaters suggests that economic motivations concealed deep underlying anger among the rank and file of North Carolina troops. A near mutiny took place over the fate of ''two squaws and a lad,'' the only captives taken alive by the soldiers. After the troop ''vandued off all our Plunder,'' an officer later recalled,

> there arose a dispute Between me & the whole Body, Officers & all, Concerning Selling off the Prisoners for Slaves. I allowed it was our Duty to Guard Them to prison, or some place of safe Custody till we got the approbation of the Congress Whether they should be sold Slaves or not, and the Greater part swore Bloodily that if they were not sold for Slaves upon the spot they would Kill and Scalp them Immediately. Upon which I was obliged to give way. Then the 3 prisoners was sold for £242. The Whole plunder we got including the Prisoners Amounted Above £1,100.[38]

The South Carolina troops seemed subconsciously to justify their interest in human ''vendue'' by attributing a similar motivation to their adversaries. A diarist of the 1776 expedition reported an incident in which the slave of a colonel was assaulted by a Cherokee, ''thinking to have a Negro to wait on him.''[39]

Though unable to engage a force of tribal men, the white troops victimized tribal women and children and blacks who were caught in the net. After crossing the ''Narrows,'' Williamson's troops:

> espied an Indian squaw; at her they fired two guns, which put us all in an alarm . . . although she was wounded in the shoulder and leg, yet she could speak . . . hearing this account we started, and the informer being unable to travel, some of our men favored her so far that they killed her there, to put her out of pain.[40]

A bit further along another ''squaw'' was taken, ''an easy prey because she was lame.''[41] The style of reports of attacks on women (''put her out of pain'') sometimes seem to reflect a fatal ambivalence toward Cherokee women. As Klaus Theweleit writes with reference to the acts and imagination of the German *Freikorps* in the years after World War I: ''Representations of murders committed against women frequently end on this peculiar note of satisfaction ('—and there was peace again in the land'). It pushes feelings of disorientation and horror that also surround the event into the background. The dominant emotion is a passionate rage that will not leave this object until the object lies dead on the ground.''[42]

Blacks were also at risk—if sometimes accidentally. For instance, the Presbyterian chaplain of the North Carolina troops along on a scouting party encountered an unnamed black man who was shot by the minister ''as he ran mistaking him for an Indian.''[43] In acting against Cherokees and Scovilites in 1776, the colonial elite revisited, and suppressed, those groups—white Indians, squaws, and slaves—which challenged their fragile standing both in politics and in familial relationships. Though strands of interracial and intercultural boundary-keeping ran from the Regulation, they were twisted in the Revolution into the slave-catcher's rope: a call for Cherokee genocide, the depersonalization of the tribal society in the minds of white Carolinians. The Cherokees, like black slaves, had become less than a people.

Through the Narrows: Carolinians Come of Age in the Revolution

Though the Cherokees were to face at least seven major offensives before the Revolutionary period was over, each attack followed, on a smaller scale, the severe precedent of the 1776 campaign. And none was to be more important for the Americans, in the eyes of postwar historians sympathetic to the Whigs, than the 1776 attack. For the Whig leadership, the campaign of 1776 was in part a drama of political competence. In the first campaign, during the combined expeditions, the Whigs re-enacted the strategy and mission of the Cherokee War expeditions. However, this time the former colonials were in charge, and they were conscious of the need to redeem their country from both the insecure peace of 1761 and its postscript.

Williamson's troops followed a path taken fifteen years earlier by colonial soldiers under the chafing command of the British leaders Grant and Montgomery. One soldier's journal suggests that the march through the ''Narrows,'' along the Little Tennessee River, where the colonial troops had been assaulted, was particularly momentous, a test of colonial abilities at the very spot where the British command had faltered. ''We expected to have an engagement with our enemies,'' Arthur Fairie wrote,

> being the spot where they repulsed General Grant the last war with killing upwards of fifty men, a great many horses and lost a vast deal of provision; so much that a great many suffered before they returned. But to be short: we came through these narrows with great courage and continued our march to the first town in the Middle Settlements.[44]

Refusing to be cowed, they went on to victory. A distance down the path, the force walked into an ambush at a ''place by the name of Black Hole.'' After losing thirteen men, the troops, "through mercy, defeated our enemies."[45] The "Map Showing the Marchings of the Army" included in John Drayton's *Memoirs of the American Revolution* precisely details the points at which Grant's and Montgomery's troops had been attacked while leaving out all other references to the Cherokee War expeditions.[46]

Whereas Grant's march had failed, in 1776 the Carolinians succeeded. While the "lack of an intelligent pilot" had at first threatened to reveal the colonial commanders as incompetents,[47] the troops recovered to march confidently through the "Narrows" and "Black Hole" in a collective rite of passage.

The campaigners of 1776 operated with a degree of consensus about South Carolina's cultural agenda. There was considerable unity of intention—a determination both to act against overt threats to the colony as well as to confront troubling issues. Revolutionary society attempted to come into its own through the disparate actions of backcountry men and low country Whigs in countering the threat of political dependency posed by their status as a colony of Britain and a neighbor of the Cherokees. In this sense, the action of 1776 was partially independent of Whig political goals for the Revolution against Britain. Of course, the Revolution would have occurred without this western context, but it would have taken a different shape. The southern theater of the Revolution superimposed an intercultural conflict over a seaboard political contest in 1776. The western war of the same year was more than a grab for land. Instead it was an effort to gain control finally, to finish the work begun with the Cherokee War. It was, as will be seen, the war of a generation against its history.

The Act of a Generation

The formation of the Provincial regiments in 1775 drew on a pool of colonial men who could themselves remember the unease of the Cherokee War days. The backbone of the South Carolina regiment partially replicated the command personnel of fifteen years before. Owen Roberts, Christopher Gadsden, and Francis Marion were recommissioned by Colonel William Moultrie, who had himself served as captain under Henry Laurens during the Cherokee War.[48] Barnard Elliott, a substantial merchant and former member of Christopher Gadsden's Artillery company, rejoined as a captain in the Second Regiment. There were other connections outside of this rather closed circle of Charlestown-based planters. For instance, William Thompson had been charged with leading an expedition during the Cherokee War in relief of Fort Prince George, and Andrew Williamson had also been involved in the war.[49] Still others, like Thomas Sumter, had participated in the Snow Campaign.[50] These were men who, in many cases, knew each other and could remember the events of the Cherokee War as part of their youth, and who had built friendships, businesses, and political careers on the foundations of this experience. They shared war stories as Henry Laurens did, when he remarked to a former comrade in arms that "the receipt of your letter afforded me a good deal of pleasure as it informed me that you were safe under the roof of a more substantial edifice than those that we were wont to erect by night between Keowih and the Catooshi!"[51] However, the doubts and afterthoughts resulting from that war were far from easy to bear, and the experiences of these men mixed their coming of age with deep conflicts concerning their personal standing in the world—as well as the position of their homeland.

When the Revolution came, not all Cherokee War veterans who had grown up in—or had recently entered—the colonial upper-class, became Whigs. Some were Loyalists and others remained "disaffected" during most of the course of the Revolution. However, the 1776 campaign, more than any other time during the Revolution, was a high point of unification among these various factions. For some of Loyalist sympathy, the Indian War erased their partisan lines of allegiance to one side of the Revolutionary conflict. "Several who called themselves Tories in 1775," David Ramsay wrote,

> became active Whigs in 1776 and cheerfully took up arms in the first instance against the Indians, and in the second against Great Britain, as the instigator of their barbarous devastations. Before this some well-meaning people could not see the justice or propriety of contending with their formerly protecting parent-state.[52]

Others temporarily aligned themselves with the Whigs, only to switch allegiances after 1776. Andrew Williamson was himself a prominent example.[53,54] Cultural opposition to the Cherokees overrode the Whig and Tory political agendas during the first phase of the Revolution in the South. For men like Williamson, the end of the major inter-tribal engagements of the war apparently brought comfort in a Loyalism finally free of substantial alliances with the tribes.

The Indian War of 1776, as it was sometimes labeled, has for the most part been shunted to the side of recent historical accounts of the Revolution because it seemed an interlude from confrontation with the British, lacking reference to the political issues that motivated Whigs and Tories. However, its very real meaning to the Revolution had to do first with South Carolina's intercultural past, and only in reference to this history can its centrality in the Revolution become clear. The Whig historian David Ramsay was particularly attentive to the personal, and thus political, significance of that war. In his general *History of the Revolution in South Carolina,* Ramsay dedicated a special section to "Reflections on the Indian War" which he believed marked a collective coming of age.

> The expedition into the Cherokee settlements diffused military ideas, and a spirit of enterprize among the inhabitants. It taught them the necessary arts

of providing for an army, and gave them experience in the business of war. The new arrangements, civil and military, were followed with that energy and vigour, which is acquired by an individual or a collective body of people acting from the impulses of their own minds. From causes like these we shall find in the course of this history, the peacable inhabitants of a whole state transformed from planters, merchants, and mechanics, into an active, disciplined military body, and a well-regulated, self-governed community.[55]

Ramsay's stress on the maturation of the Whig generation is echoed in other contemporary memoirs and histories. Joseph Johnson, in his *Traditions and Reminiscences,* put 1776 in the context of past conflicts. "None of the previous Indian wars, even when aided and supported by British Regulars, had been as decidedly successful as this, the first Warfare of our young republic."[56] And Joseph Williams, battalion commander in 1776, late in life gave his own retrospective assessment of the campaign:

> The expedition in 1776 may be considered as the first exciting cause, in the breast of the Indians, of that awe and dread of the power of the white people which prevented an active and general co-operation on their part with the British during the Revolution; and, so far as this was the case, it certainly had a very salutary effect. The spirit displayed by the soldiers engaged in it was a sure augury, a certain pledge of the triumph which awaited both them and their fellow-citizens in the war just then undertaken against Great Britain.[57]

Fullness came to the colony's Revolutionary generation in the "Great Cherokee War."[58] By retracing in 1776 the steps of the British-led campaigns of the earlier conflict, the Whigs gutted the memory of imperious James Grant and British militarism. The campaign of 1776 was on the simplest level a first victory in their uneven relationship with both tribe and empire, one aimed at the empowerment which the overthrow of dependency would bring.

Backcountry Images

The mobilization against the tribe left its mark on many of the men it carried along. Especially in the western backcountry, where hard-core partisan leaders such as Francis Marion, Thomas Sumter, Andrew Pickens, and others found their support, the decision of when and how to enter the fight had a profoundly intercultural context.[59] The intercultural dimension of the war not only entered into individual decisions about which side to stand on but also created a strong matrix for the behavior of troops and their leaders.

The image of the white hunter, an analogue of warrior folklore, provided an egalitarian metaphor for the troops as well as a way of strengthening their resolve. For instance, the outfits chosen by the Surry County militia, part of Rutherford's column of North Carolina troops in 1776, suggest the way in which assuming this pose worked to release the troops' inhibitions. The Surry County men adopted a hunter's uniform, worn with special attention to its connotations of equality in the Revolutionary effort: "if a gentleman could procure a hunting shirt made of good tow linen," one of its commanders recalled,

> died black, with a motto across the breast in large white letters "LIBERTY OR DEATH" and a pair of stout breeches and leggins . . . and a buck's tail on his wool hat for a cockade he was fine enough for anything, and in fact our good Gen'l's hunting shirt was inferior, it was a dingy colored ordinary looking one.[60]

Uniformly mimicking the egalitarianism as well as the demeanor of white hunters, the North Carolina troops, wearing a "buck's tail" on their cap as a symbol of defiance, marched their way into the tribal country. Elements of this marching costume made an explicit political statement. In 1776, British authorities among the Cherokees heard that the Whig militiamen were marching with "deertails in their hats in defiance of Mr. Cameron."[61] Cameron, as a British agent charged with policing the Boundary Line, was identified with restrictions on deer-hunting in the backcountry. Thus, the "deertails" asserted the rights of small farmers and hunters to the tribal gamelands.

The costume seemed also to free the troops of important restraints. In one incident, a member of the expedition named Roberson took personal revenge for a family member murdered in a tribal raid by killing "an old Indian prisoner, as he marched along under guard." When Griffith Rutherford, the commander, took the killer into custody "the troops were so incensed against the Indians that the thought of seeing Roberson punished seemed rather disgusting . . . and Roberson was released."[62] In this and other incidents, boundaries of decency which both white and Cherokee farmers usually respected were suspended.

The campaign led by Andrew Pickens in 1782 was one of several small but intensely violent attacks on the tribe. It is especially suggestive of the way in which individual partisan leaders, as well as rank and file troops, temporarily released restrictions on their own actions. Preparations for this campaign were elaborate, though justification for the march was thin in light of the waning war. On Pickens's order the blacksmith shops "of the country" had perfected tools, "short cutlasses,"[63] for the expedition's use. The long knives were less "a new mode of warfare," as Pickens's grandson was later to claim, than an archaism, a killing tool which was consistent with hunting garb and horseback. At Saiita, an Overhill town, the appropriateness of the new weapon to surprise attack was tested; as the villagers, awakened at daybreak, attempted to flee across the "savanna" surrounding the town, Pickens's

> troops broke generally in squads and pursued, cutting down Indians with their swords. If one blow failed in the object, a second and 3rd from some of the others did the work . . . one William Green, a very large and powerful man had a sword of great size and would cleft upon the head of the flying Indians like so many pumpkins. Young Zack Clarke, not more than 17 or 18, finely mounted particularly distinguished himself in pursuing and killing the enemy. He subsequently became Governor of Georgia.[64]

During the search for survivors of the first raid, hand-to-hand combat ensued. The narrative continues while invoking the powerful theme of racial ambiguity in the face of the enemy. Thus, a "very dark looking young Indian," fled into a ravine followed by General Pickens and ten or fifteen men. Standing on the ravine rim, they "shot at him twenty times." The man survived the barrage "dancing like a defying turkey" and then fought with a soldier named Parata who had entered the ravine,

> he with his sword and the Indian with his clubber gun. The sword struck the Indian's throat, his head fell upon his bosom and his body to the ground. Parata chopped the head of his fallen foe to pieces saying with each blow, "God d— you" and Pickens, who was always as humane as brave, remarked, "Parata acts like a fool."[65]

The split-image in Pickens's later presentation of his life—as prosperous planter and leading Whig on the one hand, warrior on the other—offers a dramatic example of how many white leading men, subjected to the pressures of the war, reshaped themselves. Along with other prominent men from the same region and time, Andrew Pickens overcame contradictions to shape a stable identity. As young members of a self-conscious backcountry elite, these men had been impressed by the violence of the Cherokee War, yet they also profited materially from the war both in terms of income and status and found in the experience new materials for the presentation of self—as veterans, seasoned fighters, or aggrieved patriarchs. In northwestern Carolina, Andrew Pickens, the Calhouns, Andrew Williamson, all owed some measure of their prosperity to their postwar ties to the Cherokee trade. Like the others, Pickens achieved personal independence in the Revolutionary decade not only by establishing himself as a Whig leader and planter but also through denial of his troubling, but profitable, economic connection to the Cherokees coupled with memories of family disaster during the Cherokee War.

Paradoxically, he achieved his psychological wholeness through the temporary embrace of one element of Cherokee culture, disembodied from the rest:

the violence of the warrior. This fusion of the image of warrior and the paternal role of the planter-partisan resembled "introjection," a psychological process in which "conflictual figures" are "swallowed whole in a distorted way."[66] In this way the aspect of the opposing and conflicted figure—in this case the violence of the warrior, which had long threatened men such as Pickens—was renewed and expressed in his own personality.[67] This mechanism assisted as well in the denial of violent acts for which Pickens and others like him were culpable. Like a uniform which could be taken off at the end of the war in a willful act of forgetting, Andrew Pickens's warrior *alter ego* was, after the war, subordinated to Andrew Pickens, the planter and patriarch. It was this second Pickens who would write contemplatively that it was in the Cherokee War that he had "learned something of British cruelty which I always abhorred."[68] In this fashion, the most radical partisans rediscovered their legitimacy, which in a sense they had never left behind, in order to take their place in the peacetime "community of leadership."[69] This was no mean accomplishment in a country which, even after "Regulation," found itself savagely disordered during the Revolutionary War. The misbegotten images of warriorhood blended with the indigenous idioms of violence in colonial culture, and turned violence against itself in a striking "uncivil war" across the western settlements. (Fig. 10)

Pickens's life history provides an extreme example of the personal dynamic which contributed to the behavior during the Revolution of his backcountry neighbors. For a time during 1782 Andrew Pickens became a warrior. In a sense, this was an act of love for qualities which he had discovered in the life of the Cherokees—radical individualism, the striking visual images of male autonomy in warriorhood, the personalization of violence. At the same time, Pickens's perceptions were selective, ignoring the routines of conciliation and male dependency within Cherokee society, borrowing only those elements of indigenous society which, isolated from the whole of society, could be turned to destruction. Out of these materials Pickens fashioned wartime hatred. In putting on the mask of the Cherokee warrior, Pickens fatally embraced the real-life people of the mountain villages, took lives, and in doing so killed the conflicted elements of his personal history as well.

Though less dramatic, the same process took place throughout the margin of the South, among the many and varied constituencies of the region, whether elite upper-class men remembering and reapplying the emotions of the Cherokee War or hill farmers asserting a right to land by thrusting a buck's tail in their caps. By its nature, the 1776 war transformed the assumptions white society would bring to understanding itself and the future place of its tribal neighbors.

16

The Wall and the Path

THE passing and repassing of hostile armies altered the relationship between the Cherokees and Carolina even before the Revolution began. During the early 1770s the Cherokee village councils moved farther apart from their neighbors. Some steps away were forced by colonial military actions, while others were taken at the tribe's own initiative and reflected a uniquely Cherokee response to changes in their heartland. The 1760s and 1770s saw the Cherokees begin to clear a new and separate path for themselves.

All Cherokees had been caught up in a drama of redefinition after the Cherokee War. The colonial invasions had broken the rules, brought immense armies in sustained marches of destruction through their towns, and touched nearly all Cherokees. The war and the troubled 1760s had strained Cherokee routines of economic and social accommodation with colonial society, but not the tribal majority's will to coexist. The idea of a barrier between colonial and Cherokee settlements fit the lessons of the 1760s for the Cherokee elders as well as for the planners in the colonial bureaucracy. Agreements to divide contested lands had long been a means of resolving conflicts between the Cherokees and their Creek neighbors. However, this time the stakes were higher than the control of hunting grounds. Loss of control here threatened another war, the prospect of which alarmed the tribe's leading men and bureaucrats alike. The beginnings of the movement for a Dividing Line reach back into the decade before the Revolution. The first such line was called for in the treaty of 1762, which closed the Cherokee War. The idea of a region-wide division, alternately called the Indian Dividing Line, Boundary Line, or Proclamation Line, was approved a year later in the Indian Congress at Augusta, which closed the southern war, and ratified in a series of colony-level conferences between 1766 and 1771.[1]

The Line was marked in segments over time. After the treaty of Hard Labor, signed at Alexander Cameron's plantation in South Carolina in 1768, a delegation of Cherokees and colonial officers together marked a strip fifty feet wide—with the large trees "blazed on both sides." At one turning of the Line on the ridge of White Oak Mountain near the South and North Carolina border, Cherokee leaders "Judd's Friend, Sallowee Ecoy" cut their marks into the boundary tree.[2] In the fixing of the Boundary Line, the strongest voices were those of the Beloved Men of the Cherokee towns. As spokesmen at councils, they negotiated the agreements. For instance, in 1766 during discussions over the North Carolina segment of the Proclamation Line, the headman Ustenaka, or Judd's Friend, laid down "a string of beads," a symbol of peace, along "the course the line was to run."[3]

Setting of the Line entailed a series of Cherokee land grants. These have long been portrayed among whites as either the mistakes of shortsighted leading men or corrupt personal sell-outs. On the contrary, the cessions represented a deeper kind of demarcation by Cherokee leadership, a design creatively to re-establish both safe relations with their neighbors as well as new limits within their own towns. Unlike colonial leading men, however, the Cherokee Beloved Men and their supporters lacked sufficient tools of economic or social coercion to silence their own people. Young men and Cherokee women, two groups which constituted important and articulate voices in village councils, would also soon be heard pleading their own special perspectives as fences were built between colonist and Cherokee.

Leading Men, Trade, and Land

The treaties confirming the Boundary Line between 1766 and 1768 are the most visible—but most often misunderstood—of Cherokee actions of the era. For Cherokee leading men the concept of the Boundary Line offered an opportunity for reshaping Cherokee-Carolina relations. While the complicated mix of public justification and private self-interest on the colonial side of the negotiations has received scrutiny for many years, Cherokee understandings of the Line, and of the purposes which it could serve, have remained, for the most part, a puzzle.

The series of Line markings underscored the Cherokee desire for a boundary, but a semi-permeable boundary. The road of diplomacy was to remain open—as were the routes to backcountry trade warehouses—but protected from the antipathy of swelling farmer settlements. The Cherokee leading men in the Boundary Line negotiations strove to win two points. On the one hand, they desired to keep open economic and trade contacts where they wished and on their own terms, but, on the other, they wanted to put obstacles between their towns and the intruding backcountry population. The goals were nearly contradictory, as described a decade later in a talk by the Raven of Chota: "The path shall last forever," the Raven said, "and I shall sit at home safe, and confide that my elder Brothers will put it out of the power of all people to cross it, as if it was a wall that reached up to the skies."[4] The path between the two cultures had to be paradoxically both a barrier, a "wall," and an entryway, a "path."

At no place were the intentions of Cherokee leading men such as the Raven clearer than in the upper Savannah River country, where the horizon of contact with whites was deepest and recent trauma most severe. There the South Carolina Boundary Line intersected the old northern segment of the Dividing Paths between Keowee and Long Cane. Negotiations in this vicinity saw the Cherokees purposefully cutting off older paths recently made dangerous after the Cherokee War. When Governor Bull of South Carolina jumped the gun and proposed a settlement boundary farther west than John Stuart thought proper, the Superintendent of Indian Affairs argued the tribal case by objecting that the proximity of settlers "would expose us to perpetual Broils."[5] Employing the derogatory vocabulary which would soon be heard in the South Carolina Regulation, Stuart continued: "the Inhabitants of those back Countries are in general the lowest and worst Part of the People, and as they and the Indians live in perpetual Jealousy and Dread of each other, so their rooted Hatred for each other is reciprocal."[6]

With only a few exceptions the Cherokees seem to have identified the small farmers who arrived in their territory in the 1760s as an almost separate ethnic group, the 'Virginians,' distinguished less by their place of origin than by their attitudes. The "Englishmen and Scotch Men, I have been long acquainted with, and always found them to be good men," a Creek chief remarked, "but these 'Virginians' are very bad people, they pay no regard to your laws."[7] It was against these new neighbors that the Cherokees wished to erect a wall while still providing a gateway to the "good men" of the colony.

Though the Cherokees focused their animosity toward the 'Virginians,' they also understood that these settlers had made such "bold inroads," coming at times "within an easy day's march of our towns," only because colonial governments had turned a blind eye toward their movements.[8] For instance, the grants of land which had encouraged these settlers to relocate to the Holston and Watauga rivers, "they [knew] to be the acts of whole provinces."[9] In addressing this problem, lobbying for a boundary was only a first step, and the Cherokees realized that measures which depended upon colonial enforcement of the law would be insufficient. The Cherokee Beloved Men attempted another, bolder solution in western South Carolina, in the zone between Cherokee Lower Towns and the Long Cane settlements.

Though the paths in this region were still, out of necessity, frequently traversed, the war and postwar settlement had made this passage hazardous. And a specific postwar act of South Carolina had threatened to make the Dividing Paths impassable: after the peace concluded by James Grant, the governor— Thomas Boone—had authorized the creation of a township, Boonesborough, out of the margin of land ceded by the tribe at the head of Long Cane Creek.[10] The new township covered territory alongside the trading path from Keowee to Long Cane and began rapidly to be settled after 1762.[11]

In the late 1760s a group of Cherokee leading men offered two blocks of land to the sons of two traders, Alexander Cameron and Richard Pearis. The first was made to Cameron before the Hard Labor conference in October 1768 during which the Boundary Line in North and South Carolina was also confirmed. Pearis's grant was made a year later. A clue to the underlying logic of the grants lies in the stipulation that both gifts were made not to the men themselves, but to their mixed-blood offspring.[12]

In the case of the first, to Cameron, the Cherokees transferred land to a man who had been among them since the end of the Cherokee War, first as trader and then as political agent for John Stuart. The Cherokee spokesman Oconostota justified the gift before John Stuart (who had protested) by retorting that "Mr Cameron has lived amongst us as a Beloved Man, he has done us justice and always told us the truth . . . we all Regard and Love him; and we hope he will not be taken away from us. When a good Man comes among us we are sorry to part with him."[13] As a "Beloved Man," Cameron was viewed as an official ambassador, and his presence was valued as proof of colonial good faith. Oconostota's wish was to guarantee Cameron's continued residence, but the gift also entailed a safeguard, beyond the life of the agent. Cameron himself attempted to convince the tribe not to make the gift, but they insisted. The Cherokees were specific in their talks at the Hard Labor Conference. "Our beloved Brother, Mr. Cameron, has got a son by a Cherokee woman," Oconostota spoke. "We are desirous that he may educate the boy like the white people, and cause him to be able to read and write, that he may resemble both white and red, and live among us when his father is dead. We have given him for this purpose a large piece of land."[14] In the case of the gift to Pearis, the political motivation was clouded by the issue of trade debts, but Pearis, like Cameron, had children by a Cherokee wife. The favoritism shown to both Cameron and Pearis was thus grounded in Cherokee kinship. Pearis's household, a "rendezvous for the Indians and Scopholites," was to become a first target of Williamson's troops.[15]

Because the grants were very large, roughly twelve miles square each, the recipients' motives, more so than the gift-givers', became the subject of controversy.[16] John Stuart was quick to condemn the two men, demanding that Cameron refuse his grant, and taking legal action against Pearis.[17] From Stuart's administrative perspective, the Cherokee leadership was guilty of foolishness and even dishonesty. Stuart linked the gifts to the settlement of debts.[18] Though the Cherokees were doubtlessly in debt to Pearis, debt in this instance may have been construed by the leading men as less a burden than an opportunity. Cherokee concepts of debt were always flexible; villagers were much more likely to satisfy their obligations to their Cherokee kindred than to white traders, and debt was endemic in the intercultural trade of the 1760s.[19] Judged by Cherokee assumptions, indebtedness, whether in gift-giving within the villages or in purchasing goods from colonial traders, could be desirable, tolerated as part of the reciprocal relationship between trader and purchaser.

In the most favored trading relationships, the bond between debtor and creditor, purchaser and trader, overlapped into a broader relatedness that sometimes approached kinship. This does not mean that individual white traders did not attempt to strong-arm villagers. However, large-scale indebtedness to major traders, especially those with *métis* families, was an institution which could tie together the Cherokees and colonial leadership. The ambassadorial status of Beloved Man Cameron did much the same thing in the political arena. Indebtedness provided a kind of leverage for Cherokee leading men. In these transactions they were thus doing more than simply swapping land for debt.

In essence, the Cherokee headmen involved in the transactions attempted to create *métis* leading men on the margin of white and Cherokee societies through cessions of land that directly enhanced the economic standing of chosen red/white families. In accomplishing this goal, debts seem to have been creatively used by the village leading men as a way of installing traders related by blood to the Cherokees as literal middlemen. Thus, they hoped to create a buffer between the Cherokee towns and the growing backcountry farmer-hunter populations.

The Cherokee cessions to Pearis and Cameron lay west of the Boundary Line on Cherokee land, and protected against friction from the growing white backcountry settlements expanding from Long Cane. These Cherokee gifts were also tailored to guarantee open paths of trade and diplomacy through the buffer-zone. Both lay along the Saluda River, just northeast of Long Cane Creek, and encompassed an alternate trade route parallel to the Dividing Paths. In the case of Pearis's land, the property was near a spur from the Great Trading Path to the Catawbas.[20] The shape and position of the grants were carefully delineated along the Saluda, just north of these communities, in a manner which gave the Cherokees access to the Charlestown road and to the Great Trading Path. The choice of Saluda also had historical and perhaps deeper cultural significance, as the town of Saluda had been an ancient broker town and was the site chosen by the headmen when they invited James Glen to the interior. Saluda was customarily (if not literally) halfway, a meeting ground between Charlestown and the Lower Towns.[21] These grants allowed the Cherokees control of alternate land routes which bypassed the 'Virginians.'

The Closing Door, 1771–73

During deliberations at the Conference of Augusta in 1773, the Cherokees appear to have followed a similar strategy of attempting to wrest control in *métis* families,[22] while these negotiations were muddied by the complex wheeling and dealing of the traders, their Savannah-based backers and the Georgia government, as well as by Creek rivalry. At the conference the Creek speakers derided the Cherokees publicly as "old women . . . saying they had long ago obliged them to wear petticoats" during their last war together in the early 1750s. In fact the Creeks had conspicuously gained against their neighbors by avoiding war in 1759. The Cherokees, John Stuart wrote, are "on the other hand much reduced . . . They look with an eye of envy on the prosperity of the Creeks." Their standing with the colonies was visibly eroding at the same meeting. New voices were raised in the audience at Augusta, when the Cherokees suffered the "laughter and jeers of the assembly, especially the young men of Virginia, their old enemies and dreaded neighbours."[23] In the end, the Conference itself served to remind Cherokee leading men of the depth of ethnic hostility—colonial and Creek—and the fragility of their efforts to buttress the Boundary Line.

The voices of the 'Virginians' at the Augusta Conference threatened to drown out residual intercultural respect, the notion that tribal men and women were, in James Adair's phrase, "freemen and equals."[24] Yet this concept of coexistence was at the heart of the message of Cherokee leading men to both their own young men and to white authority. Attakullakulla at the Lochaber treaty signing in 1770, forcefully evoked this sense of equality with an image of separate rooms occupied by Cherokees and whites. Trouble had come between the people because whites had failed to respect the integrity of the tribal claims to their territory and had darkened the thresholds of their "rooms":

> It seems like stepping out of the door to be at the white people's settlements
> . . . it seems like coming into our houses and encroaching on us greatly . . .
> The old warriors are all dead, [and now] there are young people grown up in
> their room. Yet the white people want to come into their doors, but the Great
> Being above is looking down to see no injustice done us.[25]

While the Cherokees firmly resisted losing their house, they left their doors open to visitors and intermediaries from the other side.

Traditional Cherokee diplomacy offered many ways of receiving the friendship of equals. Adopting hostages, appointing Beloved Men of other tribes to live in their towns as ambassadors, and accepting *métis* children as their own, were among these avenues of political accommodation. Euroamerican notions of accommodation were more abstract and, at both a personal and collective level, more absolute. The separate understandings brought to the Dividing Line negotiations suggest this critical difference between the two societies. When the Cherokees proposed to grant land to the *métis* offspring of white traders, they wished that the children could live in both worlds. Even as sympathetic an administrator as John Stuart, on the other hand, in his reply to the Cherokee talks offering the land, suggested that this interracial doorway between the two people would remain closed and not open. Stuart reminded the headmen that the son of a trader could not live between the two societies, but if he took up residence "without the line now ratified, he may hold it of you as an Indian but not as a white man or one of His Majesty's white subjects."[26] He could not live, as the Cherokees had suggested, as a middleman with ties to both societies. Stuart's reply must have reminded the Cherokees of how racial distinctions within colonial society shaped the rules that they were expected to play by. There could be no open door, no structures of relatedness, to make the boundary passable.

The Cherokees came away from the conference at Augusta in 1773 with disconcerting insight into the closing of the door. Deep attitudes toward ethnicity and deepening fractures within white colonial society limited their ability to negotiate compromise. The New Cession which resulted from the Treaty of Augusta created tremendous tension between established traders and upper-class merchants eagerly attempting to tie down western lands by sympathetically dealing with both the tribespeople and the anti-tribal recent arrivals in the backcountry, who were themselves anxious to own a piece. Events soon reminded the Cherokees of the increasing exclusivism which threatened to show itself in the backcountry. A few months after the close of the Augusta Conference, the dissatisfied Creeks, perhaps aided by Cherokee young men, attacked western settlements in Georgia. In quick response, whites from the backcountry rescued Thomas Fee—who had murdered a Creek headman—from jail in upper South Carolina, and brought danger right to the front door of the Lower Towns. Cherokee headman Chinisto of Sugar Town quickly wrote British Indian Department authorities to disavow any involvement with the Creeks and added, "if they are for war let them go where the white people are and not to come near our towns. We have made good houses and we desire that they may remain so, but they are kindling up fire for theirs."[27]

The Cherokee leading men were sensible that the acts of the 'Virginians,' directed against both the sovereignty of the tribe and the authority of prominent men in colonial society, cast shadows in the doorways of their villages. Up into the mid-1770s Cherokee leading men continued to respond, though less hopefully, to demands for land or other concessions with specific actions as well as with talks. The issue now confronted by the village leadership was much more complex than access to land. Instead the Cherokee leading men faced the difficult task of negotiating with a people whose cultural limits were becoming more rigid. Even among their friends there were problems. The cultural categories which John Stuart attempted to impose on Cherokee-American relations in setting the Dividing Line closed out traditional Cherokee institutional solutions, such as working through brokers or ambassadors in order to keep lines of contact. The problem of creating peaceful—or at least open— relations between the two peoples was more deeply threatened by the radical racial animosity toward the southern tribes expressed in the outpouring of support for Thomas Fee in Ninety-Six. Mob actions denied the legitimacy of the Cherokees as a people, just as surely as Stuart's regulations attempted artificially to contain and isolate the tribes as a sealed unit of politics and production. Against these threats posed by friends and enemies, however, the village leaders persisted in instituting stronger ties with the colonial middlemen whom they felt could be trusted, and in backing away from those people whom they felt they could not trust, whether in the Creek villages or the colonial settlements.

The Landscape Politics of Hunting

The Cherokee strategy for dealing with the rapidly changing politics of the 1770s was determined by events within their own villages as well as in the outside world. The words of the leading men in the talks were directed both toward whites and toward the village audience of their peers, of women and especially of discontented young men. Their words addressed not only the issues posed by whites but spoke as well to the problematic changes within their own country. Around this inner boundary of change within Cherokee society clustered hopes and fears concerning the tribe's future. These expectations profoundly affected the negotiating positions and choices made by the Cherokees in the late 1760s and early 1770s, when pressures were mounting from both outside and inside the villages.

The health of the Cherokee domestic economy, especially of hunting, was one of the compelling factors with which the Cherokees were forced to wrestle during the negotiations over land grants to whites. The debate over major land transactions of the 1770s on the northwestern boundary of the Cherokee lands reflected pressures related to the occupation of Cherokee men. The logic behind the land cessions revealed tensions related to the identity of men as hunters and to the special stresses to which this element of the village domestic economy was being subjected during the 1760s and 1770s.

At the simplest level the situation faced by the tribe involved geography. John Stuart amplified the remarks of Judd's Friend concerning the problems facing tribal hunting: "the extension of our boundaries into the Indian hunting grounds," Stuart wrote,

> has rendered what the Indians reserved to themselves on this side the ridge of mountains of very little use to them, the deer having left those lands, fright-

ened by numberless white hunters and the settlements so near them. This the
Cherokees are sensible of and therefore are easily induced to compliment away
great tracts.[28]

However, something more than the distribution of deer and the mechanics
of hunting pressure was involved. The scarcity of game often mentioned by the
Cherokees and their defenders probably reflected less actual scarcity than the
psychological threat felt by Cherokee hunters in the pre-emption of their hunting grounds, the economic territory most tied to the domain of male pride.[29]
The Cherokees had often faced challenges from white hunter-farmers whose
population had swelled the once isolated colonial settlements. In the hunting
grounds the commercial competition had grown into organized hostility. A succinct entry in the journal of a Moravian town which brokered deerskins speaks
clearly of this contest: "Was a busy day, as hunters came in with deerskins.
They reported that several parties of hunters had fought with the Cherokees,
and that some were killed on both sides. If this is true it is likely to make
trouble."[30] At the Lochaber Conference in 1770, the Cherokees complained of
mass intimidation by a large hunting party: "Captain Guess comes into our
grounds and hunts with fifty men and kills our deer and when we tell him of it
he threatens to shoot us down."[31]

There were more serious threats growing from within. Increasingly, the
biotic health of Cherokee hunting grounds was being compromised by the same
social forces at work in the Cherokee domestic economy. Many of the habitats
of Cherokee hunting, far from raw land, had been modified by years of pur-
poseful intervention. Some of the most productive areas east of the mountains
were the "old fields and planting land." At Oakmulgee Old Fields these extended "fifteen or twenty miles," but most were smaller.[32] These patches—
soil licks, sand ridges, canebrakes, and old fields, maintained in a sere of young
growth by light burning—provided habitat where deer could be predictably found.
However, competition from white hunters, disturbances of the careful timing
necessary to track pulses of deer and other animals, had added to the inherent
unpredictability posed by natural fluctuations in deer populations. Further, as
the Cherokee population declined, the time villagers had for hunting or farming
declined, and these village strictures added to the perception of problems in the
yield of village hunting. While deer takes seem to have remained substantial,
these limitations had caused the pull-back of Cherokee hunting territories closer
to the villages. Judd's Friend, speaking at the Carolina negotiations in 1767,
pointed out that Cherokee hunting grounds were by then "small and but a little
way from the nation."[33] Its best landscapes out of reach or underproductive,
Cherokee hunting had become more difficult.

The economic undertow in Cherokee negotiating positions shows up dramatically in the cessions of the faraway, and thus increasingly out of reach,
western hunting grounds of the tribe. The Lochaber Conference in 1768 took a

first wedge out of the wide arc of shale and limestone northwest of the Cherokee homeland. By hunters' measures, the cost of long distance travel to reach
this country had long been offset by the rich and predictable animal congregations, especially at licks, usually open seams of mineral rich dirt, and frequently burned, grassy cedar barrens.[34] This country offered access to deer and
salt, the latter of which had been a critical element of inter-tribal trade before
the disruptive wars of the 1750s and 1760s.[35] However, the most reliable hunting territories of the region, especially the licks, were beginning to be fenced
off for the cattle and horses of white colonists by the late 1760s. When a
delegation of tribal co-claimants to the Ohio lands reported in 1776 that "their
salt Springs and their Buffaloe grounds . . . had numbers of Inhabitants and
fortified places round them," they simply were describing the end of a decade-
long process of exclusion of the Cherokees.[36] The Dividing Line agreed to at
the Lochaber Conference in 1770 was unexpectedly pushed westward when
Attakullakulla agreed to make the Kentucky River serve as the boundary. This
transaction of 1771, called the "Donelson Purchase" after the Virginia colonial
agent who negotiated it, subtracted approximately ten million acres from
Cherokee-claimed lands on the middle Ohio tributaries.[37]

Thus, the land transfers bore witness to the discarding of rights and to the
slow breakage of economic and ecological templates: knowledge of the land
and its animals. And the talks spoke of the sense of worry among Cherokee
men about the health of their most central economic activity, the space necessary for it, and thus of their own status. The Cherokee leading men who spoke
at the conferences of the Revolutionary era urgently made clear that the underlying boundary between colonial and Cherokee society was biocultural, that
Cherokees and colonists had made different choices of the land and that either
way carried fundamental natural possibilities—and limitations— of its own.
Most often, the statements made by the spokesmen of the tribe underscored the
importance of maintaining male occupations—and space for them—as the first
issue of the tribal political agenda. Corn Tassel's famous words spoken at the
Long Island of the Holston Conference in 1777 fused the work of men and
Cherokee culture.

> You say: Why do not the Indians till the ground and live as we do? May
> we not, with equal propriety ask, Why the white people do not hunt and live
> as we do? You profess to think it no injustice to warn us not to kill our deer
> and other game from the mere love of waste; but it is very criminal in our
> young men if they chance to kill a cow or a hog for their sustenance when
> they happen to be in your lands . . . *We are a separate people!* He has given
> each their lands, under distinct considerations and circumstances; he has stocked
> yours with cows, ours with buffalo; yours with hog, ours with bear; yours
> with sheep, ours with deer. He has, indeed, given you an advantage in this,
> that your cattle are tame and domestic while ours are wild and demand not
> only a larger space for a range, but art to hunt and kill them; they are, never-

theless, as much our property as other animals are yours, and ought not to be taken away without our consent, or for something equivalent.[38]

All Cherokee men, but especially the young, had a stake in the preservation of hunting territories. Continuing to hunt against economic and demographic odds preserved the distinctiveness of the economic roles of Cherokee, as opposed to white men. Their "wild" prey, versus "tame and marked" stocks distinguished them from the colonists.[39] Tribal men stayed on one side of the Line and hunted, or wanted to continue to hunt, deer and bison or bear.

While they seem to have remained silent in the initial treaty discussions that led to land cessions, their objections to the release of land were actively expressed elsewhere. This urgent mission of male culture protection was apparent in the course of village farm adaptation. While women actively fit new crops and even domestic animals into their garden plots, most Cherokee men, with the encouragement of traditional "priests and prophets," resisted accepting cattle, the domesticate of white men. In an incident reported by James Adair, a group of young men who had stolen and eaten a trader's cattle became ill with what they called *"Wahka Abeeka,* or 'the cattle distemper.' " Adair wrote that the sick young men

> imagined they had thus polluted themselves, and were smitten in that strange manner, by having their heads, necks, &c. magnified like the same parts of a sick bull. They first concluded, either to kill all the cattle or send them off their land to prevent the like mischief, or greater ills from befalling the beloved people—for their cunning old physicians or prophets would not undertake to cure them, in order to inflame the people to execute the former resolution; being jealous of encroachments, and afraid the cattle would spoil their open corn fields.[40]

This incident reflects the degree to which the symbols of subsistence—'red' deer versus 'white' cattle—had become critical to Cherokee identity. The prescription given the young men, accordingly, required the young men to reaffirm their allegiance to the proper animals of the tribe. Only in this way could a safe boundary be re-established and the threat to the spiritual as well as physical health of the village allayed. The rejection of cattle portrayed here, as literal contaminants borne by an enemy society, had at its core the rejection of borrowed elements of material culture, and a return to simpler traditional ways and clarity in human-animal relationships.

Cherokee men, especially young men active as hunters and warriors, had felt the centripetal pull created by population decline on their distant hunting territories, the contraction of the space which they could call their own. Compounding the psychological effect of this loss of male territories was the fact that young men as a class had tolerated the compromises made by leading men during negotiations with the colonies, compromises in which the rights to some of their hunting grounds were transferred away. Eventually these lands ended up under the de facto control of competing white hunters, sacrificed, in their eyes, for the broad collective need of achieving coexistence with the whites. However, the failure of conciliation to stem the problems facing the tribe on its borders with the whites began to pull young men toward conflict. Consensus within their own villages began to break down, and the hostility toward white incursions, complained of in undertones during the 1760s, began to be spoken out loud in the speeches and actions of the mid-1770s.

17

From Sycamore Shoals to Chickamauga

A Cherokee hunter surprised Quaker naturalist William Bartram as he paused near Jore in the summer of 1775, to pull a lunch of "biscut and cheese, and a peace of neat's tongue" from his wallet. "Upon sight of me he stood, and seemed a little surprised, as I was very much . . . Speaking in the Cherokee tongue, our conversation was not continued to a great length . . . I presented him with some Tobacco" and "parted in friendship; he descended the hills, singing as he went." Bartram quickly set out again too, around him a world of "mountains piled upon mountains," but felt a chill in the unfolding distance: "an alteration in the air, from warm to cold."

The next day, on the trail through the Nantahala gorge, Bartram unexpectedly met Little Carpenter on horseback, on his way to meet Indian Superintendent John Stuart. Bartram "turned off of the path, to make way, in a token of respect" and Little Carpenter himself "clapped his hand on his breast, and offered it" saying "I am Ata-cul-culla . . . and asked me if I knew it." They parted peacefully, Bartram reassuring Attakullakulla that he "was of the tribe of white men, of Pennsylvania, who esteem themselves brothers and friends to the red men." Little Carpenter's party moved on, and Bartram continued, shaken by the meeting. The Cherokees were on their way to the Augusta Conference, and even the high country seemed tense. Spring had not penetrated these ridges, nothing was in bloom—bad news for a botanist, Bartram jotted in his journal. Only then, admitting to himself that "I could not, with entire safety, range the

Overhill settlements until the treaty was over," he turned back to Cowee town and the path to Charlestown.[1]

Attakullakulla's mission, part of the search for treaty and land cessions made in the decade before 1775, reflected a Cherokee desire for stability in their relationship with whites. But the conciliatory debates carried on in the villages during the hopeful Boundary Line markings were soon followed by more divisive councils. Efforts at coexistence were tested to the breaking point in the critical years of 1775 and 1776, when the Cherokees first perceived the preface to the Whig "Indian War." At this time the Cherokees renewed their debates with urgency and simultaneously were confronted with new demands for major land cessions in the west. The pressures which these requests brought to bear on the towns forced the Cherokees to choose between direct or indirect resistance to Carolina, a choice which involved fundamental decisions over the direction of life in the mountain towns.

The sequence of peacetime land cessions culminated in 1775 at Sycamore Shoals on the Watauga River with the Henderson Purchase. In this treaty (and in a second postwar agreement in 1777 at Long Island in which a peace was signed by Virginia and North Carolina with the Cherokees), most tribal lands north of the Cumberland River were granted to whites, vastly extending earlier territorial concessions made in the negotiations over the Boundary Line, such as at the Donelson Conference of 1771.[2] The deliberations at both the 1775 and 1777 conferences brought more issues than land to the reaction point. It was at Sycamore Shoals in 1775 that fracture lines began to split apart the face of Cherokee consensus, and these would deepen in 1777 after the destructive first campaign of the colonial forces.

In March of 1775 a group of North Carolina land speculators represented by Richard Henderson had purchased the territory between the Cumberland River on the south and the Kentucky River on the north for £10,000 worth of trade goods.[3] However, during the twenty days of the discussion, there was unusually sharp public disagreement among the Cherokees. Those Cherokee leading men led by Little Carpenter, who agreed to cede the lands, faced objections from the warrior Tsi.yu Gansi.ni, or Dragging Canoe.[4] When the tribal spokesman had offered to sell the group the land north of the Kentucky River, Henderson countered that it was the Cumberland, closer to the Cherokee towns, which he wished. Dragging Canoe "got angry and withdrew himself from the Conference—And the other Indians immediately followed him and broke up the Conference for that day."[5] When the conference reconvened, without Dragging Canoe, the Cherokee negotiators objected, telling Henderson, that the "Country which he wanted, was of great Service to them as hunting Ground & that they looked upon their Cattle or game in it, to be as beneficial to them as the Tame Cattle were to the white people."[6]

The debate between the radical dissidents and signers had long been expressed in counterposed terms of occupation and age: hunters versus nonhunters, young men versus old men. In replying to the questions of a British official relating to prior Cherokee land cessions, of which the Sycamore Shoals agreement was the most recent and largest, Dragging Canoe admitted that

> they themselves were to blame for making private Bargains . . . but Blamed some of their Old Men who he said were too old to hunt and who by their Poverty had been induced to sell their Land but that for his part he had a great many young fellows that would support him and that were determined to have their Land.[7]

From the perspective of the dissidents, the Henderson agreement had been a fatal appeasement of genocidal backcountry whites by irresponsible old men. Dragging Canoe spoke for the ambitious hunters and warriors of the tribe. The Cherokees, he had argued to his own town leaders, "had but a small spot of ground left for them to stand upon and that it seemed to be the intention of the white people to destroy them from being a people."[8]

The linkage here between a "spot of ground" and "being a people" reflects the occupational importance of hunting grounds for the identities of young men. The loss of the Cumberland hunting grounds was an economic and psychological blow, and the dissent of Dragging Canoe from the actions of men "too old to hunt" reflects the generational tensions of Cherokee society. At Sycamore Shoals and Long Island the young men lost an important part of their own ground, and inherited a long war of resistance.

The Politics of Survival

In the spring of 1776, Dragging Canoe traveled to Mobile to inquire of Henry Stuart, then Deputy Superintendent of Indian Affairs, "into the cause of the present quarrel and disorders in the Colonies," and to express support for the British.[9] Afterwards Stuart proceeded overland to Mussel Shoals on the southern bend of the Tennessee River, with a gift of "thirty Horse load of Ammunition" to cement this show of support for the British. Soon after his arrival in the Cherokee country, a delegation of northerners "came in all black," advocating war against the colonies, and "a lasting bond of true friendship with their red Brethren"[10] the Cherokees. The Shawnee representative "produced a War Belt about 9 feet long and six inches wide of purple Whampum strewed over with vermillion."[11] Still, many of the young men expressed "their uneasiness" with the idea of engaging the provincials in war. But the momentum of events prevailed in the Lower Towns, where word of engagement with Carolina arrived, and the "principal Chiefs, who . . . remembered the Calamities brought on their Nation by the last war, instead of opposing the rashness of the young people with spirit, sat down dejected and silent."[12]

Soon afterwards, the Watauga settlements were attacked by Cherokees led by Dragging Canoe, and a new cycle of invasion began. The July 1776 attack on the Holston colony was unsuccessful: "there were streams of blood every way," the Holston colonists reported to the Virginia Whig commander, "and it was generally thought there never was so much execution done in so short a time on the frontiers. Never did troops fight with greater calmness." [13] Both the Cherokees and Watauga settlers had tipped their hands, and in retaliation for the attack, William Christian, a veteran of the engagement with the Shawnee two years prior, marched in support of the Holston and Watauga settlements. When the Cherokees fled their towns, Christian established a base of operation at Fort Patrick Henry, across from Long Island of the Holston River and began what amounted to a six months' long occupation of the Overhill Towns. Though all Cherokee regions were damaged during the war, the Lower Towns received the most severe blow. These townspeople fled first to the Middle Towns, and some eventually took up the Creek invitation issued first at the end of the Cherokee War to establish a new town, called Willstown, a safe harbor in the Creek and Cherokee borderland.

The Revolutionary columns had come and gone; months of burning and sniping had left the Cherokees in need. The 3,000 cattle reportedly along with Rutherford proved an effective weapon, as these "tame stock" helped win a victory for their masters. "Where we encamped," a pensioner later recorded, in "one night the beeves destroyed the whole of it [the surrounding growth], even to the stumps, and destroyed the grass to the bare ground." [14] A variation on scorched earth.

A new set of negotiations began. Convened in the summer of 1777 at Long Island of the Holston and just a few miles from Sycamore Shoals, a familiar Cherokee debate resurfaced with greater clarity. [15] In the negotiations, the Virginians began by reading the treaty signed two months earlier between the Lower Towns and South Carolina, which boldly claimed "Cherokee lands, eastward of the Unacay Mountain" by conquest. [16] The leading men at Long Island learned that Keowee had been abandoned, along with Tugaloo, and the old trading territory of the upper Savannah headwaters apportioned to Revolutionary officers in Williamson's army. [17]

At the outset, Corn Tassel acknowledged the futility of conflict. In answer to a group of northern warriors urging war, he told the assembly that he had warned that while "even four, five or six thousand" Americans could be killed "as many more will come in their place. But the red men cannot destroy them." [18] However, the Cherokee leadership still stood united in refusing to concede the right of the Americans to their land by conquest. In referring to the land claims of the South Carolinians, which had been newly stretched to the Tennessee River, Corn Tassel noted "I don't see how they can claim the land by that, for we drove the white people from their houses too." [19] The negotiations were thus to be conducted without an acknowledgment of Cherokee defeat. "It seems

misterious to me why you should ask so much land near me," Corn Tassel
remarked as the negotiations concluded,

> I am sensible that if we give up these lands they will bring you more a
> great deal than hundreds of pounds. It spoils our hunting ground; but always
> remains good to you to raise families and stocks on, when the goods we
> receive of you are rotten and gone to nothing.[20]

The eventual willingness of the Cherokees to convey lands at this treaty, as
well as earlier at Sycamore Shoals, suggests another interior division in Cherokee society. At tribal councils, especially during wartime, women often provided a refrain of peace. In a peace talk with the Six Nations in 1768, Oconostota offered the sachems "a Belt from our Women to yours, and we know
that they will hear us—for it is they who undergo the pains of childbirth and
produce men, surely therefore, they must feel mother's pains for those killed
in war, and be desirous to prevent it."[21] Near the close of the Revolution, a
Six Nations representative concluded a speech to the British by noting that
"Father, After having spoken to you on behalf of the warriors I must beg of
you to have patience until I speak for the women, from whom all Warriors
spring forth at the beginning of Things. Father: Tho' we do not go to war yet
it subjects us women to many misfortunes."[22]

Most Cherokee women appear to have opposed the hostilities threatening
the survival of their decimated families and villages. They seem to have lobbied for compromise while on journeys to council with the British and northern
allies. In one such journey to the Delaware in 1779, the two women in the
party offered items of their own work, "curiously made tobacco pipe bowls,
small baskets made of cane, &c." as ritual gifts when "the chiefs of both
nations . . . made a covenant, not to join in the war, but to maintain the
peace."[23] One of the lessons of the scorched earth warfare of the Cherokee
War had been the vulnerability of the villages, their standing cornfields and
stores of food, and women wished to avoid another forced reconstruction of
the domestic economy.

The gifts were also offered by the Cherokee women as ritual symbols of
their position in Cherokee society, and their part in its politics, as well as of
their pride in the health of those elements of the village economy under their
control. The relative stability of women's village farming, as opposed to indigenous hunting, may have brought tribal women into subtle opposition with
hunters. Women continued to innovate in agriculture in part as a way of protecting the core values of Cherokee society.[24] Perhaps their own success at
tending the tame stock eschewed by their men made them more willing to
contemplate the loss of territory. The chicken houses, hog pens, and corn bins
rebuilt for the second time in less than two decades in the Cherokee villages,
may have convinced Cherokee women farmers that continued innovation, along

with trade through the channel of *métis* traders, could securely provide food enough. At Sycamore Shoals, an unusually high percentage of women, relative to other treaty conferences, were in attendance. One white observer "frequently tried to count the number of Indians which he could not do exactly, but from his best observations, there was about one thousand in all counting big and little; and about one-half of them were men."[25] Women, as well as leading men, seem to have been particularly interested in keeping order among the attendees. At one point in the Sycamore Shoals conference, women hid the guns of a few inebriated warriors and convinced the Raven of Chota to have them tied up.[26] Yet the underlying order which women and leading men wished to maintain went far deeper than keeping peace in the meeting.

Sympathetic leading men (as well as priests and prophets, men who had traditional ties to agriculture and its ritual management) seem to have joined with women. Corn Tassel interjected the desires of women, when, at the Long Island treaty gathering in 1777, he reported that a delegation of his people, "chiefly women and children," had just returned from the South Carolina negotiations "naked as my hand and crying with hunger by which it appeared that they [the Carolinians] only wanted our land and not to make peace."[27] Corn Tassel pointed out the sufferings of women and children in wartime, a critical motivation for real peace. Echoing this theme, the Raven closed the first talk of the conference by offering an image of cultivation rather than hunting or war: "I have now said all I can say to the purpose. I don't care how soon I could be going home for I have a bad enemy in my corn field, I want to go and turn him out (meaning weeds)."[28] The Raven's words suggest that he and like-minded Cherokees believed that the vital task ahead for the mountain people was to return to the security of the village, even at the price of lost hunting grounds.

Women had other reasons to shut themselves off from Carolina. Just as Dragging Canoe correctly recognized the genocidal intention of some Whigs "to destroy them from being a people," Cherokee women may have sensed the threat colonial men posed to their own political personhood. In council talks, trade, and even in marriages, they had encountered resistance on the part of some to their strong economic and political roles. Thus it is not surprising that at least some women, perhaps fearing the violent agenda of both Cherokee and Euroamerican men, actively sought to aid their leaders in creating a buffer between whites and the mountain villages at traditional zones of peaceful intercultural intersection. The most central of these meeting places in the north was Long Island of the Holston, a sacred place for the Cherokees.[29] "Here is the Long Island where we are talking the peace talks and where we have the white seats of justice, the beloved fire," the Raven reminded the 1777 conference; "let the place never be removed but kept for Justice, and for Peace talks; let these seats and this fire always remain fast here on this particular spot of ground."[30]

In fact, the Cherokees had worked at the Lochaber Conference and then at the Henderson Purchase to exempt this spot of ground from colonial control. After attempting to convince the Cherokees to cede the island at the Lochaber negotiations, John Stuart reported that "no persuasion could induce the Indians to give up Long Island on Holston's River . . . it is the first instance of any nation having shown a reluctancy to treat with me, it is the only one of my having failed in carrying a point with the Cherokees."[31] When trader Richard Pearis, along as an interpreter, became concerned during the negotiations with Henderson that leading men had signed away rights to Long Island, he

> informed Oconostota's Wife that the Chiefs had given a deed for land upon this River, upon which she appeared to be very Uneasy & went away . . . to acquaint some of the Chiefs with it—Next morning the deponent and sd Paris met at Oconostota's Tent, and found a Number of Chiefs at it, who the Deponent saw (as he apprehended) marking out sundry Water Courses, which he took to be the main branch of Holstein River, seeing the Great [Long] Island laid down, and the North Fork, with sundry others . . . Said Paris then asked the Indian Chiefs if they had sold Col: Henderson the lands upon them waters— The Indians reply'd . . . they had not, nor would not.[32]

The motives of the Cherokees became clear in 1777, when they requested the removal of the Watauga settlements[33] and asked that the Long Island be reserved for the residence of a white trader, Nathaniel Gist, who was married to a Cherokee woman:[34]

> The Island you see there belongs to Col. Gist. It is to keep the beloved fire on, to bring the Cherokees to talk by. No man shall hold any right thereto but Col Gist. Your beloved fire shall be on this side the River last war your beloved fire was on this side and ours on the Island, so it must be reserved for him . . . don't stop your ears, but hear and remember well.[35]

As in earlier gifts to South Carolina traders, the Cherokees wanted to install a Cherokee-controlled gatekeeper at sacred, strategic places. The Cherokees conceded the new boundaries to the Commissioners unhappily. The Raven hoped "that the line shall be made firm and lasting as I give up the land."[36] However, they added stipulations about Long Island as insurance that boundary-keeping would be workable.

Ani-Yun'wiya: The Real People

The conference at Long Island in 1777 drove a wedge between Dragging Canoe's followers and the leading men and women who had compromised with the Commissioners. Dragging Canoe himself boycotted the conference. When trader Robert Dews asked him if he planned to attend, he said that "he had already heard all the talks . . . [and] supposed he was looked upon as a boy and not as a warrior."[37] Though Dragging Canoe's remarks suggest that a personal slight was behind his absence from the conference, Dews soon found Dragging Canoe had a broader and more concrete agenda, and expected to receive material help from the British in attacking the American settlements. Alexander Cameron, with the aid of Thomas Brown of Georgia, was organizing Tory resistance in the backcountry. And Dragging Canoe understood that Henry Stuart, John Stuart's brother, was on his way from Mobile with ammunition, a force of Creeks allied to the British, and "a belt in order to get the Western and the Northern Indians to assist the King."[38] When trader Dews observed Dragging Canoe's son sitting silently "mending his moccasins, his gun and a small bundle standing near him," he asked another tribesman, Bench, what his intentions were. Bench, after warning Dews that young Dragging Canoe "understands a great deal of English," said "I expect as much Christian blood will be spilt as will fill that (pointing to an iron pot which would hold about two gallons)." Dews remembered that "I told him he talked as trifling of Christian's blood as though it was bullock's blood."[39]

After the conference, many young Cherokee warriors followed Dragging Canoe in seceding from the Cherokee nation. Pulled by village allegiance and belief in their leader's stance toward the unfolding conflict, men and women of three major island towns—Tellico, Toqua, and Chilhowee—affiliated with Dragging Canoe's town of Great Island, followed him south down the Tennessee River.[40] The settlement of new towns, called Chickamauga, was the result of more than a determination violently to resist the territorial compromises made in 1777 at the Long Island and Dewisse's Corner conferences.

Dragging Canoe's strategy was built around a radically Cherokee justification. Unlike the path taken by the leading men who made the agreement at Long Island, Dragging Canoe's way was designed to maintain the prerogatives of Cherokee young men in diplomacy, war, and economy. In symbolic as well as practical terms, Dragging Canoe wished to keep the paths open which the negotiators at Long Island had choked off. The leading men's solution compromised the free access and flow of communication, trade and war, which were the materials out of which young Cherokee men fashioned their identity and status. Keeping each of these channels open and unbuffered was Dragging Canoe's central goal.

Cherokees such as Dragging Canoe offered a metaphor which evoked their fears concerning the direction their leading men were taking: the Cherokees were being "surrounded." The power of this image of political and social emergency is suggested by the remarks of an Iroquois sachem in 1761 when, perhaps alluding to Cherokee suffering in the Cherokee War, he caustically remarked that "you brethren of the several Nations are penned up like Hoggs. There are forts all around us and therefore we are apprehensive that Death is coming upon us.''[41] The first year of the Revolution had given the threat grave specificity. The danger was from the "the Virginians, or *new* American people," who wished "nothing short of . . . total destruction" of the tribes.[42]

In 1777, the same symbol recalled earlier Cherokee fears of encirclement, of isolation from their tribal neighbors. In his remarks to Henry Stuart in 1776 at Mobile, Dragging Canoe spoke of the fact that the Cherokees "were almost surrounded by the White People," and he repeated the image in 1779 to a Shawnee delegation.[43] The land cessions along the Boundary Line in the late 1760s had triggered this alarm, which had very real implications for both the survival of the Cherokees and the conduct of inter-tribal diplomacy. In peace negotiations with the Six Nations at Albany in 1768, Conaghgwayeson, an Oneida chief, reported to the entire assembly that "the Cherokees have told us that the Line was run in their country last year and that it has surrounded them so that they cannot stir.''[44] At issue was both a literal inter-tribal pathway and also, at a deeper level, a threat to the traditional openness of inter-tribal communication.

In fact, Conaghgwayeson questioned the genuineness of British promises to protect the path between the Cherokees and the Six Nations from settlement: "We have large wide Ears and we can hear that you are going to settle great numbers in the very heart of our country.''[45] He pointedly referred to the pathway to and from the Cherokees, the Warrior's Path, which, along with western roads to the Ohio, Wabash and beyond, was the main connecting route between the northern and southern native peoples:[46] "If you will not keep the People away from the Rivers near Ohio, and keep the Road open, and make Pennsylvania and Virginia quiet, we must get tired of looking to you and turn our faces the other way.''[47] The essential issue was one of countering the hostility of the *"new* American people" while at the same time maintaining free access to traditional routes of war, diplomacy, kinship, and trade.

The fact that a literal path as well as a symbol for the whole Cherokee condition was involved was clearly, if indirectly, indicated during Henderson's Purchase in 1775. The Cherokee headmen stubbornly refused to cede Long Island, a major intersection of pathways, including those to the Warrior's Path. However, two years later at the Treaty of Long Island, they came very close to ceding Long Island, and with it control of the surrounding land crossed by the paths to the north. Yet Dragging Canoe resisted and was unwilling to allow white settlements to push closer and cut off the critical intersections at Long Island.

The pathway to the Six Nations was more than just a path; it was perhaps the most significant and ancient route of Cherokee geopolitics. The paths which clustered at Long Island governed major routes north to the traditional enemy, the Six Nations, and west. As a warning, the leading men described the dangers of the proposed Henderson Purchase by recalling: "that a black cloud hung over the country . . . that their enemies came over the ground, on the way to war with them, and would perhaps kill some white people, which they feared would be laid on them, the Cherokees, as the Indians were all red people."[48] Dragging Canoe invoked this history by warning Henderson that the land he had purchased below the Kentucky River was "the bloody Ground, and would be dark, and difficult to settle it,"[49] proper borderland, intended to be shared and not possessed, as Henderson proposed to do. In the past, such challenges to shared occupancy had been countered with warfare to restore balance, and this, in Dragging Canoe's eyes, was to be the future for whites who would come to live in the region.

Before the end of 1779, Dragging Canoe's followers had settled eleven towns south of the Overhill villages, where the Tennessee turns sharply west to cut along the base of the Cumberlands. Dragging Canoe's village was Chickamauga, after the historical name of the place, the next important stop of the Warriors' Path after Long Island, and, like Long Island, an intersection of many paths west and south to potential allies or traditional enemies. Chickamauga had a tradition as a place of fresh starts as far back as the sixteenth century, and a recent history as dissenters' ground. At a crisis time nearly twenty years earlier, the anti-English Creek headman Mortar had chosen a location nearby for his new town as well, and Dragging Canoe was depending on existing lines of supply and support from the Creeks.[50] His move also put the Cherokee colonists closer to Pensacola, where Stuart had moved operations in 1775, and thus nearer to a point of supply for arms shipments. Over the next two decades, Dragging Canoe's Chickamauga settlers followed the paths west and north to engage whites.[51]

Appropriate to the long history of cultural intersection of the place, the Chickamauga towns included many *métis* members as well as Cherokees from the tribal heartland. Dragging Canoe's village found a black farmer there when they first arrived, and from the beginning the Kituwan dialect was mixed with the English of white Tories, traders, and black refugees. The ethnic openness at Chickamauga contrasted to the barriers to cultural intermixing erected by the Cherokee negotiators who made peace in 1777. The Chickamauga were ethnically open in a way that the older towns were not. Their gatekeepers were less selective than the core town leaders who strove to stop unwelcome black and white folk at the door. Thus, ironically, it was the Chickamauga towns which, while actively opposing the 'Virginians,' yet remained more receptive to racial diversity within their towns than the mainstream Cherokees. This social openness was an expression of cultural confidence, mixed with pragmatism.[52]

Ultimately the debate at Long Island, the discussion of game scarcity, of the paths, and of the Cherokee claim to the ceded land, all related to debates within Cherokee councils about how to respond to whites, and in the end, about being Cherokee. The Chickamauga townspeople called themselves Ani-yuni'wiya, or "real people," and ridiculed the conciliatory Cherokees they had left behind with the name 'Virginians.'[53] In a sense their actions—continuing warfare with

whites, resistance to the diminishment of the resource base of young men,
tolerance of ethnic diversity within their towns—were an expression of Cherokee traditionalism.

The Chickamauga at War

The departure of the Cherokee Chickamauga was guided by the culture and
political agenda of young men and their vision of the tribal future. It was a
vision imbued with the deep generational division at the core of Cherokee society but one which also represented the breakdown, under the extreme pressures of the Revolutionary decade, of processes of accommodation and compromise within tribal councils. Like their counterparts in the colonies, the leaders
of the Chickamauga towns represented a generation touched by the dramatic
intercultural hostility underlying the Cherokee War and memories of the vulnerability of their own people to disaster. As they grew into leadership during
the 1760s, Cherokee men of the Revolutionary generation found their status
threatened by anti-tribal incidents and the difficulties of their hunting economy.
At the same time, they witnessed the adaptive innovations of tribal women and
may have felt their pride equally challenged from within the village. And economic change within the village economy would provide the basis of differing
strategies during the 1770s to achieve a shared cultural objective: survival.

The Chickamauga have been described as "militant-nationalists,"[54] and
their choice of strategy was war. In 1776 and again in 1777, Dragging Canoe
launched the earliest in a series of raids against white settlements which would
continue through the Revolution and into the next decade.[55] The "Indian War"
of 1776 stands apart from the seven major campaigns and the numerous rear-
guard actions against the tribe which were to follow in its wake. However, the
post 1776 campaigns probably had a cumulative physical impact on the tribe
which far surpassed that of the first "Indian War."

Seventeen-eighty saw the most substantial of the Revolutionary era raids by
the tribe, coordinated action with the British and tribes in the Ohio Valley.[56]
Whites countered in kind. John Stuart's successor as British Indian Superintendent, former trader Thomas Brown, used his close ties with the Creeks to negotiate tribal alliances and waited for the moment of unification of loyal backcountry men and Indian allies. However, the Loyalist defeat at King's Mountain
in October began to turn the tide as "Overmountain" men returning from King's
Mountain carried destruction indiscriminately through the Cherokee country.
The violence of the attacks was unusual, and the Raven of Chota later reported
to Thomas Brown that "the Rebels from Virginia attacked . . . in such numbers last fall there was no withstanding them, they dyed their hands in the
blood of many of our Women and children, burnt seventeen towns, destroyed

all our provisions by which we and our families were almost destroyed by famine this spring.''[57]

The campaigns which came afterwards see-sawed between local centers of anti-tribalism and the equally estranged Chickamauga. Propelled by reciprocal hostility dating from 1776, raiders moved back and forth between the Chickamauga and the newly occupied Cumberland settlements at Nashville (the Cherokee Dagu'nawe'lahi or ''Mussel-liver place''). This conflict was to persist into the 1790s.[58] Smallpox, which carried away Dragging Canoe in 1778, returned in 1783, and cut away at Chickamauga resistance.

With the exception of the Chickamauga, it seemed that ''exertions in war were not so great as might have been expected'' from the Cherokees and other southern tribes.[59] By 1781 the peace parties of most towns had either retained or regained control, and, minus the Chickamauga, signed a preliminary peace treaty with the Tennesseans at Long Island in 1781. The Cherokees, after nearly a decade of conflict, negotiated a final treaty with the new American state at Hopewell, South Carolina, in 1785. Though hostilities would continue chiefly between the Chickamauga and their enemies into the 1790s,[60] the leading men began to gradually command the attention of the young again. In spite of active negotiation by the Chickamauga and sporadic contact from other towns with traditional tribal partners in the north, inter-tribal diplomatic traffic along the paths began to dwindle. Though memories and traditions remained, the Cherokees were eventually surrounded by white settlement on the north, and the ancient conduit of the Warriors' Path was gradually closed off. When John Norton, a Seneca leader, visited the Cherokee town of Seneca early in the nineteenth century, only the very old remembered the days when common interchange created kinship between the Six Nations and the Cherokees. Norton was surprised to find that ''any of their old Chiefs'' could recite the genealogy of his Cherokee father, who had been captured ''when the British burned the town,'' and later adopted by the Senecas.[61] The slow slippage of social and diplomatic ties binding the Cherokees to other tribes began during the years of the Revolution as the Cherokees were indeed surrounded by new American settlements.

Some Cherokees attempted to back out of this box. As early as 1782 a group of Cherokees explored with Spanish officials the possibilities of emigrating to the trans-Mississippi country, and the westward movement swelled at the beginning of the nineteenth century.[62] The most mobile and active of the Cherokee traditionalists, especially those men who wished to remain hunters, often Kituwan speakers, were among the first to look west, appraising the possibilities of settlement with a hunter's eye, finding new game, salt, and unencumbered space to replace that given up in the Revolutionary era land cessions. These immigrants followed the path of Yunwi usga' se'ti, ''Dangerous Man,'' who, according to tradition, had, out of a vision of weariness ahead, followed the Tennessee River west after the first treaty with the colonists.[63]

But the most pervasive shift among the tribe was less a single change than an intention, a determination of the Cherokees to set themselves apart from whites *in place* by peaceful means. This intention was consistent with their certainty about the necessity of maintaining their separateness from white society. At the treaty of Dewisse's Corner between the Cherokees and South Carolinians in 1777, a "Beloved Woman in the Valley" had sent a message to be spoken at the conference by the warrior, the Bird of Noewee. He offered her ancient and rich image of the path between these two peoples as a symbol of clarification, condolence, and peace: "A Beloved Woman in the valley said the Great Man above directed all things; that he had sent fire down and spoiled the path; but he hoped it would be made clear again." The Bird emphasized her remarks by adding that "a white cloth was now spread over the path and he hoped all would walk on it and dirty it no more." [64]

Yet, even before the events of 1776, the path walked by the Cherokees and colonists had been "spoiled," and the white cloth of the Beloved Woman in the Valley stained. The Cherokee War had served as an emphatic, but not final, notice of the divergence which had taken place between colonial and Cherokee societies. With few exceptions, neighborliness filled their respective historical traditions with warnings of their differences. The Cherokee leading men who wished to put an end to confrontation with whites offered a compromise, a political solution to the problem of coexistence in the same land. In the hope that the Dividing Line would be respected, they placed a buffer between themselves and whites. In the realistic expectation that this was not enough to keep the path clear, they attempted to invest *métis* families with enough power to control the traditional points of intersection and trade, at Saluda, the white peace-making ground at Long Island, and perhaps even Augusta. The Chickamauga derisively labeled these Cherokee leading men 'Virginians' for their compromises with white authorities. However, the resistance of these 'Virginians' was equally profound. By closing, for the most part, the paths to war and to active interaction with surrounding white society, they had begun to follow other routes toward cultural survival.

The Chickamauga dissent fashioned a different solution out of Cherokee tradition. From their gateway town they kept open the red paths to war and to hunting grounds and welcomed those non-Cherokees who wished to incorporate themselves into the tribe. Their active military resistance to the Americans was costly, though Dragging Canoe and the Chickamauga accepted the risks of war. The Chickamauga, the "Real Cherokees," believed they walked a truer path than that taken by the Beloved Men, but by the 1790s the Chickamauga had for the most part mixed again with the Cherokee majority. For on a deeper level, both initiatives had succeeded in the fundamental goal of maintaining separateness between white and Cherokee society. Each had contributed to fulfilling the imagery of Attakullakulla in 1770 and the words of Corn Tassel at Long Island of the Holston in 1777: "We are a separate people!"

Setting the Dance

B Y 1785, the year of the Treaty of Hopewell, the first of many such documents between the United States and the Cherokees, the blazes cut twenty
years earlier into the boundary trees marking the Dividing Line had healed
over. But underneath the calloused bark the wood remained distorted. Scarred
by years of violence during the Revolutionary War period, and
even earlier in the events of the Cherokee War, the heart grain of Cherokee-
American relations was twisted against itself. The trauma experienced between
the Cherokee War and the Revolution marked thirty years of troubled time for
the two peoples. Their paths had never intersected fully: even when Cherokees
and colonists were walking the same trading route their steps were to a different
cultural pace and cadence. Yet in spite of this there had remained enough mutual respect, even up to the eve of the Revolution, for individuals on both sides
to work to bring about the mutual profit which coexistence promised. Certainly
the effort of Cherokee elders to put gatekeepers on the path between the mountain villages and the Americans had suggested that they still sought stable peace.
And, to a degree, some counterparts in American society shared this intention
to find a political solution within difficult circumstances.

Among the most genuine of the voices for conciliation was trader James
Adair, whose *History of the American Indian* was written from the vantage of
a career spent in the tenuous middle ground between white colonial and Amerindian societies. Adair's *History* contains a long ethnographic proof that the
southern tribespeople were a lost Tribe of Israel, which has caused it to be
persistently ridiculed by critics from Adair's time onward. In fact, the aim of

achieving remotely biblical social redemption in the colonies through reconciliation with the southern native Americans represents in some ways a restatement of Alexander Cuming's mission, and, at a deeper historical level, a medieval strain of thought recurrent in European ideas about the New World. Adair's book was as complex as his life, mixing eccentric political theory, self-interest, and the biases of the author. Outside the mainstream of public opinion, Adair insisted on the legitimacy of the related *histories* as well as destinies of native and "British Americans." By providing a careful account of tribal life, Adair wanted to strip away misconceptions of folklore or prejudice and bring his readers face to face with their indigenous neighbors. "I sat down to draw the Indians on the spot," Adair wrote, "had them many years standing before me—and lived with them as friend and Brother." [1]

The rambling *History* contained a powerful and focused political message. In the last of many revisions of the book, on the eve of the Revolution, Adair suddenly borrowed from the rhetoric of the moment to urge recognition of the tribes as "freemen and equals." [2] Perhaps sensing the condescending, destructive drift of the Whig disposition toward the tribes, Adair countered by adding a new conclusion to the book reporting the pointed critiques of the "red majii" toward materialism and even marriage in colonial society. As the Revolution neared, Adair rushed to offer a political solution: intercultural "union," as he termed it. "It must be evident," he wrote, "that with proper cultivation, they [tribespeople] would shine in higher spheres of life; and it is not an easy matter to seduce them from their supposed interests, to the incoherent projects that our home-bred politicians confidently devise over their sparkling bowls and decanters. The friendly and warlike Indians have an intense affection to their country and so have the British Americans." [3] Both the "British-Americans" and the tribespeople held a legitimate claim to the country, a claim which, even as Adair wrote these words, was being undermined by the "home-bred" agenda of the Whigs.

Adair's search for financial backing in the early 1770s to publish his book, and thus to spread its message, yielded only sympathetic endorsements. Perhaps out of desperation, remembering the Cherokee public relations coup of Alexander Cuming thirty-five years before, Adair even unsuccessfully sought for permission to travel to England with a group of Chickasaw warriors and put his case for cultural accommodation before the Court. [4] In what appears to have been an effort to find support in Georgia, Adair became enmeshed in land speculations in 1774 and endorsed the establishment of "Georgiana" on ceded tribal lands. [5] Whatever thin hope Adair may have had in these unlikely activities for finding a solution to maintaining tribal sovereignty by establishing a new province, as the backers of Georgiana proposed, was compromised by self-interest on the part of the speculators. Disappointed, Adair finally sailed alone to England to see to the printing of his book in 1775. His voice, along with those of like-minded leading men among the Cherokees, was drowned out in the cacophony of revolution. The *History of the American Indians* appeared in London in 1775, just as the hope for the realization of its philosophical message was on the verge of dissolving into war.

Other voices which seemed equally outside the mainstream in 1775, though quite different in tone from Adair's, prevailed. Andrew Pickens emerged from the Revolution as the unlikely political middleman between the Cherokees and the new nation. Pickens grew increasingly comfortable in his role as Commissioner of Indian Affairs and proud of the Cherokee honorific title "Skiagusta," or Warrior, given him by his foes after a Revolutionary fight. Years later, as Commissioner, Pickens heard the case of a Cherokee accused of murder in 1788 and confidently asserted his knowledge of tribal law by insisting that "nothing but the blood of the men who spilled the blood of that white man could atone for the crime." [6] Confirming his place as intercultural broker, Pickens built his plantation house, Hopewell, on the banks of the Keowee River, across from the old Cherokee town of Seneca, which had been destroyed for the final time in 1776, and from there acted as one of the United States Commissioners who negotiated the Treaty of Hopewell. It was the warriors of both societies who took control of the path.

A strain of ethnic exclusiveness, present from the beginning of intercultural contact, encouraged by events, won out against alternative visions of the future South. Working on both sides against real interaction had been sheer distance, both physical and cultural, misunderstanding, mistrust, and sometimes, obvious self-interest. From the beginning of conversation with Euroamericans, the Cherokees warily insulated themselves by concealing rituals from the unwelcome eyes of whites. When Alexander Longe, a trader among the Cherokees in the early decades, persisted in a dialogue with a Cherokee priest, Longe's questions were politely evaded until he asked whether "if some of our priests were to come hear and teach you, would you renounce your ways of worship?" The frustrated Cherokee sarcastically answered "yes, we would gladly for then we should be as wise as you and could do and make all things as you do . . . and peradventure the great god of the English would cause us to turn white as you are." [7]

Change was everywhere, but it still affected the form more than the content of Cherokee village life. It was thus the combination of necessity, group and individual choice, which still guided Cherokee decisions ranging from the limited acceptance of Euroamerican pottery forms in late eighteenth-century households, to the persistent rejection of the plow and cattle, to partisan village debates and dissent regarding land cessions. Even in the troubled deerskin economy, the center of Cherokee economic behavior based on gift exchange and redistribution of subsistence items seems to have held. For example, in 1784, a Moravian missionary, journeying through the Cherokee countryside, was told that "twice or more times during the year a special dance was held in each town; no one might come without bringing at least one skin; and so they gather a large number of skins, which are sold for the benefit of the poor who can no longer take care of themselves."[8] The dance, originating in both an older tradition of mutual aid and the commercial experience of the Cherokees, was emblematic of the manner in which the Cherokees were able to accommodate institutional change without abandoning their cultural tenets.

The cultural logic which insisted on the protection of the core of Cherokee identity, was visited during the Revolution by urgent challenges. Village events were more than the simple sum of economic or demographic forces, for the late-century transformation had a separate and ultimately personal reality. What among the mountain villages had been a relaxed distaste for non-Cherokee things and peoples deepened as the result of the trauma visited on them from inside and outside their country. The effects of two major episodes of warfare touched everyone in the villages, and the populations of the towns struggled to recover. The most discouraging sign of this time was not a numerical abstraction; rather it was felt in the sorrow of lost neighbors, and in the unrelenting emptiness of towns left behind. Each generation from the 1730s, and perhaps much earlier, onward had to bear exigencies of crisis years brought on by smallpox, sometimes famine, and war. As Cherokee numbers showed little recovery even at the end of the century, a surging white and black population transformed the tribal homeland into a minority enclave. The reversal between 1700, when the Cherokees greatly outnumbered the colonists, and 1790, when the numbers of new American people had grown exponentially larger, weighed heavily on the tribe. (Fig. 11)

The Revolutionary decade was perhaps not the least of the crises contributing to the demographic decline of the Cherokee people. In 1776 more men marched against the villages than there were Cherokee males of any age. After "moving to the woods" during the invasion, the exposed Lower Towns never regrouped. The land around Keowee and Tugaloo was divided up into bounties for South Carolina officers who had taken part in the Indian War of 1776, and Lower Towns people began to move south. They carried away haunting memories. In 1796, when United States Agent Benjamin Hawkins visited Willstown, a town settled by these refugees, he found that the "children were exceedingly alarmed at the sight of white men, and here a little boy of eight years old was excessively alarmed and could not be kept from screaming until he got out of the door, and then he ran and hid himself."[9]

The mountain people confronted their troubled history and their neighbors by choosing either to acculturate or to isolate themselves. In the nineteenth century the Cherokees would gain the admiration of sympathetic whites for their efforts at 'civilizing' themselves. And it was in these progressive, as opposed to the traditional, farming regions of the tribe that a minority, perhaps 20 percent, presented itself as proof of the tribal will to conform, at least to the norms of its neighbors. Here Cherokee planters, often from *métis* families, would come to possess the accoutrements of large landowners—cattle, slaves, land—and manage their families in the style of white patriarchy.[10] Early in the nineteenth century, mainly in northern Georgia and the Tennessee River valley, some Cherokee men and women erected respectable white clapboard houses with the help of black hands. In doing so, they emulated the white leading men of the colonial backcountry of two generations before.

At least through the Revolutionary decade there is little evidence that Cherokees had adopted the racial attitudes of their neighbors along with their architecture. The lack of references to blacks as blacks—not as colonists—in the historical record is striking. Only one Revolutionary-era talk mentioned color boundaries. When Attakullakulla during the Revolutionary buildup spoke metaphorically of a house of cultural accommodation, blacks had a room of their own—as servants but still under the same roof. This lack of racial reference, a passage from Adair's *History* suggests, had less to do with tolerance toward black people in particular than with a tendency reinforced by colonial encounters toward indifference to all non-Cherokees:

> The Indians are of a copper or red-clay colour—and they delight in every thing, which they imagine may promote and increase it: accordingly they paint their faces with vermilion, as the best and most beautiful ingredient. . . . All of the Indians are so strongly attached to and prejudiced in favour of, their own colour, that they think as meanly of the whites, as we possibly can do of them.[11]

The adoption of black slavery by progressive, often *métis,* Cherokees would seem to suggest an inevitable reversal of racial indifference. Slavery also seems consistent with undoubtedly real, rising paternalism and female suppression as male planters took on white ways.[12] And, obliquely, slavery could have been a tactical victory for Cherokee women, who had always controlled the destiny of captives: putting slaves to work in the field meant that Cherokee men had not taken over entirely; they were still kept out of the fields.[13] Both interpretations make sense in light of the pattern of Cherokee response to eighteenth-century challenges. Male and female control remained counterposed in the nineteenth century but was increasingly pushed by the outside world. What exactly went on in the houses of the Cherokee elite remains for the most part out of sight but was in all likelihood consistent with what had gone before.

The lives of the tribal majority, however, remained quite different, though not completely apart. Most Cherokee communities (perhaps three-quarters of the population in 1820) chose a route of self-isolation rather than full-scale integration—or imitation—of American social patterns.[14] Cherokee farming was not radically altered in traditional households, and the reins of domestic economic authority were still held by women. These Cherokees moved deeper into the Appalachian valleys and built farmsteads much like those of their American neighbors.[15] Though polarization would later occur between the conservative tribal mainstream and themselves, the Cherokee progressives may have served the purposes of the traditionalists. They functioned as a screen of the kind which Judd's Friend and other Cherokee leaders had wished to create in the 1760s during the Boundary Line negotiation, half Cherokee and half white, a broker presence which deflected the attention of neighbors.

Nevertheless, individual Cherokees, especially in the conservative areas, began to strengthen the personal defenses which protected them from disturbing one-on-one contact with whites. Language had long been used as a shield to conceal anger. Some English-speaking Cherokees after the Revolution simply refused to talk with whites. When a Cherokee leader was accosted by missionaries, he "took hold of his ears and shook his head as if he did not understand the language, though circumstances showed that he could understand very well when he chose." [16] Even *métis* Cherokees who had been exposed to English in their families registered their own resistance by failing to learn, or forgetting, the language of their fathers. For instance, when a visitor from the Six Nations met the widow and the *métis* children of a Highlander named Campbell, a Loyalist in the Revolution, he found that "none of them that I saw could speak English." [17] When Sequoyah, a non-English speaking son of the trader to whom the leading men had entrusted Long Island in 1777, developed his syllabary for Cherokee writing, this new tool was rapidly adopted by traditional men and women who had been indifferent to learning written English. [18]

It is not surprising that missionaries found the Cherokees a poor seedbed for their gospel; the Cherokees had practiced resistance too long. As a resident of the Cherokee country told two Moravians, the "Cherokees were already too civilized and good, and too well acquainted with white people, to be converted easily." [19] In spite of the exertions of many missionaries in the early nineteenth century, the number of Cherokee converts to Christianity remained "relatively small." [20] The hostilities of the Cherokee War and Revolution had re-emphasized the negative insights gained over a century into the culture of Carolina.

Perhaps as a result, their own faith exhibited a strain of rejection of white subsistence, of the things of the opposing culture among them. Articulated in the rhetoric of Cherokee warriors, this rejection was strongly stated in the message of the Ohio Valley "Woodland Prophet" of the 1760s. It eventually had its most clear-cut statement during the "Cherokee Ghost Dance" which reached its height from 1811 to 1813. This movement was inspired by a vision: "a whole crowd of Indians arriving on the hill from the sky: 'Don't be afraid; we are your brothers and have been sent by God to speak with you. God is dissatisfied that you are receiving white people in your land without any distinction. You yourselves see that your hunting is gone—you are planting the corn of the white people—go and sell that back to them and plant Indian corn and pound it in the manner of your forefathers.'" [21] While the Cherokees could not do without the agricultural accommodations of the prior hundred years, they found ways to remind themselves of their apartness.

A Dance of Defiance

Inside Cherokee communities ritual dances projected the attitudes shared by Cherokee villagers toward the outside. There was laughter alongside anger. During the Booger Dance, a Cherokee winter ceremony, villagers donned masks to ridicule their neighbors, black and white.[22] In the earliest eye-witness account, from the 1830s, the Booger dancers were reported to consist of "three or four men disguised in masks, made of large gourds, with openings for the eyes, nose, and mouth, and painted in a hideous manner." These men are revealed as travelers, strangers, and when the onlookers at the dance ask where they are from, they reply "from a far distant land . . . They are invited to dance, and accordingly, perform. . . . Their dancing and accompanying gestures, are so ludicrous, and at the same time, so exactly in imitation of the characters they represent that the giddy multitude are almost convulsed with laughter."[23] The identity of the dancers as intruders, and of the people which they ultimately represent, becomes clearer as the dance progresses.

In early twentieth-century enactments, the masked men represented both old Indians as well as outsiders, dancers who are identified as Germans, French, Chinese, and others "from far away or across the water." The audience suggested derisive names: Black Buttocks, Frenchman, Big Testicles, Sooty Anus, or Penis.[24] Carved wood and gourd masks animated a burlesque. When the dancers were asked what they wanted in the second phase of the dance, they answered "Girls." Before the "sexual pantomime" which concluded, the outsider figures had their names called, and began solo dancing with "awkward and grotesque steps, . . . clumsy white man trying to imitate Indian dancing."[25] The final phase carried out the mock erotic theme. The dancers, some of whom had gourd phalli concealed under their clothing, thrust toward their female partners, but the women, dancing around a corn mortar, "proceeded serenely and the Boogers [did] not insist upon touching them during the dance movement."[26] (Fig. 12)

The Booger Dance was, on one level, an overtly political dance, a private statement of the "Cherokee estimate of the European invader as awkward, ridiculous, lewd, and menacing, a dramatic perpetuation of the tradition of hostility and disdain."[27] In this aspect, however, it may well reflect not only a tradition of instant cultural disdain but also a specific historical etiology—lessons brought forcibly home during the traumatic decades spanned between the Cherokee War crisis years and the end of the Revolution. The Booger Dance, insofar as it was a mechanism for coping with the new American society, represented a way of masking, and thus controlling, the disturbing acts of their neighbors. With the masks on, it was not necessary to deal with confusing individuality. Instead, Americans became a manageable category—fools ignorant of basic Cherokee civilities—whose threat could be dismissed with laughter and indifference. Racial distinctions were subsumed into the American "other"; while the black-mask was swollen and distorted, it was no more unattractive than the 'white' dancer who wore his penis on his face.

The laughter in the midst of the Booger Dance has deep echoes within Cherokee tradition and suggests the degree to which, in spite of extreme disruption, it accommodated itself to a new world. Such laughter, and the dance itself, was regenerative.[28] Old men became revitalized as they danced, and the preoccupation of young men with sexual conquest was on exhibit.[29] The laughter was also a self-healing kind of humor. The Booger Dance was prescribed as a cure for the sick, and the dance helped resolve the inner tensions of Cherokee life—between men and women, young and old, insiders and outsiders, the healthy and the sick.[30] In times such as the Revolutionary era, when the economic and occupational traditions in Cherokee society were threatened, the performance of rituals such as the Booger Dance had a particular, healing intensity.

In the Booger Dance, rural Cherokees set their past outside of the historical record. The Booger Dance, according to tradition, was learned before whites entered the mountains, in the days in which mythical monsters such as Stone Coat, a giant with an invulnerable "stony skin," were on the earth.[31] Stone Coat had warned of the coming of "Caucasians in company with Negroes and strange Indians from the East," and offered the dance as a defense against military onslaught and cultural contamination.[32] Stone Coat's warning held true for the colonial era wars but also kept its application across the eighteenth century. The association of the Booger Dance with the colonial assaults suggests that the Cherokees employed this dance to subsume the events of their recent history in the constancy of myth and thus to steady their collective balance.[33] Perhaps this drama continued to be a source of resilience, even in severe times such as the Revolutionary War period. Whether through communal dances, personal silences, or by building backcountry big houses, Cherokee society masked its core against American society.

Cherokees kept their autonomy, but with certain costs to their society as well. The idea of obligation that lay behind Cherokee gift-giving and rules of hospitality was gradually turned inside out, and white visitors, even if tolerated, were kept at a distance. The love of exchange of all sorts which had fueled trade demands and political involvements gradually dwindled as well. Neither the strategy of accommodation nor that of evasion undertaken respectively by Cherokee progressives and conservatives would eventually succeed without loss.

The Deliverance of John Marrant

After the Revolutionary War, white society chose to put a different face on Cherokee society by fashioning reassuring caricatures. The harsh white-on-white civil war which raged in the western backcountry of South Carolina, together with recurrent threats from the Cherokees, created a climate of Revolutionary crisis. In its wake, backcountry folk, like the mountain villagers, sought refuge in sacred visions fitting their mythic and moral traditions. *A Narrative of the Life of John Marrant,* the story of his captivity among the Cherokees in the years just before the Revolution, was originally published at the close of the Revolution in 1785 in London.[34] Marrant's *Narrative,* one of the most popular of its genre in the post-Revolutionary era,[35] provides a rare insight into the way in which the Great Awakening defensively absorbed disturbing intercultural memories. The story of Marrant suggests that an awareness of the dangers posed by the Cherokees for South Carolina extended even into the unconscious of a religious movement usually understood as purely an internal crisis of faith.

The story straightforwardly relates the Christian conversion and self-discovery of a black fourteen-year-old, and follows his life through dreamlike wanderings in the backcountry, a country where "savage despotism exercised its most terrifying empire."[36] After a charismatic conversion in a Charlestown meeting, Marrant is shunned by his family so far "as to threaten my life." In this crisis, the youth thinks of suicide. Realizing that "if I did destroy myself I could not come where God was," the boy took "to the fields," and "went over the fence about half a mile from our house, which divided the inhabited and cultivated parts of the country from the wilderness."[37]

After befriending an "Indian hunter," Marrant, who has by then taken on the persona of a wild man, enters a Cherokee town, where he is taken hostage and sentenced to death. However, the executioner is converted at the last minute through Marrant's prayers and takes him to the Cherokee king. Accused of witchcraft, Marrant is told that unless he can heal the king's sick daughter, the execution order will be reinstated. The events which follow—the healing of the girl, the conversion of the king, Marrant's visit to three other tribes, his eventual return to his family, and his reunification with the Cherokee king in Charlestown—are significant.

Marrant is a Carolina Everyman, and his message relies on shared experience to communicate the urgency and personal emotion of his story. Thus, beneath the superficial layer of scrambled biblical images in the *Narrative* lies a cluster of references to historical events and tensions which ground Marrant's work firmly in the backcountry history of South Carolina. At the beginning of the parable, Marrant crossed the fence between tame and wild land—an image which offered particular connotations in the perceptual landscape of Carolinians, where the possibilities of Indian war or slave insurrection had invested the wilderness, especially the Cherokee Mountains, with an intense darkness. The same image had recurred in sources as various as Henry Lauren's recollections or in the militiaman's powderhorn from the Grant campaign. Similarly, Marrant returns to his family from the Cherokees dressed as a wild man, in the "skins of wild beasts . . . without breeches, and a tomahawk by my side," [38] resembling the costumed actors of the Booger Dance. The reunion plays on the threat posed to the Euroamerican ideal of proper family relationships by Cherokee society:

> My affections to my family were not dead . . . and at last strengthened into an invincible desire of returning home . . . in two days I reached the settlements, and on the third I found a house; it was about dinner-time, and as I came up to the door the family saw me, were frightened and ran away.
>
> I sat down to dinner alone and ate very heartily, and after returning God thanks, I went to see what had become of the family. I found means to lay hold of a girl that stood peeping at me from behind a barn. She fainted away, and it was upwards of an hour before she recovered; it was nine o'clock before I could get them all to venture in, they were so terrified. [39]

The political message of the story also touches on aspects of the relationship between the English and Cherokees, in which the Cherokees had long been assumed to hold a special place—for good or for ill—in the future of the colony. Marrant's visits to other tribes, the Creeks, Catawbas, and Housaws, who, unlike the Cherokees, were not "savingly wrought upon," were unsuccessful. [40] Furthermore, his failure among these tribes ("who often united and murdered all the white people in the back settlements which they could lay hold of, man, women and child") echoes the experience of the Yamassee and Cherokee wars. True to their history of dangerous centrality in the life of the colony, the Cherokees were singled out for salvation, while, in reality, more faithful, but less potent, allies such as the Catawbas were not. Whereas Charlestown had always feared the hostile mobilization of the western tribes by Afroamericans, Marrant, a black man, had become the instrument of red spiritual detente. In the Marrant parable, history was retold and reversed. The fact that the king had allied himself to the British was less important in the narrative than the underlying drama of saving reunification. If the historical tradition of the mingled fates of colony and tribe was still alive, the decisive punitive actions against the tribe in 1776 finally made the Cherokees safe to employ as reassuring symbols for sacred work.

Like Marrant, the Cherokees had been saved for higher things and donned a mask of Christian civility, as reassuringly comical as the Booger Dance players. Awakened readers of the *Narrative* could rest easier with the knowledge that the old and frightening terrain across the fence, in the mountains to the west, had been tamed. In both cases, for both societies, the masking served to diminish the power of their neighbors and to acknowledge the rightness of whoever was calling the dance.

An Upcountry Dance

The period of the Revolution brought to a climax the worst of the hostilities and disappointments which were to come between the two peoples during the eighteenth century. During the period from the Cherokee War through the Revolution, the deciding movements were set in a complicated choreography played out between the two peoples. Dances were set and masks donned which would continue to be seen well into the nineteenth century and beyond.

There were many versions of such movements on both sides, and ironic reversals of identity. Some nineteenth-century Cherokee warriors would eventually transform themselves into planters and slaveholders, just as the ambitious eighteenth-century planters of western South Carolina had for a time put on warrior-masks. Some of these masked men would later reappear to haunt the Cherokees. Those places most directly experiencing intercultural violence during the Cherokee War and Revolutionary era—for instance Long Cane and Waxhaws or, later, the Cumberland settlement at Nashville—were the epicenters of cultural antagonism.[41] The unique intercultural matrix of family and individual conduct evident in the careers of the men of influence in western communities such as Long Cane during the 1760s, also persisted into the nineteenth century. John C. Calhoun, who remembered the manner in which the life of his father, Patrick Calhoun, had been fated by conflict with the Cherokees, in another context offered a view of moral life which suggested a long tradition of building imperfect barriers: "The moral is like the physical world," Calhoun wrote, "Nature has incrusted the exterior of all organic life, for its safety. Let that be broken through, and all is weakness within."[42] The psychosocial legacy of eighteenth-century intercultural relations in backcountry South Carolina contributed to the formation of rigid, defensive poses designed to protect the autonomy of individual men and their families. The patriarchal pose, as well as the personalized idiom of violence it defended against, still characterizes white ethnicity in the region. Whatever mode of Southern behavior was originally received, was quickly reshaped through the decades of the eighteenth century; inheritance was recast by history, including the intercultural experience central to the story of the Cherokees and Carolina.

The rural society that came to surround the Appalachian Cherokees was given great torque against the land and its neighbors by its technology, market ties, and weight of population. However, the most violent intrusion of American power was inspired by an individual's legacy, a personal inheritance of community anger rooted in the colonial middle ground. Andrew Jackson, marked by growing up in the tense world of the Waxhaws and a young adulthood lived in a Nashville harassed within general memory by Chickamauga raids, would as President mastermind the genocidal Removal of the Cherokees in 1838.

The Cherokees were forced off their land and made to march to mid-continent from their mountains under brutal military guard. There was controversy and ineffective protest among sympathetic whites, philosophical heirs of James Adair. Four thousand of the 13,000 Cherokee men, women, and children would die. In the mountains, small groups of traditional Cherokees resisted and stayed, as they have to this day. There, from time to time, habits of fear returned to the white majority; when, for instance, John Brown planned to bring his army of black liberation from the Adirondacks down the spine of the Appalachians to the old rear launching place of interracial attack.[43] Yet the bluish haze of the mountain coves, deepened and thickened by the hydrocarbons of nineteenth-century coal fires, had little that was frightening left to hide.

The colonial-period South was a profoundly tri-cultural society, and the pervasive consciousness of this fact among whites powerfully formed the colonial sense of self. A significant, but overlooked, source of reinforcement was the long intersection of a slaveholding colonial society with an indigenous culture in which autonomy and dependency were handled in radically different fashion. Issues of personality, of race and gender, of the proprieties of violence and love were all mingled in this intersection. But the continuing vulnerability at the center, of elite ambitions especially, was protected against by a loss of latitude in personal, family, and community relationships. And narrowing life required narrowing history, just as maintaining personal autonomy sometimes required forgetting the past. A reworked memory concerning the red, white, and black of the colonial period was gradually, in the late nineteenth and twentieth century, reabsorbed into the simplified contours of southern ethnicity, especially of black-white relationships. The sense, shared by mid-twentieth-century white southerners, of an "edgy blackness and whiteness of things . . . the metaphors we created and turned ourselves into," no longer included,[44] in all but the most out of the way places, redness—an Amerindian past or present.

This absence of part of the story reflects, to a large degree, the way in which particular events of the colonial period resulted in the willful collective distancing of red and white people from the reality of one another's lives. After the Revolution, and before the Removal, the Cherokees would engage in a remarkable renaissance, managed and presented to the American public by *métis* Cherokee planters and white sympathizers and missionaries. Yet these families remained profoundly in the middle, between two societies whose drift apart already had a long history and momentum behind it. The Removal, in the end, ensured that this divisiveness would continue against the best and most imaginative efforts of a new generation to resist it.

The Cherokee Removal only gave physical reality to the already existing cultural alienation of Cherokees and whites. For the majority of Americans who lived outside of the foothills of Georgia or South Carolina and the plateaus and low basins of central Tennessee, the Cherokees were more and more out of mind. For both societies the most comfortable course had become to put aside the other's existence or to control what was visible. Among the traditional Cherokees, who were becoming a minority in their own country by the end of the century, such escape sometimes meant tension and effort, as they often lived next to white settlements. There was familiarity and friendship between neighbors, a shared mountain identity, but always with the sense in mixed gathering that lines had been crossed. Old ambivalent admiration for the Cherokees persisted in atrophy. For instance, prosperous farmers were likely to have turned to *The Cherokee Physician, or Indian Guide to Health,* published in western North Carolina in 1849, for medical advice. And in the Removal year of 1838, while the Cherokees were being rounded up, South Carolina novelist William Gilmore Simms aimed at the Charleston literary set a new volume of "tales of the imagination" which included "Jocassee," a Cherokee romance set around "Keowee old Ford . . . a fine antique ruin and relic of the Revolution."

Each society had served as a mirror for the other, revealing weaknesses and strengths in an intense comparative light, but at the same time distorting the underlying humanity of each. In the reflected image, each saw projected fears concerning its own failings as well as real and profound differences of interest. The images caught in this brittle mirror represented losses on both sides which would never be recaptured. Eventually, along the Dividing Path of Cherokee-Carolina history, the mirror shattered, its pieces reflecting bits of lost sky.

The political reality facing the tribe could not be presaged by old metaphors. The "white cloth" offered by the Beloved Woman in the valley and her messenger, the Bird, at Dewisse's Corner, near the original Dividing Line in 1777, was intended symbolically to cover over the scars left by the fire in the path in 1776. The Beloved Woman's offering came too late to effect conciliation between Americans and Cherokees. For most Cherokees and Americans the path would soon be gullied and unused. Whereas the Cherokees would remember the Removal as a central event in their history, for the vast majority of Americans there was forgetfulness, as if memory itself was removed west. When a white visitor walked in the 1830s over the site of the old village of Nequassee, where Alexander Cuming had negotiated his 1730 treaty, and not far from isolated but still-occupied Cherokee communities, he speculated on its future: "this most delightful place is now owned by an enterprising gentleman of Macon County . . . by whom we may expect the site of the old Indian town to be converted into a paradise." [45]

Notes

INTRODUCTION

1. Mark Van Doren, ed., *Travels of William Bartram* (1791; reprint, New York: Dover Publications, 1955), 283. Christopher French, "Journal of an Expedition to South Carolina," *Journal of Cherokee Studies* 2 (Summer 1977): 289.

2. "With an Indian Mound for his pulpit," William Hall preached a "most affecting and thrilling sermon, insomuch that, as the good man's voice echoed through the surrounding woods, there was scarcely a dry eye to be seen." "Historical Sketch of the Indian War of 1776," *North Carolina University Magazine* 1 (May 1852): 136.

3. Louis Philippe, *Diary of My Travels in America,* trans. Stephen Becker (New York: Delacorte Press, 1977), 70.

4. A note on terms. The story proves hard to tell without relying on words like tribe and colonist, terms weighted by history and therefore somewhat biased for the present-day reader. The Cherokees regularly called themselves a people—never tribe with its implications of political solidarity and uniformity. And colonist cloaks the experience of many peoples: African, English, Scot, German. Like colonist, even the label Cherokee was a new word that implied the experience and conditions of the new world faced by both sides. Carolina is used throughout as shorthand for South Carolina, unless North Carolina is specified.

5. Albert Memmi, *Dependence: A Sketch for a Portrait of the Dependent,* trans. Phillip A. Facey (Boston: Beacon Press, 1984).

6. Society for the Propagation of the Gospel Mss., A, II, 156, quoted in Verner W. Crane, *Southern Frontier, 1670–1732* (1929; reprint ed., New York: W. W. Norton, 1981), 136.

7. Peter H. Wood, "The Changing Population of the Colonial South: An Overview by Race and Region, 1685–1790," in *Powhatan's Mantle: Indians in the Colonial South* (Lincoln: University of Nebraska Press, 1989), 47. For a longer view of Cherokee population, see Russell Thornton, *The Cherokee: A Population History* (Lincoln: University of Nebraska Press, 1990).

8. John Drayton, *A View of South Carolina* (Charleston: W. P. Young, 1802), 14.

9. George Hunter, "This Represents the Chareeke Nation by Col. Herberts Map and My own Observations, with the Path to Charles Town," 1730.

CHAPTER ONE

1. Alexander Longe, "A Small Postscript on the Ways and Manners of the Indians called Cherokees," ed. David H. Corkran, *Southern Indian Studies* 11 (October 1969): 40–42.

2. Ibid., 42.

3. James Mooney, *Myths of the Cherokees* in *Nineteenth Annual Report of the Bureau of American Ethnology,* 1897–98. Part 1 (Washington, D.C.: Government Printing Office, 1990; reprint ed., Nashville, Tenn.: Charles and Randy Elder—Booksellers, 1982), 329–30.

4. A nineteenth-century retelling of the story located the lost town at a place called Kanasta on the French Broad River. Mooney, *Myths,* 341–42, 479.

5. Ibid., 523; James Mooney, "The Sacred Formulas of the Cherokees," in *Seventh Annual Report of the Bureau of American Ethnology,* 1885–86 (Washington, D.C.: Government Printing Office, 1891; reprint ed. Nashville: Charles and Randy Elder—Booksellers, 1982), 342.

6. Alfred W. Crosby, "Virgin Soil Epidemics as a Factor in the Aboriginal Depopulation in America," *William and Mary Quarterly* 33 (April 1976): 289–99; Ian W. Brown, "A Study of the Stone Box Graves in Eastern North America," *Tennessee Anthropologist* 6 (Spring 1981): 14–9; Nancy Teppen Baker, "From Fort Ancient to Shawnee," paper presented at the Annual Meeting, American Society for Ethnohistory, Chicago, October 15, 1977.

7. For an important though controversial discussion of the demographic disaster which spilled over into the north, see Henry L. Dobyns, *Their Number Become Thinned* (Knoxville: University of Tennessee Press, 1983). For the southeast as a whole, see Marvin T. Smith, *Archaeology of Aboriginal Culture Change in the Interior Southeast: Depopulation During the Early Historic Period* (Gainesville: University of Florida Press, 1987).

8. This judgment is offered in Charles R. Hudson, "The Genesis of Georgia's Indians," in Harvey H. Jackson and Phinizy Spalding, eds., *Forty Years of Diversity: Essays on Colonial Georgia* (Athens: University of Georgia Press, 1984), 31. See also Marvin T. Smith, "Aboriginal Population Movements in the Early Historic Period Interior Southeast" in *Powhatan's Mantle,* ed. Peter H. Wood, G. Waselkov, and T. Hatley (Lincoln: University of Nebraska Press, 1989). For the *entradas,* see Charles Hudson, *The Juan Pardo Expeditions: Exploration of the Carolinas and Tennessee, 1566–1568* (Washington, D.C.: Smithsonian Institution Press, 1990).

9. Charles Hudson, "Some Thoughts on the Early Social History of the Cherokees," in *The Conference on Cherokee Prehistory,* assemb. David G. Moore (Swannanoa, N.C.: Warren Wilson College, 1986), 139–53; David J. Halley, "The Cherokee Archaeology of Georgia," in *The Conference on Cherokee Prehistory,* 95–121.

10. [George Chicken], "A Journal from Carolina in 1715," ed. Langdon Cheeves, *Year Book of the City of Charleston* (1894), 330. During a 1727 conference, the Long Warrior of Tunisee recalled that the Yamassee had once lived with the Lower Cherokees. Old Cherokee men still spoke their language. Discourse with the Long Warrior, January 24–25, 1726/27, C.O. 5/387/237 (microfilm in Western Carolina University Library).

11. Duane H. King, "Vessel Morphology of Eighteenth-Century Overhill Ceram-

ics,'' *Journal of Cherokee Studies* (Winter 1977), 154–69; David Halley, "Cherokee Archaeology,'' 115.

12. Crane, *Southern Frontier*, 142.

13. See Peter H. Wood, "The Impact of Smallpox on the Native Population of the 18th Century South,'' *New York State Journal of Medicine* 87 (January 1987): 30–36.

14. John Lawson, *A New Voyage to Carolina*, ed. Hugh T. Lefler (London: 1709; reprint ed. Chapel Hill: University of North Carolina Press, 1967) 232.

15. Mark Catesby, "Of the Aborigines of Carolina and Florida,'' ms. in Royal Society, Decade I, #19, 13 (microfilm at the Library of Congress).

16. See Chapter 3 for more discussion of the impact of the slave trade on the Cherokees.

17. See Daniel K. Richter, "War and Culture: The Iroquois Experience,'' *William and Mary Quarterly* 40 (October 1983): 528–59.

18. Crane, *Southern Frontier*, 254.

19. [John Barnwell], Map of Southern North America, by W. Hammercon, 1721, Map Folio B, IR-237, Yale Center for British Art, Collection of Paul Mellon; the much better known colonial office copy is in P.R.O., C.O., N.A.C., General 7.

20. Wilbur R. Jacobs, *Indians of the Southern Frontier: The Edmond Atkin Report and Plan of 1755* (Columbia: University of South Carolina Press, 1954), 57.

21. Samuel Cole Williams, *Adair's History of the American Indian* (London: 1775; reprint ed. New York: Promontory Press, 1973), 39.

22. Van Doren, *Bartram's Travels*, 68; Williams, *Adair's History*, 236.

23. Klinch and Talman, *Norton's Journal* (Toronto: Champlain Society, 1970), 82.

24. Francis Varnod to the Secretary, Society for the Propagation of the Gospel in Foreign Part, April 1, 1723, Letters from the Carolinas, Letter Book 18, Doc. 173 (microfilm in the Western Carolina University Library).

25. Wood, "The Changing Population of the South,'' *Powhatan's Mantle*, figure 1.

26. Anne Matthews, "Memoirs,'' typescript in South Carolinian Library, Columbia, 5; for an anthropological perspective see Fred Gearing, "The Structural Pose of 18th Century Cherokee Villages,'' *American Anthropologist* 60 (December 1958): 1149.

27. Richard A. Yarnell and Jean M. Black, "Temporal Trends Indicated by a Survey of Archaic and Woodland Plant Food Remains from Southeastern North America,'' *Southeastern Archaeology* 4 (1985): 93–106.

28. Thomas Hatley, "Holding Their Ground: Eighteenth-Century Cherokee Women's Farming,'' in *Appalachian Frontiers*, ed. Robert Mitchell (Lexington: The University Press of Kentucky, 1990.)

29. Antoine Simon Le Page du Pratz, *History of Louisiana* (London, 1774), 204–5. Charred black-eyed peas have recently been discovered in excavations at the Creek town of Fusihatchee. Gregory A. Waselkov, "Seventeenth-Century Trade in the Colonial Southeast,'' *Southeastern Archaeology* 8 (1989), 127.

30. For village names see Mooney, *Myths*, 517–25.

31. Mark Catesby to Sir Hans Sloane, November 27, 1724, British Museum, Sloane Ms. 4047/290 (microfilm copy in Western Carolina University Library).

32. Price Hughes to the Duchess of Ormonde, October 13, 1715, quoted in Crane, *Southern Frontier*, 103, fn 101.

33. John Stuart to BOT, March 9, 1764, C.O., 323/17/240 (microfilm copy in Western Carolina University Library).

34. Talk of the Cherokee Indians to Governor Glen, November 14, 1751, in *Documents Relating to Indian Affairs, May 21, 1750–August 7, 1754,* ed. William M. McDowell, Jr. (Columbia: South Carolina Archives Department, 1958), (*DRIA,* I), 177.

35. Longe, "A Small Postscript," 46.

36. Old Hop's Reply to Captain Demere's Speech at Tomatley, October 3, 1756, in *Documents Relating to Indian Affairs, 1754–65,* ed. William M. McDowell, Jr. (Columbia: South Carolina Department of Archives and History, 1970), (*DRIA,* II), 224.

37. Ludovic Grant to Governor Glen, May 4, 1752, *DRIA,* I, 238.

38. Eleanor Leacock, "Ethnohistorical Investigation of Egalitarian Politics in Eastern North America," in *The Development of Political Organization In Native North America,* 20, 25–29.

39. Ibid., 20.

40. Raymond D. Fogelson, "Who Were the Ani-Kutani? An Excursion into Cherokee Historical Thought," *Ethnohistory* 31 (Winter 1984): 255; Leacock, "Ethnohistorical Investigation of Egalitarian Politics," 1–16.

41. Gearing, "Structural Poses," 1148.

42. Stuart to BOT, March 9, 1764, 256.

43. Ludovic Grant to Governor Glen, July 22, 1754, *DRIA,* II, 18.

44. Captain Raymond Demere to Governor Lyttelton, July 30, 1757, *DRIA,* II, 392.

45. Stuart to BOT, March 9, 1764, 268.

46. Proceedings of the Council Concerning Indian Affairs, July 5, 1753, *DRIA,* I, 441. An incident described in the early phase of the Georgia settlement illustrates the egalitarian politics of such speech. "One of the Indians of the Cherokee Nation being come down to the governor, [the Governor] told him, that he need fear nothing, but might speak freely. He answered smartly, 'I always speak freely, what should I fear? I am now among my friends and I never feared among my enemies.' " An Honorable Person, "A Curious Account of the Indians," *Collections of the Georgia Historical Society* 2 (1842), 63.

47. Stuart "Of Indians in General," 265.

48. Ibid., 255.

49. A Cherokee town delivered to a Virginia agent a gift of "pipes (of great value among them)," intended for the King of England, along with special instructions. As the pipes were colored red, the agent wrote, "they have ordered me to cover them over with Chaulk as everything that comes from them in peace must be white." Report from John Cary on the Cherokees, September 18, 1728, C.O., 5/1337/128; See also Gearing, "Structural Poses," 1152–55.

50. [Chicken], "Journal, 1715," 330.

51. Longe, "A Small Postscript," 14; Williams, *Adair's History,* 90–93.

52. Fogelson, "Who Were the Ani-Kutani? 255–63.

53. Ibid.

54. James Mooney, "The Cherokee River Cult," *The Journal of American Folklore* 9 (January–March 1900): 1.

55. Ludovic Grant to Governor Glen, February 8, 1754, *DRIA,* I, 474.

56. Captain Raymd. Demere to Governor Lyttelton, October 29, 1756, *DRIA*, II, 237.

57. Mankiller of Tellico to Raymond Demere, February 6, 1757, *DRIA*, II, 333; Examination of James Beamer by the Governor and Council, [1754], *DRIA*, I, 516.

58. Samuel C. Williams, *Lieut. Henry Timberlake's Memoirs* (Johnson City, Tenn.: Watauga Press, 1927).

59. Catesby, "Of the Aborigines"; see also Mark Catesby, *Natural History of Carolina, Florida and the Bahamas Islands* (London, 1754), II, 57.

60. Catesby, "Of the Aborigines," 6.

61. Ibid. During the English encampment in Tugaloo town in 1715 the local headman estimated that of 2,370 "gunmen," he "beleiv'd half of them had Guns." [Chicken], "Journal," 343; Mary Rothrock, "Carolina Traders Among the Cherokees," *East Tennessee Historical Society Publication* (1929): 4–5. See also Donald F. Worcester and Thomas F. Schilz, "The Spread of Firearms Among the Indians on the Anglo-French Frontiers," *American Indian Quarterly* 8 (Spring 1984): 103.

62. "A Map Describing the situation of the several Nations of Indians between South Carolina and the Mississippi; was Copied from a Draught Drawn upon a Deer Skin by an Indian Cacique and Presented to Francis Nicholson Esqr. Governor of Carolina," C.O., 700, 6 (2); Gregory Waselkov, "Indian Maps of the Southeast," in *Powhatan's Mantle*.

63. Waselkov, "Indian Maps."

64. Stuart to BOT, June 8, 1764, C.O., 323/17/255. For Nairne's account of the Chickasaw *fane mingo,* as this office was called, see Alexander Moore, *Nairne's Muskhogean Journals: The 1708 Expedition to the Mississippi River* (Jackson: University of Mississippi Press, 1988), 40–41.

65. One of the first historical writers on the Iroquois emphasized this connection by noting that "nothing is more distinct in the existing traditions of Iroquois, than their wars with some of the southern tribes, particularly the Cherokees." Henry Schoolcraft, *Notes on the Iroquois* (Albany: Erastus H. Pease and Co., 1847), 252. See also Anthony F. C. Wallace, *The Death and Rebirth of the Seneca* (New York: Knopf, 1969), 101, and Richter, "War and Culture," 557–58.

66. Thomas Nairne to the BOT, July 10, 1708, C.O., 5/382/24 (microfilm in Western Carolina Library).

67. Catesby, "Of the Aborigines," 14.

68. [Barnwell], Manuscript Map (1721).

69. David G. Anderson, "Stability and Change in Chiefdom-Level Societies: An Examination of Misissippian Political Evolution on the South Atlantic Slope" (xeroxed), November 1986, p. 22.

CHAPTER TWO

1. Henry Woodward, "A Faithful Relation of My Westoe Voyage," December 31, 1764," in *Narratives of Early Carolina*, ed. Alexander S. Salley, Jr. (New York: Scribner's, 1911), 127–34.

2. [Barnwell], Manuscript Map [1721].

3. William P. Cumming, *The Southeast in Early Maps* (Princeton: Princeton University Press, 1958), 47.

4. [Barnwell], Manuscript Map, [1721].

5. Verner W. Crane, "The Tennessee River as the Road to Carolina: The Beginnings of Exploration and Trade," *The Mississippi Valley Historical Review* 3 (June 1916): 9. For background on Nairne's attitudes, see Moore, *Nairne's Muskhogean Journals*.

6. For the location of the fort (near present-day Tallahassee) and a discussion of the Spanish presence in the area in the eighteenth century, see John J. TePaske, *The Governorship of Spanish Florida, 1700–1763* (Durham: Duke University Press, 1964), 6, and facing map.

7. Cumming, *Southeast in Early Maps*, 68.

8. Mooney, *Myths*, 201; C. D. Huneycutt and Roy Blalock, Jr., *The Pardo Expeditions, 1566–1567* (New London, N.C.: Gold Star Press, Star Press, 1981), 38–41; Chester DePratter, Charles Hudson, Marvin T. Smith, "The Route of Juan Pardo's Expeditions in the Interior Southeast, 1566–1568," *Florida Historical Quarterly* 62 (October 1983): 134–35; Charles C. Jones, *Antiquities of the Southern Indians, Particularly of the Georgia Tribes* (New York: Appleton and Company, 1873), 48–49.

9. "In hoc lacu Indigenae argenti grani invenieunt." Le Moyne, "Floridae Americae Provinciae . . . descriptio," 1565.

10. DeBry, *America*. (Frankfurt, 1591), plate XLI.

11. John Lederer, *The Discoveries of John Lederer from Virginia to the West of Carolina and other parts of the Continent*, ed. William P. Cumming, Jr. (1672; reprint, Charlottesville: University of Virginia Press, 1958). Crane, *Southern Frontier*, 14–15. Lederer never actually left the Piedmont. See Alan V. Briceland, *Westward from Virginia: The Exploration of the Virginia-Carolina Frontier, 1650–1710* (Charlottesville: University Press of Virginia, 1987).

12. Lederer, *Discoveries*, 43. A new map, produced especially for the Proprietors, dovetailed with Lederer's description by depicting mines at the base of the mountains. See John Ogilby, "A New Description of Carolina, [1672], in Cumming, *Southeast in Early Maps*, plate 37.

13. Ibid., 4.

14. See Peter H. Wood, "La Salle: Discovery of a Lost Explorer," *American Historical Review* (April 1984).

15. Lederer, *Discoveries*, 17.

16. Crane, "River Road," 5.

17. James Moore to Edward Randolph, [1699], C.O., 5/1258/19 quoted in Crane, *Southern Frontier*, 40–44; Charles C. Jones, *Antiquities of the Southern Indians, Particularly of the Georgia Tribes* (New York: Appleton and Company, 1873), 50–51.

18. Quoted in Crane, "River Road," 5.

19. Ibid., 14.

20. Between 1702 and 1713 the Carolina colonists were pulled into Queen Anne's War between England and Spain and France.

21. Crane, *Southern Frontier*, 74–80.

22. Lederer, *Discoveries*, 11.

23. Thomas Nairne to [Secretary of State], July 10, 1708, P.R.O., C.O., vol. 620 (typescript in South Carolina Department of Archives), quoted in ibid., 18, n. 44.

24. Marcel Giraud, *Histoire de la Louisiane française,* vol. II (Paris: Presses Universitaires de France, 1958), 177; John B. Fortier, "New Light Fort Massac," in *Frenchmen and French Ways in the Mississippi Valley,* ed. John F. McDermott (Urbana: University of Illinois, 1969), 58.

25. Cf. Pierre François Xavier de Charlevoix, "Historical Journal," in *Historical Collections of Louisiana* (New York: Appleton and Company, 1851), 122.

26. Giraud, *Histoire de la Louisiane,* 171; Norman Caldwell, "Fort Massac During the French and Indian War," *Journal of the Illinois State Historical Society* 43 (Summer 1950): 101.

27. Guillaume Delisle, "Carte d'Amérique," 1703.

28. The best narrative of the complicated Yamassee conflict is in Crane, *Southern Frontier,* 164–86.

29. Ibid., 172.

30. Gideon Johnson to the Secretary, October 13, 1715, reprinted in Frank Klingburg, ed., *Carolina Chronicle,* University of California Publications in History (Berkeley: University of California Press, 1956), 147.

31. Francis Le Jau to the Secretary, November 28, 1715, SPG B4, doc. 32.

32. George Chicken, "Letter from Carolina, 1715," 321. Also see [Chicken], "Journal, 1715," 324–54.

33. [Chicken], "Journal, 1715," 331.

34. David H. Corkran, "Introduction to Alexander Longe's 'Small Postscript,' " *Southern Indian Studies* 11 (October 1969): np; [Chicken], "Journal, 1715," 334.

35. Crane, *Southern Frontier,* 17.

36. James Moore, Sr., "An Account of What the Army Did Under the Command of Colonel Moore . . . in a Letter," May 1, 1704, *Boston News,* in Carroll, *South Carolina Historical Collections,* II, 574–76; Crane, *Southern Frontier,* 75–81; TePaske, *Governorship of Spanish Florida,* 115.

37. [Chicken], "Journal, 1715," 331.

38. Ibid., 331.

39. Ibid., 342.

40. Ibid.

41. LeJau to Secretary, November 28, 1715, SPG B4, doc 32.

42. [Chicken], "Journal, 1715," 343.

43. Assembly to Agents, March 15, 1715/16, quoted in Crane, *Southern Frontier,* 182.

44. LeJau to SPG, March 19, 1715/16, quoted, ibid., 183.

45. LeJau to SPG, March 19, 1715/16, quoted, ibid., 184.

46. Ibid., 180.

47. South Carolina Council to Dinwiddie, November 1, 1753, *DRIA,* I, 467, noted that the Creeks "are very attentive to the punctillioes of form" and suggested that the Creeks would turn down an invitation to a conference in Winchester "unless they previously received some token from the several tribes . . . as an invitation to them."

48. Report of John Cary on the Cherokees, September 18, 1728, C.O., 5/1337/128.

49. Mark Boyd, ed., "Diego Peña's Expedition to Apalachee and Apalachicolo in 1716," *Florida Historical Quarterly* 28 (July 1949): 10; Similar reports came from English sources: "The Creeks came upon a town called Nogoulchee and destroyed it, carrying off an abundance of slaves." [William Hatton?, "Some Short Remarks on the

Indian Trade in the Charikkes and the Management there of Since the Year 1717, [1725?], ms. in the Historical Society of Pennsylvania, 13.

50. William Hatton to Governor Nicholson, November 14, 1724, S. C. Governor's Papers, folio 1266–88, C. O. 5/359/421 (microfilm copy in South Carolina Department of Archives and History).

51. Ibid.

52. Talk of the Headmen of Tenassee to Governor Glen, August 9, 1751, *DRIA,* II, 101.

53. Talk of the Overhill Cherokees to Governor Glen, April 9, 1751, *DRIA,* I, 64.

54. Abstract of Letter to Joseph Boone, June 24, 1720, C.O. 5/358/7.

55. Crane, *Southern Frontier,* 263.

56. Samuel C. Williams, ed., "Introduction," "Cuming's Journal" in *Early Travels in the Tennessee Country* (Johnson City: Watauga Press, 1928), 117; Alexander Cuming, [1764], "Memoir of Alex. Cuming," British Museum Add. Mss. 39855, folio 1, 25; William O. Steele, *The Cherokee Crown of Tannassy* (Winston-Salem: John F. Blair, Pub., 1977).

57. These figures are quoted in James Glen, *A Description of South Carolina,* in Chapman J. Milling, ed., *Colonial South Carolina: Two Contemporary Descriptions* (London, 1761; reprint ed. Columbia: University of South Carolina Press, 1951), 89.

58. [Barnwell], "Manuscript Map [1721]." However incomplete, Barnwell's mapping of the Appalachians was used as the baseline for maps of the mountains until the mid-1750s. Cumming, *The Southeast in Early Maps,* 48–49.

59. Mooney, *Myths,* 528. A Grant campaign map of 1761 employed the term potato-hills for the Knobby County in the Little Tennessee and French Broad headwaters.

60. For instance, in February 1730, North Carolinian John Brickell set out on a journey to the "Charokee Mountains." John Brickell, *The Natural History of North Carolina,* ed. Carol Urness (Dublin, 1737; reprint ed. New York: Johnson Reprint, 1969), 387. Cf. Plat of Wilkinson Grant, December 8, 1770, C.O. 5/74/38.

61. [Chicken], "Journal, 1715," 341.

CHAPTER THREE

1. From a sixteenth-century beginning, the Spanish trade with indigenous southeasterners was already over a century old by the time of English colonization. For archaeological and ethnohistorical insights into this commerce see Waselkov, "Seventeenth-Century Trade;" Crane, *Southern Frontier,* 21. Manakin Town was at the falls of the James River near present-day Richmond, while Savannah Town and the Waxhaws were located, respectively, near the future locations of Augusta, Ga., and Fort Mill, S.C.

2. Crane, *Southern Frontier,* 41.

3. In North Carolina, an innkeeper's lawsuit with a guest listed significant losses on stolen goods including "Buckaneer gun," "two pistols" and an "Indian or Cherokee basket." N.C. General Court, July 1725, in *Colonial Records of North Carolina,* ed. William Saunders, 2nd Series, I, 138.

4. Williams, *Adair's History,* 456.

5. Indian Trade Commissioners Journal, November 16, 1716, in William L. Mc-Dowell, ed., *Journals of the Commissioners of the Indian Trade, September 20, 1710–*

August 29, 1718, in *Colonial Records of South Carolina, Series 2: The Indian Books* (Columbia: South Carolina Archives Department, 1955), 126–28.

6. Estimates of the dimensions of Indian slavery in the English colonies vary widely. For a conservative account, see the William R. Snell, "Indian Slavery in Colonial South Carolina, 1671–1795" (Ph.D. Thesis, University of Alabama, 1972).

7. In 1716 a group of Cherokees attacked another tribe solely for the purpose of obtaining slaves for sale to the colony. Crane, *Southern Frontier,* 146. See Moore, *Nairne's Muskhogean Journals,* 13.

8. The manuscript copy of this treaty no longer exists. Cf. Mooney, *Myths,* 30–31.

9. John Woort to John Bee, July 30, 1723, C.O. 5/359/67.

10. For a discussion of the transformation in the commercial culture of the pre-Yamassee War trade as it existed in trading centers such as the Catawbas, see James H. Merrell, " 'Our Bond of Peace': Patterns of Intercultural Exchange in the Carolina Piedmont" in *Powhatan's Mantle,* 196–223.

11. See W. Neil Franklin, "Virginia and the Cherokee Indian Trade, 1673–1752," *East Tennessee Historical Publications* 4 (January 1933): 3–21.

12. See Crane, *Southern Frontier,* 179, 196.

13. Memorial of Robert Bunning and Others, November 22, 1751, *DRIA,* I, 149.

14. Jacobs, *Atkin's Report,* 36; see also, Maj. Gen. Gage to Earl of Shelburne, January 17, 1767, C.O. 323/25/36.

15. Trade Commissioners Journal, July 24, 1716, *Journals of the Commissioners of the Indian Trade,* 84.

16. Rothrock, "Carolina Traders," 1.

17. Trade Commissioners Journal, July 24, 1716, *Journals of the Commissioners of the Indian Trade,* 85.

18. Ibid., November 7, 1716, 123.

19. See George Chicken, "Colonel Chicken's Journal to the Cherokees, 1725," in *Travels in the American Colonies* (New York: Macmillan, 1916), 97–172.

20. For 1731 law see Thomas Cooper, *The Statutes at Large of South Carolina* (Columbia: A. S. Johnston, 1838), III, 330. For black labor in the trade, see Peter H. Wood, *Black Majority: The Negro in Colonial South Carolina from 1670 Through the Stono Rebellion* (New York: Knopf, 1974), 114–19.

21. Negroes were housed in a separate Cherokee town from white troops. [George Chicken], Letter from a Gentleman in Charlestown to the Carolina Agents in London, July 19, 1715, ed. Langdon Cheeves, *Yearbook of the City of Charleston,* 321; [Chicken], "Journal, 1715," 339, 351.

22. See Peter H. Wood, *Black Majority,* 114–19.

23. Cooper, *Statutes at Large,* III, 330; Cherokee lobbying contributed to the repeal of the restrictive public monopoly created in 1717, cf. John P. Reid, *A Better Kind of Hatchet: Law, Trade and Diplomacy in the Cherokee Nation in the Early Years of European Contact,* (Philadelphia: Temple University Press, 1976), 96.

24. [Chicken], "Journal, 1715," 344.

25. Ibid., 348.

26. Raven of Hiawassee to Governor Glen, May 14, 1751, *DRIA,* I, 75.

27. Memorial of Robert Bunning and Others, *DRIA,* I, 150.

28. *Journal of the Commons House of Assembly* January 17, 18, 1716/17, quoted in Crane, *Southern Frontier,* 196.

29. William L. McDowell, Jr., "Introduction," *DRIA*, II, xxxvii; for continuing Creek resentment of this post-Yamassee War policy, see the Talk of Oakfuskee, May 31, 1753, *DRIA*, II, 398.

30. Crane, *Southern Frontier*, 188, 195. The Congaree fort was near present-day Columbia, S.C.

31. [William Hatton?], "Some Short Remarks on the Indian Trade," 2.

32. Crane, *Southern Frontier*, 195.

33. See Franklin, "Virginia and the Cherokee Indian Trade," 3–21. The western tribes may have been the first source of horses for the Cherokees. By the 1750s the Chickasaw town was surrounded by "open, rich Champain plaine about ten miles in circumference," which would have been the natural outcome of both fire and grazing over many years. Wilbur R. Jacobs, *Indians of the Southern Frontier: The Edmond Atkin Report and Plan of 1755*, (Columbia: The University of South Carolina Press, 1954), 70. Samuel C. Williams quoted an early nineteenth-century observer as noting that "the Indians . . . toward the middle of the last century, discovered that their horses were a valuable article of commerce . . . the traders in all cases brought their largest horses," Williams, *Adair's History*, 340–41.

34. [Hatton], "Short Remarks," 3.

35. *Journals of the Commissioners of the Indian Trade*, 311.

36. William Richardson, "An Account of My Proceedings Since I Accepted the Indian Mission on Oct. 2d, 1758—Mar. 17, 1759, Wilberforce Eames Collection, N.Y. Public Library (photocopy in the Southern Historical Collection, UNC-Chapel Hill), 9.

37. Williams, *Adair's History*, 242–43.

38. By 1735 as many as 800 horses, in the hands of both traders and tribesmen, were used in the trade. P.R.O, C.O., 17 (1735), 412–25. (Sainsbury transcript in the South Carolina Department of Archives and History, Columbia, S.C.)

39. [Chicken], "Journal, 1725."

40. Talk of the Cherokee Towns to Governor Glen, May 6, 1751, DRIA, I, 173; Van Doren, *Bartram's Travels*, 288; Williams, *Adair's History*, 241; by mid-century, traders kept large stocks of horses in the Cherokee villages; James Glen reported one man "having 200 horses in the nation, and goods to most of several thousand pounds." James Glen, Letterbook, April 23, 1748, Dalhousie Muniments, Scottish Record Office, General Register House, Edinburgh (microfilm in the Western Carolina University Library).

41. [Hatton], "Short Remarks," 15–16.

42. Ibid., 17.

43. Ibid., 17–19.

44. Stuart to BOT, March 9, 1764, 264.

CHAPTER FOUR

1. Glen, *A Description of South Carolina*, 87. Compare Lawson's observation that though there were few traders in North Carolina, "the Dealers therein have throve as fast as any Men, and the soonest rais'd themselves of any People I have known in Carolina." Lawson, *A New Voyage*, 93.

2. Rothrock, "Carolina Traders," 8.

3. A State of the Province of Georgia attested upon Oath, In the Court of Savannah, November 10, 1740 (London: Printed for W. Meadows, 1742), in *Georgia Historical Collections,* Vol 2. (Boston: Freeman and Bolles, 1850), 72.

4. See Testimony from Michael Rowe, October 11, 1743, C.O. 5/370/150; Testimony from Thomas Murray, October 11, 1743, C.O., 5/370/151.

5. Robert Pringle to [], October 19, 1743, *Letterbook of Robert Pringle,* ed. Walter B. Edgar (Columbia: University of South Carolina Press, 1972), II.

6. Van Doren, *Bartram's Travels,* 270.

7. [Hatton], "Short Remarks," 12.

8. Ludovic Grant to Governor Glen, May 3, 1752, *DRIA,* I, 262–63; Anthony Dean to Governor Grant, April 13, 1752, *DRIA,* I, 260.

9. Jacobs, *Atkin's Report,* 86.

10. Speech of Little Carpenter, July 13, 1756, *DRIA,* II, 138.

11. Cf. Ludovic Grant to Governor Glen, February 8, 1754, *DRIA,* II, 475.

12. Jacobs, *Atkin's Report,* 53.

13. William Hatton to Francis Nicholson, November 14, 18, 1724, C.O. 5/359/266; John Sharp to Governor Nicholson, November 12, 1724, C.O. 5/359/265 (microfilm in Western Carolina University Library).

14. Longe, "A Small Postscript," 36–38. Will West Long, a twentieth-century Eastern Band Cherokee, reported that the Cherokees had previously produced an explosion during the second movement of the Green Corn Dance by striking a mound of charcoal on a "big white rock." Frank Speck and Leonard Broom, in collaboration with Will West Long, *Cherokee Dance and Drama* (Norman: University of Oklahoma Press, 1983), 47.

15. [Chicken], "Journal, 1715," 332, 344.

16. Mary Douglas criticized the shortcomings in the treatment of the behavior of consumers in economics, and of the reasons people desire goods—conventionally for "material welfare, psychic welfare or display." Douglas advances the broader concept of goods as "information systems." This view of the demand for and exchange of goods as a form of communication can aid in understanding both Cherokee demand and the linkage of trade to political communication and status in Cherokee society. Mary Douglas and Brian Isherwood, *The World of Goods* (New York: Basic Books, 1979), 3.

17. See Christopher C. Miller and George R. Howell, "A New Perspective on Indian White Contact: Cultural Symbols and the Colonial Trade," *Journal of American History* 73 (September 1986): 311–28. For examples of Cherokee "substitutions," see Michael A. Harmon, "Eighteenth-Century Lower Cherokee Adaptation and Use of European Material Culture," in *Volumes in Historical Archaeology,* II, ed. Stanley South (Columbia: South Carolina Institute of Archaeology and Anthropology, 1986).

18. William Bartram, "Observations on the Uses of Plants by the North American Indians," n.d., Benjamin Smith Barton Papers, American Philosophical Society, Philadelphia; also Catesby, "Of the Aborigines," 6; Williams, *Adair's History,* 187.

19. Douglas, *World of Goods,* 3.

20. Cf. Harmon, "Cherokee Adaptation," 49. Harmon notes that the "novelty" of first purchases soon diminished.

21. [Chicken], "Journal, 1715," 343; Virginia adventurers James Needham and Gabriel Arthur found in 1673 that the Cherokees had already obtained Spanish muskets.

Cf. Alvord and Bidgood, *First Explorations,* 5; for archaeological data relating to this early trade horizon, see G. Waselkov, "Seventeenth-Century Trade."

22. Leila Sellars, *Charleston Business on the Eve of the American Revolution* (Chapel Hill; University of North Carolina Press, 19343), 173.

23. Quoted in Harmon, "Cherokee Adaptation," 50.

24. James Merrell describes this kind of hybrid behavior among the Piedmont trading tribes, particularly the Catawba, before the Yamassee War. See Merrell, "Our Bond of Peace," *Powhatan's Mantle.*

25. Connecortee to Governor Glen, March 20, 1756, *DRIA,* II, 108–9; Affidavit of Charles Banks, *DRIA,* I, 23–24.

26. Williams, *Adair's History,* 460–61; cf. Anthony Dean to Governor Glen, April 13, 1752, *DRIA,* I, 259.

27. Williams, *Adair's History,* 461; "They will hear nothing patiently of loss and gain" (179).

28. This becomes clearest during the 1750s, when trade good "dependency" is most often cited as driving the politics of the Cherokees and other western tribes. (See Chapter 12.)

29. Alcohol abuse among tribespeople, as well as colonists, was a killing disease, and recent critics have criticized historians for underestimating its impact. See Robin Room, "Alcohol and Ethnography: A Case of Problem Deflation?," *Current Anthropology* 25 (April 1984): 169–91.

30. Williams, *Adair's History,* 237.

31. The Mankiller of Tellico to Captain Rayd. Demere, January 25, 1757, *DRIA,* II, 329.

32. Williams, *Adair's History,* 326.

33. Stuart to BOT, March 9, 1764, 258.

34. Jacobs, *Atkin's Report,* 26.

35. The disintegration created by alcohol consumption in the social organization of tribes such as the Cherokees was seen to parallel the disturbance created in village economies by European trade goods, and these ideas in turn affected the perceptions of colonists. For instance, George Milligen, a Carolina historian of the 1760s, quoted Montesquieu to support his own observations on the degeneration brought by the entrance of tribes into the cash economy. George Milligen, *A Short Description of the Province of South Carolina* in Milling, *Colonial South Carolina,* 185.

36. Raymond Demere to Gov. Lyttelton, October 26, 1756, II, 229.

37. Stuart, "Of Indians in General," 257.

CHAPTER FIVE

1. Carlos Fuentes, *The Old Gringo* (New York: Farrar, Straus and Giroux, 1985), 5.

2. See Thomas Hatley, "Holding Their Ground," 37–52.

3. Affidavit of James Maxwell, June 12, 1751, *DRIA,* I, 70.

4. Lawson, *Voyage to Carolina,* 189.

5. Longe, "Small Postscript," 30.

6. Ibid., 32.

7. Williams, *Adair's History*, 152–53. In the first decade of the nineteenth century, John Norton observed that the Cherokees had no severe punishments for adultery relative to those applied by their neighbors, the Creeks. Klinch and Talman, "Journal of John Norton," 78. For further discussion of comparative sexual behavior, see Theda Perdue, "Southern Indians and the Cult of True Womanhood," in *Web of Southern Social Relations: Women, Family and Education,* ed. Walter J. Fraser, Jr., R. Frank Saunders, Jr., and Jon L. Waeklyn (Athens: University of Georgia Press, 1985), 35–52, and "The Traditional Status of Cherokee Women," *Furman Studies,* New Series, 26 (December 1980).

8. John Tobler, "John Tobler's Description of South Carolina," ed. and trans. by Walter C. Robbins, 74 (October 1970): 260; Milligen, *A Short Description,* 185; cf. Lawson, *Voyage to Carolina,* 194; Ludwik Krzywicki, *Primitive Society and Its Vital Statistics* (London: Macmillan, 1934), 161.

9. Williams, *Adair History,* 134–35.

10. *South Carolina Gazette,* August 15, 1743.

11. Governor Nicholson to BOT, December 4, 1723, 5/359/115.

12. "The old magii and religious physicians who were consulted . . . reported the sickness had been sent among them on account of the adulterous intercourses of their young married people, who the past year, in the most notorious manner, violated their ancient rules of marriage in every thicket, and broke down and polluted many of their honest neighbors' bean plots, by their heinous crimes." Williams, *Adair's History,* 244.

13. Wallace, *Death and Rebirth,* 90–93.

14. Ibid., 101. For a Cherokee incident, see Captain Raymond Demere to Governor Lyttelton, August 21, 1756, *DRIA,* II, 164–65.

15. Trade Commissioners Journal, *Journals of the Commissioners of the Indian Trade,* November 16, 1716, pp. 125–28.

16. Mooney, *Myths,* 360; Schoolcraft, *Notes,* 256–57.

17. Williams, *Timberlake's Journal,* 94; on the role of war-women, see John G. W. DeBrahm, *Report of the General Survey in the Southern District of North America,* ed. Louis De Vorsey, Jr. (Columbia: University of South Carolina Press, 1971), 109; Bartram, "Observations," 32.

18. Wallace, *Death and Rebirth,* 103; Stuart, "Of Indians in General," 248; Mooney, *Myths,* 388–89.

19. William L. Anderson, ed., "Cherokee Clay from Duche to Wedgwood: The Journal of Thomas Griffiths, 1767–1768," *North Carolina Historical Review* 63 (October 1986): 504.

20. Longe, "Small Postscript," 34.

21. Matthews, "Journal," 5.

22. Richardson, "An Account of My Proceeding," 20.

23. John D. Hammerer, "An Account of a Plan for Civilizing the American Indians (1766)," ed. Paul L. Ford, *Winnowings in American History, Indian Tracts 1* (Brooklyn: Historical Printing Club, 1890). A Society for the Propagation of the Gospel missionary reported his frustration in this regard in 1714: "I cannot as yet prevail on our neighboring Indians to send their children, not withstanding all the encouragement I offered 'em and their continual promising that they will. I find they are very desirous their children should learn, but they generally leave them to their own will." Ben Dennis to Secretary, March 21, 1714, A/10/83.

24. The reputation for permissive parenting among the tribespeople made an early and also quite persistent impression among influential early colonial observers and their "natural histories," which usually included informal ethnographies. Mark Catesby observed that "the women particularly are the most patient and most innocent creatures living: I never saw a scould amongst them and to their children they are most kind and indulgent." Catesby, "Of the Aborigines," 22; Lawson's *A New Voyage,* reported that "Mildness being a vertue the Indians are in love withal, for they do not practice beating and correcting their Children as we do" (p. 245). Thus, at least among the book-owning elite of Carolina, the idea of tribal parenting, as well as of sexually permissive but politically strong women, was part of the image of the western tribespeople from early in the century on.

25. Williams, *Timberlake's Journal,* 90.

26. Dennis to Secretary, Society for Propagation of the Gospel, March 21, 1714.

27. Quoted in Robert L. Meriwether, *The Expansion of South Carolina,* (Kingsport, Tenn.: Southern Publishers, 1940), 132.

28. In council speeches during times of hostility, the warriors were even more damning: "Nothing is the most favorable name they give us in set speeches: even the Indians who formerly lived in amity with us and in enmity to the French used to call us in their war orations, *hottuk ookprosse,* 'the accursed people.' " Williams, *Adair's History,* 38–39; see also p. 1.

29. Ibid., 132.

30. Affidavit of James Maxwell, June 12, 1751, *DRIA,* I, 68.

31. Ft. Loudoun Association, "Contemporary Newspaper Accounts of the Massacre . . . and Plight of the Survivors," typescript in the Tennessee State Library and Archives, 16, (10), 89–91; Captain Christopher French, "Journal of an Expedition to South Carolina," *Journal of Cherokee Studies* 2 (Summer 1977): 280–81. French, "Journal of an Expedition," 286; *South Carolina Gazette,* September 13–20, 1760; January 24–31, 1761; Intelligence from Indian Nancy to Captain Rayd. Demere, December 12, 1756, *DRIA,* II, 269.

32. Talk of Attakullakulla to John Stuart, [1766]; C.O. 5/67/246; Cf. Alexander McKee's *Journal of Transactions with the Shawnees,* October 12 to November 27, 1762, Public Archives of Canada, R.G. 10 C1221/5/327 (microfilm in the Western Carolina University Library).

33. Cf. Carol I. Mason, "Eighteenth-Century Culture Change Among the Lower Creeks," *The Florida Anthropologist* 16 (1963), 65–81; Perdue, "Southern Indians," 1–26.

34. Octavio Paz, "Monologue," trans. Enrique Fernández, *Village Voice,* New York, March 19, 1984.

CHAPTER SIX

1. "Historical Relation of Facts, Delivered by Ludovic Grant, Indian Trader, to His Excellency the Governor of South Carolina," *South Carolina Historical and Genealogical Magazine (SCHGM)* 10 (January 1909): 56–57.

2. Of an earlier seventeenth-century treaty, and another negotiated with the tribe in

1721, there is only an odd reference. Cf. Charles C. Royce, *The Cherokee Nation of Indians,* Smithsonian Institution, Bureau of American Ethnology, 144. In 1734, the Lower Towns villages made a transfer of land to South Carolina, partly in response to Carolina demands for the satisfaction of trade debts. Mabel L. Webber, "An Indian Land Grant in 1734, *SCHGM* 19 (October 1918): 157.

3. The events surrounding the Cherokee visit are told, unfortunately with few hints of the reactions of the Cherokees themselves to the attempts of their hosts to overawe them, Carolyn Thomas Forman, *Indians Abroad, 1493–1938* (Norman: University of Oklahoma Press, 1943), 44–55.

4. Cuming, viewed as a Scottish outsider in the court, was locked out of the royal negotiations with the tribe, and this slight was to dog him the rest of his life. Cuming's own retrospective account of his journey was filled with apocalyptic imagery connecting the defeat of the Scottish clans (whom Cuming associated, at least metaphorically, with the Jews) and the redemption of these lost people through bringing another people lost in the wilderness—the Cherokees—into the English fold. Cuming wrote concerning his trip to the Cherokees, "the *Plowman* Chapter of the Prophet Isaiah under the Designation of an Al-Camon the Chief of the *Cumin seed* was beat out of this Kingdom with a *Shebet,* the *Rod,* of oppression, and the *Sign* of the *Scepter,* to manifest the Power of that Mighty Being, who to Display his over-ruling Power, and as a proper lesson to Britons, rose up in mount *Perazim,* the place of Breaches, the *Cherekee* mountains & the mountain of the Wild men that inhabit the Wilderness." Alexander Cuming, "Memoir." 1. For Cuming's *Journal,* see Williams, *Early Travels,* 115–43.

5. Cuming's trip to England opened a window of opportunity for the Board of Trade and for the schemes of the newly appointed royal governor, Robert Johnson, for creating a buffer of settlements developed in connection with eleven townships. The Cherokee visit generated great interest in the affairs of the southern colony in the court and furthered Johnson's efforts to "transform the garrison-colonies of the revived Barnwell scheme [post-Yamassee War] into a full-fledged barrier province." Crane, *Southern Frontier,* 292–302.

6. Thomas Nairne to BOT, July 10, 1708, C.O. 5/382/24.

7. Peter Henry Bruce, *Memoirs of Peter Henry Bruce, Esq.* (1783; reprint London: Frank Cass and Co., 1970), xii, 518–20.

8. Jacobs, *Atkin's Report,* 10–11, 28.

9. Captain Rayd. Demere to Governor Lyttelton, November 28, 1756, *DRIA,* II, 259.

10. [McDowell], February 4, 1757, *DRIA,* II, 330.

11. James Adair reported that Attakullakulla was particularly alienated by Glen's action. He later asked Adair to "but count . . . the lying black marks" on one of Glen's messages. Williams, *Adair's History,* 351.

12. Deposition of Richard Smith, July 12, 1751, *DRIA,* I, 102.

13. "Map Drawn by Chegere (An Indian) who Says he has Travell'd Through Kentuckey" [1755], Library of Congress Map Collection. For possible sites of this lead mining, see Ruben G. Thwaites, "Early Lead Mining in Illinois and Wisconsin," *Annual Report, American Historical Association* (1893), 192–93.

14. Figures are from Glen, *Description of South Carolina,* 58–62. Crane, *Southern Frontier,* 110–12.

15. Robert Weir, " 'The Harmony We Were Famous For': An Interpretation of Pre-Revolutionary South Carolina Politics," *William and Mary Quarterly*, 3rd Series, 26 (October 1969): 479–80.

16. Roger G. Kennedy, *Architecture, Men, Women and Money in America, 1600 to 1860* (New York: Random House, 1985), 115.

17. Jacobs, *Atkin's Report*, 27. So persistent was the problem of raiding by northern tribesmen on their southern adversaries—especially the long-running conflict between the Iroquois and the Catawbas—that Glen unsuccessfully attempted to mediate between the two, and sent Lt. Governor Bull to Albany in 1751 in an attempt to secure the backcountry from harassment. See William Bull, Jr., to Governor Glen, June 15, 1751, *DRIA*, I, 110–12.

18. Mooney, *Myths*, 36; see also S.C. Correspondence with Board of Trade, [1731], folios 172–79, C.O. 5/364/D42.

19. "Their Country is the Key of Carolina and from thence may be made frequent Incursions." Governor Glen to Lieutenant Governor Dinwiddie, June 1, 1754, *DRIA*, I, 525.

20. See John R. Alden, *John Stuart and the Southern Colonial Frontier* (Ann Arbor: University of Michigan Press, 1944), 20–37.

21. Glen to Secretary of State, [ ], *DRIA*, I, 553. For a fuller discussion, see Chapter 8.

22. Glen to BOT, February 1750, C.O. 5/372/282.

23. Glen was the butt of the growing anti-Scottish prejudice evident in Charlestown. Cf. Robert M. Weir, *Colonial South Carolina: A History* (Millwood, N.Y.: KTO Press, 1983), 286. "A very polished courtier," Irishman James Adair remarked scornfully of Glen. See Dobbs to BOT, November 9, 1754, in William L. Saunders, ed., *The Colonial Records of North Carolina* (Raleigh: Josephus Daniels, 1887), V, 148.

24. Glen was quick to point out evidential errors on the part of his colleagues in other colonies. At one point, Glen, somewhat ingenuously, suggested that Dinwiddie and other Virginia officials had been misled by relying on incorrect historical sources on which to base their claim to precedence in relations with the Cherokees. "A book of no great Authority may have misled some Gentlemen of Virginia," he wrote to the Board of Trade, "the book is Keith's *History of Virginia*, page 181 are the following words: the most ancient though not the most considerable Branch of Commerce in Virginia is its Indian Trade &c., and in the same Paragraph he says but if ever the English . . . extend their settlements in Virginia beyond the Great Mountains . . . then will the Indian Trade be considerable indeed." Governor Glen to [Sir Thomas Robinson, Secretary of State], [1754], *DRIA*, I, 534–35.

25. Glen to the Secretary of State, August 1, 1754, *DRIA*, I, 535.

26. Atkin, Charlestown trader like Glen, gained wide readership in the Board of Trade with his paper, and he was installed as Superintendent of Southern Indian Affairs a year later, just after Glen had himself been removed from office. For the trade involvement of Glen and Atkin, see tables of export firms in W. O. Moore, "The Largest Exporters of Deerskins from Charlestown, 1735–1775," *South Carolina Historical Magazine* 74 (October 1973): 144–51.

27. Governor Glen to Dinwiddie, June 1, 1754, *DRIA*, I, 526.

28. Governor Glen to Lt. Governor Dinwiddie, June 1, 1754, *DRIA*, I, 525. Underlying this outlook were recollections of the Yamassee War and the more recent Stono

slave revolt, along with a concern for the poor performance of Carolina in the border wars with Spanish Florida during the 1740s. Glen, *Description of South Carolina,* 265.

29. Jacob F. Price, "Economic Function and the Growth of American Port Towns in the Eighteenth Century," *Perspectives on American History* 8 (1974): 162–63.

30. Carolina rice production was to remain profitable until competition from southeast Asian rice cut into the demand for rice from the [European] low countries, where it was used to supplement the winter fare ("when pease and pulse &c. are scarce") of growing populations. Quote is from James Glen, *Description of South Carolina,* 99. See also Wood, *Black Majority,* especially 35–63. For an overview of the rice economy see Peter A. Colconis, "Bitter Harvest: The South Carolina Low Country in Historical Perspective," *Journal of Economic History* 45 (June 1985); Daniel C. Littlefield, *Rice and Slaves: Ethnicity and the Slave Trade in Colonial South Carolina* (Baton Rouge: Louisiana State University Press, 1981).

31. [Committee of the South Carolina Commons House], July 1, 1741, *Statements Made in the Introduction to the Report on General Oglethorpe's Expedition to St. Augustine,* in Bartholomew R. Carroll, *Historical Collections of South Carolina; embracing many rare and valuable pamphlets . . . relating to the history of that state from its first discovery to its independence, in the year 1776* (New York: Harper and Brothers, 1836), IV, 359.

32. See the videotape entitled "The Strength of these Arms," produced by North State Public Video (Durham, 1988).

33. Lieut. Governor Bull to Earl of Hillsborough, November 30, 1770, C.O. 5/394/5.

34. John Bartram, September 2, 1765, "Diary of a Journey Through the Carolinas, Georgia and Florida from July 1, 1765 to April 1, 1766," ed. Francis Harper, *Transactions of the American Philosophical Society,* n.s., XXXIII, pt. 1 (December 1942), 22.

35. Herbert Aptheker, "Maroons Within the Present Limits of the United States," *Journal of Negro History* 29 (April 1939): 168. In the aftermath of a "Negro insurrection" in 1766, the participants took cover in "large swamps." Governor Bull to BOT, January 25, 1766, C.O. 5/378/54.

36. Cf. Bull to Glen, June 7, 1751, June 15, 1751, *DRIA,* I, 33–35; Alden, *John Stuart,* 33.

37. The so-called Jamaican Maroon Wars took place between 1720 and 1739. The rugged Blue Mountains, which provided an easy escape for slaves, were one of the reasons for the prolonged and strong slave resistance in Jamaica. Cf. Richard S. Dunn, *Sugar and Slaves: The Rise of the Planter Class in English West Indies, 1624–1713* (New York, Norton, 1972), 261–62. See also Michael Craton, *Testing the Chains: Resistance to Slavery in the British West Indies* (Ithaca: Cornell University Press, 1982), 81–96.

38. The association between the mountain strongholds of the Cherokees and the Jamaican maroons led Alexander Cuming to the Blue Mountains five years after his visit to the Appalachians. In Jamaica, where the maroons were in an on-and-off war with the white settlers, Cuming suggested a "scheme of attacking them in their strongest settlement." He then proposed cementing the peace much as he had done on the mainland: "to give them their liberty upon very easy terms of making them useful both to themselves and to the rest of the Island." Cuming, "Memoir," 31.

39. Lt. Gov. Bull to BOT, May 8, 1760, C.O. 5/377/11.

40. "Extract of a Letter from Frederica in Georgia," *South Carolina Gazette,* August 15, 1743, Verner Crane, "A Lost Utopia of the First American Frontier," *The Sewanee Review* (January 1919), 53–54.

41. George Milligen, *A Short Description,* 136.

42. For incidents of such cooperation in the late 1720s see Crane, *Southern Frontier,* 185, 287.

43. Edmund Gray to John Fallowfield, May 15, 1751, *DRIA,* I, 83.

44. "Deposition of Richard Smith," July 12, 1751, *DRIA,* I, 103.

45. Quoted in Herbert Aptheker, *American Negro Slave Revolts* (1943; reprint New York: International Publishers, 1974), 20. For incidents in Virginia, see Chester A. Young, "Effects of the French and Indian War in Virginia" (Ph.D. dissertation, Vanderbilt University, 1969), 287.

46. Charles F. Adams, ed., *The Works of John Adams,* II, 428, quoted in Aptheker, *Slave Revolts,* 21.

47. McDowell, "Introduction," *DRIA,* II, xxii; Eugene Sirmans, *Colonial South Carolina: A Political History, 1663–1763* (Chapel Hill: University of North Carolina Press, 1966), 299–300.

48. James Francis to Glen, October 7, 1754, *DRIA,* I, 20–22.

49. *Historical Chronicle* XXV (October 1755): 468.

50. *South Carolina Gazette,* July 24–31, 1755.

51. Two years earlier, during negotiations over the location of Fort Prince George at Keowee, the Cherokee leader Connacautee at Keowee, had (according to one of Glen's allies) promised that "the little piece of Land that I now Give [for the Keowee fort] you is as nothing. It is like a small bit cut off from a great piece of cloth, but I propose soon to go round the whole Nation to every town in it and to get them to give up all their lands to you." Ludovic Grant, "Historical Relation," 62–63. Grant suggests that the generous offer made by Connacautee stemmed from his determination to recoup prestige after his exclusion a decade earlier during negotiations over land in the upper Savannah drainage which was 'sold' in 1747 to Carolina. Grant reported that negotiations had "cost a great expense to the Government & these Gentlemen [the negotiators] were at great pains before they could prevail with the Indians to part with it tho' that land lay a hundred miles from their Nation. The sale was made by the Lower Towns only. And they were many months about it, and after all Coll: [Colonel] Pawley was told by Connacautee that he had been doing nothing and that the Lower Towns had no right to sell these Lands for tho they lay nearest them Yet they belonged to the nation in general." See also Cherokee Headmen to Governor Glen, September 21, 1754, *DRIA,* II, 7–8.

52. *South Carolina Gazette,* July 24–31, 1755. In fact, Connacautee, or Old Hop, faced substantial dissent within his own circle of Overhill villages. Attakullakulla, or Little Carpenter, disliked James Glen intensely and was carrying on negotiations with both the French and Virginians at the time of the conference.

53. Ludovic Grant, "Historical Relation," 63.

54. *South Carolina Gazette,* July 24–31, 1755.

55. *Historical Chronicle,* (London) October, 1755, 470.

56. Quoted in Crane, *Southern Frontier,* 180.

57. C. Vann Woodward, "Preface to the First Edition," in *The Strange Career of Jim Crow*, 3rd edition (New York: Oxford University Press, 1974).

58. Jacobs, *Atkin's Report*, 18.

59. Glen, *Description of South Carolina*, 69.

60. An English fort near the mouth of the Tennessee-Wabash-Ohio confluence, in southwestern Kentucky-Illinois, would so block French communication that "a single Canow could not pass without leave." *South Carolina Gazette*, July 24–31, 1755; cf. Glen to Board of Trade, [n.d.], *DRIA*, I, 538. The *Gazette* used Charlevoix as an authority to point out the strategic position occupied by the tribe in the river system of the mid-continent.

61. *South Carolina Gazette*, July 24–31, 1755.

62. *Historical Chronicle*, 470.

63. Moses Thompson to Governor Glen, January 16, 1756, *DRIA*, II, 115.

CHAPTER SEVEN

1. S.C. Council Journal, August 14, 1759; John Milligen commented in 1763 that "wheat is cultivated by the German Protestants . . . [who] would have been able to supply all the flour we consume by this time had they not been interrupted by the Cherokee War." Milligen, *A Short Description*, 138.

2. John Murray to [ ], February 5, 1756, A512. Dalhousie Muniments (microfilm in South Carolina Department of Archives and History).

3. Meriwether, *Expansion of South Carolina*, 256; Rachel Klein, "The Rise of the Planters in the South Carolina Backcountry, 1767–1808" (Ph.D. dissertation, Yale University, 1979), 59–62.

4. Anthony Dean to Cornelius Doharty, May 1, 1751, *DRIA*, I, 73.

5. Peter Wood estimates that the Cherokee population stood at 10,500 in 1730; 9000 in 1745; and 7200 in 1760. Wood, "Changing Population" in *Powhatan's Mantle*, Table I.

6. Williams, *Adair's History*, 244.

7. Memorial of Robert Bunning and Others, November 21, 1751, *DRIA*, I, 148.

8. According to one knowledgeable observer "the Creeks have for many years past . . . enjoyed peace [and that] means greatly increased in numbers. Many young men have arrived at a state of manhood since they had a war with their neighbors . . . the Cherokees on the other hand by Col. Montgomery's and Grant's expedition, their war with the northward Indians and the smallpox in 1759 and 60 [are reduced]. They look with an eye of envy on the prosperity of the Creeks and would gladly see them humbled themselves." Stuart to BOT, 323/17/170; Wood, "Changing Population," in *Powhatan's Mantle*, 56–66.

9. "The Creeks have already planted Corn at Old Estertoe and thirty of them are now hunting in those parts." Lieutenant Coytmore to Governor Lyttelton, May 8, 1759, *DRIA*, II, 488.

10. French overtures may have encouraged the Creek-related faction at these towns to settle in this area in 1756. "If we suffer the Tellico people, the Savannahs, and the French traders to settle at Highwassey Old Town," one source wrote, "we may as well

give up the whole Nation of Cherokees to the French.'' Captain Raymd. Demere to Governor Lyttelton, November 18, 1756, *DRIA*, II, 248; Daniel Pepper to Governor Lyttelton, November 30, 1756, *DRIA*, II, 295. The shifting settlement of this region continued into the 1770s. The Creeks seem to have also sanctioned the continuing existence of Cherokee settlements such as Little Chota, a town of one hundred houses, reported in the 1770s to have been "given to the Cherokee Indians" by the Creeks. A. Wm.son to W. H. Drayton, August 22, 1776, in Robert W. Gibbes, *Documentary History of the American Revolution . . . Chiefly in South Carolina* (New York: 1853), II, 32; [Arthur Fairie?], "Journal, Williamson's Expedition, 1776," in Draper Collection, 2W199.

11. C. G. Holland, *An Archaeological Survey of Southwest Virginia*, Smithsonian Contributions to Anthropology, Number 12 (City of Washington: Smithsonian Institution Press, 1970), 117.

12. At the fork of the Holston and North rivers, Thomas Walker found houses resembling Cherokee dwellings ("five Indian Houses built with logs and covered with Bark") as well as a "large Indian Fort" nearby. Thomas Walker, *Journal of an Exploration in the Spring of the Year 1750* (Boston: Little, Brown, 1888), 43–44, 49.

13. This trail was called the "Warriors Path," and Walker described it as "an Indian Road, much frequented," along the Powell River. Walker, *Journal*, 51.

14. Lt. Governor Burwell to Glen, October 26, 1751, *DRIA*, I, 160.

15. Captain Fairchild to Governor Glen, September 29, 1751, *DRIA*, I, 131. David Corkran, *The Cherokee Frontier: Conflict and Survival, 1740–1762* (Norman: University of Oklahoma Press, 1962), 34. Lyman Chalkey, *Chronicles of the Scotch Irish Settlement in Virginia*, III, 40–41. This evanescent settlement may have been linked to reports from the Logstown conference in 1752, where 500 tribespeople from the Lower Towns had suggested that they might move *en masse* to the mid-Ohio River. William Trent, *Journal of Captain William Trent from Logstown in Pickawillany, A.D. 1752*, (1871; reprint New York: Arno Press, 1971), 100. See also Memorial of Robert Bunning, November 22, 1751, *DRIA*, I, 150–51; see also Helen H. Tanner, "Cherokees in the Ohio Country," *Journal of Cherokee Studies* (Spring 1978): 95–96.

16. Ludovic Grant to Glen, May 3, 1752, *DRIA*, I, 261; Corkran, *Cherokee Frontier*, 34.

17. James Patton's land included a grant of "3,000 acres on which Saml. Stalnaker and others is living, known by the name of Indian Fields, on the waters of Houlston's River, a branch of the Mississippi." *Abstracts of Wills*, Augusta County, September 1, 1750, 131. Patton to Dinwiddie [1753], Draper Collection, IQQ73. The "Indian Fields" settlement was "above 40 miles from our outmost settlement at which Place the Cherokees meets our traders," Patton wrote.

18. Thomas Walker met Stalnaker in 1748 when he was "on his way to the Cherokee Indians," and two years later he "helped him raise his house." In 1753 the Cherokees upbraided Stalnaker for "asking an Extravagant Price for some Corn," and eventually the issue was settled when "Starnicker Provided he would let his people have Provisions at the same rate he sold to white People." James Patton to [ ], [January 1753], Draper Collection, 1QQ72; James Patton to Dinwiddie [1753], 1QQ73.

19. Patrick Brown to Governor Glen, April 25, 1752, *DRIA*, I, 246–47.

20. William J. Hinkle and Charles E. Kemper, "Moravian Travel Diaries Through Virginia," *Virginia Magazine of History and Biography* 6 (October 1903): 123. Donald

F. Durnbaugh, *The Brethren in Colonial America* (Elgin, Ill.: The Brethren Press, 1967), 156, 163. Walker, *Journal,* 1.

21. See Patricia G. Johnson, *James Patton and the Appalachian Colonists* (McClure Press, 1973), 89–100; for background on the complicated legal and commercial ties of the region, see Robert Mitchell, *Commercialism and Frontier: Perspectives on the Early Shenandoah Valley* (Charlottesville: University of Virginia Press, 1977), 134–35, 180–83; for areas of western North Carolina, see Paula H. Anderson, "The New River Frontier Settlement on the Virginia-North Carolina Border, 1760–1820," *Virginia Magazine of History and Biography* 86 (1978): 413–31.

22. Robert W. Ramsey, *Carolina Cradle: Settlement of the Northwest Carolina Frontier, 1747–1762* (Chapel Hill: University of North Carolina Press, 1964), 31–37; "Morgan Bryan," *Dictionary of North Carolina Biography,* vol. 1, ed. William S. Powell (Chapel Hill: University of North Carolina Press, 1979), 257–59.

23. See the discussion in Ramsey, *Carolina Cradle,* 94–137.

24. See H. Roy Merrens, *Colonial North Carolina in the Eighteenth Century: A Study in Historical Geography* (Chapel Hill: University of North Carolina Press, 1964).

25. "Petition of the Inhabitants of the Frontiers of Anson County in North Carolina upon the Catawba River above the Catawba Indians," South Carolina Council Journal, April 7, 1752. As late as 1757 the settlers of the same locality were complaining that Cherokees had stolen horses "out of the woods." "Petition," September 3, 1757, North Carolina Treasurer's Papers, North Carolina State Archives, Department of Archives and History, Raleigh.

26. Meriwether, *Expansion of South Carolina,* 132.

27. Ibid., 119–21.

28. Like these men, Thomas Steel, a prosperous landowner, in 1763 set out on a long trading journey to New Orleans, even though the recent hostilities of the Cherokee War would seem to have made his route uninviting. See Elizabeth F. Ellet, *The Women of the American Revolution* (New York: Baker and Scribner, 1850), III, 58–59.

29. Meriwether, *Expansion of South Carolina,* 23, 131.

30. For the settlement history of this area, see ibid., 117–35 and Map Six; Louis De Vorsey, Jr., *The Indian Boundary in the Southern Colonies* (Chapel Hill: University of North Carolina Press, 1966), 114–15. John C. Calhoun, who grew up near Long Cane, remembered these stores as representing the only other settlements worth mentioning near his family's land. The stores literally stood out on an otherwise blank countryside, and in this sense the perceptual map of the region reflected and validated the social standing of his family. See John C. Calhoun to Charles H. Allen, November 21, 1847, *Gulf States Historical Magazine* 1 (May 1903): 440.

31. Long Cane settlement was near present-day Abbeville, S.C.

32. Calhoun to Allen, *Gulf States Magazine,* 440. The cane (a woody grass adapted to regular burning) in Long Cane apparently had been burned on a fairly regular basis up until the 1760s. In the absence of man-caused fire, the canebrakes would have been diminished. See Ralph C. Hughes, "The Fire Ecology of Canebrakes," *Proceedings, Fifth Annual Tall Timbers Fire Ecology Conference* (March 1966): 149–59. Other sources corroborate the widespread existence of vigorous cane stands in western Carolina in the 1760s. Cf. John H. Logan, *A History of the Upper Country of South Carolina* (Charleston: G. Courtenay and Company, 1859), I, 158. Cattle-grazing and hog-rooting, as well as a shift in the duration of burn-intervals from the three-year optimum practiced by the

tribespeople to annual burning by white farmers and cattle keepers, contributed to the rapid disappearance of canebrakes in the upper Savannah valley. See F. A. Michaux, *Travels to the West of the Allegheny Mountains* (London: B. Crosby and Company, 1805), 251.

33. Meriwether, *Expansion of South Carolina,* 169; Logan, *Upper Country of South Carolina,* 82; Cf. Cooper, *Statutes at Large,* V, 647.

34. Meriwether, *Expansion of South Carolina,* 124–25; Mitchell, *Commercialism and Frontier,* 46–47.

35. Meriwether, *Expansion of South Carolina,* 133.

36. Draper Collection, 1VV10; David Ramsay, *History of the Revolution in South Carolina from a British Colony to an Independent State,* (Trenton: Isaac Collins, 1785), 209; "Data Relative to Major Andrew Hamilton," typescript in South Caroliniana Library, 2; for a general perspective on the family migrations, which may reflect vestiges of "clan" organization and leadership and "clachan" settlements, see Tyler Blethen and Curtis Wood, Jr., *From Ulster to Carolina: The Migration of the Scotch-Irish to Southwestern North Carolina* (Cullowhee, N.C.: Western Carolina University, 1983), 8.

37. Joseph Waddell, *Annals of Augusta County* (Richmond: Wm. Ellis Jones, 1886), 27.

38. Mitchell, *Commercialism and Frontier,* 46.

39. Meriwether, *Expansion of South Carolina,* 124. The roots of the "siege mentality" which marked the religion and the clannishness of such settlements reflected actual events and memories of displacement and persecution for "Ulster Presbyterians" in Ireland. Blethen and Wood, *From Ulster to Carolina,* 9.

40. William Calhoun, "Journal of William Calhoun," June 10, 1769, ed. Alexander S. Salley, *Publications of the Southern History Association* 8 (May 1904): 179–95.

41. Richard Maxwell Brown, *South Carolina Regulators* (Cambridge: The Belknap Press of Harvard University, 1963), 21. By 1768 there were twenty-one Presbyterian churches in the western backcountry; the church at Long Cane was the largest, serving "over five hundred families."

42. Joseph Wesley Brinsfield, *Religion and Politics in Colonial South Carolina* (Easley: Southern Historical Press, 1983), 61; *South Carolina Gazette,* September 8, 1758; "Sketch of the Caldwell Family," typescript in the South Caroliniana Library, 3. Leading "New Light" ministers in South Carolina, such as Craighead, David Caldwell, and William Tennant, also had a memory of dissension they had faced in Virginia's Hanover Presbytery, where clergymen were split between conservatives, or "Old Side" pastors, who held to an older clericism and those caught up in the Awakening; Young, "The Effect of the French and Indian War," 371.

43. Brown, *South Carolina Regulators,* 21.

44. The subtle and detailed interplay between family and political control, particularly in New England and Virginia, is examined in Philip J. Greven, *The Protestant Temperament: Patterns of Childrearing, Religious Experience, and the Self in Early America* (New York: Knopf, 1977).

45. John Craig, *Autobiography* [n.d.], Virginia State Library; on his defense role, see *South Carolina Gazette,* March 4, 1756.

46. The pressure continued in South Carolina, where Anglicans such as Charles

Woodmason condemned the "Bigotry and Zeal of the Church of Scotland" imported into upper South Carolina. Richard J. Hooker, *The South Carolina Backcountry on the Eve of the Revolution: The Journal and Other Writings of Charles Woodmason, Anglican Itinerant* (Chapel Hill: University of North Carolina Press, 1953), 132–34.

47. Calhoun to Allen, *Gulf States Magazine,* 439–41.

48. It is easy to overstate the common inheritance of the Scotch Irish; for a critical assessment of their solidarity, see Kenneth W. Keller, "What Is Distinctive about the Scotch Irish?," in Mitchell, *Appalachian Frontiers,* 69–87.

49. Quoted in De Vorsey, *Indian Boundary,* 133.

50. Patrick Calhoun to Lyttelton, September 21, 1759, ms. in William L. Clements Library, University of Michigan.

51. Matthews, "Memoirs of Ann Matthews," 2. Ellet, *The Women of the American Revolution,* III, 59.

52. The story of Nancy Ward, who according to tradition learned how to make milk and butter from Mrs. Bean, a settler in the region north of the Overhill Towns, suggests the same underlying female to female transactions concerning subsistence matters. John P. Brown, *Old Frontiers: The Story of the Cherokee Indians from Earliest Times to the Date of Their Removal to the West, 1838* (Kingsport, Tenn.: Southern Publishers, Inc., 1938), 148–49, 153–54.

53. Williams, *Adair's History,* 447–48.

CHAPTER EIGHT

1. "Talk of Tistoe," March 5, 1759, ms. in Lyttelton Papers, William L. Clements Library, University of Michigan.

2. Cherokee Headmen to Governor of Virginia, December 21, 1756, *DRIA,* II, 228. Other geographical divisions of the tribe contested the attention received in the 1750s by the Overhill villages.

3. Intelligence from Captain Raymond Demere, November 8, 1756, *DRIA,* II, 248.

4. Initially, Lower Town leaders, such as the broker-figures the Conjurer and Caesar, captured the attention of the English. Later in the 1730s and 1740s English-Cherokee diplomatic contact was dominated by the Tanasee and Tellico families, especially the kin-lineage of Moytoy and his son, Ammouscossittee.

5. Prince of Jore to Lyttelton, April 13, 1758, *DRIA,* II, 452.

6. Several studies offer a parallel, though different perspective, on this period of Cherokee history. See David Corkran, *Cherokee Frontier* and *The Creek Frontier* (Norman: University of Oklahoma Press, 1962); also useful is John Philip Reid, *A Law of Blood: Primitive Law of the Cherokee Nation* (New York: New York University Press, 1970).

7. Patrick Brown to Glen, April 24, 1752, *DRIA,* I, 246. While this proved to be a threat, the Creek hostilities were amplified by the sporadic attacks of other tribes, and the perceived danger represented by the colonies as well. Thus, the headmen of Chota and Tanasee in 1751 voiced fears of encirclement in response to a rumor "that the

Creeks have declared war against us and the Yuchees, Chickasaws and Catawbas, with a body of white men, also to form in all about the number of one thousand who were to cut them off . . . and so throughout the nation, burning and destroying everywhere they went along." Talk of Caesar to Raymond Demere, December 21, 1756, *DRIA*, II, 280.

8. Jean-Bernard Bossu, *Travels in the Interior of North America, 1751–62,* ed. Seymour Feiler (Norman: University of Oklahoma Press, 1962), 152–55. Fort Toulouse, located 300 miles from its base of supply at Mobile, was chronically underfunded and understaffed (there were never more than fifty in the garrison). In the 1750s, the commander wrote: "there are several French families whose children are raised among the Indians, and acquainted early with their customs." Gregory A. Waselkov, Brian M. Wood, Joseph M. Herbert, *Colonization and Conquest: The 1980 Archaeological Excavations at Fort Toulouse and Fort Jackson, Alabama,* Auburn University, *Archaeological Monograph #4,* Auburn University at Montgomery, April 1982, pp. 67–82, 103–9, 119–27.

9. James Mooney, *Myths,* 38, 384–85, 533; William Sludders to Commissioner Pinckney, November 11, 1750, *DRIA,* I, 1.

10. Malatchi to Governor Glen, May 7, 1754, *DRIA,* I, 508.

11. Milo B. Howard and Robert R. Rea, *The Memoire Justicatif of the Chevalier Montault de Montberaut* (University: University of Alabama Press, 1965), 70.

12. Glen to Secretary of State, [], *DRIA,* I, 533.

13. French authorities were preoccupied with Cherokee raiding against French-allied tribes along the Mississippi. The long-projected Fort Massac, on the Ohio bluffs near the confluence of the Cherokee (Tennessee) and Shawnee (Cumberland) rivers, reflected this concern, as well as the inability of the French to muster sufficient resources to "capture" the country in their interest. In 1751, at the height of conflicts between these tribal groups as well as the Creeks, French authorities were moved to recommend that *voyageurs* not be allowed to hunt in the Ohio in order to avoid conflict with the Cherokees. See Bill Barron, ed., *The Vaudreuil Papers* (Polyanthos: New Orleans, 1975), 108, also 169–70, 190–91, 208–10. On the complex problem of synonymy in the mid-Mississippi Valley (which creates problems of interpretation of records, whether French, English, or Cherokee) see Charles Callender, "Illinois," *Handbook of American Indians, Northeast,* 15: 673–81.

14. As late as 1752, a trader, observing continuing Creek hostilities to the south, and raiding northern tribes at the back of the Cherokees, noted "they have Enemy on all Sides." Patrick Brown to Governor Glen, April 25, 1752, *DRIA,* I, 246. See Talk of the Cherokee Head Men to Governor Glen, September 21, 1754, *DRIA,* II, 7–8. Cf. Old Hop's Talk to Captain Stuart and Lieutenant Wall, November 15, 1756, *DRIA,* II, 246–47. Judge's Friend to Captain Raymond Demere, October 16, 1752, *DRIA,* II, 228.

15. McDowell, "Introduction," *DRIA,* II, xiii, xxii; Captain Rayd. Demere to Governor Lyttelton, November 7, 1756, *DRIA* II, 240.

16. The Overhill fort, Fort Loudoun, was constructed in 1756; Fort Prince George was used as a staging point. The Virginia fort was begun in 1755. Old Hop to Captain Raymond Demere, October 3, 1756, *DRIA,* II, 223–24.

17. Connacorte of Chote *et al.* to Governor Glen, February 19, 1754, *DRIA,* II, 486. During the same time that the fort was under construction, Old Hop fended off

English requests for Cherokee assistance against allied northern tribes by stating that "his town belongs to the Nuntaways and the Nuntaways belong to him." Old Hop to Captain Raymond Demere, October 26, 1756, *DRIA,* II, 235.

18. Major Lewis to Captain Demere, July 7, 1756, *DRIA,* II, 138.

19. Captain Raymond Demere to Governor Lyttelton, October 13, 1756, *DRIA,* II, 214. The "French" referred to were Huguenots.

20. Dinwiddie called the Winchester Conference to seek Cherokee support for planned northern offensives against the French allied tribes because recruitment efforts among Virginia colonists had been "disappointed from our colonies." Dinwiddie had requested Glen's assistance in obtaining 800 warriors. Later, Dinwiddie complained that tribal leaders had been told that "South Carolina desired them to remain at home, to care for their families and hunting . . . for I was only going to build a fort." Dinwiddie to Glen, August 5, 1754, *DRIA,* I, 529.

21. Andrew Lewis to Raymond Demere, August 15, 1756, *DRIA,* II, 167.

22. Governor Lyttelton to Board of Trade, December 25, 1756, C.O. 5/375/155.

23. Captain Raymond Demere to Governor Lyttelton, September 12, 1756, *DRIA,* II, 199.

24. De Brahm, *Report of the General Survey,* 125. Cf. Jacobs, *Atkin's Report,* 70.

25. See Henry Timberlake, "Draught of the Cherokee Country," in Williams, *Timberlake's Memoirs.*

26. Danl. Pepper to Governor Lyttelton, December 21, 1756, *DRIA,* II, 298–99.

27. The Mankiller of Highwassee's Answer, September 27, 1756, *DRIA,* II, 221.

28. Old Hop to Captain Raymond Demere, October 3, 1756, *DRIA,* II, 224.

29. Captain Rayd. Demere to Governor Lyttelton, June 23, 1756, *DRIA,* II, 126.

30. Ibid., 127.

31. Raymond Demere to Governor Lyttelton, October 13, 1756, *DRIA,* II, 218.

32. *South Carolina Gazette,* October 11–18, 1760. For a fuller discussion of the dual nature of food exchange among the tribe (involving both giving and selling), see Hatley, "The Three Lives of Keowee," in *Powhatan's Mantle.*

33. Captain Rayd. Demere to Governor Lyttelton, July 28, 1756, *DRIA,* II, 150.

34. Captain Rayd. Demere to Governor Lyttelton, June 15, 1756, ibid., 121.

35. Sergeant Harrison to Governor Glen, March 27, 1754, ibid., 485.

36. The first cession—or gift—of tribal land to the Carolinians was in 1721, and others followed in 1734 and 1747. The first two specified the transfer of a "small spot of ground" to the Carolinians. L. Grant, *Historical Relation of Ludovic Grant,* 157.

37. Captain Rayd. Demere to Glen, October 16, 1756, *DRIA,* II, 225.

38. James May to Governor Glen, September 27, 1755, ibid., 80–81. These towns were among the smallest of the Cherokee villages in 1761. Cf. Christopher French, "Journal," 300.

39. Williams, *Adair's History,* 444.

40. Fort Loudoun Association, "Contemporary Newspaper Accounts," 16(10)58.

41. Governor Glen of South Carolina collected testimony from a member of Washington's march in 1754 that while employed in the "Merchant's Service in the Virginia Trade" he read "Proposals [which] were made and published to give Encouragement for settling some lands on the Ohio and that he was one amongst many others that embraced the said Proposals, and he believes there might be 100 in all. But it being found necessary that some Force should be raised they were thrown into the Virginia

Regiment as few or none would enlist and were called Volunteers. There were also twenty-two Gentlemans' Sons or thereabouts that made a part of the Said Regiment as Cadetts, but he believes they were to receive no Pay, but all the Virginia Volunteers who were to settle the Lands were to have eight Pence per Day Virginia Currency, but that he never received one Farthing.'' ''Affidavit of John Shaw,'' August 21, 1754, *DRIA*, II, 3–5.

42. Ludovic Grant to James Glen, January 1, 1756, *DRIA*, I, 91–92.

43. Chuchecha to Glen, August 4, 1755, *DRIA*, II, 73.

44. After observing this scene Chuchecha settled the matter directly (''he talked to Branham and he has promised to be good and there should be no more bad talks of him'') without recourse to ineffective colonial ''paper.'' James May to Glen, September 27, 1755, ibid., 80–81.

45. Anthony Dean to Cornelius Doharty, May 1, 1751, *DRIA*, I, 73.

46. For origins of the alienation of the Shawnees from the Carolinians see ''Old Hop's Talk to Captain Stuart and Lieutenant Wall,'' November 15, 1756, *DRIA*, II, 246–47; for the locations of this band, led by half-blood Peter Chartier, see ibid., 162, 164, 226, 295.

47. Raymond Demere to Governor Lyttelton, June 13, 1757, *DRIA*, II, 383–86.

48. Ibid., 384.

49. Geo. Turner to Governor Lyttelton, July 2, 1758, *DRIA*, II, 471.

50. Bouquet to Johnson, RG10/C1222/128.

51. Governor Lyttelton to Board of Trade, October 2, 1758, C.O. 5/376/55.

52. George Milligen, *Short Description*, 187; for a full account see David Corkran, *Cherokee Frontier*.

53. John Echols, ''An Extract of a Journal—'Concerning a March That Capt: Robt. Wade took to the New River'—In search of Indians,'' August 12, 1758, *Virginia Calendar of State Papers*, volume I, ed. William P. Palmer (Richmond: Superintendent of Public Printing, 1875), 254–57.

54. Young, ''The Effect of the French and Indian War,'' 104–5.

55. Echols, ''Concerning a March,'' 254.

56. Ibid., 255.

57. Little Carpenter to Governor Glen, March 20, 1759, ms. in William L. Clements Library, University of Michigan.

58. Samuel C. Williams, ''Richardson's Diary,'' 134.

59. Cf. Leach, *Roots of Conflict: British Armed Forces and Colonial Americans, 1677–1763* (Chapel Hill: University of North Carolina Press, 1986), 110–13.

60. Glen to Lord North, [1765], ms. in South Caroliniana Library, Columbia; See also Alden, *John Stuart*, 78–79. Attakullakulla, out of an old grudge, later blamed Governor Glen for his trouble with Forbes. ''Talk of Little Carpenter to Governor Lyttelton,'' March 29, 1759, Lyttelton Papers, William L. Clements Library, University of Michigan.

61. Stuart, ''Of Indians in General,'' 257.

62. William Preston, ''Diary, February 9-March 13, 1756,'' Draper Collection, 1QQ122–23; also Otis K. Rice, ''The Sandy Creek Expedition of 1756,'' *West Virginia History* 13 (January 1953): 5–19.

63. Ibid., 4.

64. Old Hop and the Great Warrior to [Raymond Demere], April 5, 1757, *DRIA,* II, 409.

65. Ibid., 410.

66. Governor Glen to Little Carpenter, February 17, 1756, *DRIA,* II 100.

67. "Talk of the Nottaway Indians," [May 2, 1751], *DRIA,* I, 47.

68. *South Carolina Gazette,* October 11, 1760.

69. Quoted in Crane, *Southern Frontier,* 300; Williams, "Cuming's Journal," 143.

70. Captain Rayd. Demere to Governor Lyttelton, January 15, 1757, *DRIA,* II, 315; "The Mankiller of Highwassee's Answer" [September 27, 1756], *DRIA,* II, 221.

CHAPTER NINE

1. For more information on Richardson's sponsorship see Alden, *John Stuart,* 351–52.

2. Williams, "Richardson's Diary," 134; ibid., 126.

3. Ibid., 134.

4. Ibid., 133.

5. Ibid., 136.

6. Old Hop was responding to the news from Little Carpenter and reports from other returning warriors that their presents had been taken away by Forbes.

7. "Intelligence from Nancy Butler to Captain Rayd. Demere," December 20, 1756, *DRIA,* II, 276.

8. "Intelligence from Indian Nancy to Captain Rayd. Demere, December 1756, *DRIA,* II, 269.

9. Williams, *Adair's History,* 261; S.C. Journal of Council, October 19, 1759 (SCDAH).

10. Maud Wyndham, *Chronicles of the Eighteenth-Century, Founded on the Correspondence of Sir Thomas Lyttelton and His Family* (London: Hodder and Stoughton, 1924,), 190–201. See also Michael Kammen, *A Rope of Sand; The Colonial Agents, British Politics and the American Revolution* (Ithaca: Cornell University Press, 1968).

11. Walter L. Dorn, *Competition for Empire* (New York: Harper and Row, 1963), 346.

12. Richard Lyttelton to William Lyttelton, March 7, 1758, Lyttelton Letterbooks (microfilm in the South Carolina Department of Archives and History.)

13. James Grant to [   ], September 22, 1757, ms. in South Caroliniana Library, Columbia.

14. Journal of the Upper House, January 1757, *Colonial Records of Georgia,* XVI, 161.

15. Journal of the Commons House, July 1757, *Colonial Records of Georgia,* XVI, 219.

16. Jack P. Greene, *The Quest for Power; The Lower Houses of Assembly in the Southern Royal Colonies, 1689–1776* (Chapel Hill: University of North Carolina Press, 1963), 323. For a different perspective, see Weir, *Colonial South Carolina,* 265–68.

17. Ibid.

18. Vaudreuil and his colleagues had left a substantial paper trail concerning their

attempts to keep the English in the southern colonies preoccupied on one of many fronts in *la petite guerre* which he advocated. "Some Facts Stated, That Prove the French To Have Been the Aggressors in North America, for Four Years Successively, Before the English were Obliged to Take Up Arms in their Own Defense," John Appy to Earl of Loudoun, [1756] summarized in Barron, *Vaudreuil Papers,* 433–38. Significantly, the English fort in the Overhill was named for Loudoun, a gesture which suggests the degree to which the English occupation of this ground represented the territorial ambitions of the home office.

19. For an informed discussion of Fort Toulouse, see Daniel H. Thomas *Fort Toulouse* (Tuscaloosa: University of Alabama Press, 1989). Fort Toulouse was "but seven days' march from Fort Loudoun." Captain Raymond Demere to Governor Lyttelton, October 28, 1756, *DRIA,* II, 233.

20. "Letter from William Henry Lyttelton Esq. Gov. of South Carolina, to the Board dated the 22nd of April 1757, inclosing Copies of Dispatches in writing and Cypher from ye Govr. of Louisiana and other Papers, taken out of a French Prize Ship bound from New Orleans to la Rochelle, brought in by His Majesty's Sloop the Jamaica," C.O. 5/375/D 437.

21. William Pitt to Governor Lyttelton, March 7, 1758, Lyttelton, Letterbook (SCDAH).

22. Lyttelton to BOT September 15, 1757. Lyttelton to Raymond Demere, September 28, 1757, ibid. (SCDAH). Lyttelton's reference was to the "Negro fort," Fort Mosa, at St. Augustine. See John J. TePaske, "The Fugitive Slave: Intercolonial Rivalry and Spanish Slave Policy, 1687–1764" in *Eighteenth-Century Florida and Its Borderlands,* ed. Samuel Proctor (Gainesville: University Presses of Florida, 1975), 1–39.

23. Lyttelton to Paul Demere, June 7, 1759, Lyttelton Letterbook (SCDAH).

24. The correspondence between Paul Demere, his brother, who commanded Fort Loudoun in 1757–59, is similarly important in this regard.

25. Raymond Demere to Lyttelton, June 13, 1757, *DRIA,* II, 385.

26. Raymond Demere to Lyttelton, August 10, 1757, *DRIA,* II, 398.

27. Daniel Pepper to Lyttelton, November 30, 1756, *DRIA,* II, 297.

28. Daniel Pepper to Lyttelton, May 25, 1757, *DRIA,* II, 377.

29. Raymond Demere to Lyttelton, January 2, 1757, *DRIA,* II, 302.

30. Ibid., 301–2.

31. *South Carolina Gazette,* August 18, 1759.

32. Ibid., August 25, 1759.

33. Ibid.

34. Lyttelton to BOT, September 7, 1759, S.C. Governor's Papers. (SCDAH)

35. S.C. Journal of Council, July 9, 1759, C.O. 5/474/536. "Buckraa" was an African-derived term for "white."

36. Aptheker, *Slave Revolts,* 20; see also Ruth A. Hudnut and Hayes Baker Crothers, "Acadian Transients in South Carolina," *American Historical Review* 43 (April 1938): 500–503.

37. Robert L. Meriwether, *The Expansion of South Carolina,* 154–55.

38. Robert Mitchell, working in the Shenandoah Valley (where ethnically segregated settlements were the rule), has described the pattern as developing from "self-choice." Mitchell, *Commercialism and Frontier,* 155–56.

39. 'Filius Gallicae' to the Duke de Mirepoix, January 12, 1756, in "Intercepted Letters to the Duke de Mirepoix," *American Historical Association Annual Report,* 1896, I, 675.

40. Glen to Stanwix, November 6, 1759, W.O. 34/29 (microfilm in SCDAH).

41. S.C. Lower House Journals, July 5, 1759. The Lower House argued for "a consideration of the heavy charges the Province has labored under during the present war" (July 7, 1759). As a conciliatory gesture, Amherst offered to pay the cost of carriage to the "Out-Posts" (July 14, 1759).

42. Lyttelton to Governor Dobbs, October 19, 1759, Lyttelton Letterbook (SCDAH).

43. Lyttelton to Amherst, February 22, 1760, Lyttelton Letterbook (SCDAH).

44. *South Carolina Gazette,* August 9–11, 1759.

45. Ibid.

46. Corkran, *Cherokee Frontier,* 174; *South Carolina Gazette,* September 1, 1759.

47. S.C. Lower House Journal, October 4–5, 1759 (SCDAH).

48. Ibid., October 12, 1759 (microfilm copy in South Carolina Department of Archives and History).

49. S.C. Journal of Council, October 10, 1759.

50. Ibid., October 4, 1759.

51. *South Carolina Gazette,* October 13, 1759.

52. Ibid., October 17, 1759; See account in Corkran, *Cherokee Frontier,* 173–75.

53. S.C. Journal of Council, October 19, 1759 (SCDAH).

54. Ibid. See account in Milligen, *A Short Account,* 189.

55. *South Carolina Gazette,* Extraordinary, October 13, 1759. "When the news of our glorious success in North America reaches them, we hope to receive different accounts of their mood."

56. Ibid., September 1, 1759.

57. Journal of Council, October 22, 1759; George Milligen noted that the headmen were finally put under formal arrest at Congarees on November 7, 1759. Milligen, *A Short Account,* 190.

CHAPTER TEN

1. Other recent accounts include: David Corkran, *Cherokee Frontier,* chap. 5; Robert Weir, *Colonial South Carolina: A History,* chap. 11, and Marion Sirmans, *Colonial South Carolina,* chap. 14.

2. William I. Thompson, *The Imagination of an Insurrection, Dublin, Easter 1916* (New York: Harper and Row, 1967), v–vi. The lengthy contemporary newspaper accounts of the campaigns, especially in the *South Carolina Gazette,* provided a self-consciously dramatic sense of the conflict to readers. Thus, the ongoing stories published through the period, especially the "Journal from Fort Prince George," provided a lengthy interior view of the campaigns, segments of which were later condensed and published in Continental as well as American almanacs, such as John Tobler's *Almanac* of 1763, and an Italian almanac of the period: M. De Filipis ed. and trans., "An Italian Account of the Cherokee Uprisings at Fort Loudoun and Fort Prince George, 1760–61," *North Carolina Historical Review* (1943), 247–58. These almanac accounts of the Cherokee-English war almost immediately began to be supplanted by more retrospec-

Notes

tives. George Milligen's narrative, incorporated into *A Short Description of South Carolina*, written in 1763, contains the thread of analysis which has been followed by modern historians. Alexander Hewatt, another historian of the time, gave prominence to the war in his *An Historical Account of the Rise and Progress of South Carolina and Georgia* (London, 1779). James Adair also provided a long account of the war in his *History of the American Indians*.

3. *South Carolina Gazette,* November 1–3, 1759.

4. Ibid.

5. Ibid., November 3–10, 1759.

6. Milligen, *A Short Account,* 189–90.

7. S.C. Journal of Lower House, October 5, 1759. On colonial fighting technology see John K. Mahon, "Anglo-American Methods of Indian Warfare, 1696–1794," *Mississippi Valley Historical Review* 45 (September 1958): 254–59; Meriwether, *Expansion of South Carolina,* 216.

8. *South Carolina Gazette,* November 3–10, 1759.

9. Ibid.

10. Ibid., January 8–12, 1760.

11. Estimates of fighting strength varied widely. Cf. *South Carolina Gazette,* November 3–10, December 1–8, 1759.

12. Williams, *Adair's History,* 265–66.

13. Milligen, *A Short Account,* 190.

14. Historians have generally followed Milligen's assessment of the importance of this action in catalyzing the Cherokee violence. All of the headmen's retinue (excepting the "women and children") were eventually confined to a "small hut" at Fort Prince George at Keowee. Milligen, *A Short Account,* 192.

15. Williams, *Adair's History,* 265.

16. *South Carolina Gazette,* December 1–8, 1759.

17. Ibid., December 22–29, 1759.

18. Milligen, *A Short Account,* 190. The disease had been appearing in pockets around Charlestown and in the backcountry during the march. *South Carolina Gazette,* June 30, 1758.

19. Ibid., January 8–12, 1760.

20. Williams, *Adair's History,* 266. The "gentleman" was a purported French agent.

21. *South Carolina Gazette,* January 8–12, 1760.

22. "Second Conference with Attakulla Kulla," December 19, 1759, ms. in William L. Clements Library, University of Michigan.

23. Lyttelton posted sentinels at the fords leading to the village, and the tribespeople, acquiescing to Lyttelton's request, "burned their houses and removed the people to a valley four miles distant." *South Carolina Gazette,* January 8–12, 1759.

24. Milligen, *A Short Account,* 194–95.

25. Summaries of these events were reported in *South Carolina Gazette,* January 8–12, 1760.

26. Williams, *Adair's History,* 264.

27. *South Carolina Gazette,* January 8–12, 1760.

28. Thomas Mante, *History of the Late War in America* (London, 1772; reprint New York: Arno Press, 1970), 268.

29. *South Carolina Gazette,* January 8–12, 1760.

30. Ibid., March 15–22, 1760. Lyttelton's brother, George, reflected on the appointment to Jamaica (which he had engineered), and on the quality of his brother's reputation: "my dear Governor, I suppose you won't leave a dry eye in your Province. If I did not love you as well as I do I should envy you the Reputation you have acquired." George Lyttelton to W. H. Lyttelton, *Papers of William Henry Lyttelton* (London: Southeby's, 1978), 78.

31. *South Carolina Gazette,* March 29 to April 7, 1760.

32. Milligen, *A Short Account,* 195.

33. Ann Manigault, "Extracts from Journal of Mrs. Ann Manigault, 1754–1781," *South Carolina Historical Magazine* 20 (January 1919): 135.

34. *South Carolina Gazette,* March 29–April 7, 1760.

35. Ibid.

36. A similar act passed during the Yamassee emergency of 1715 had prohibited the export of "corn and peas." Thomas Cooper, *Statutes at Large of South Carolina* (1836), II, 634–41, #356, IV, 109, #893; *South Carolina Gazette,* June 10–24, 1760.

37. *South Carolina Gazette,* April 1, 1760.

38. Cooper, *Statutes at Large,* IV, 109.

39. Alexr. Miln to Lyttelton, February 24, 1760, *DRIA,* III, 499.

40. Milligen, *A Short Account,* 196.

41. Alexr. Miln to Lyttelton, February 28, 1760, *DRIA,* III, 503.

42. *South Carolina Gazette,* May 22–29, 1760.

43. Ibid., May 17–24, 1760.

44. Ibid., June 10–14, 1760.

45. E. Pinckney to [Mrs. Evance], March 15th, [17]60, *The Letterbook of Eliza Lucas Pinckney, 1739–1762,* ed. Elise Pinckney (Chapel Hill: University of North Carolina Press, 1972), 147–48.

46. *South Carolina Gazette,* July 19–26, 1760.

47. Milligen, *A Short Account,* 196.

48. John Pearson to Lyttelton, February 8, 1760, *DRIA,* III, 495–96.

49. *South Carolina Gazette,* February 10, 1760.

50. Alexander S. Salley, "The Calhoun Family of South Carolina," *South Carolina Historical and Genealogical Magazine* 7 (April 1906): 86.

51. North Carolina, Treasurer's Records, May 30, 1777, Box 1, North Carolina Department of Archives and History, Raleigh.

52. *South Carolina Gazette,* March 8–11, 1760.

53. Ibid.

54. *South Carolina Gazette,* June 10–14, 1760.

55. Milligen, *A Short Account,* 197.

56. *South Carolina Gazette,* August 9–13, 1760.

57. Patrick Calhoun to Lyttelton, February 25, 1760, ms. in Clements Library, University of Michigan.

58. William Richardson to [], [1760], ms. in Draper Collection, 2VV177–78.

59. Patrick Calhoun to Lyttelton, February 25, 1760, Clements Library, University of Michigan.

60. Cf. Memorial from Merchants to William Pitt, [1760], C.O. 5/65, pt. 1.

61. *South Carolina Gazette,* April 7–12, 1760.

62. Richard Richardson to Lyttelton, February 26, 1760, *DRIA,* II, 501–502.

63. *South Carolina Gazette,* April 1, 1760.

64. Ibid., March 24–31, 1760.

65. Ibid., March 24–31, 1760.

66. Ibid., July 19–26, 1760; also Robert Weir, *Letters of Freeman* (Columbia: University of South Carolina Press, 1977), "Introduction."

67. James Grant to William Bull, letter reprinted in *South Carolina Gazette,* June 7–16, 1760 (Extraordinary); ibid., June 10–14, 1760. The British scorched-earth tactics—aiming at dwellings and stored food—were long practiced in Ireland and perfected at the last stop of Montgomery's troops in Canada, where rapid nighttime raids targeted the native villages of Trois Rivères. Reports from Quebec had noted "we are daily taking their sheep and cattle by the hundreds, and they can't have any benefit from any crop this year . . . they must perish in the winter," ibid., October 13, 1759.

68. Ibid., July 12–19, 1760; a few of the backcountry men owned rifles as well, and were tagged "rifle-barrel men" (ibid., November 24–December 1, 1759.) For another short account of the action at Echoe, see Philip M. Hamer and George C. Rogers, *The Papers of Henry Laurens* (Columbia: University of South Carolina Press, 1972), III, 308–9.

69. *South Carolina Gazette,* October 18–26, 1760. In reality, a few Creeks acted in concert with the Cherokees, often in the most violent incidents.

70. Ibid.

71. Ibid., July 5–12, 1759.

72. Ibid., July 19–26, 1760. Weeks later, a Cherokee War leader was reported to have spoken of Captain Williams as "a brave man" (ibid., August 13, 1760).

73. "Second Letter of James Grant," July 3, 1760, ibid., quoted in Gadsden, "Some Observations of the Two Campaigns Against the Cherokee Indians in 1760 and 1761 in a Second Letter of Philopatrios" (Charlestown: Peter Timothy, 1762; microprint Readex Microprint, #9242, #9243), 286.

74. Ibid., 87.

75. *South Carolina Gazette,* July 12–19, 1760.

76. Corkran, *Cherokee Frontier,* 214.

77. *South Carolina Gazette,* August 13–16, 1760.

78. Amherst to Pitt, August 26, 1760, C.O. 5/54/1.

79. Alexander Hewatt, *An Historical Account,* II, 29.

80. *South Carolina Gazette,* August 20–30, 1760.

81. S. C. Lower House Journal, February 9, 1760.

82. *South Carolina Gazette,* August 13–16, 1760. For financial measures and the Artillery Company see Cooper, *Statutes at Large,* IV, 119, 128, 144, 664–70 and IX, 894, 897–99. Financing included funds raised by subscription from prominent merchants such as Henry Laurens. See Hamer and Rogers, *Papers of Henry Laurens,* III, 16.

83. Lachlan Shaw to Lyttelton, *DRIA,* II, 506.

84. Bossu, *Travels,* 83.

85. *South Carolina Gazette,* September 10–27, 1760.

86. Ibid., August 16–23, 1760.

87. Alexander Moneypenny, "Daybook," *Journal of Cherokee Studies* 2 (Summer 1977): 327.

88. Saunders, *CRNC,* VI, 136–37; Jerry C. Cashion, "North Carolina and the

Cherokee: The Quest for Land on the Eve of the Revolution, 1754–1776'' (Ph.D. dissertation, University of North Carolina at Chapel Hill, 1979), 41.

89. Cashion, ''North Carolina and the Cherokee Indians,'' 43. For the social context of desertion in colonial militia, see John Shy, ''A New Look at the Colonial Militia,'' *William and Mary Quarterly*, 3rd Series, 20 (April 1963): 175–85.

90. Williams, *Adair's History*.

91. *South Carolina Gazette*, June 14–21, 1760.

92. Ibid., September 20–27, 1760.

93. Hamer and Rogers, *Papers of Henry Laurens*, III, 297.

94. Mante, *History of the War*, 347.

95. Weir, *Colonial South Carolina*, 289.

96. Hamer and Rogers, *Papers*, III, 318–19.

97. There was not total unanimity about the wisdom of the coming expedition; after all, Montgomery and Lyttelton had taught the Cherokees a lesson and not everyone indulged in Cherokee-hating rhetoric. Some were still concerned with the possibility of losing the advantage of trade with the tribe, or still more important, the strategic value of its former friendship. This lack of unanimity was given occasional expression in the *Gazette*. For instance, one reader complained that ''The words SCOURGING AND CHASTISEMENT have been lately very frequently used.'' *South Carolina Gazette*, August. 23–30, 1760.

98. Ibid., September 13–20, 1760.

99. Ibid., August 30, 1760.

100. Ibid., October 18–26, 1760.

101. Ibid., August 12, 1760.

102. Richard G. Stone, ''Captain Paul Demere at Fort Loudoun, 1757–60,'' *East Tennessee Historical Society Publications* 41 (1969): 29.

103. *South Carolina Gazette*, July 11–18, 1761.

104. Ibid., May 31–June 7, 1760; William Bull to BOT, May 21, 1761, 5/377/5. During the Yamassee War and afterwards, blacks had been essential elements in defense. Cf. Peter Wood, *Black Majority*, 127–28. Cooper, *Statutes at Large*, II, #356.

105. French, ''Journal'': 277.

106. Mainstream German clergy seem to have attempted to downplay the heresy among their people, and as a result, few reports of the Webber affair have survived. Henry M. Muhlenberg quoted in Goddard Bernheim, *History of the German Settlements and the Lutheran Church in North and South Carolina* (Philadelphia, 1872; reprint Baltimore, 1975), 197–201.

107. John Ettwein to Henry Laurens in Hamer and Rogers, *Papers of Henry Laurens*, III, 356. Ettwein was a member of the Moravian Wachovia settlement and his remarks seem to refer to non-communitarian backcountry populations on the North and South Carolina border, west of the Catawba settlements.

108. *South Carolina Gazette*, May 2–May 9, 1760.

109. Hewatt, *An Historical Account*, 242–53.

110. Hamer and Rogers, *Papers of Henry Laurens*, III, 311.

111. French, ''Journal,'' 278. Public killings were used to enforce discipline among the King's troops, and made a strong negative impression upon the colonial troops. Cf. Leach, *Roots of Conflict*, 112–13.

112. Hamer and Rogers, *Papers of Henry Laurens*, III, 300–301.

113. James Grant, "Journal of Lt. Colonel James Grant, Commanding an Expedition Against the Cherokee Indians," *Florida Historical Quarterly* 12 (July 1933): 25.

114. French, "Journal," 279.

115. Ibid., 284.

116. Ibid., 291.

117. Ibid., 285.

118. Ibid., 283–85, 90–91.

119. "Letter of James Grant," quoted in Gadsden, "Philopatrios," 87.

120. James Grant, "Journal," 36.

121. French, "Journal," 288.

122. Corkran, *Cherokee Frontier*, 256–65.

123. Ibid., 258.

124. Hamer and Rogers, *Papers of Henry Laurens*, III, 343.

125. French, "Journal," 266, 292.

126. The preliminary peace was resisted for a time by the Commons House, which appointed a committee whose report labeled the treaty (minus Article One) as "useless and dishonorable." Weir, *Colonial South Carolina*, 273.

CHAPTER ELEVEN

1. An excellent description of the 1760 epidemic, from which these estimates are taken, appears in an unpublished paper by Suzanne Krebsbach, "The Great Charles Town Smallpox Epidemic of 1760," 1981 (xeroxed).

2. Milligen, *Short Account*, 195. See also, Sirmans, *Colonial South Carolina*, 348. In the last year of the war, the "tax per adult," (white or free taxpaying adult) in South Carolina was the highest of any province. Weir, *Colonial South Carolina*, 288. During the Stamp Act Crisis, Christopher Gadsden argued that the "long and expensive war with the Cherokee Indians" had left the colony "burdened with a very heavy balance of debt." Gibbes, *Documentary History*, III, 3. Though the fiscal burden of the war was substantial, colonial complaints reflected as much emotional frustration with the wartime experience as they did an actual financial crisis. Cf. Lawrence H. Gipson, *The Coming of the Revolution* (New York: Harper and Row, 1954), 149–51. Gipson notes that tax bills were postponed from one year to the next between 1762 and 1766.

3. Sirmans, *Colonial South Carolina*, 348–49; Cooper, *Statutes at Large*, IV, 187–88.

4. Edward McCrady, *History of South Carolina under Royal Government* 1719–1776 (New York, 1889), 378–379; Cooper, *Statutes at Large*, IV, 187–88.

5. Black numbers were double the white population of 20,300 in 1745, and by 1760 black population had risen to 57,900, while whites counted 38,600. Wood, "Changing Population," Table 1.

6. *South Carolina Gazette*, May 31–June 7, 1761; 7–13 June, 1761.

7. Ibid., May 31–June 7, 1761. The same issue reprinted the proposed text of "An Act for Laying an Additional Duty on All Negroes Hereafter to Be Imported into This Province."

8. Ibid., May 31–June 7, 1761.

9. Robert Weir stresses the embarrassment suffered by the provincials: "men of

property in South Carolina were, perhaps for the first time since the seventeenth century, being closely measured against British standards and by and large they were found wanting'' (*Colonial South Carolina*), 284–85.

10. *Lloyd's London Evening Post*, June 21–23, 1762 (transcription in the Draper Collection, 3W137).

11. After their departure, the captain of the ship on which the tribesmen returned, wrote to reassure Egremont that they had been "treated in a proper and suitable manner" on their return to Charlestown. Peter Blake to Lord Egremont, November 27, 1762 (transcript in Draper Collection, VV167223).

12. *Lloyd's London Evening Post*, July 30–August 2, August 4–6, 1762 (transcript in Draper Collection, 3VV137).

13. One commentator worried about the effect of the Cherokees being "made a shew of instead of cementing the peace." If the chiefs were offended by the conduct of the crowds "it might only serve to raise implacable hatred." *Lloyd's London Evening Post*, July 26–28 (transcript in Draper Collection, 2VV 137).

14. *Boston Gazette*, December 6, 1762.

15. *London Chronicle*, July 6, 1762 (transcript in Draper Collection, 2VV).

16. Middleton technically outranked Grant and complained that being forced to receive orders from him had been like swallowing a "Choak Pear." Hamer and Rogers, *Papers of Henry Laurens*, III, 295.

17. Quoted in George Rogers, "The Papers of James Grant of Ballindaloch Castle, Scotland," *South Carolina Historical Magazine* (February 1976): 147–48; Alexander Moneypenny, "Diary," 323.

18. Rogers, "The Papers of James Grant," 146–48.

19. Weir, "Harmony" 473–501.

20. Hamer and Rogers, *Papers of Henry Laurens*, III, 350. Alexander Hewatt, *An Historical Account*, II, 249–51. Hewatt interpreted the clash as inflaming largely pro-Scottish and Angloamerican interests in Charlestown, but also pointed out the growth of "party spirit," which in a "growing province, where the utmost harmony and liberality of sentiment ought to have prevailed . . . was attended . . . with the most pernicious consequence."

21. Laurens's "A Letter Signed Philolethes, May 2, 1762" was privately circulated but never published. Hamer and Rogers, *Papers of Henry Laurens*, III, 275–355. Gadsden's writings were printed by anti-Scottish, and therefore anti-James Grant, *Gazette* editor Peter Timothy in the pamphlet titled "Some Observations of the Two Campaigns against the Cherokee Indians in 1760 and 1761 in a Second Letter of Philopatrios." For an abstract and more on versions of the Philopatrios letters see Richard Walsh, *The Writings of Christopher Gadsden* (Columbia: University of South Carolina Press, 1966), 14–15, 52–63.

22. In the same vein, Laurens was particularly critical of the attempt of his former commander to create a *show* of competence with "pompous & Cumbrous equipage . . . well enough indeed for a Campaign in Flanders." Hamer and Rogers, *Papers of Henry Laurens*, III, 297.

23. Ibid., III, 309.

24. Walsh, *Writings of Christopher Gadsden*, xix.

25. For Christopher Gadsden, the debate over the war initiated the redirection of his interests and his discovery of a new political vocabulary that would be deployed in the

sequence of controversies in which he was embroiled by 1763. Walsh, *Writings of Christopher Gadsden*, xix–xx. Also see Jack P. Greene, "The Gadsden Election Controversy and the Revolutionary Movement in South Carolina," *Mississippi Valley Historical Review* XLIV (1959): 469–92. The consequences of the debate would persist through the 1760s for Laurens as well. During the Stamp Act crisis in 1765, Laurens's house was attacked by a mob of "Jacks" angry over the manner in which he had "held sway" with Grant during the Cherokee War. Weir, *Colonial South Carolina*, 283. The Grant-Middleton controversy and its aftermath also coincide with a "turning point" in Laurens's career in 1764 in which he put aside his commercial interests and adopted the style and preoccupations of the major landowner and planter which he had become.

26. For a list of South Carolinians who served as officers on the Grant expedition, see "officers in the South Carolina Regiment in the Cherokee War, 1760–61," *South Carolina Genealogical and Historical Magazine* III (October 1902): 202–6.

27. Rogers, "Papers of James Grant of Ballindalloch," 148. See also McCrady, *The History of South Carolina Under the Royal Government*, 350.

28. *South Carolina Gazette*, September 20–27, 1759.

29. Williams, *Adair's History*, 265.

30. French, "Journal," 323–24.

31. Hamer and Rogers, *Papers of Henry Laurens*, III, 351.

32. Andrew Pickens to William H. Lee, [], Draper Collection, IVV107.

33. Williams, *Timberlake's Journal*, 28.

34. Just prior to Montgomery's march the Assembly passed, at the request of William Bull, "An act to enforce a due subordination and observance of military discipline among the forces employed in the service of this Province." Cooper, *Statutes at Large*, IV, 104–6. The *Gazette* reported a year later that, just after Grant's arrival at Congarees, "some examples have been lately made both of regulars and Provincials for desertion." *South Carolina Gazette*, April 25–May 2, 1761. Grant ordered the execution of at least two men in front of the assembled troops. French, "Journal of an Expedition," 278. Cf. Leach, *Roots of Conflict*, 112.

35. Quoted in Hamer and Rogers, *Papers of Henry Laurens*, III, 353.

36. Ibid., 342.

37. Williams, *Timberlake's Journal*, 79; John Stuart found that he could not receive full respect from the warriors he negotiated with without having "military rank" himself. John Stuart to Hillsborough, July 30, 1769, C.O.5/370/264.

38. This Virginia regiment had clear class markings. As Henry Timberlake wrote, "about 100 of Our Gentlemen are entered into an Association at their own expense, properly accoutered on Horse Back, to go to our frontier against the enemy." Williams, *Adair's History*, 28.

39. *South Carolina Gazette*, February 14–21, 1760.

40. Ibid., July 12–14, 1760. See also Hamer and Rogers, *Papers of Henry Laurens*, III, 336.

41. The son of a close friend remembered that the incident reflected his personality—"a proud, supercilious, extravagant young man, as he was when he was old." William Martin to Lyman Draper, Draper Collection, 2VV77.

42. Williams, *Adair's History*, 262.

43. *London Gazette*, #10140; James Grant, "Journal," 25.

44. In the exchange between Henry Laurens and Christopher Gadsden, Laurens ex-

plained away Grant's remarks while Gadsden furiously rebutted the British version of what had occurred at the battle of Echoe: The Rangers, "did not give the least reason to be even **SUSPECTED** of fearing the Indians." Gadsden, *Philopatrios,* 21.

45. Williams, *Adair's History,* 152–53; Alexander Longe, "Short Account," 30. John S. Reid's history of Cherokee legal governance stresses the absolute equality of women in councils and other deliberative bodies during the eighteenth century. Cf. Reid, *A Law of Blood,* 30. For historical assessments which stress the decline of strong women's status during the colonial and early national period and discuss the contrast between Cherokee and Euroamerican female sexual behavior, see Theda Perdue, "The Traditional Status of Cherokee Women," *Furman Studies,* New Series, 26 (December 1980): 19–26; and "Southeastern Indians and the Cult of True Southern Womanhood," 35–52; for another treatment see Eleanor Leacock, *Myths of Male Dominance* (New York and London: Monthly Review Press, 1981), 234–41.

46. Tobler, "Tobler's Description," 260. George Milligen echoed the same theme of women "committing" abortion as a spiteful punishment to unfaithful men. In his *A Short Description of South Carolina,* Milligen wrote: "Polygamy is permitted among them; yet few have more than one wife at a time, possibly on account of the expense of supporting them; for he is accounted a good Gunman that provides well for one; besides, the Indians are not of an amorous Complexion: It is common with them however to repudiate their wives, if disobliged by them or tired of them; the rejected woman generally revenges herself after the affront by taking Herbs to procure an abortion, an operation that destroys many of them and greatly contributes to depopulate them" (185). Though Milligen in a sense blames tribal men of nothing more than non-support, economic and sexual impotence, women are depicted as committing what must have impressed his readers as a much more considerable crime against the family, child-killing.

47. Williams, *Timberlake's Memoirs,* 91; see also Reid, *A Law of Blood,* 68–71.

48. Ibid., 88–89.

49. French, "Journal," 284, 285.

50. Hamer and Rogers, *Papers of Henry Laurens,* III, 279.

51. Gadsden, "Philopatrios," 34.

52. Hamer and Rogers, *Papers of Henry Laurens,* III, 279–80.

53. Talk of Attakullakulla, quoted in John Reid, *A Better Kind of Hatchet,* 69.

54. Henry Timberlake, *Gentleman's Magazine* 34 (1765): 142.

55. Richard Beale Davis, *Intellectual Life in the Colonial South, 1585–1763* (Knoxville: University of Tennessee Press, 1978), I, 215. Davis argues that the narrative of Mary Ingle's captivity was the most popular such story disseminated in the South. This female motif is missing by and large in the post-Cherokee war imaginative literature—broadly considered—and male suffering and anxieties concerning tribal women take their place. Annette Kolodny's study of imaginary landscapes argues that the key to narratives such as Ingle's (which is in the genre of the New England captivity story) is to understand that the female protagonist "vicariously displaced onto the dark and dusky figure of the Indian a projection of her husband's darker side." By the same token, such stories are often marked by an admiration for the "Squaws" who coped with the wilderness, and whom captive white women could never equal. Thus, the captivity novel has at its core a story of "women's suffering in the wilderness." Cf. Annette Kolodny, *The Land Before Her: Fantasy and Experience of the American Frontiers, 1630–1860* (Chapel Hill: University of North Carolina Press, 1984), 18, 33.

56. David Menzies, "A true Relation of the unheard of Sufferings of DAVID MENZIES, Surgeon, among the CHEROKEES, and of his surprizing Deliverance," in Alexander Kellett, *A Pocket of Prose and Verse: Being a Selection from the Literary Productions of Alexander Kellet, Esq.* (Bath: Printed by R. Cruttwell, 1778; reprint Garland Publishing, 1975), 197.

57. Menzies, "A true Relation," 197–204.

58. Ibid.

59. *South Carolina Gazette,* June 3, 1732. Cf. June 20–27, 1748.

60. A broadside copy of "Song on the Chiefs" is in the Manuscript Collection, Library of Congress.

61. ". . . in what posture their partners may fancy, which makes me still hope thay have the preference of the black ladies in the esteem of widowers and bachelors." *South Carolina Gazette,* July 24, 1736; also June 20–24, 1748.

62. Anderson, "Cherokee Clay," 504.

63. Van Doren, *Bartram's Travels,* 263. Hewatt, *An Historical Account,* II, 245.

64. Hewatt, *An Historical Account,* II, 245.

65. Glen to Board of Trade, [1751], C.O. 5/372/294–95. Glen stresses the image of "Paterfamilias." Cf. Kellett, "Letter from North America," 4.

66. Though the public discussion of diplomacy during the 1750s had tended to assume that the benevolence of the Cherokees during the Yamassee War, in interceding against the Creeks, provided a precedent for alliance, after the war history was rewritten. In George Milligen's *A Short Account* and Hewatt's *An Historical Account* the Cherokees were cited as enemies of South Carolina in 1715. Milligen, *A Short Account,* 186; Hewatt, *An Historical Account* II, 216–18.

67. This resolution came in the low point after Lyttelton's return from his failed expedition. *South Carolina Gazette,* February 8, 1760.

68. The linkage of domestic image and political stance was to evolve rapidly over the decade and a half leading up to the Revolution. The exploration of this theme within the context of colonial society (and apart from the intercultural context examined here) has been a major contribution of recent historical scholarship. For a recent treatment which stresses literary as well as social aspects of this problem, see Jay Fleigleman, *Prodigals and Pilgrims: The American Revolution Against Patriarchal Authority, 1750–1800* (New York: Cambridge University Press, 1982).

CHAPTER TWELVE

1. The total population loss may have, conservatively, approached 10 percent. See Wood, "Changing Population," *Powhatan's Mantle,* 64–65.

2. Hamer and Rogers, "A Letter Signed Philolethes," [March 2, 1763], *Papers of Henry Laurens,* III, 313.

3. Ibid., 286; *London Chronicle,* "Report from Charlestown," June 24, 1762.

4. Williams, *Adair's History,* 169.

5. For a discussion of the Cherokee case see Hatley, "Three Lives of Keowee," in *Powhatan's Mantle.* The smallpox outbreak apparently resembled the "prodigious havoc" of the 1738 outbreak among the tribe. Wood, "The Impact of Smallpox," 244. "Half" the Catawbas were to die of the disease, and before it was over the epidemic had spread

from the Appalachians to Bermuda. *South Carolina Gazette*, December 8–15, 1759; for the measles outbreak which accompanied smallpox ("measles rage"), see *South Carolina Gazette*, December 9–11, 1759.

6. Ibid., October 11–18, 1760.

7. Ibid., September 29, January 1–February 7, May 23–30, 1759.

8. Ibid., January 31–February 7, 1761.

9. Grant, "Journal," 35. Thomas Mante, *History of the Late War*, 284. In addition to uprooting standing corn crops, the burning of stored reserves ("astonishing magazines of corn") made the villages vulnerable to postwar famine.

10. Hamer and Rogers, "A Letter Signed Philolethes," *Papers of Henry Laurens*, III, 341; Moneypenny, "Diary," 321.

11. Grant, "Journal," 25, 33.

12. For instance, some Lower Towns, which had suffered most during the Creek conflict a decade earlier, hesitated. Their headmen addressed this point in a conciliatory message to the English, before the outbreak of the Cherokee War, blaming the "last war" with the Creeks on the "warriors over the Hills" who "made their road through our towns to the settlements." As a consequence, they noted, "our nation was thinned by it." Lower Towns to John Stuart, March 16, 1757, C.O. 5/68/106.

13. Williams, *Adair's History*, 263. For Adair's account of the origins of the war and Cherokee political divisions see *Adair's History*, 256–73; for detailed recent accounts see Corkran, *Cherokee Frontier*, and J. S. Reid, *A Law of Blood*.

14. *South Carolina Gazette*, March 29–April 7, 1759.

15. The French were particularly active through the "Coweeta" Creeks, a group whose leader, "The Wolf" (called "The Mortar" by the English), was closely tied to the French presence on the Coosa and Tallapoosa rivers, near Fort Toulouse. The majority of Creeks remained uncommitted, and met Edmond Atkin in order to cement a peace during 1760.

16. *South Carolina Gazette*, June 14–21, 1760. The Mortar persuaded warriors in Tellico and Settico to attack English settlements in 1759, and, participated in the massacre of the Fort Loudoun garrison a year later. Bossu, *Travels*, 83.

17. The promises of the French stemmed from long negotiations through Creek intermediaries. Repeated visits to Fort Toulouse and to New Orleans in the late 1750s and in 1760 confirmed among some Cherokees the sense that the French would provide support, an important promise as ammunition became scarce after the English trade embargo in the backcountry continued. See Kerlerec to Minister, June 12, 1760, AC, C12A/42. Chevalier Montault de Monberaut and his friend, the Mortar, played a particularly important role, as did the bureaucratic maneuvering of Kerlerec. See Milo B. Howard and Robert R. Rea, *The Memoire Justificatif de Chevalier Montault de Montberaut* (University: University of Alabama Press, 1965), 16–19, 69–71.

18. Kerlerec to Minister, December 15, 1761, AC, C13A/267.

19. For the native Americans allies along with Grant in 1761 see French, "Journal," 279.

20. *South Carolina Gazette*, October 18–26, 1760.

21. During the treaty at Albany in 1768 the Cherokees acknowledged the long condition of war between towns such as Chota and the Onondagas. "Brother" Oconostoa spoke to the northern tribe's representative, "it is a long time since the Sachem of Chotee made peace with the Onondaga, but that Sachem is now dead . . . here is a

belt [of peace] . . . which we have carefully preserved in our town these twenty years past." Proceedings of a General Congress at Albany, March 5, 1768, Public Archives of Canada (PAC), R.G. 10, C1222/8. A heavily edited transcript of this conference is in E. B. O'Callaghan, *Documents Relative to the Colonial History of the State of New York* (Albany: Weed, Parsons, and Co, 1849–51), 8, 38–53. See also Proceedings of a General Congress at Albany, March 6, 1768, PAC, R.G. 10, C1222/8.

22. Laurens to Willis Martin, August 29, 1763, Hamer and Rogers, *Papers of Henry Laurens*, III, 553.

23. Williams, *Timberlake's Memoirs*, 60.

24. Col. Stephen to Boquet, November 7, 1763, PAC, MG 21, BM Add Mss. 21649; John Stuart to Lt. Governor Bull, June 1, 1766, C.O. 323/23/306.

25. John Stuart to Board of Trade, March 9, 1764, C.O. 323/17/240.

26. Francis Parkman, *Conspiracy of Pontiac* (Boston: Little Brown, 1933), I, 182–88; *South Carolina Gazette*, October 17–24, 1761.

27. Sir William Johnson to Hillsborough, February 10, 1770, April 4, 1772, in O'Callaghan, *Documents Relative to the Colonial History of New York*, VIII, 203, 291. See also Randolph C. Downes, *Council Fires on the Upper Ohio: A Narrative of Indian Affairs in the Upper Ohio Valley Until 1745* (Pittsburgh: University of Pittsburgh Press, 1940), 146–47.

28. Governor Wright to Earl of Hillsborough, March 2, 1771, C.O. 5/661/25.

29. Talk of Sauy to Governor Boone, January 26, 1764, C.O. 323/17/172

30. Cf. Corkran, *Cherokee Frontier*, 194; *South Carolina Gazette*, January 24–31, April 12–19, 1761; Brown, *Old Frontiers*, 115.

31. North Carolina. Treasurer's Records, Box 1, 1770.

32. Draper Collection, 5XX52, 1–2; DeFillipis, "An Italian Account," 256; *South Carolina Gazette*, August 24, 1761.

33. Little Carpenter's status as village leader had substantial swings during the Cherokee War. As conflict with the colonies had escalated, his support of conciliation with the colonies on the eve of the war had become a liability. For instance, Standing Turkey, who opposed his leadership, accused him of "Englishness." *South Carolina Gazette*, June 28–July 5, 1760.

34. According to one source, Attakullakulla was actually a Nipissing captive adopted by the Cherokees. Later in life, as a Cherokee, he had been held hostage again by the Ottawas. Klinch and Talman, *Norton's Journal*, 32.

35. During the Cherokee War, his son, Selukukigh Wohellengh, was living among the Shawnee towns on the Ohio. For the role of Attakullakulla in Cherokee-Virginia diplomacy in the 1750s see Philip M. Hamer, "Anglo-French Rivalry in the Cherokee Country, 1754–57," *North Carolina Historical Review* 2 (1925): 303–22.

36. Talk from the Cherokee Chiefs to John Stuart, September 22, 1766, C.O. 323/24, pt. I/98.

37. Martin Schneider, "Journey of Br. Schneider from Salem to Long Island of the Holston, December 1783–January 24, 1784," in S. C. Williams, *Early Travels in the Tennessee Country*, 257.

38. For a more detailed discussion see Hatley, "Holding Their Ground"; Van Doren, *Bartram's Travels*, 284; Williams, *Adair's History*, 443.

39. Compare Jeanne Kay, "The Fur Trade and Native American Population Growth," *Ethnohistory* 31 (Winter 1984): 265–87.

40. Williams, *Adair's History*, 241–42.

41. Ibid.

42. Cf. Frederick Barkalow, "Vertebrate Remains from Archaeological Sites in the Tennessee Valley of Alabama," *Southern Indian Studies* 24 (October 1972): 21–22.

43. DeBrahm, *Report*, 126; Mooney, *Myths*, 265.

44. Williams, *Adair's History*, 17.

45. Raymond Demere to Governor Lyttelton, December 8, 1756, *DRIA*, II, 264. For archaeological evidence of Cherokee pig-keeping, see Arthur E. Bogan, "Faunal Remains from the Historic Cherokee Occupation at Citico" (40MR7), *Tennessee Anthropologist* 34 (Spring 1983); R. Newman, "The Acceptance of European Domestic Animals by the 18th Century Cherokee," *Tennessee Anthropologist* 4 (1979): 101.

46. Williams, *Timberlake's Memoirs*, 72.

47. Gary Goodwin, *Cherokees in Transition: A Study of Changing Culture and Environment Prior to 1775, Research Paper #181*, Department of Geography, University of Chicago, 1977, 135.

48. Williams, *Adair's History*, 262–63.

49. James Francis to Glen, October 7, 1754, *DRIA*, II, 21.

50. Williams, *Adair's History*, 1–2, 17.

51. "Talk between Judd's Friend and Governor Boone," November 3, 1762, C.O. 5/390/1–3.

52. Anthony Dean to Governor Glen, *DRIA*, I, 259–60; Williams, *Adair's History*, 242; Ludovic Grant to James Glen, *DRIA*, II, 41–42; John Stuart reported that "for many years there has not been a Trader in that Nation but was Bankrupt." John Stuart, "Observations on the Plan for the Future Management of Indian Affairs," December 8, 1764, in "Observations of Superintendent John Stuart and James Grant on the Proposed Plan of 1764 for the Future Management of Indian Affairs," *American Historical Review* 20 (July 1915): 822.

53. Cf. figures in Crane, *Southern Frontier*, Table IV, 330, and R. Nicholas Olsberg and Helen Craig Canon, *Duties on Trade at Charlestown, 1784–89*, South Carolina Microcopy #6 (Columbia: South Carolina Department of Archives and History, 1972). Statistics on the exports through Georgia are contained in Louis De Vorsey, Jr., "The Colonial Georgia Backcountry," in Edward J. Cashin, *Colonial Augusta: "Key to the Indian Countrey,"* (Macon: Mercer University Press, 1986), Tables I and II.

54. McDowell, *Introduction, DRIA*, II, xvii–xxi, xxxvii; Table of Trade for the Indian Trade;" also *DRIA*, II, 567. In general the prices prevailing at the Carolina Keowee "factory," or trading post during the 1760s, were half those charged fifty years earlier. See Leila Sellars, *Charleston Business on the Eve of the Revolution* (Chapel Hill: University of North Carolina Press, 1934), 173.

55. John Stuart to Earl of Hillsborough, June 12, 1772, in *Documents of the American Revolution;* V, 116.

56. Williams, *Adair's History*, 242. Trade good prices were from the 1730s widely felt to be too low. Stuart, "Observations . . . on the Proposed Plan of 1764 for Future Management of Indian Affairs," 822; Mr. Beaufain to Georgia Trustees, January 31, 1734, *Colonial Records of Georgia*, XXIV, 126.

57. Franklin, "Virginia and the Cherokee Indian Trade, 1753–1775," *East Tennessee Historical Society's Publications* 4 (January 1933): 22–38.

58. A State of the Province of Georgia, *Georgia Historical Collections*, II, 72.

59. One of the factors which may have leveled off local variations in hunting success was that Cherokee hunters did not depend on the 'take' of a single year. Cherokees and other tribes banked surplus leather during good years in order to follow fluctuations in trade prices and to carry over through poor hunting seasons. Cf. William Bartram's description of a "skin ware-house," Bartram, "Observations." Colonial trade administrators realized that getting access to these caches was as important as praying for a good hunt in a particular year. James Grant to Board of Trade, December 1, 1764, in "Observations of Superintendent John Stuart and Governor James Grant of East Florida on the Proposed Plan," 830.

60. Raymond Demere to Lyttelton, January 2, 1757, *DRIA*, II, 303. Inter-tribal trading was conducted in indigenous currencies—deerskins or "beeds and Wampon, which are valued by the Indians." Affidavit of David Dowey, May 25, 1751, *DRIA*, I, 58. Excavated trade-goods exhibit a limited replacement of the material culture among the Cherokee Lower Towns, and the pervasive presence of jewelry and beads strongly suggests that the bulk of tribal demand was based on a distinctly Cherokee taste for non-utilitarian goods. See data in Michael A. Harmon, "Eighteenth-Century Lower Cherokee Adaptation."

61. Williams, *Adair's History*, 245. See discussion in Chapter 3.

62. Raymond Demere to Governor Lyttelton, March 26, 1757, *DRIA*, II, 348; "List of Prices of Goods for the Cherokee Trade," November 1, 1751, *DRIA*, I, 146; Table of Goods and Prices for the Indian Trade, Journal of the Directors of the Cherokee Trade, November 20, 1762, *DRIA*, II, 576.

63. Grant, "Observations . . . on the Proposed Plan of 1764 for the Future Management of Indian Affairs," 829.

64. Table of Goods and Prices, November 20, 1762, *DRIA*, II, 576.

65. Williams, *Adair's History*, 32. Five hundred pounds of leather was the price of a "just" killing of an accused murderer. See Stuart, "Of Indians in General," 257–58; and Demere to Lyttelton, August 10, 1757, *DRIA*, II, 398.

66. Anderson, "Cherokee Clay," 503, 507.

67. Stuart, "Of Indians in General," 257.

68. Within the villages there were, however, counter pressures working to limit production. Competition with white hunters and the difficulty of traveling long distances in towns hard pressed for work-time due to depopulation, began during this period to refocus hunting activities away from more distant hunting territories and nearer the towns. In this context, hunting was probably less productive in economic terms. See Hatley, "The Three Lives of Keowee," in *Powhatan's Mantle*.

69. John Stuart, "Observations . . . on the Proposed Plan of 1764 for the Future Management of Indian Affairs," 821; Lud. Grant to Governor Glen, March 27, 1755, *DRIA*, II, 41, noted that traders were cheating Indians and that tribespeople were petitioning for redress that "the Trade at Present is at such a low Ebb and the Price of Skins so small." But he observed that the cost of such cheating to the tribe was probably exaggerated.

70. Sellars, *Charleston Business*, 169–71. While the opportunistic Moravians of Wachovia had begun to ship deerskins from Wachovia in 1761, by the middle of the decade they were forced to interrupt shipments because prices had fallen. Adelaide L. Fries, ed., *Records of the Moravians in North Carolina* (Raleigh: Historical Commission, 1942), 762.

71. Sellars, *Charleston Business*, 170.

CHAPTER THIRTEEN

1. *Georgia Gazette,* April 12, 1763, quoted in Sellars, *Charleston Business,* 29.

2. With this population growth the western backcountry, the Piedmont and foothills soon reached a parity with the population of the older settled inner coastal plain and sandhills districts. Meriwether, *Expansion of South Carolina,* 259–60; cf. Klein, "Ordering the Backcountry," 665. Richard M. Brown estimated that the Afroamerican population across the entire backcountry approached 10 percent by the middle 1760s, while Rachel Klein suggests that the figure was nearer 20 percent. Brown, *South Carolina Regulators,* 18; Klein, "Ordering the Backcountry: The South Carolina Regulation," *William and Mary Quarterly,* 3rd Series, 38 (October 1981): 665, n. 10.

3. Meriwether, *Expansion of South Carolina,* 260; "Ownership of a few slaves was quite common among more prosperous farmers"; and some blacks, runaways from the low country, were held illegally. Meriwether, *Expansion of South Carolina,* 49; Klein, "Ordering the Backcountry," 665, 666.

4. Edward J. Cashin, "Sowing the Wind: Governor Wright and the Georgia Backcountry on the Eve of the Revolution," in *Forty Years of Diversity: Essays on Colonial Georgia,* ed. Harvey H. Jackson and Phinizy Spalding (Athens: University of Georgia Press, 1984), 231, 236; Jack P. Greene, "The Travails of an Infant Colony: The Search for Viability, Coherence and Identity in Colonial Georgia," in *Forty Years of Diversity,* 296.

5. Richard R. Beeman, "The Political Response to Social Conflict in the Southern Backcountry: A Comparative View of Virginia and the Carolinas During the Revolution," in *An Uncivil War: The Southern Backcountry During the American Revolution* (Charlottesville: University of Virginia Press, 1985), 219.

6. Mitchell, *Commercialism and the Frontier,* 96.

7. Historian Jack Greene, in prefacing a collection of articles on the southern backcountry at the time of the Revolution, notes that all the authors share the common perception, rooted in Frederick Turner's frontier stages, that the west was somehow freer from the emotional and social baggage of the settled seaboard colonies. Furthermore, while the fear of blacks in the eastern regions tied together the different classes of white colonial society, such emotional unification did not exist in the west. Jack P. Greene, "Independence, Improvement, and Authority: Toward a Framework for Understanding the Histories of the Southern Backcountry During the Era of the American Revolution," in Hoffman, *An Uncivil War,* 9. In this vein, Richard M. Brown writes that "until the Cherokee War the backcountry had been primarily an Indian frontier . . . all this changed with the humbling of the powerful Cherokees in 1761. As a result of the white victory, the future difficulties of the backcountry would stem from the tensions of settlement alone." Brown, *The South Carolina Regulators,* 13.

8. Beeman, "Political Response," 217; see also Mitchell, *Commercialism and Frontier,* 46–48.

9. Sirmans, *Colonial South Carolina,* 348; Weir, *Colonial South Carolina,* 288.

10. Moneypenny, "Diary," 325.

11. *South Carolina Gazette,* January 8–12, 1761; Meriwether, *Expansion of South Carolina,* 143.

12. These efforts were not restricted to the boundary of South Carolina with the Cherokees. In western Virginia troops took time to construct the "Island Road" linking the New River to the Long Island of the Holston, and the periodic river crossings of the

troops enabled one local entrepreneur to establish "Ingles Ferry" on the New. The fork of the Great Wagon Road south of Staunton was also improved after 1755. Mitchell, *Commercialism and Frontier, 149. Meriwether, Expansion of South Carolina,* 246.

13. For the nature of the provisioning business in Virginia, see Mitchell, *Commercialism and Frontier,* 144–45; "Gist's Instructions from Edmond Atkin, November 16, 1757," in Kenneth P. Bailey, *Christopher Gist: Colonial Frontiersman, Explorer, and Indian Agent* (Hamden, Conn.: Archon Press, 1976), Appendix Four, 207–17.

14. Meriwether, *Expansion of South Carolina,* 170.

15. Fries, *Moravian Records,* I, 49, 232.

16. For similar social effects of the war in the north, see Gary Nash, *Urban Crucible: Social Change, Political Consciousness and the Origins of the American Revolution* (Cambridge: Harvard University Press, 1979).

17. John Stuart, "Of Indians in General," C.O. 323/17/240; Christopher French noted that "the chief commodities of this country are Rice . . . Indigo, and Deerskins, but the Quantity of the latter depends on the Inhabitants being at Peace or War with the Indians." French, "Journal," 277.

18. Sellars, *Charleston Business,* 170.

19. Ibid., 114–17.

20. Meriwether, *Expansion of South Carolina,* 252–56. On Boonesborough, see De Vorsey, *Indian Boundary* 124.

21. De Vorsey, *Indian Boundary,* 123.

22. Ibid., 124.

23. Lachlan McIntosh to Lyttelton, February 17, 1758. *DRIA,* II, 447; *South Carolina Gazette,* September 6–13, 1760. "Andrew Williamson," in *Dictionary of American Biography,* ed. Dumas Malone (New York: Charles Scribners, 1936), 20, 296–97.

24. Meriwether, *Expansion of South Carolina,* 127.

25. Anderson, "Cherokee Clay," 501.

26. Talk of Mankiller, quoted in David Ramsay, *History of the Revolution in South Carolina from a British Colony to an Independent State* (Trenton: Isaac Collins, 1785), 350. John C. Calhoun remembered hearing of Williamson, "a Scotch Trader" near his family's settlement at Long Cane. "Calhoun to Allen," *Gulf States Historical Magazine,* 440. Williamson's example was not unique. For instance, in Virginia, Thomas Walker and Christopher Gist, late important land speculators, played a similar role as Washington's Commissaries during the western wars of the 1750s. See Bailey, *Christopher Gist,* 213.

27. Sellars, *Charleston Business,* 58–60.

28. Rachel Klein, "The Rise of the Planters in the South Carolina Backcountry, 1767–1808" (Ph.D. Dissertation, Yale University, 1979), 84–87; Brown, *South Carolina Regulators,* 16–17. Through these low country contacts Williamson, for instance, became associated with Joseph Salvador, a scion of the DeCosta family, who owned a nearby plantation called Cornacre. See also B. H. Levy, "The Early History of Georgia's Jews," in *Forty Years of Diversity,* 164–65.

29. Roger G. Kennedy, *Architecture, Men, Women and Money,* 115.

30. See Alexander Cameron, "A Return of Traders in the Cherokee Nation," May 1, 1765, C.O. 5/323/23/254.

31. Though the term "farmer" was used more often than "planter" in colonial South Carolina, recent historical work has stressed the latter term as connoting the social

goals of these who would transform themselves into community leaders during the post-Cherokee War era. See Klein, "Ordering the Backcountry," 667; Greene, "Independence, Improvement and Authority," 13, 17–18; and compare Brown, *The South Carolina Regulators,* 183, n. 28.

32. Greene, "Independence, Improvement, and Authority," *Uncivil War,* 29–31.

33. Meriwether, *Expansion of South Carolina,* 145.

34. Klein, "The Rise of the Planters," 17–19; "Ordering the Backcountry," 663, 667.

35. Andrew Pickens to Lyman Draper, [], Draper Collection, 3XX141.

36. At Augusta, Pickens was in contact with factors for leading Savannah and Charlestown merchants. F. W. Pickens to Charles H. Allen, March 26, 1848, "Transcripts of Dr. John H. Logan," *Historical Collections of the Joseph Habersham Chapter of the Daughters of the American Revolution,* III, 96.

37. Alexander Cameron, "A Return of Traders in the Cherokee Nation," C.O. 323/23/254. "Mr. Parks" and "Mr. Tinker" together sponsored four traders, three of whom were "half-breeds," in the Valley Towns and at Great Island. It is also possible that Mr. Parks was, in turn, employed by Lt. Governor Bull at this time.

38. Alden, *John Stuart,* 298–301.

CHAPTER FOURTEEN

1. See Rachel N. Klein, *Unification of a Slave State: The Rise of The Planter Class in the South Carolina Backcountry, 1760–1808* (Chapel Hill: University of North Carolina Press, 1990); Richard M. Brown, *The South Carolina Regulators;* and Richard M. Brown and D. E. Fehrenbacher, eds., *Traditional Conflict and Modernization: Perspectives on the American Revolution* (New York: Academic Press, 1977), chap. 13. Also see Weir, *Colonial South Carolina,* 275–83. The South Carolina Regulation was a complex amalgam of social unrest and class ambition, and though scholars differ in their interpretations of the nature of this elusive movement, they agree that its leadership and agenda were distinctly elite. As Brown summarizes: "The South Carolina Regulators were ambitious Back Country property holders determined to end lawlessness; to discipline the lower people; and to establish an orderly society" (*South Carolina Regulators,* 135).

2. David Ramsay, *A Chronological Table of the Principal Events* (New York: J. Hoff, 1811), 28. It is important to differentiate the North and the South Carolina Regulations, events which, though often confused, were quite different. North Carolina's Regulation, in the most general terms, was a broader popular insurgency opposing, rather than the South Carolina equivalent.

3. Klein, "Ordering the Backcountry," 660. These men have been variously labeled, among others, important men, men of influence, as well as leading men. Cf. Meriwether, *Expansion of South Carolina,* 132. When William Henry Drayton visited the upper Broad and Saluda valleys in 1775, near the Cherokees, he noted the absence of "a leading man of his neighborhood" in the audience. Mr. Drayton to Council of Safety, August 12, 1774, Gibbes, *Documentary History,* I, 141. Especially in the western backcountry during the pre-Revolutionary years, the term "leading man" was not

without intercultural connotations, as the same phrase was commonly used to describe village authority figures among the Cherokees.

4. Pressure on such civil issues had been building in the backcountry since at least the early 1750s. See Address from an Inhabitant of Saxegotha to Governor Glen, [July–August, 1754], C.O. 5/375/12.

5. For instance, Andrew Pickens's friend, relative, and fellow Regulator Patrick Calhoun marched in 1769 with a force of armed men gathered from the kindred Dissenter communities of Waxhaws and Long Cane to Prince William Parish where, in a primarily reform-oriented action, the men voted Calhoun a member of the Assembly. Klein, "The Rise of the Planters," 82; Brinsfield, *Religion and Politics,* 54.

6. See De Vorsey, *Indian Boundary,* 128–29.

7. For a vivid account of backcountry conditions during the Cherokee War, see Brown, *South Carolina Regulators,* chap. 1.

8. Salley, "Calhoun Family," 441.

9. Anderson, "Cherokee Clay," 501.

10. As early as 1766, John Pickens, Andrew's brother, represented South Carolina in the survey party which began to mark the Line in 1766. De Vorsey, *Indian Boundary,* 130. The involvement of leading men in creating the Boundary continued throughout the Regulation. The conferences during which the Cherokees and colonial officials negotiated the Boundary Line were major events, attended by many backcountry leading men and lower-class observers. For instance, during the Lochaber Conference in 1770, as at Saluda in 1755, "a number of back-inhabitants of the province of South Carolina" watched as the treaty documents were signed. Report of Congress with the Cherokees, October 18, 1770, in *Documents of the American Revolution,* ed. K. G. Davies (Shannon: Irish University Press, 1974), II, 210.

11. Message of the Governor, Commons House, October, 1759, *Colonial Records of Georgia,* XVI, 219.

12. See discussion in Klein, "Ordering the Backcountry," 668–72.

13. Commons House, *Colonial Records of Georgia,* November 2, 1759. Cooper, *Statutes at Large,* IV, 50, see Klein, "Rise of the Planters," 56–58. Evidence of the way in which this issue counterposed the claims of landowners and non-landed hunters was commonplace. For instance, one citizen advertised through the *Gazette* (1758) that: "my stock of cattle has been often disturbed and drove out of my old fields . . . by hunters with their dogs." *The South Carolina Gazette,* July 12–19, 1760, offers a fifty-pound reward for timber trespassers and a similar notice the next summer (July 11–18, 1761) states: "All persons are forewarned from cutting trees, hoop poles, or other wood on Mr. Colleton's land." For a law concerning slaves collecting lightwood and cutting of timber for the Charlestown firewood market, see Cooper, *Statutes at Large,* V, 131.

14. Rachel Klein "Ordering the Backcountry."

15. Governor Glen to Board of Trade, October 25, 1753, C.O. 5/374/225.

16. Quoted in Klein, "Rise of the Planters," 46; see also pp. 68–69.

17. Hooker, *The South Carolina Backcountry on the Eve of the Revolution,* 68–70.

18. See also Klein, "Rise of the Planters," 46, 68–69; "Ordering the Backcountry," 661.

19. Klein, "Rise of the Planters," 59; The settlement of backcountry Georgia had broadened this complaint to the "Cracker" settlers in general. Mr. Barnard, a prominent trader, informed James Habersham of the arrival of "several idle People from the

Northward, some of whom . . . are great Villains, Horse Stealers &c. and were amongst the North Carolina Regulators.'' Habersham to Hillsborough, August 12, 1772, *Letters of Hon. James Habersham, 1756–1775, Collections of the Georgia Historical Society* (Savannah: The Savannah Morning News Print, 1904), VI, 201. On the Cherokee side, horse numbers probably had climbed steadily after the 1750s, and as killing and capture became more hazardous after the Cherokee War, horse-stealing became the moral equivalent of warfare for warriors. This substitution is first suggested in Carol I. Mason, ''Eighteenth-Century Culture Change Among the Lower Creeks,'' 72–73; also Thomas B. Ford, ''An Analysis of Anglo-American/Cherokee Culture Contact During the Federal Period, the Hiwassee Tract, Eastern Tennessee'' (M.A. thesis, Department of Anthropology, University of Tennessee, 1981).

20. Jacobs, *Atkin's Report,* 36; Klein, ''Ordering the Backcountry,'' 676.

21. Quoted, ibid., 672.

22. *South Carolina Gazette,* [January 1758].

23. Cf. T. H. Breen, ''Horses and Gentlemen: The Cultural Significance of Gambling Among the Gentry of Virginia,'' in *Puritans and Adventurers: Change and Persistence in Early America* (New York: Oxford University Press, 1980), 148; Rhys Isaac, *Transformation of Virginia, 1740–1790* (Chapel Hill: University of North Carolina Press, 1983), 100–101.

24. George Cadogan to Governor Glen, March 27, 1751, *DRIA,* I, 12.

25. Cf. ''Affidavit of Charles Banks, June 1, 1751'' and ''Deposition of James Francis, [July 11, 1751],'' *DRIA,* I, 23–27. Vann and Burgess, along with George Downing, reappeared in the late 1760s working as traders out of Long Cane. Alexander Cameron, ''A Return of Traders in the Cherokee Nation,'' C.O. 323/23/254. Jack Greene suggestively writes that such men had put themselves ''beyond dependence'' on leading men. Greene, ''Independence, Authority and Autonomy,'' 15. In far western South Carolina, however, many of these men were alternately competing with or working for the agents of such men through their involvement in the deerskin trade.

26. Alexander Cameron, ''A Return of Traders in the Cherokee Nation,'' May 1, 1765, C.O. 323/23/254. Cameron estimated the number of packhorsemen equal to the number of traders (''reckoning at a modest computation a packhorseman for each trader''), and the percentage of mixed-blood packhorsemen was probably even greater than that among the traders. See also Klein, ''The Rise of the Planters,'' 60, 70–74.

27. Affidavit from John Bowie, May 21, 1767, C.O. 5/68/151; see also Affidavit from James McCormick, May 21, [1767], C.O. 323/25/111.

28. Aptheker, *Slave Revolts,* 40.

29. Young, ''French and Indian War'', 129, 323; see also Louis K. Koontz, ''The Virginia Frontier, 1754–1763,'' *Johns Hopkins Studies in Historical and Political Science,* Series 43, n. 2, 1925: 100.

30. Francis Fauquier to Board of Trade, August 1, 1765, *The Official Papers of Francis Fauquier,* ed. George Reese (Charlottesville: Virginia Historical Society, 1983), III, 1266; Fauquier to Lewis, May 14, 1765, *Papers of Fauquier,* III, 1238.

31. Andrew Lewis to Fauquier, May 9, 1765, ibid., 1234. Lewis knew the Cherokees, as he had commanded the construction of the Virginia fort in the Overhill Towns.

32. Andrew Lewis to Fauquier, June 3, 1765, ibid., 1248.

33. Francis Fauquier to Andrew Lewis, May 14, 1765, ibid., 1238.

34. Fauquier to Board of Trade, August 1, 1765, ibid., 1266.

35. "Proclamation of the Augusta Boys," [ca. June 4, 1765], ibid., 1255.

36. The Augusta Boys' protest linked political complaints with the memory of the harsh dislocations of the border fighting of the 1750s. "We Augusta Boys in heart are and do profess ourselves his present Majesty's (King George the third) true and liege Subjects, and unhappy we living on this Verge of his Majesty's Dominion have by the unparaled deceit of an Insidious and Cruel Heathen Enemy have been repeatedly distressed, and find it Impracticable to maintain the legal rights granted us by his Majesty." Ibid.

37. Fauquier to Thomas Gage, July 6, 1765, ibid., III July 6, 1765.

38. Harvey H. Jackson, "Georgia Whiggery: The Origins and Effects of a Many-Faceted Movement," in Spalding and Jackson, *Forty Years of Diversity*, 263.

39. Van Doren, *Bartram's Travels*, 382. White elites used similar terms and some of their own—"Cracker," for instance—to distinguish themselves from recent arrivals. Cf. Habersham to Hillsborough, August 12, 1772, Habersham to Wright, August 20, 1772, *Correspondence of James Habersham*, 201–3, 204. Traveling to the Cherokee country during the South Carolina Regulation, clay collector Thomas Griffiths was warned of "Virginia crackers, & Rebells; a set of Theives that wer joined together to Rob Travillers." Anderson, "Cherokee Clay," 500.

40. Cashin, "Sowing the Wind," 248; in Georgia, as opposed to South Carolina, the emerging Whig leadership based in Savannah was strongly oriented toward alliance with the tribes. This political reversal of the Whig position stemmed in part from the continued strong economic role of intercultural trading in the Georgia economy (as opposed to South Carolina where the trade, partly due to competition with Georgia after the Cherokee War, had faded in importance), and the ties of many Savannah merchant families to mixed-blood and Creek "brokers" such as the McIntosh family. See Janet and David G. Campbell, "The McIntosh Family Among the Cherokees," *Journal of Cherokee Studies* (Spring 1980), 4–8; Martha C. Searcy, *The Georgia-Florida Contest in the American Revolution* (University: University of Alabama Press, 1985), 20–21, 31, 201.

41. Quoted in Cashin, "Sowing the Wind," 242.

42. Ibid.; Searcy, *Georgia-Florida*, 30. When Governor Wright, in order to placate backcountry leaders, banned the Indian trade in 1774, a "canvass for signatures" to support his ban was begun in the western region. Edward Cashin notes that this action "might be regarded as the first throughgoing effort to organize the backcountry politically." Cashin, "Sowing the Wind," 242.

43. Alexander Cameron to John Stuart, February 4, 1774, MG21, BM Add Mss. 21672.

44. Charles Callendar, "Shawnee," *Handbook of North American Indians*, 631. For documents and standard interpretations of Dunmore's War, see Ruben G. Thwaites and Louise P. Kellogg, eds., *Documentary History of Lord Dunmore's War* (Madison: Wisconsin Historical Society, 1905), especially 110–33; Randolph C. Downes, "Dunmore's War: An Interpretation," *Mississippi Valley Historical Review* 21 (December 1934): 311–30.

45. See discussion in Jackson, "Georgia Whiggery."

46. Ian C. Cargill, *Colonists from Scotland: Emigration to North America, 1707–1783* (Ithaca: Cornell University Press, 1956), 132.

47. This document, dated September 12, 1775, is reprinted in Gibbes, *Documentary History,* I, 179–80. The "Loyal Frontier Friends Club," formed in 1766 in the region around Long Cane, may have predated the group which signed the Resolves. Jacob Summeral to John Stuart, November 10, 1768, *CRNC,* VII, 866, quoted in Klein, "Rise of the Planters," 52.

48. Ronald Hoffman, "Introduction," xiv-vx; Klein, "Frontier Planters and the American Revolution: The South Carolina Backcountry, 1775–1782," in *An Uncivil War,* 51; Crow, "Liberty Men and Loyalists: Disorder and Disaffection in the North Carolina Backcountry," 125; Ekirch, "Whig Authority and Public Order in Backcountry North Carolina, 1776–1783," in *An Uncivil War,* 110.

49. Reflecting long-standing ethnic prejudices, Whig leaders failed to approach the German settlers with an open mind, and the German communities, perhaps reflecting the experience of the Webber movement and the Cherokee War, were unresponsive. When Drayton was coolly received at the "Dutch Church" at Saluda, he jotted in his journal that they were "a stiff-necked congregation," and concluded that "the Dutch are not with us." Mr. Drayton to Council of Safety, August 16, 1775, Gibbes, *Documentary History,* I, 141. For a map of his journey, see Hamer and Rogers, *Papers of Henry Laurens,* X. See also Ramsay, *History of the Revolution in South Carolina,* 64–65.

50. See comments in "Fragment of a Journal Kept by the Rev. William Tennent," *Yearbook of Charleston,* 1894, 304–5; Mr. Drayton to Council of Safety, August 16, 1775, Gibbes, *Documentary History,* I, 140–43; Ramsay, *History of the Revolution in South Carolina,* 66–67; Thomas Fletchall to Henry Laurens, in Gibbes, *Documentary History,* I, 123–24.

51. "Mr. Drayton's Talk to the Cherokees, September 25, 1775," reprinted in Draper Collection, 2UU89–92; "A Talk from the Hon. William H. Drayton," September 25, 1775, in Peter Force, *American Archives: Consisting of a collection of authentick records . . . forming a documentary history of the origin and progress of the North American colonies; of the causes and accomplishment of the American Revolution; and of the Constitution of government for the United States, to the final ratification thereof* (Washington, D.C.: Peter Force, 1837–53), 4th Series, 3, 790–93.

52. Long Cane Resolves, in Gibbes, *Documentary History,* I, 179–80. The disputed land was that settled by white small-farmers beyond Long Cane.

53. News of Lewis's strategy was probably communicated through informal family networks to South Carolina, where many prominent backcountry families had known the Lewis family and their associates. This family dimension was highlighted during the war itself. "Nothing connected with General Lewis' army is more remarkable than the kinship existing among the men composing it," observed an historian and descendant of Andrew and Charles Lewis. Virgil A. Lewis, *History of the Battle of Point Pleasant* (Charleston, W. Va.: Tribune Printing Company, 1909), 130–31. See also "Andrew Lewis," *Dictionary of American Biography,* 11: 206–7. During the five years prior to the engagement, Lewis and his associate, Jacob Hite, had cooperated in an effort to obtain Cherokee lands near the backcountry settlements of Long Cane, and the implications of Lewis's efforts against the Shawnees must have been made clear to leading men on the South Carolina border with the Cherokees. Cf. Alden, *John Stuart,* 299.

54. Henry Hampton to John Hampton, [1775], ms. in South Caroliniana Library.

55. However, Whig fears were not entirely unfounded. Though the Cherokees for their part had continued to be observers rather than intervene in support of the traders and Tories on their borders, a deeper involvement for the tribes was pushed by General Gage as well as Thomas Brown, working with Governor Patrick Tonyn of Florida. John Stuart, as the principal regional contact of the tribe, remained more equivocal about tapping tribal aggressions. And local traders in the upper Savannah, such as John Vann, were reported to have directly incited the villagers, cf. "Deposition of Robert Gowdy to John Caldwell," "96" District, July 10, 1775, ms. in South Caroliniana Library. Also see James H. O'Donnell, III, *The Cherokee of North Carolina in the American Revolution* (Raleigh: North Carolina Department of Archives and History, 1976), 30, 36–38, and *Southern Indians in the American Revolution,* 17–33. Stuart, for his part, denied that he had instructions "to arm the Negroes and Indians," and rumors that "I had sold Fort London [*sic*]," John Stuart to Committee of Intelligence, in Force, *American Archives,* Series 4, vol. 2, 1681–82.

56. "Declaration by the Authority of Congress, South Carolina, Charleston District," November 19, 1775, in Gibbes, *Documentary History,* I, 211–15; Col. Richardson to Mr. Laurens, December 22, 1775, in Gibbes, *Documentary History,* I; 242.

57. "There is still a camp which we cannot come up with, consisting of the principal agressors, which were . . . camped on Cherokee land." Col. Richardson to Mr. Laurens, December 22, 1775," in Gibbes, *Documentary History,* I, 242. The list of 136 prisoners eventually taken at Cane Brake included many German surnames as well as individuals from leading families, such as the Alexanders and Caldwells, though the Whig troops focused their energy on apprehending the bandit element within this larger group.

58. Col. Richardson to Mr. Laurens, December 22, 1775, in Gibbes, *Documentary History,* I, 243; Cf. Crow, "Liberty Men and Loyalists: Disorder and Disaffection in the North Carolina Backcountry," in *An Uncivil War,* 127–30.

59. Fifteen inches of snow fell in the mountains during the action. Col. Richardson to Hon. H. Laurens, January 2, 1776, in Gibbes, *Documentary History,* I, 247.

60. David Ramsay, *History of South Carolina* (Charleston: David Longworth, 1809), I, 215. The term "Scovilite," or "Scopholite," was derived from the name of Joseph Scoffel, a leader of "bandits" and "anti-Regulator" forces. Klein, "Frontier Planters and the American Revolution: The South Carolina Backcountry, 1775–1782," in Hoffman, Tate, and Albert, eds., *An Uncivil War,* 43.

61. "Prisoners Sent to Charles Town by Col. Richardson," in Gibbes, *Documentary History,* I, 249–53.

62. Ibid.

63. Klein, "Frontier Planters and the American Revolution," 89. Klein argues further that this connection, which emerged out of the confusing interplay of backcountry political infighting, was as much "by default as by design." See also Cashin, " 'But Brothers, It Is Our Land We Are Talking About,' Winners and Losers in the Georgia Backcountry," in *Uncivil War,* 240.

CHAPTER FIFTEEN

1. For a collection of articles reflecting prevailing scholarly perspectives on the Revolution, see the Jack P. Greene, ed., *The American Revolution: Its Character and Limits* (New York: New York University Press, 1987).

2. O'Donnell, *The Cherokees . . . in the American Revolution,* 39.

3. For the Fort Charlotte meeting and its outcome, see Ganyard, "Threat from the West," 55. Not long after the Fort Charlotte Conference, the North Carolina Commissioner gave the news credence. Willie Jones to Richard Caswell, June 2, 1776, *CRNC,* XXII, 743.

4. For an account of actions by Afroamericans across the region that contributed to the very real fears of the coastal elite of the seaboard colonies, see Peter H. Wood, " 'The Dream Deferred': Black Freedom Struggles on the Eve of White Independence," in *In Resistance: Studies in African, Caribbean, and Afro-American History,* ed. Gary Y. Okihiro (Amherst: University of Massachusetts Press, 1986), 167–87.

5. Peter H. Wood, "Impatient of Oppression: Black Freedom Struggles on the Eve of White Independence," *Southern Exposure* 12 (November/December 1984): 10–16; Aptheker, *Slave Revolts,* 87–88.

6. Such a letter was published by David Ramsay in his *History of South Carolina,* 279, and *History of the Revolution in South Carolina,* 346–54. Also see O'Donnell, *The Cherokees . . . in the Revolution,* 37, 41–42; Saunders, *Colonial Records of North Carolina,* X, 665.

7. John R. Alden, *The American Revolution* (New York: Harper and Row, 1954), 200.

8. Bethania Diary, May 1, 1776, Fries, *Moravian Records,* III, 1105; quoted in Robert L. Ganyard, "Threat from the West: North Carolina and the Cherokee, 1776–1778," *North Carolina Historical Review* 45 (1968): 47–51.

9. See Ganyard, "Threat from the West," 46–67; Philip M. Hamer, "The Wataugans and the Cherokee Indians in 1776," *Tennessee Historical Society Publications* III (1931): 108–27. John P. Brown, *Old Frontiers: The Story of the Cherokee Indians from the Earliest Times to the Date of Their Removal to the West, 1838* (Kingsport, Tenn.: Southern Publishers, 1938), 148–54.

10. Henry Hampton to John Hampton, [1776], ms. in the South Caroliniana Library.

11. James Creswell to W. H. Drayton, Gibbes, *Documentary History,* II, 81.

12. Searcy, *Georgia-Florida,* 722–25.

13. Henry Laurens to John Laurens, August 14, 1776, quoted in "A Letter from John Laurens to his Uncle James Laurens," October 24, 1776, *South Carolina Historical and Genealogical Magazine* 10 (1910): 51.

14. W. H. Drayton to Francis Salvador, July 24, 1776, Gibbes, *Documentary History,* II, 29.

15. Quoted in O'Donnell, *Southern Indians,* ix.

16. Charles Lee to Edmund Pendleton, July 7, 1776, in Force, *American Archives,* Series 5, volume 1, p. 95.

17. Griffith Rutherford to Council of Safety, July 5, 1776, *CRNC,* X, 652.

18. Letter from the North Carolina Delegates in the Continental Congress to the

North Carolina Provincial Council, *CRNC*, X, pt. 2, pp. 730–32. Also see O'Donnell, *Southern Indians*, 51–53.

19. A detailed account of the staging and operations of the 1776 campaigns can be found in O'Donnell, *Southern Indians*, 34–69.

20. A Williamson to [], July 22, 1776, in Gibbes, *Documentary History*, II, 27.

21. Ramsay, *History of South Carolina*, 279; Joseph Johnson, M.D., *Traditions and Reminiscences; Chiefly of the Revolution in the South* (Charleston: Walker and James, 1857), 143.

22. Johnson, *Traditions and Reminiscences*, 143–44. [Fairie], "Journal, Williamson's Cherokee Campaign, 1776," 177–83. One of the most comprehensive sources for the 1776 campaign is a journal, probably by Arthur Fairie, which has survived in three related but distinctive copies. The first, and most extensive, is [Arthur Fairie], "Journal, Williamson's Campaign, 1776," Draper Collection, 3VV176–203. The second, which differs at some points and contains nineteenth-century editorial embellishment is in E. F. Rockwell, ed., "Parallel and Combined Expeditions Against the Cherokee Indians in South and in North Carolina, in 1776," *Historical Magazine and Notes and Queries*, New Series, II (October 1867): 212–20. Both versions are cited in the following discussion. A third copy of Fairie's "Journal" is in the National Archives.

23. Brown, *Old Frontiers*, 154. Whig leaders in Georgia used their persuasion to hold off any joint Cherokee-Creek attack. George Galphin reported that the Creeks had "not only refused aid to the Cherokees, but threatened them if they persisted in assisting the enemy [the British] against us." George Galphin to Willie Jones, October 26, 1776, in Force, *American Archives*, Series 5, volume 3, p. 650.

24. Francis Salvador to Hon. Chief Justice Drayton, July 19, 1776, ibid., 25–26.

25. O'Donnell, *Southern Indians*, 44. William Lenoir, June 1835, "An Account of the Expedition Against the Cherokee Indians in 1776, Under Gen'l Griffith Rutherford, from 17th August to 7th Oct. 1776," typescript in the North Carolina Collection, Wilson Library, University of North Carolina at Chapel Hill, 1; William Lenoir, "The Revolutionary Diary of William Lenoir," ed. J. G. DeRoulhac Hamilton, *Journal of Southern History* (May 1940): 249–59. Joseph Williams, "Col. Joseph Williams' Battalion in Christian's Campaign," ed. Samuel C. Williams, *Tennessee Historical Magazine*, New Series, 9 (April 1925): 108; O'Donnell, "The Virginia Expedition Against the Overhill Cherokee, 1776," *East Tennessee Historical Society's Publications* 9 (April 1925): 21–23. Williams, "Joseph Williams' Battalion," 109–10.

26. William Moore to Brigadier General Rutherford, November 7, 1776, in "Rutherford's Expedition Against the Cherokees," in *The University Magazine* [University of North Carolina], New Series, 7 (February 1888): 93.

27. Rockwell, "Parallel and Combined Expeditions," 217; Willie Jones to Patrick Henry, October 25, 1776, *CRNC*, X, pt. 2, pp. 860–61; Lenoir, *Journal*, 255.

28. O'Donnell, "Virginia Expedition, 1776," 16–18.

29. Moore, November 7, 1776, in "Rutherford's Expedition," 90.

30. Williams, "Williams' Battalion," 108.

31. [Fairie], "Journal, Williamson's Campaign, 1776," 198.

32. Rockwell, "Parallel and Combined Expeditions," 220.

33. Williams, "Williams' Batallion," 112.

34. Ibid.

35. Williamson to [], July 22, 1776, in Gibbes, *Documentary History*, II, 27.

36. Ramsay to Drayton, September 1, 1779, ibid., 212. While Williamson's proposal was refused, at least one captured tribal woman was sold as a slave by the South Carolina troops. See Klein, "Frontier Planters and the American Revolution," in *Uncivil War,* 67.

37. Ibid., 67–68; "Rise of the Planters," 131–32.

38. Moore, November 7, 1776 in "Rutherford's Expedition," 92–93.

39. Rockwell, "Parallel and Combined Expeditions," 215.

40. Ibid., 218–19; Cf. [Fairie], "Journal, Williamson's Campaign, 1776," 189.

41. Fairie, *Journal,* 191; Lenoir, *Journal,* 255.

42. Klaus Theweleit, *Male Fantasies,* trans. Stephen Conway (Minneapolis: University of Minnesota Press, 1986), I, 191.

43. "Historical Sketch of the Indian War of 1776," *North Carolina University Magazine,* 133.

44. Rockwell "Parallel and Combined Expeditions," 216.

45. Ibid., 217.

46. John Drayton, *Memoirs of the American Revolution . . . Relating to the State of South Carolina* (Charleston: A. E. Miller, 1821), II, 242–43.

47. Extract of a Letter from North Carolina, dated October 25, 1776, in Force, *American Archives,* 5th Series, 2, p. 1235.

48. Walsh, *Writings of Christopher Gadsden,* 13; *South Carolina Gazette,* November 1, 1759.

49. Ibid., October 11, 1759. "General Orders by Col. Moultrie," in Gibbes, *Documentary History,* I, 105.

50. Anne K. Gregorie, *Thomas Sumter* (Columbia: R. L. Bryan Company, 1931), 40–44. Before he came to South Carolina Sumter seems also to have been a friend of North Carolina partisan leaders Joseph Martin and Benjamin Cleveland, both important figures during the Revolution. Stephen B. Weeks, "General Joseph Martin and the War of Revolution in the West," *Annual Report American Historical Association,* 1893, 410–11; "Benjamin Cleveland," in *Dictionary of North Carolina Biography,* ed. William Powell (Chapel Hill: University of North Carolina Press, 1979), I, 385–86.

51. Henry Laurens to Willis Martin, August 29, 1763, *Papers of Henry Laurens,* III, 553.

52. Ramsay, *History of the Revolution in South Carolina,* 160.

53. Cf. Draper Interview with Andrew Pickens, Draper Collection, 3VV135–41.

54. See Crow, "Disaffected," 157; cf. John Walker et al. to Safety Committee in Rowan County," June 12, 1776, *CRNC,* X, 609–10; Clarence W. Griffin, *History of Old Tryon and Rutherford Counties, 1730–1936* (Asheville: Miller Printing Company, 1937), 36–37; Lyman C. Draper, *Kings Mountain and Its Heroes* (Cincinnati, 1881; Lyman C. Draper, *Kings Mountain and Its Heroes* (Cincinnati, 1881; rpt. Baltimore: Genealogical Publishing Company, 1971). See also Klein, "Frontier Planters and the Revolution," 53–54.

55. Ramsay, *History of South Carolina,* I, 284–85; Ramsay, *History of the Revolution in South Carolina,* 159–61.

56. Joseph Johnson, *Traditions and Reminiscences,* 144.

57. Williams, "Williams' Battalion," 113.

58. The son of the North Carolina agent to the Cherokees after the Revolution recalled this term. William Martin to Lyman Draper, June 1, 1842, in "Biographical

Sketch of General Joseph Martin," *Virginia Historical Magazine* 8 (April 1901): 355. Historian David Corkran has labeled the conflict the "Second Cherokee War." Corkran, *The Creek Frontier,* 298.

59. The guerilla activities of these men were to be critically important in keeping alive Whig hopes during the period 1779–81, when the British had the upper hand in the south. For a description of their activities on the British-colonial, rather than intercultural, front of the Revolution, see Alden, *The American Revolution,* chap. 15; Lucien Angiel, *Rebels Victorious: The American Revolution in the South,* 1780–81 (New York: Ballantine Books, 1975).

60. Lenoir, "Rutherford's Expedition," 2.

61. Henry Stuart, "Account of His Proceedings," 771.

62. Lenoir, "Rutherford's Expedition," 3, Lenoir, "Journal," 255.

63. Pickens's grandson noted that the Cherokees "were so thoroughly overrun and conquered by the terrible slaughter in this new mode of warfare (but few firearms were used) that they sued for peace." Hon. F. W. Pickens to Charles H. Allen, in "Transcripts of Dr. John H. Logan," 95.

64. Andrew Pickens, Fayette County, Tennessee, to Lyman Draper, "Pickens Campaign," 3VV142–43.

65. Ibid.

66. Samuel Osherson, *Finding Our Fathers: The Unfinished Business of Manhood* (New York: Free Press, 1986), 20. For a fuller definition, see Robert M. Goldenson, ed., *The Longman Dictionary of Psychology and Psychiatry* (New York: Longmans, 1984), 391.

67. The so-called pioneers—land speculators and Indian fighters and small farmers—who in successive generations would lay claim to trans-Appalachia during the nineteenth century would follow a pattern much like that of Pickens. In fact many of them, such as Andrew Jackson, were descendants of colonial upper Savannah and Catawba—Long Cane and Waxhaws—families. In the attack against the Creeks which followed the Battle of New Orleans, Michael Paul Rogin writes, "War against the Indians would permit Jackson to reexperience his feelings of primitive violence, purify the self of them, and establish a legitimate title to the land. He could destroy lingering fears of feminine domination and grow securely into manhood . . . to acquire, in violence, authority." At another point Rogin suggests the special role of Jackson's ethnicity: "Was the 'Savage Tribe that will neither adhere to Treaties, nor the Law of Nations,' the Cherokees or the American Scotch-Irish?" Michael P. Rogin, *Fathers and Children: Andrew Jackson and the Subjugation of the American Indian* (New York: Random House, 1976), 128–30, 133.

68. Andrew Pickens to General Lee, August 28, 1815, Draper Collection, 1VV1077. A similar passage occurs in Francis Marion's biography. "We proceeded, by Colonel Grant's orders, to burn the Indian cabins. Some of the men seemed to enjoy this cruel work . . . I saw everywhere the footsteps of the Little Indian children, where they had lately played . . . 'Who did this?' They will ask their mothers, and the reply will be, 'The white people did it—the Christians did it!' Thus, for cursed Mammon's sake the flowers of Christ have sowed the selfish tares [weeds] of hate in the bosoms of even Pagan children." Quoted in *Journal of Cherokee Studies* 2 (Summer 1977): 333.

69. Robert M. Weir, " 'The Violent Spirit,' the Establishment of Order and the

Community of Leadership in Post-Revolutionary South Carolina," in *Uncivil War*, 70–99.

CHAPTER SIXTEEN

1. The most important of the negotiations between the Cherokees and South Carolina authorities occurred during 1765 and 1766. A year later the same sequence of council discussions followed by actual line-marking occurred during 1766–67 in North Carolina. Both boundaries were ratified in October 1768, at a Southern District Indian Congress held at Hard Labor in South Carolina. For a detailed and insightful discussion of the Indian Boundary, see Louis De Vorsey, *Indian Boundary*.

2. Ibid., 102.

3. Ibid.

4. Archibald Henderson, ed., "The Treaty of Long Island of the Holston, July, 1777," *North Carolina Historical Review* 8 (Spring 1931): 96–97.

5. Stuart to Board of Trade, August 24, 1765, C.O. 5/66/369, quoted in De Vorsey, *Indian Boundary*, 128.

6. Ibid.

7. Quoted in Cashin, "Sowing the Wind," 236. Cf. Duane H. King, "Lessons in Cherokee Ethnology from the Captivity of Joseph Brown, 1788–98," *Journal of Cherokee Studies* (Spring 1977): 222–23.

8. Talk from Kittagusta (Prince of Chote) to Alexander Cameron and Ensign Price, May 8, 1766, C.O. 323/23/302.

9. John Stuart to John Pownall, August 24, 1765, C.O. 5/323/176.

10. De Vorsey, *Indian Boundary*, 124.

11. In 1769, two years after marking the boundary, John Stuart found "that County is full of inhabitants which in my memory was considered by the Indians as their best hunting grounds; such is the rage for settling far back." John Stuart to Earl of Hillsborough, January 3, 1769, C.O. 5/70/105; De Vorsey, *Indian Boundary*, 116.

12. Historian John Alden suggests that this was simply a tactic to overcome John Stuart's objection to the Cherokee gifts of land beyond the Proclamation Line to Whites. According to Alden, the "chiefs adroitly argued that the proclamation did not apply, since Cameron's son was an Indian." Cameron apparently had three *métis* children (Alden, *John Stuart*, 298, 187). In any case, Stuart was entirely circumvented in this action, and as Alden notes, the Commissioner's objections stemmed in part from his loss of "prestige" (303). The motives of Richard Pearis were questioned by Stuart, and in 1770 the Overhill headmen strongly stated, under pressure from Stuart, that they had viewed the transaction as "no more than . . . application to trade." John Stuart to Hillsborough, October 25, 1770, *Documents of the American Revolution*, II, 238. Pearis was well known to the tribe, having established a store at Long Island in the 1750s, and the headmen may have, in repudiating Pearis, simply been accommodating Stuart's statements of concern. See Duane H. King, "Long Island of the Holston: Cherokee Sacred Ground," *Journal of Cherokee Studies* (Fall 1976), 113–127.

13. Talk of Cherokee Headmen, Minutes of a Congress at Hard Labor, October 15, 1768, C.O. 5/74/39. A year later, Oconostota, was contacted by The Mortar, who told

them that "a man who had been appointed a Beloved Man by the Cherokees in the Creek nation had died lately." The Mortar "requested that they would send some of their headmen in order to invest another with the same honour." Alexander Cameron to John Stuart, March 19, 1771, *Documents of the American Revolution*, III, 70–71. See Chapter 1 for a discussion of the function of inter-tribal ambassadors.

14. Minutes of Congress Held at Hard Labor, October 15, 1768, C.O. 5/74/39.

15. At the initial confrontation of the South Carolina troops in the summer of 1776 at "Lindley's fort" the *métis* Cherokee wife of trader Pearis, branded a "Scophilite Adjutant," was captured. Francis Salvador to Hon. Chief Justice Drayton, July 18, 1776, *Documentary History of the American Revolution*, II, 25.

16. Alden, *John Stuart*, 298–301.

17. De Vorsey, *Indian Boundary*, 135.

18. In concluding a discussion of Pearis's purchase, Louis De Vorsey notes disapprovingly that "a disturbingly large number of Cherokees showed an unusual willingness to part with tribal lands" (*Indian Boundary*, 135); see John Stuart to Hillsborough, April 27, 1771, *CRNC*, VIII, 553–54; John Alden follows Stuart's appraisal. (*Southern Colonial Frontier*, 301).

19. The collapse of the Carolina trading system in 1765, followed by a debt forgiveness, suggested to the Cherokees that colonial concepts of debt were also flexible: the loss to South Carolina over the two years of the trade amounted to over £3500. Alden, *John Stuart*, 208.

20. Map of Creek and Cherokee Country, Enclosure in John Stuart to Hillsborough, June 12, 1772, C.O. 5/73/162. A portion of the map is reproduced in De Vorsey, *Indian Boundary*, Fig. 13.

21. *Historical Chronicle* XXV (October 1755): 468.

22. John Stuart to the Earl of Hillsborough, June 12, 1772, *Documents of the American Revolution*, V, 113–14; Cashin, "Sowing the Wind," 240; Memorial of the Traders to the Creek and Cherokee Nations to Governor James Wright, [June?, 1771], *Documents of the American Revolution*, III, 125–27, transcript of 5/651/127. The traders (among them the substantial traders on the mid-Savannah River, George Galphin and Lachlan McGillivray) were because of kinship ties relatively 'safe' for the tribespeople to deal with. For more detailed accounts of the politics of the Great Cession, see De Vorsey, *Indian Boundary*, 157–72; *Southern Frontier*, 301–13. Augusta, though much newer, had become a broker town, like ancient Saluda. Augusta had remained open to tribal visits after 1763, when settlements in Carolina had been closed. Here, "they were entertained, sometimes lavishly, by the principal Augusta traders . . . they considered Augusta their town." Cashin, "Sowing the Wind," 235–36.

23. Van Doren, *Bartram's Travels*, 382.

24. Williams, *Adair's History*, 222.

25. Report of Congress with Cherokees, October 18, 1770, *Documents of the American Revolution*, II, 213.

26. Minutes of a Congress Held at Hard Labor, October 15, 1768, C.O. 5/74/39. Stuart's trade regulations of 1765 made a similar distinction in attempting to establish control of the trade. Stuart prohibited Indian traders from employing "any negro or Indian or half breed, who from the manner of his life shall in the conscience of a jury be considered as living under the Indian government." Alden, *John Stuart*, Appendix A, 342.

27. Talk of Wolf of Seneca and Chinisto, February 24, 1774, MG 21, BM Add Ms 21672, folio 309.

28. Stuart to Hillsborough, April 27, 1771, *CRNC,* 553–54.

29. For instance, the Cherokees complained before the Cherokee War that white settlers "kill all our deer so that we cannot find meat to eat." Warriors of Keowee to Lyttelton, March 2, 1758, *DRIA,* II, 444. However, during Grant's march near Keowee in 1761, the troops encountered "a great abundance of Deer every Place we came to, in so much that they came amongst us, & were sometimes affrightened from the grounds where we encamped." Wolf populations were also healthy. The invading English camp in 1761 was "a little alarm'd one Night by a vast howling of Wolves, [and] our Indians, screaming at the same time, making it impossible to judge for some Time what it was." French, "Journal," 280–81, 290.

30. "Bethabara Diary, December 1, 1766," in Fries, *Moravian Records,* I, 337. The Moravians had begun to ship deerskins from their Wachovia settlement to Charlestown in 1761 at the suggestion of Henry Laurens. "An Account of the Rise and Progress of the United Brethren's Settlement," in Fries, *Moravian Records,* VI, 2454.

31. Report of Congress with Cherokees, October 18, 1770, *Documents of the American Revolution,* II, 213.

32. Bartram, "Observations," 68.

33. Talk of Judd's Friend, June 7, 1767, *CRNC,* VII, 465.

34. The trans-Appalachian country was nutrient-rich compared with the weathered terrain of the foothills and Piedmont. As a result, deer body size was in all likelihood larger. See data in Robert L. Jones and Harold C. Hanson, *Mineral Licks, Geophagy, and the Biochemistry of the North American Ungulates* (Ames: Iowa State University, 1985).

35. See discussion of changes in the salt trade in Hatley, "Three Lives of Keowee," in *Powhatan's Mantle.*

36. "The Deputy Henry Stuart's Account of his Proceedings with the Cherokee Indians about Going against the Whites," August 26, 1776, *CRNC,* X, 773. The Ohio lands granted in the Boundary Line negotiations were shared hunting grounds. First ceded by the Six Nations at the treaty of Fort Stanwix in 1768, the Cherokees soon followed suit. This situation soon resulted in a tangle of claims and co-claims by other tribes—as well as colonial land speculators, whose projects depended on treaties with one party or another. John Stuart offered a succinct southern perspective on the Fort Stanwix cession: "Sir William Johnson, by having suffered the claims of the 6 Nations and other northern tribes to extend to the southward of the Conowhay [Kanawha] as far up to the source of the Cherokee [Tennessee] River, has in great measure given rise to the pretensions of Virginia." John Stuart to Hillsborough, February 12, 1769, C.O. 5/70/124.

37. For the Donalson cession, which was a 1771 revision of the Virginia segment of the Boundary Line negotiated at Lochaber the year before, see discussions in De Vorsey, *Indian Boundary,* 74–85; also Alden, *John Stuart,* 344–50.

38. Corn Tassel, "Cherokee Reply to the Commissioners of North Carolina and Virginia," *Journal of Cherokee Studies* (Fall 1976), 128–29. For similar statements, see "Deposition of John Lowrey," April 16, 1777, *Calendar of Virginia State Papers,* ed. William P. Palmer (Richmond: R. F. Walker, 1875), I, 283. This distinction was made by the Cherokees at least by the 1720s. Cf. Longe, "A Small Postscript," 28.

39. Henderson, "Treaty of Long Island of the Holston," 91.

40. Williams, *Adair's History,* 138–39. Adair goes on to relate that a head warrior had "a few cattle soon presented to him, to keep off the wolf; and his reasoning proved so weighty, as to alter their resolution, and produce in them a contrary belief." However, in the internal debate over the propriety of cattle ownership, the warnings of the priests and of women gardeners prevailed. A Moravian visitor among the tribe recorded that "no cattle are kept, except by a few traders," in the Overhill Towns he visited in the 1780s. Schneider, "Journey of Br. Schneider," 1985. Archaeological evidence bears this out. See R. D. Newman, "The Acceptance of European Domestic Animals by the 18th Century Cherokee," *Tennessee Anthropologist* 4 (Spring 1979): 101.

CHAPTER SEVENTEEN

1. Van Doren, *Bartram's Travels,* 293–96.

2. The Lochaber Line, the original boundary line agreed to between the Cherokees and Virginia, was modified during the actual survey by John Donelson, with the agreement of Attakullakulla. Though the new line earned Virginia, which Donelson was representing, millions of acres in the west, the critical element was the Island itself. Attakullakulla received £500 for the change, and attributed the decision to his concern for the Holston settlements ("my brothers were settled upon it and I pittied them"). De Vorsey, *Indian Boundary,* 83.

3. Actually, three separate claims were dealt with at the conference: the disposition of the Watauga settlement, which has "leased" land from the tribe; the reimbursement of a storekeeper for goods presumably stolen by tribespeople at Carter's Valley; and the Henderson request proper. For detailed accounts of the politics of the Henderson purchase see Jerry C. Cashion, "North Carolina and the Cherokees"; for a clear depiction of these transactions see map titled "Cession of Indian Lands to States and Private Parties, 1775–1790," Lester J. Cappon, Barbara B. Petchenik, John H. Long, *Atlas of Early American History* (Princeton: Princeton University Press, 1976); Charles Royce, *Indian Land Cessions in the United States, Bureau of American Ethnology, Annual Report 18, 1896–97, Part 2.*

4. The controversy is well recorded because it was used as a basis for discrediting Henderson's title to the land by Virginia, which appointed a commission to examine outstanding land claims in the area. *Calendar of Virginia State Papers,* I, 272–316.

5. "Deposition of James Robinson in behalf of Richard Henderson," April 16, 1777, *Calendar of State Papers,* I, 286. At least one deposition from the Virginia hearings provides the basic, though often contradictory, view of the events at Sycamore Shoals. One deposition made by the Watauga representatives has Dragging Canoe return later and, stamping his foot on the ground, confirm their claim as well as that of Henderson and Carter. "Deposition of Charles Robertson," October 3, 1777, ibid., 292.

6. "Deposition of John Lowry &c on behalf of the Commonwealth," April 16, 1777, ibid., 283.

7. Henry Stuart, "Account of his Proceedings," 764. This dissent between Cherokee young and old men was not new. At the Lochaber Conference in 1770 the young men at Chote refused to accept the cession. Oconostota, who had signed the agreement, communicated the dissent of the young to Alexander Cameron, who reported: "he does

not choose to stand out against these young men as they have an equal right to the land.'' Promises of goods partially smoothed over this rift. Alexander Cameron to John Stuart, March 19, 1771, *Documents of the American Revolution,* III, 72.

8. Henry Stuart, "Account of his Proceedings," 764.

9. Ibid., 765.

10. Ibid., 777. Tribespeople described the backcountry settlers who, in small incidents, took many Cherokee lives during the 1760s, as colored with the same hostile black paint. Thus, when Indian Stephen was killed in 1770, headmen asked "what sort of men the Black Boys were." Adam Stephen to Governor Lord Botetourt, February 9, 1770, *Documents of the American Revolution,* II, 47.

11. Ibid., 778.

12. Ibid., 779.

13. James Thompson et al. to Anthony Bledsoe and Colonel Preston, August 2, 1776, in Force, *American Archives,* 5th Series, vol. 1, p. 464.

14. Mary E. Lazenby, *Catawba Frontier, 1775–81* (Washington, D.C.: published by the Compiler, 1950), 73.

15. Convened in July, enough time had passed for the tribal participants to hear of similar treaty negotiations held three months earlier, at Dewisse's Corner, South Carolina, and of substantial cessions, including the land between the Keowee River and Saluda and, with it, the traders' cessions earlier made by the tribe.

16. This claim was the doctrine of *uti possidetis,* the right of conquest to land. For the assumption by Georgia backcountry Whigs that this doctrine would hold, see Cashin, "But Brothers," 269.

17. Though claims of conquest were not made by the American Commissioners at Long Island, they demanded the land in the headwater reaches of the Holston and Powell rivers and, over Cherokee protests, eventually received them.

18. Henderson, "The Treaty of Long Island," 66.

19. Ibid., 81. In fact, the Cherokees had achieved their objectives; "the settlers had been rolled back and only two or three isolated settlements were left intact." Pate, "The Chikamauga," 253; Thomas L. Connelly, "Indian Tactics on the Tennessee Frontier, 1776–1794," *East Tennessee Historical Society's Publications* 36 (1964).

20. Henderson, "Treaty of Long Island of the Holston," 91.

21. Proceedings of a General Congress of the Six Nations, March 6, 1768, PAC, RG 10, C1222/8/9.

22. Minutes of a Meeting of DePeyster with Cherokees from Chota, June 15, 1782, RG 10, C1223/13/134.

23. John Heckewelder, *Narrative of the Mission of the United Brethren Among the Delaware and Mohegan Indians* (Philadelphia: McCarty and Davis, 1820), 203.

24. Like all other aspects of Cherokee society, there was a wide range of responses among women. While some Cherokee women held to tradition, others made radical changes—both in the fields and in politics. For instance, *métis* Nancy Ward was "rich in stock," meaning cattle, by the time of the Revolution, and provided cattle to the American troops. Ward, perhaps out of loyalty to her family, actively supported the American cause and warned the Watauga settlements of the attack in 1776 which Dragging Canoe was planning. See Mooney, *Cherokee Myths,* 203–4; Hatley, "Holding Their Ground," in *Appalachian Frontiers,* n. 67.

25. Deposition of Charles Robertson, *Calendar of Virginia State Papers,* I, 291.

26. Williams, *William Tatham*, 109.

27. Henderson, "Treaty of Long Island," 81.

28. Ibid.

29. For a review of the history of Long Island, see Duane H. King, "Long Island of the Holston."

30. Ibid., 83.

31. John Stuart to Governor Lord Botetourt, *Documents of the American Revolution*, II, 237, transcript of C.O. 5/1349/20. See also Joseph Martin to Governor Caswell, December 17, 1779, *NCCR*, XIV, 234–35.

32. Deposition of Mr. John Reid on behalf of the Commonwealth, April 16, 1777, *Calendar of Virginia State Papers*, I, 284–85.

33. Henderson, "Treaty of the Long Island of the Holston," 83. The Watauga settlements, which were alongside a tributary river to the Holston, could not be moved. Though the tribe had "leased" land to them, and the settlers had sought and claimed to have received fee simple title at Sycamore Shoals in 1775, the Cherokees remained concerned. After the conference, the settlers had apparently "talked of building or had already built a Fort on the Cherokee Land at the mouth of the Watoga River," and this action may have inspired Dragging Canoe to initiate hostilities here (Henry Stuart, "An Account of His Proceedings," *CRNC*, X, 765). The Wataugans were singled out by Dragging Canoe. When trader Robert Dews received news that his life was in danger, he was informed that he was threatened because he "was looked upon as a Watauga man" (Dews, "The Deposition of Robert Dews, taken at Fort Patrick Henry the 21 January 1777," *NCCR*, XXII, pt. 2, p. 997).

34. By the time of the conference, Gist and his wife may have had a *métis* son, Sequoyah. See Samuel C. Williams, "Nathanial Gist, Father of Sequoyah," *East Tennessee Historical Society's Publications* 5 (January 1933): 39–45.

35. Henderson, "Treaty of Long Island," 102.

36. Ibid., 103.

37. Dews, "Deposition of Robert Dews," 996.

38. Ibid., 1000. This promise echoed that of 1776, when Stuart did visit the Cherokees, but real assistance from the British was slow to materialize.

39. Ibid., 1002. When the attack finally materialized in 1779, it was launched from the new Chickamauga towns. Mooney, *Myths*, 55.

40. According to Richard Pearis's 1775 estimate of town populations, these four towns included 370 men, though the total number of dissident men was probably much larger. Force, *American Archives*, 4th Series, vol. 2 (1775), 793–94.

41. Parkman, *Conspiracy of Pontiac*, I, 184.

42. Heckewelder, *Narrative of the Mission of the United Brethren*, 179.

43. Henry Stuart, "An Account of His Proceedings," 764. Referring to the 1776 invasion of the Cherokee towns, Dragging Canoe later reported that "our nation was alone and surrounded by them. They were numerous and their hatchets sharp." Quoted in Brown, *Old Frontiers*, 176.

44. Reply of Conaghgwayeson to William Johnson, March 8, 1768, RG 2333/8.

45. Ibid.

46. William E. Meyer, "Indian Trails of the Southeast," *Forty-Second Annual Report of the Bureau of American Ethnology for 1924–1925* (Washington, D.C.: Smithsonian Institution, 1928), 749–51.

47. Reply of Conaghgwayeson to William Johnson, March 8, 1768, PAC, RG 2333/8.

48. Deposition of John Lowry, April 16, 1777, *Calendar of Virginia State Papers,* I, 315.

49. Deposition of Samuel Wilson, &c., April 16, 1777, ibid., 283.

50. Meyer, "Indian Trails," 749–51. This region, occupied by the "Mouse Creek Culture," which had disappeared by the beginning of the seventeenth century, also saw passing Spanish occupation. See Raymond Williams, "Williams' Island," *Journal of Cherokee Studies* (Spring, 1984): 11–17. On The Mortar, Williams, *Adair's History,* 271–72; Ludovic Grant, *Memoir,* 59.

51. See Randolph C. Downes, "Cherokee-American Relations in the Upper Tennessee Valley, 1776–1791," *East Tennessee Historical Society's Publications* (1936), 35–53.

52. Klinch and Talman, *Norton's Journal,* 62, 149; Dews, "Deposition of Robert Dews," 996, 999; Evans and Karhy, "Williams' Island," 17–18; for an account of ways of 'adoption' at Chickamagua, see Joseph Brown, "Captivity Narrative"; and Duane H. King, "Lessons in Cherokee Ethnology from the Captivity of Joseph Brown, 1788–1790," *Journal of Cherokee Studies* 3 (Spring 1977): 208–29.

53. Brown, *Old Frontiers,* 161.

54. The phrase is from Pate, "The Chickamauga," 56.

55. The Chickamauga rejoined their old towns only after 1794. See Pate, "The Chickamauga," 255; Mooney, *Myths,* 61–79. For a valuable summary and appraisal of Chickamauga tactics, see Thomas L. Connelly, "Indian Tactics"; Klinch and Talman, *Norton's Journal,* 59.

56. For a brief account of the continuing, but sporadic, contact among the Cherokees, the Shawnees and Delawares, see Helen H. Tanner, "Cherokees in the Ohio Country," *Journal of Cherokee Studies* (Spring 1978): 94–101.

57. Quoted in O'Donnell, *Southern Indians,* 118–19.

58. Mooney, *Myths,* 46–48. One of the reasons for continuing counteraction by whites in the west against the Chickamauga was the effectiveness of their efforts in blocking the Tennessee River communications artery. This in turn hampered Whig visions, derived in part from the conviction of early traders of the critical connection made by the Tennessee with the Mississippi, of the "flattering prospects of trade which were opening to our view at New Orleans." Governor Henry to Governor Caswell, January 8, 1779, *NCCR,* XIV, 244.

59. Klinch and Talman, *Norton's Journal,* 59. For an account of these campaigns, see Chapter 15; Mooney, *Myths,* 53–61.

60. See Pate, "The Chickamauga" and Connelly, "Indian Warfare," 17–21; also, George Christian, "The Battle of Lookout Mountain: An Eye Witness Account," ed. Raymond Evans, *Journal of Cherokee Studies (Winter 1978), 49–53.*

61. Klinch and Talman, *Norton's Journal,* 37–38.

62. Ibid., 149; see also Mooney, *Myths,* 99–101.

63. Mooney, *Myths,* 99, 391–92.

64. This version of the talk is in John Drayton, *Memoirs of the American Revolution* (Charleston: A. E. Miller, 1821), II, 361. A second, slightly different version is in Ramsay, *History of the Revolution in South Carolina,* 347.

CHAPTER EIGHTEEN

1. Williams, *Adair's History,* xxxvi.

2. Samuel C. Williams suggests that this final revision was made when Adair was in England in 1775 completing the publication of the book. Williams, *Adair's History,* 222.

3. Ibid., 459.

4. William Johnson to General Gage, December 10, 1768, quoted ibid., xxiii.

5. See Adair, "Appendix. Advice to Statesmen," ibid., 481–97. Adair was a signatory to Jonathan Bryan's "second lease" with the Creeks, which transferred "Apalachee Old Fields" and other land north of West Florida to Bryan. See "Indenture of the Indian Creek Nation," October 28, 1774, reprinted in *Selected Eighteenth-Century Manuscripts,* ed. Albert S. Britt, Jr. and Anthony R. Deees, *Georgia Historical Society Collections* (Savannah: The Society, 1980), 146–49.

6. Andrew Pickens to Thomas Pinckney, March 26, 1788, ms. in Charleston Library Society.

7. Longe, "A Small Postscript," 18.

8. Williams, "Schneider Report," 259.

9. Mooney, *Myths,* 209.

10. For examples of the rapidly developing literature on the nineteenth-century Cherokees, which has recently begun to balance the earlier stress of historical accounts on Cherokee "progressives" rather than "traditionals," see William G. McLoughlin, *Cherokee Renascence in the New Nation* (Princeton: Princeton University Press, 1986) and Theda Perdue, *Slavery and the Evolution of Cherokee Society* (Knoxville: University of Tennessee Press, 1979). For excellent articles on Cherokee traditionalism in the nineteenth century, see Satz, "Cherokee Traditionalism, Protestant Evangelism, and the Trail of Tears, Part II," *Tennessee Historical Quarterly* XLIV (Winter 1985): 380–402; and Theda Perdue, "Traditionalism in the Cherokee Nation: Resistance to the Constitution of 1827," *Georgia Historical Quarterly* 66 (Summer 1982): 159–70.

11. Adair, *History,* 1.

12. See Perdue, *Slavery and the Cherokee Indians.*

13. See Gregory E. Dowd, "North American Indian Slaveholding and the Colonization of Gender: The Southeast Before Removal," *Critical Matrix* 3 (Fall 1987).

14. Not more than 25 percent of the Cherokees censused in 1820 seem to fit in the progressive category. See data in William G. McLoughlin and Walter H. Conser, "The Cherokees in Transition: A Statistical Analysis of the Federal Cherokee Census of 1835," *Journal of American History* 64 (1977): 678–703.

15. Richard Pillsbury, "The Europeanization of the Cherokee Settlement Landscape Prior to Removal: A Georgia Case Study," *Geoscience and Man* 22 (1983); and Douglas C. Wilms, "Cherokee Settlement Patterns in Nineteenth Century Georgia," *Southeastern Geographer* 14 (1974).

16. "Report of Brethren Steiner and von Schweinitz," *North Carolina Historical Review,* 344.

17. Klinch and Talman, *Norton's Journal,* 63.

18. Sequoyah, the son of Nathanial Gist and a Cherokee woman, "could neither read, write or speak English." Satz, "Cherokee Traditionalism," 383–84.

19. "Report of Brethren Steiner and von Schweinitz," 348.

20. Satz, "Cherokee Traditionalism," 385.

21. William G. McLoughlin with Walter H. Conser, Jr., and Virginia Duffy Mc-Loughlin, *The Cherokee Ghost Dance: Essays on the Southeastern Indians, 1789–1861* (Macon: Mercer University Press, 1984), 142.

22. The earliest description of the Booger Dance Dates from the 1830s. Similar dances were described much earlier among other tribes, and the Cherokees themselves described the dance as ancient. See J. P. Evans, *Sketches of Cherokee Characteristics,* ms. in Payne Manuscripts, Ayer Collection, Newberry Library. Evans's Booger Dance description is reprinted in *Journal of Cherokee Studies* (Winter 1979), 19–20.

23. Evans, *Sketches,* 19.

24. Frank G. Speck and Leonard Bloom in collaboration with Will West Long, *Cherokee Dance and Drama* (Norman: University of Oklahoma Press, 1983), 28.

25. Ibid., 32.

26. Ibid., 34.

27. Ibid., 36–39.

28. Raymond D. Fogelson and Amelia B. Walker, "Self and Other in Cherokee Booger Dances," *Journal of Cherokee Studies* V (Fall 1980): 90.

29. Fogelson and Walker, "Self and Other," 98.

30. Fogelson and Walker understand the dance as a drama of Cherokee society itself. "The Booger Dance highlights certain problematics of Cherokee Life: the uncontrolled excessiveness of young men, the nagging moral authority of elders, and the unappropriated behavior of non-Cherokees" (ibid., 98). For a related argument concerning another historical tradition, the mythical Ani-Kutani, see Fogelson, "Ani-Kutani," 256–63.

31. Mooney, *Myths,* 529.

32. This was the explanation offered by Will West Long, the Cherokee informant of Speck and Broom. *Cherokee Dance,* 38; Mooney, *Myths,* 67.

33. In this respect, the Booger Dance is similar to the myth of Augustoge, the edenic town of refuge revealed in a whirlpool "twenty years before the English came." See discussion in Chapter 1. Cf. Fogelson and Walker, "Self and Other," 97.

34. The text cited is *A Narrative of the Life of John Marrant . . . Giving an Account of His Conversion,* ed. William Aldridge (London, 1786; rpt. Leeds: Davies and Co., 1810).

35. Van der Beets, *Held Captive by Indians* (Knoxville: University of Tennessee Press,), 180.

36. Marrant, "Preface," in *Narrative.*

37. Ibid., 10–12.

38. Ibid., 20.

39. Ibid., 22.

40. Ibid., 18–19.

41. For a development of this idea, see the psychobiography of Jackson in Rogin, *Fathers and Children.*

42. John C. Calhoun quoted in Bertram Wyatt-Brown, *Southern Honor: Ethics and Behavior in the Old South* (New York: Oxford University Press, 1982), 54.

43. Steven B. Oates, *To Purge This Land with Blood: A Biography of John Brown* (New York: Harper and Row), 279.

44. Lillian Smith, "A Letter to My Publisher," in *Killers of the Dream* (Garden City, N.Y.: Anchor Books, 1963), 2.

45. [], "Historical Sketch of the Indian War of 1776," 134.

Index